Finding Afro-Mexico

In 2015, the Mexican state counted how many of its citizens identified as Afro-Mexican for the first time since independence. *Finding Afro-Mexico* reveals the transnational interdisciplinary histories that led to this celebrated reformulation of Mexican national identity. It traces the Mexican, African American, and Cuban writers, poets, anthropologists, artists, composers, historians, and archeologists who integrated Mexican history, culture, and society into the African Diaspora after the Revolution of 1910. Theodore W. Cohen persuasively shows how these intellectuals rejected the nineteenth-century racial paradigms that heralded black disappearance when they made blackness visible first in Mexican culture and then in post-revolutionary society. Drawing from more than twenty different archives across the Americas, this cultural and intellectual history of black visibility, invisibility, and community-formation questions the racial, cultural, and political dimensions of Mexican history and Afro-diasporic thought.

Theodore W. Cohen is Associate Professor in the History and Geography Department at Lindenwood University, Missouri.

Afro-Latin America

Series editors

George Reid Andrews, *University of Pittsburgh*
Alejandro de la Fuente, *Harvard University*

This series reflects the coming of age of the new, multidisciplinary field of Afro-Latin American Studies, which centers on the histories, cultures, and experiences of people of African descent in Latin America. The series aims to showcase scholarship produced by different disciplines, including history, political science, sociology, ethnomusicology, anthropology, religious studies, art, law, and cultural studies. It covers the full temporal span of the African Diaspora in Latin America, from the early colonial period to the present and includes continental Latin America, the Caribbean, and other key areas in the region where Africans and their descendants have made a significant impact.

A full list of titles published in the series can be found at:
www.cambridge.org/afro-latin-america

Finding Afro-Mexico

Race and Nation after the Revolution

THEODORE W. COHEN
Lindenwood University

CAMBRIDGE
UNIVERSITY PRESS

CAMBRIDGE
UNIVERSITY PRESS

University Printing House, Cambridge CB2 8BS, United Kingdom

One Liberty Plaza, 20th Floor, New York, NY 10006, USA

477 Williamstown Road, Port Melbourne, VIC 3207, Australia

314-321, 3rd Floor, Plot 3, Splendor Forum, Jasola District Centre, New Delhi - 110025, India

79 Anson Road, #06-04/06, Singapore 079906

Cambridge University Press is part of the University of Cambridge.

It furthers the University's mission by disseminating knowledge in the pursuit of education, learning and research at the highest international levels of excellence.

www.cambridge.org
Information on this title: www.cambridge.org/9781108730310
DOI: 10.1017/9781108632430

First published 2020
First paperback edition 2021

A catalogue record for this publication is available from the British Library

Library of Congress Cataloging in Publication data
NAMES: Cohen, Theodore W., 1983– author.
TITLE: Finding Afro-Mexico : race and nation after the Revolution / Theodore W. Cohen.
DESCRIPTION: First edition. | New York : Cambridge University Press, 2020. | Series: Afro-Latin America | Includes bibliographical references and index.
IDENTIFIERS: LCCN 2019051671 (print) | LCCN 2019051672 (ebook) | ISBN 9781108493017 (hardback) | ISBN 9781108632430 (ebook)
SUBJECTS: LCSH: Blacks – Mexico – History. | Blacks – Mexico – Social conditions. | Blacks – Race identity – Mexico. | Mexico – Race relations. | Mexico – History – 1810–
CLASSIFICATION: LCC F1392.B55 C64 2020 (print) | LCC F1392.B55 (ebook) | DDC 305.800972–dc23
LC record available at https://lccn.loc.gov/2019051671
LC ebook record available at https://lccn.loc.gov/2019051672

ISBN 978-1-108-49301-7 Hardback
ISBN 978-1-108-73031-0 Paperback

For Michael and Cynthia Cohen and Joanna Varrone

Contents

Figures and Maps

Acknowledgments

Finding Afro-Mexico has accompanied me for my entire adult life. It was with me when my wife, Joanna, and I moved; when we attended graduations, weddings, and funerals; when we did just about anything no matter how exciting or ordinary. The words in this book tell more than the history of African-descended communities, cultures, spaces, and identities in Mexico; they also remind me of the many friendships I made and the conversations I had while *Finding Afro-Mexico* went from an ill-formed idea to a book. I think of my family, friends, and colleagues when I read the pages that follow, since each of you accompanied me, at least metaphorically, when I waded through archives, read books and articles, and wrote and edited drafts of papers, presentations, a dissertation, and these pages. *Finding Afro-Mexico* would not have been possible without any of you.

Institutions in Mexico and the United States gave me the resources necessary to complete *Finding Afro-Mexico*. The History Department and the Latin American Studies Center at University of Maryland, College Park; the Carter G. Woodson Institute of African-American and African Studies at the University of Virginia; Lindenwood University; the Conference on Latin American History; and the Gilder Lehrman Institute for American History funded trips to archives and conferences in Mexico and across the United States. The hard work of archivists and librarians in both countries made this research possible, both during the process of digging through archival boxes and then in acquiring the rights to reproduce images. In Mexico, thank you in particular to Herlinda Mendoza Castillo, Claudia Jasso, Tania Martín Becerril, Rosa Maura Tapia Velázquez, and Dulce Reynoso Rosales. UDLAP's María del

Refugio Paisano Rodríquez went above and beyond the call of an archivist when I wanted six images by Miguel Covarrubias to help me to bring his immense ethnographic and artistic methodologies to life. María Covarrubias also went out of her way to ensure that I would be able to reproduce these images. Rosario Ochoa Rivera's generosity, enthusiasm for her grandfather's poetry, and love of the cultural life of the city of Veracruz has not only inspired me but also allowed me to push the boundaries of this research further than I ever could have imagined; I would never have conceived of Chapter 6 were it not for her. In the United States, Lisette Matano, Geoffery Stark, Matt Gorzalski, and Lauren Sallwasser have helped me expand the African American dimensions of this project. In the process, I have had the good fortune to work with and receive suggestions from Judith Anne Still, the daughter of William Grant Still, as well as the Katherine Biddle family.

Writing a book seemed so much easier before I actually tried doing it. The process of making these words into something that can sit on bookshelves takes so much more than just the act of reading and writing. While writing can be a solitary act, publishing certainly is not. James Oles, Melanie Anne Herzog, Mary Coffey, and Tely Duarte helped me acquire the rights to reproduce many of the images in *Finding Afro-Mexico*. Francesca Dennstedt kindly assisted with some of the translations. The University of Texas Press and Lindenwood University graciously let me reproduce parts of my articles, "Among Race, Nations, and Diasporas: Genealogies of 'La bamba' in Mexico and the United States" and "Katherine Dunham's Mexican Adventure," which I had already published in *Studies in Latin American Popular Culture* and *The Confluence*. Everyone at Cambridge University Press has worked diligently to make this process as simple as possible. Reid Andrews and Alejandro de la Fuente have supported *Finding Afro-Mexico* since I first proposed it. Debbie Gershenowitz, Rachel Blaifeder, and Ruth Boyes have answered more questions than I thought I would have asked about the publishing process. Two anonymous reviewers generously read this manuscript when it did not look quite like it does in this final form. Their extensive yet encouraging comments strengthened my arguments and helped me focus on topics that needed further reflection.

Thank you to all the people who sat in conference halls, classrooms, and other venues as I presented my research at meetings of the American Historical Association and Latin American Studies Association, at the Midwest Workshop on Latin American History, and especially at the Tepoztlán Institute for the Transnational Study of the Americas.

Comments by Eric Zolov, Nils Jacobson, Paulina Alberto, Vicram Tamboli, Shane Dillingham, and Frank Guridy have undoubtedly made this work better. Similarly, chats with my fellow Afro-Mexicanists – especially Herman Bennett, Ben Vinson III, Beau Gaitors, and John Milstead – have given me the confidence to push my ideas further than I would have otherwise considered. Niels Jacobson, David Sartorius, Jerry Dávila, Bryan McCann, Alejandro L. Madrid, Frank Guridy, and Mary Kay Vaughan deserve a special thank-you for going out of their way to read chapters of the manuscript, oftentimes when they were not ready for public consumption. In St. Louis, Deborah Cohen has constantly been a helping hand, reading book chapters and just being around when I needed to talk to someone about my research. Finally, thank you to Karin Rosemblatt and Stephen Lewis for graciously reading the entire manuscript.

I cannot say that I began my undergraduate or graduate education thinking I would be a cultural and intellectual historian of modern Mexico and the African Diaspora. Nonetheless, Gil Joseph's and Seth Fein's guidance, support, and friendship set me on this path even before I knew it existed. Similarly, all the interdisciplinary discussions I had with the other fellows at the Carter G. Woodson Institute between 2011 and 2013 continue to shape the questions I ask and the ways in which I choose to answer them. The passion that I experienced in Minor Hall has not only improved this book but also made me a better teacher and person. Deborah McDowell, Lawrie Balfour, Lisa Shutt, Cheryll Lewis, and Debbie Best deserve special mention for their tireless efforts to make that experience possible.

At the University of Maryland, College Park, I was lucky to work with and learn from a great cohort of historians, including Sarah Walsh, Shane Dillingham, Josh Walker, Daniel Richter, Reid Gustafson, and Will Burghart. Daniel Richter has always been ready to help me develop my ideas and provide advice on how I could develop my research agenda. I cannot thank Reid Gustafson and Will Burghart enough for all their support during and after graduate school; their friendship has been invaluable both personally and professionally. Professors Elsa Barkley Brown, David Sartorius, Daryle Williams, and Barbara Weinstein asked poignant questions that still shape the way I conceive of the historian's craft. Ira Berlin's deft advising, teaching, and scholarship left a bigger imprint on this book than he ever could have imagined. Most importantly, Karin Rosemblatt and Mary Kay Vaughan guided me through this entire process, helping me find sources, answering my questions, and editing more drafts than I should have asked them to read. They both deserve more thanks than I can give in these acknowledgments.

Lindenwood University has supported me while I turned my dissertation into this book. Funds to visit conferences and a course reduction during the 2016–17 academic year allowed me to polish my arguments, to reexamine my archival notes, and, most importantly, to write. Carl Hubenschmidt helped me acquire many of the images reproduced in the book. The History and Geography Department has gone beyond what I should have expected. In addition to hearing me talk about Mexican history and the African Diaspora more than they ever could have imagined, they graciously let me schedule my classes so that I had days dedicated to writing. Jeff Smith and Patrick O'Banion helped me navigate the initial stages of publishing. And, as my department chair, Kris Runberg Smith constantly went out of her way to encourage me to make sure I found time to work on *Finding Afro-Mexico*.

Finally, my parents and grandparents, my aunts and uncles, my in-laws, and especially my wife, Joanna, listened attentively as I developed this project. They have given me confidence when I needed it and distracted me when I became too engrossed in some aspect of my research. No one ever questioned the value of what historians do or why I chose to study Mexico. That support has been priceless. I dedicate *Finding Afro-Mexico* to three people: my parents, Michael and Cynthia Cohen, and Joanna Varrone. Long before I decided to be a historian, my parents encouraged me to follow my interests. Without their encouragement, I doubt I would have even attempted to write a book. Joanna deserves special mention, since she has lived with *Finding Afro-Mexico* as much as I have. Her love of film challenged me to think of all of my sources first as narratives, then as pieces of information. By asking why my research fascinates me so much, she forced me to distill my arguments and has left an indelible imprint on this book.

Abbreviations

III	Instituto Indigenista Interamericano (Inter-American Indigenist Institute)
INAH	Instituto Nacional de Antropología e Historia (National Institute of Anthropology and History)
INBA	Instituto Nacional de Bellas Artes (National Institute of Fine Arts)
INEGI	Instituto Nacional de Estadística y Geografía (National Institute of Statistics and Geography)
INI	Instituto Nacional Indigenista (National Indigenist Institute)
LEAR	Liga de Escritores y Artistas Revolucionarios (League of Revolutionary Writers and Artists)
MoMA	Museum of Modern Art
NAACP	National Association for the Advancement of Colored People
OSM	Orquesta Sinfónica de México (Mexican Symphony Orchestra)
PNR	Partido Nacional Revolucionario (National Revolutionary Party)
PRI	Partido Revolucionario Institucional (Institutional Revolutionary Party)
PRM	Partido de la Revolución Mexicana (Party of the Mexican Revolution)
SEP	Secretaría de Educación Pública (Secretariat of Public Education)
TGP	Taller de Gráfica Popular (Popular Graphic Art Workshop)

Introduction

December 8, 2015, inaugurated a new period in Afro-Mexican history. For the first time since September 16, 1810, when Father Miguel Hidalgo y Costilla declared Mexican independence from Spain, the federal government counted its African-descended population as such. According to the intercensal survey completed by the INEGI in March of that year, 1.4 million citizens identified themselves "in accordance with their culture, history, and traditions" as "Afro-Mexican or Afro-descendant." As 1.2 percent of the national populace, these numbers appear small, particularly in comparison to the 25.7 million people who self-reported as indigenous, the only other ethnic group that the government chose to include.[1] In a few coastal areas typically thought to have historical ties to

[1] Instituto Nacional de Estadística y Geografía, "Resultados definitivos de la encuesta intercensal 2015," 8 de diciembre de 2015, www.inegi.org.mx/contenidos/programas/intercensal/2015/doc/especiales2015_12_3.pdf. The 25.7 million people who claimed to be indigenous possibly overstates Mexico's indigenous population. This number is substantially larger than what is found in previous censuses. For example, using data from the 2010 census, the Consejo Nacional de Población concluded in 2013 that there were only 11.7 million people with at least moderately indigenous cultural or linguistic traits; see *La situación demográfica de México, 2013* (Mexico City: Consejo Nacional de Población, 2013), 127, www.gob.mx/cms/uploads/attachment/file/112476/La_Situacion_Demografica_de_Mexico_2013.pdf. Although the counting of indigenous peoples has been a constant feature of the modern Mexican state, popular and official definitions of indigeneity have changed, thereby leaving the possibility for the number of citizens classified as indigenous to vary substantially; see Mara Loveman, *National Colors: Racial Classification and the State in Latin America* (Oxford: Oxford University Press, 2014); and Paula López Caballero and Ariadna Acevedo-Rodrigo, eds., *Beyond Alterity: Destabilizing the Indigenous Other in Mexico* (Tucson: University of Arizona Press, 2018). All translations are my own, unless otherwise stated.

African slavery, this demographic visibility was more pronounced. On March 28, 2017, *Excélsior* explained that least 10 percent of the residents in 100 communities – including 69 in Oaxaca, 16 in Guerrero, and 12 in Veracruz – claimed an African heritage (See Map 0.1).[2]

Activists saw the INEGI's data as a necessary step to rectify the structural inequalities that the descendants of enslaved Africans encountered daily. Not looking for an enumeration of historical offenses, national newspapers described the findings with a vision toward future social justice initiatives, such as better public education, and the possibility of amending the Constitution of 1917 to give African-descended Mexicans the same institutional protections as the indigenous communities whose cultural presence the state had always counted. Scholars, artists, and public intellectuals believed that social recognition validated the humanity of African-descended Mexicans.[3] Nonetheless, in an interview for *La Jornada*, Sergio Peñaloza Pérez, President and founder of the grassroots organization Black Mexico, *México Negro*, somberly noted that this newfound visibility was merely a step in the right direction: the INEGI's statistics, he clarified, "do not truly reflect how many we are, because many preferred not to assume this identity thanks to the historical discrimination that we have endured."[4]

In the United States, remarks were equally positive but often tinged with exasperation. On January 27, 2016, in the *Huffington Post*, Krithika Varagur published "Mexico Finally Recognized Its Black Citizens, But That's Just The Beginning." In response to what many academics and activists perceived as the state's erasure of African-descended identities, she wistfully asked "Why has it taken so long?" before continuing with the more hopeful query, "What's next for Afro-Mexicans?" her article

[2] "Uno de cada cien mexicanos es afrodescendiente, revela estudio," *Excélsior*, 27 de marzo de 2017, www.excelsior.com.mx/nacional/2017/03/27/1154391.

[3] There are countless articles published in mainstream Mexican newspapers referencing these ideas, including César Arellano García, "La población afrodescendiente sufre más discriminación que la indígena: Conapred," *La Jornada*, 16 de marzo de 2015, www.jornada.unam.mx/2015/03/16/sociedad/034n1soc; and Julián Sánchez, "CNDH demanda evitar discriminación a afromexicanos," *El Universal*, 3 de julio de 2015, http://archivo.eluniversal.com.mx/nacion-mexico/2015/cndh-demanda-evitar-discriminacion-a-afromexicanos-1111784.html.

[4] Sergio Peñaloza Pérez qtd. in Blanca Juárez, "Habitan 1.4 millones de afromexicanos en el país: INEGI," *La Jornada*, 9 diciembre 2015, www.jornada.unam.mx/ultimas/2015/12/09/habitan-1-4-millones-de-afromexicanos-en-el-pais-inegi-7219.html. Also see Glyn Jemmott Nelson, foreword to Paulette A. Ramsay, *Afro-Mexican Constructions of Diaspora, Gender, Identity and Nation* (Kingston, Jamaica: University of the West Indies Press, 2016), xi.

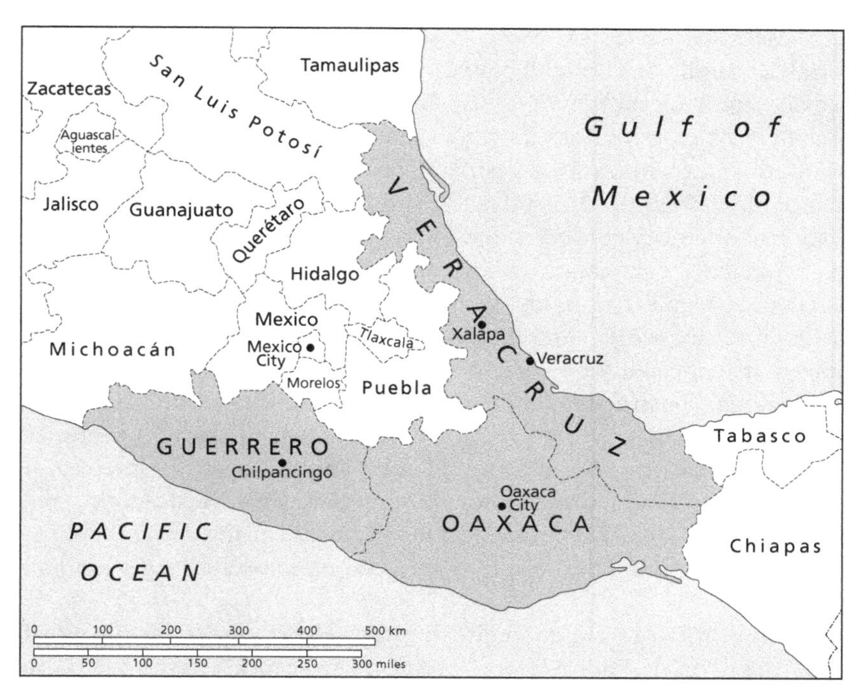

MAP 0.1 Map of Mexico.

was as much the dutiful reporting of the INEGI's data as a political statement about Mexico's insufficient constructions of blackness, which she characterized as "a still tenuous identity." Like Peñaloza Pérez, she condemned the fragmented state of Afro-diasporic identity in civil society. Too many citizens, she lamented, "use labels like 'criollo' (creole) or 'moreno' rather than the ones black Mexicans tend to prefer. Peñaloza, for instance, describes himself as 'afrodescendiente (of African descent), negro (black), or afromexicano (Afro-Mexican).'"[5]

[5] Krithika Varagur, "Mexico Finally Recognized Its Black Citizens, but That's Just the Beginning," *Huffington Post*, January 27, 2016, www.huffingtonpost.com/entry/mexico-finally-recognized-its-black-citizens-but-thats-just-the-beginning_us_568d2d9ce4b0c8beacf50f6b. For a similar perspective, see Sameer Rao, "Mexico Finally Recognizes Afro Mexicans in National Census," *Colorlines*, December 14, 2015, www.colorlines.com/articles/mexico-finally-recognizes-afro-mexicans-national-census?fbclid=IwAR0X5DUZF-WxAptzW0XPgzvh7tdAYvsAPgJlBJKcX7Akyn2JSBtfz-TRHfs. Odile Hoffmann discusses the complex social questions surrounding blackness in "Negros y afromestizos en México: Viejas y nuevas lecturas de un mundo olvidado," trans. Camila Pascal, *Revista Mexicana de Sociología* 68, no. 1 (2006): 103–35.

These responses to the INEGI's statistics point to the demographic, social, cultural, and spatial politics of African-descended identities in Mexico, the subject of *Finding Afro-Mexico*. The black body buoyed the socially visible and politically active form of diasporic subjectivity that Peñaloza Pérez and Varagur desired. Conceived through some combination of physiological, ancestral, and sociological attributes, the racialized body has often been reduced to a biological typology that scholars and policy makers can count, whether to surveil and oppress African-descended peoples, to study them, or both.[6] However, the INEGI's groundbreaking work – and the turn-of-the-century grassroots mobilizations that advocated for it – signified a stark about-face from the cultural and regional constructions of blackness that Mexican intellectuals, political officials, and cultural producers had crafted in the two centuries between Mexican independence and the publication of the intercensal survey.[7] To tell this history of how blackness became Mexican after the Revolution of 1910, this book integrates the political and cultural dimensions of the African Diaspora into Mexican nation-state formation and vice versa.

Finding Afro-Mexico contends that the celebratory refrains penned since the INEGI published its results have been erected on a false premise. The activists, scholars, and reporters who celebrated this newfound demographic visibility incorrectly assumed that Mexican

[6] There is a large literature on the black body in Anglophone scholarship on the African Diaspora, including Paul Gilroy, *Against Race: Imagining Political Culture beyond the Color Line* (Cambridge, MA: Harvard University Press, 2000); and Dorothy Roberts, *Killing the Black Body: Race, Reproduction, and the Meaning of Liberty* (New York: Vintage Books, 1999). For a Latin American perspective, see Livio Sansone, *Blackness without Ethnicity: Constructing Race in Brazil* (New York: Palgrave Macmillan, 2003), esp. 11 and 79. On the construction of the body as a political act rooted in specific historical contexts, see Emily S. Rosenberg and Shanon Fitzpatrick, eds., *Body and Nation: The Global Realm of US Body Politics in the Twentieth Century* (Durham, NC: Duke University Press, 2014). Historian Jessica Marie Johnson challenges scholars to consider the quantifiable black body not only as a foundation for the study of slavery and the slave trade but also as part of the recuperation of black humanity; see "Markup Bodies: Black [Life] Studies and Slavery [Death] Studies at the Digital Crossroads," *Social Text* 36, no. 4 (2018): 57–79.

[7] Of course, the distinction between biological and cultural race is not absolute, even when Mexican nationalists claimed it to be. As historian Laura Gotkowitz explains, scholars need to consider constructions of biological and cultural race on a continuum and in conversation with each other; see "Introduction: Racisms of the Present and the Past in Latin America," in *Histories of Race and Racism: The Andes and Mesoamerica from Colonial Times to the Present*, ed. Laura Gotkowitz (Durham, NC: Duke University Press, 2011), 8–11.

nationalists uniformly sought to silence – if not erase – the country's African heritage through *mestizaje*, a postcolonial project to craft a modern Mexico through the racial and cultural fusion of indigeneity and Spanishness.[8] The recuperation of blackness, however, was a much more piecemeal process than they have described. This history reveals the social, demographic, cultural, and spatial dimensions of racial visibility and invisibility that are all too often lumped together, represented by the racialized body. At the turn of the twentieth century, tropes of black disappearance left intellectuals, like sociologist and lawyer Andrés Molina Enríquez, assuming that African-descended peoples were, as he stated in 1909, "insignificant" to the course of Mexican history.[9] Yet, by the 1930s and 1940s, when the specter of global fascism placed the Revolution's populist aims in conversation with the New Negro Movement, Afro-Cubanism, and other similar initiatives to refashion African-descended identities in the Atlantic world, enslaved Africans, often symbolized by Gaspar Yanga, entered the national narrative as patriotic rebels who foreshadowed postrevolutionary conceptions of social justice. These transnational dialogues provided a select but immensely well connected set of Mexican anthropologists, artists, and composers with the ethnographic methodologies to perceive and to discuss the similarities between the cultural expressions found in Mexico's coastal regions and those of African-descended peoples in the United States, Cuba, and other American nations.[10] In other words, the descendants of colonial Mexico's free and enslaved black populations slowly became visible, first culturally and spatially, then socially and demographically. For the first time since independence, ethnographers could study African-descended peoples and cultures, as anthropologist Gonzalo Aguirre

[8] For example, see Laura A. Lewis, "African Mexicans," in *Concise Encyclopedia of Mexico*, ed. Michael S. Werner (Chicago: Fitzroy Dearborn, 2001), 4; and Christina A. Sue, "Hegemony and Silence: Confronting State-Sponsored Silences in the Field," *Journal of Contemporary Ethnography* 44, no. 1 (2015): 113–40.

[9] Andrés Molina Enríquez, *Los grandes problemas nacionales* (Mexico City: A. Carranza e Hijos, 1909), 292.

[10] By rooting my analysis in the intellectual strands of cultural production, I nuance B. Christine Arce's argument that there is a paradox in Mexico, where the official narrative erases blackness but popular culture celebrates it as foreign and exotic. This tension, she explains, has its origins in the discursive, cultural, and tropological process of transforming black bodies into "no-bodies"; see *México's Nobodies: The Cultural Legacy of the Soldadera and Afro-Mexican Women* (Albany: State University of New York Press, 2017), 3, 8, and 9.

Beltrán had in the decade preceding the 1958 publication of *Cuijla: Esbozo etnográfico de un pueblo negro*, the first book dedicated to blackness in postrevolutionary society.

The radicalization of Afro-diasporic politics in the 1960s, however, has cast aside Mexico's cultural and spatial visions of its African heritage. It has imposed what Pierre Bourdieu and Loïc Wacquant call "imperialist reason," a foreign brand of diasporic authenticity, on Mexican history and society.[11] Characterized by the socially visible, racially conscious communities of the Anglophone world, an Afro-diasporic ideal-type has prevented Mexico from entering global conversations about blackness on its own terms.[12] As such, I ask, how did Mexican intellectuals and cultural producers construct African-descended identities as Mexican? By highlighting how Mexicans and their colleagues abroad discussed the nation's African heritage – rather than how they did not discuss it – *Finding Afro-Mexico* illuminates an alternative history and politics of racial formation and diasporic consciousness-raising to the ones activists and scholars heralded after the publication of the INEGI's data.

The intellectual and cultural histories I tell in *Finding Afro-Mexico* reveal the transnational interdisciplinary dialogues among the historians, anthropologists, writers and poets, composers, and artists in Mexico, the United States, and Cuba who selectively integrated the African Diaspora into Mexican nation-state formation and Mexico into the African Diaspora. Their constructions of Mexico's African heritage expose the ontological boundaries of modern Mexican mestizaje and Afro-diasporic politics. The potential for blackness to be cultural or demographic, Mexican or foreign, visible or invisible gave postrevolutionary

[11] Pierre Bourdieu and Loïc Wacquant, "On the Cunning of Imperialist Reason," *Theory, Culture, and Society* 16, no. 1 (1999): 41–58. Regarding this critique for the study of Afro-Mexico, see Laura A. Lewis, "Blacks, Black Indians, Afromexicans: The Dynamics of Race, Nation, and Identity in a Mexican 'moreno' Community (Guerrero)," *American Ethnologist* 27, no. 4 (2000): 898–926; María Guevara Sanginés, "Perspectivas metodológicas en los estudios historiográficos sobre los negros en México hacia finales del siglo XX," in *Poblaciones y culturas de origen africano en México*, comp. María Elisa Velázquez Gutiérrez and Ethel Correa Duró (Mexico City: INAH, 2005), 76–77; and Luis Eugenio Campos, "Caracterización étnica de los pueblos de negros de la costa chica de Oaxaca: Una visión etnográfica," in Velázquez Gutiérrez and Correa Duró, *Poblaciones y culturas de origen africano en México*, 411–13.

[12] Paul Tiyambe Zeleza, "Rewriting the African Diaspora: Beyond the Black Atlantic," *African Affairs* 104, no. 414 (2005): 35–68; and Elisabeth Cunin, "Introducción: ¿Por qué una antología?," in *Textos en diáspora: Una antología sobre afrodescendientes en América*, ed. Elisabeth Cunin (Mexico City: Instituto Nacional de Antropología e Historia, 2008), 11–29.

intellectuals, cultural producers, and policy makers the opportunity to articulate their global visions, ideological projects, racial fantasies, and democratic yearnings more freely than they could through other racial categories. While indigeneity had to be conceived locally, where communities could negotiate with or rebel against the state, blackness first and foremost lived among abstractions, articulated to cast a positive light on state racial policies: it fed Mexico's claim to be free of the racism plaguing the United States. Blackness offered no specter of social or political revolution. No one had to write about it, and consequently every discussion of it was a radical act, pushing the boundaries of what and eventually who was Mexican and Afro-diasporic.

THE AFRICAN DIASPORA IN MEXICO

The INEGI's 2015 intercensal survey concluded a century-long project to document Mexico's cultural and racial diversity. In 1910 Francisco I. Madero led the charge to overthrow Porfirio Díaz, a dictator who had ruled Mexico since 1876. His goal was political, to create electoral democracy, but he unleashed a social revolution that transformed the relationship between civil society and the state. Calls for popular political participation, social justice, and the cultural representation of the people – whether male or female, urban or rural, indigenous or *mestizo* (racially mixed) – abounded. As anthropologist Manuel Gamio proclaimed in 1916, the histories and cultures of every community needed to be studied so that government officials could design policies to integrate each region of the country respectfully and efficiently into a modern unified nation-state.[13]

Although Mexicans gave primacy to indigeneity in their postrevolutionary ethnographic and historical accounts, they schematically wove African slavery into their narratives. Historians and social scientists constructed blackness and indigeneity in tandem. After all, the origins of the Atlantic slave trade could not be divorced from the precipitous decline of the indigenous population across the New World in the decades after Christopher Columbus set foot in the Caribbean, and Hernán Cortés, in Mexico. By the beginning of the seventeenth century, the Spanish and Portuguese colonial economies could not have prospered without African slavery. Free and enslaved blacks and their mixed-race progeny frequently worked in sugar production and silver mining, but they were also

[13] Manuel Gamio, *Forjando patria (pro nacionalismo)* (Mexico City: Librería de Porrúa Hermanos, 1916).

ranchers, artisans, urban service workers, militiamen, and sailors, among countless other occupations.[14] From 1521 to 1640, Africans outnumbered Europeans in colonial Mexico. The urban settings of Veracruz, Guadalajara, and Mérida housed at least as many African-descended individuals as Spanish settlers. In 1646, while the Atlantic slave trade turned its attention to other parts of the New World, there were approximately 35,000 Africans and another 116,000 African-descended individuals residing in Spain's most valuable colony.[15]

By the nineteenth century, the place of blackness in Mexican society had entered troublesome terrain. With the resurgence of the indigenous population, the expansion of a racially mixed caste population, and a preference for free wage labor throughout the colony, slavery had fallen out of favor. Manumission – whether through the benevolence of slave owners and abolitionists, religious or political decree, or self-purchase – accelerated. Slavery only continued as a viable institution in sugar producing regions, like Veracruz, where the economic reverberations of the Haitian Revolution (1791–1804) created the opportunity for a race-based plantation economy to expand. When Father Miguel Hidalgo y Castillo called for Mexican independence on September 16, 1810, approximately 624,000 people, or 10 percent of the population, were of African descent.[16]

[14] For example, see Ben Vinson III, *Bearing Arms for His Majesty: The Free-Colored Militia in Colonial Mexico* (Stanford, CA: Stanford University Press, 2001); and Herman Bennett, *Africans in Colonial Mexico: Absolutism, Christianity, and Afro-Creole Consciousness, 1570–1640* (Bloomington: Indiana University Press, 2003). The simultaneous crafting of indigeneity and blackness has also garnered scholarly attention; see Peter Wade, *Race and Ethnicity in Latin America* (London: Pluto Press, 1997); and Barbara Weinstein, "Erecting and Erasing Boundaries: Can We Combine the 'Indo' and the 'Afro' in Latin American Studies?," *Estudios Interdisciplinarios de América Latina y el Caribe* 19, no. 1 (2008): 129–44.

[15] Colin A. Palmer, *Slaves of the White God: Blacks in Mexico, 1570–1650* (Cambridge, MA: Harvard University Press, 1976), 40 and 46; Patrick J. Carroll, *Blacks in Colonial Veracruz: Race, Ethnicity, and Regional Development*, 2nd ed. (Austin: University of Texas Press, 2001), xiii–xv and 8–26; Bennett, *Africans in Colonial Mexico*, 1 and 21–23. Of course, the slave trade did not end in 1640 and continued until its abolition in 1824; see Adriana Naveda Chávez-Hita, *Esclavos negros en las haciendas azucareras de Córdoba, Veracruz, 1690–1830* (Xalapa: Universidad Veracruzana, 1987), 35–43; Antonio García de León, *Tierra adentro, mar en fuera: El puerto de Veracruz y su litoral a Sotavento, 1519–1821* (Mexico City: Fondo de Cultura Económica, 2011), 692–703; and Pablo Miguel Sierra Silva, *Urban Slavery in Colonial Mexico: Puebla de los Ángeles, 1531–1706* (New York: Cambridge University Press, 2018), 107–43.

[16] Carroll, *Blacks in Colonial Veracruz*, 55–56 and 65–78; and Bennett, *Africans in Colonial Mexico*, 1. On the demographic shifts in sugar producing regions, see Naveda,

During and after the wars of independence (1810–21), liberal elites proclaimed that all Mexicans should be defined by their vice or virtue, not their racial heritage. First professed by Father Hidalgo on that fateful September day, abolition blossomed into a fundamental component of Mexican nation-state formation: it signified the idea that all citizens must be treated equally under the law. Two African-descended generals, José María Morelos y Pavón and Vicente Guerrero, reasserted Hidalgo's emancipatory sentiments respectively in 1813 and 1829. In between, wartime mobilization and other presidential decrees created new pathways to freedom.[17] For liberals, slavery and caste were intrinsically bound together as a sociological problem in need of extirpation – and blackness, its most pernicious social and demographic incarnation, needed to disappear. If a postcolonial fantasy rooted in national unity and racial harmony were to become a reality, then the new nation's African heritage could only remain as a subject of historical inquiry buried in Spanish colonial archives.[18] As historian Peter Guardino explains for the state of Oaxaca in years leading up to and during the wars of independence, "Afromexicans had a symbolic weight that was much larger than their demographic weight."[19] By the end of the nineteenth century, most liberal intellectuals and policy makers assumed that mestizaje, driven by the invisible hand of progress, rendered blackness socially and demographically invisible.[20]

Esclavos negros en las haciendas azucareras de Córdoba, Veracruz, 63–65. For a discussion of slavery in a region not defined by sugar production, see Juan Carlos Reyes G., "Negros y afromestizos en Colima, siglos XVI-XIX," in *Presencia africana en México*, coord. Luz María Martínez Montiel (Mexico City: Consejo Nacional para la Cultura y las Artes, 1997), 322–28. Ben Vinson has recently made the argument that the black population was likely overestimated in census data on the eve of independence; see *Before Mestizaje: The Frontiers of Race and Caste in Colonial Mexico* (New York: Cambridge University Press, 2017), 123.

[17] Carroll, *Blacks in Colonial Veracruz*, 93–102; Naveda, *Esclavos negros en las haciendas azucareras de Córdoba, Veracruz*, 148–61; and García de León, *Tierra adentro*, 751–65.

[18] Regarding the colonial foundations of blackness, see Patrick J. Carroll, "Los mexicanos negros, el mestizaje y los fundamentos olvidados de la 'Raza Cósmica': una perspectiva regional," trans. Jeffrey N. Lamb, *Historia Mexicana* 44, no. 3 (1995): 403–38; and Álvaro Ochoa Serrano, *Afrodescendientes: Sobre piel canela* (Zamora: El Colegio de Michoacán, 1997), 21–24. On the discursive place of blackness in Mexico's postcolonial imaginary, see Vinson, *Before Mestizaje*, 182–202.

[19] Peter Guardino, "La identidad nacional y los afromexicanos en el siglo XIX," in *Practicas populares, cultura política y poder en México, siglo XIX*, ed. Brian Connaughton (Mexico City: Casa Juan Pablos, 2008), 272.

[20] Studying the history of blackness in predominately indigenous countries helps scholars interrogate the racial and cultural boundaries of indigenous assimilation and mestizaje. For a discussion of why historians and anthropologists need to question these narratives,

This liberal dedication to a race-blind society has shaped how academics search for African-descended peoples to investigate and how activists advocate for these historically ostracized communities. The claim that there are no longer any African-descended people has regularly been the point of departure for historical, ethnographic, and cultural inquiries into modern Mexico's relationship to the African Diaspora. As such, it has become fashionable to lament the state of black identity in modern Mexico.[21] Defining "nonblackness" as a pillar of mestizaje, sociologist Christina A. Sue concludes that state racial policies, theoretically ensconced in doctrines of racial harmony, guarantee "the marginalization, neglect, or negation of Mexico's African heritage." A spate of scholarly accounts contends that African-descended peoples embraced – and continue to embrace – racial identities affixed to indigeneity to downplay their African heritage. Presuming archival and demographic sources do not exist, most historians choose to remain in the comfortable confines of the colonial period or, at best, continue to abolition, when liberal scripts destined African-descended peoples to social and demographic obscurity.[22]

The historical and historiographic lacuna between abolition in 1829 and the emergence of popular organizations, like Sergio Peñaloza Pérez's Black Mexico, at the end twentieth century casts Mexico's African-descended peoples as historical spectators consigned to colonial slavery, just as the nation's founders dreamed.[23] With the discussion of blackness

see Laura Gotkowitz, ed., *Histories of Race and Racism: The Andes and Mesoamerica from Colonial Times to the Present* (Durham, NC: Duke University Press, 2011).

[21] Frederick Cooper and Rogers Brubaker unpack the social, cultural, and political dimensions of the term *identity* in "Identity," in *Colonialism in Question: Theory, Knowledge, History*, by Frederick Cooper (Berkeley: University of California Press, 2005), 59–90.

[22] Christina A. Sue, *Land of the Cosmic Race: Race Mixture, Racism, and Blackness in Mexico* (Oxford: Oxford University Press, 2013), 14. Also see María Luisa Herrera Casasús, *Presencia y esclavitud del negro en la Huasteca* (Mexico City: Universidad Autónoma de Tamaulipas, 1989); Rafael Valdez Aguilar, *Sinaloa: Negritud y Olvido* (Culiacán, Sinaloa, Mexico: Talleres Gráficos, 1993); and Francisco Fernández Repetto and Genny Negroe Sierra, *Una población perdida en la memoria: Los negros de Yucatán* (Mérida: Universidad Autónoma de Yucatán, 1995), ix–x.

[23] Ben Vinson and Matthew Restall mention the lack of research on nineteenth- and twentieth-century Afro-Mexico in their introduction to *Black Mexico: Race and Society from Colonial to Modern Times*, ed. Ben Vinson III and Matthew Restall (Albuquerque: University of New Mexico Press, 2009), 8. Thinking about these historiographical tropes for the colonial period, Herman Bennett makes a similar case for the writing of Afro-Mexican history in *Colonial Blackness: A History of Afro-Mexico* (Bloomington: Indiana University Press, 2009), 6–7. Nonetheless, these methodological questions are not unique

reduced to the dichotomy between colonial visibility and postcolonial invisibility, mestizaje becomes nothing more than a euphemism for black disappearance. The possibility that it could also nourish democratic theories of nation-state formation built on popular suffrage, social justice, ethnic heterogeneity, and cultural pluralism vanishes.[24] Accordingly, the peculiarities of blackness in nineteenth- and twentieth-century Mexico and their relationships to the broader African Diaspora meet the same fate.[25] If African-descended communities continue only to be buried in the colonial past or to be ahistorically bound to contemporary ethnographic observations, then the cultural and political meanings of blackness remain fixed. The burden of diasporic consciousness-raising is left to academics and social activists from other regions of the Black Atlantic.[26]

Census data – the clearest window into the state's classification of the national populace – similarly points to the elision of blackness as a modern Mexican social reality just as it provides a rich source base for

to Mexico. The historical gap between abolition and recent movements to recover blackness exists in many of the Spanish American countries associated more with indigeneity than with the African Diaspora; for instance, see Heidi Feldman, *Black Rhythms of Peru: Reviving African Musical Heritage in the Black Pacific* (Middletown, CT: Wesleyan University Press, 2006); Kwame Dixon and John Burdick, eds., *Comparative Perspectives on Afro-Latin America* (Gainesville: University Press of Florida, 2012); and Tianna Paschel, *Becoming Black Political Subjects: Movements and Ethno-Racial Rights in Colombia and Brazil* (Princeton, NJ: Princeton University Press, 2016).

[24] For example, see Agustín Basave Benítez, *México mestizo: Análisis del nacionalismo mexicano en torno a la mestizofilia de Andrés Molina Enríquez*, 2nd ed. (Mexico City: Fondo de Cultura Económica, 2002); Peter Wade, "Afterward: Race and Nation in Latin America: An Anthropological View," in *Race and Nation in Modern Latin America*, ed. Nancy P. Appelbaum, Anne S. Macpherson, and Karin Alejandra Rosemblatt (Chapel Hill: University of North Carolina Press, 2003), 263–81; and Rick A. López, *Crafting Mexico: Intellectuals, Artisans, and the State after the Revolution* (Durham, NC: Duke University Press, 2010).

[25] The concept of black disappearance, which scholars across disciplines often affix to racial mixture and whitening, is not confined to Mexico. It has been a common theoretical tool for research in Latin American regions less associated with the African Diaspora; for example, see Peter Wade, *Blackness and Race Mixture: The Dynamics of Racial Identity in Colombia* (Baltimore, MD: Johns Hopkins University Press, 1993); and Erika Edwards, "Mestizaje, Córdoba's Patria Chica: Beyond the Myth of Black Disappearance in Argentina," *African and Black Diaspora: An International Journal* 7, no. 2 (2014): 89–104. As Paulina L. Alberto explains, scholars need to see the concept of disappearance not purely as a social phenomenon but rather as one rooted in storytelling; see "El Negro Raúl: Lives and Afterlives of an Afro-Argentine Celebrity, 1886 to the Present," *Hispanic American Historical Review* 96, no. 4 (2016): 669–710.

[26] Sociologist Tianna Paschel explains the need to historicize black political consciousness in *Becoming Black Political Subjects*.

inquiries into colonial slavery.[27] Sociologist Mara Loveman explains that national censuses allow states "to acknowledge or champion the presence of some types of people within the nation, while rendering others officially invisible." In isolation, demographic recordkeeping does not establish political legitimacy, even if it helps the state codify certain social categories as legitimate and visible and dismiss others as dangerous, unmodern, foreign, or insignificant. As a historical outlier, twentieth-century Mexico offers a unique point of entry into questions about the relationship between racial formations and diasporic identities in the Western Hemisphere. Argentina, Chile, Uruguay, and Venezuela – like Mexico – historically rejected biological concepts of race and instead employed cultural indicators like language, religion, and clothing to categorize its citizenry. Yet, until 2015, Mexico stood out as the only Latin American state always to recognize indigenous communities and never to distinguish its African-descended population.[28]

Although scholars, policy makers, and activists cannot retroactively rectify blackness's demographic invisibility in the nineteenth and twentieth centuries, we can adjust the methodological and theoretical tools we use to study it. We have typically framed our cultural and social analyses of postindependence Mexican history in relation to the relative power of the pre- and postrevolutionary state. For the twentieth century, we ask, was the postrevolutionary state democratic? A modern Leviathan? Or, something in between?[29] The myriad relationships between local communities and the state have been the main points of departure for evaluating Mexican history and society. This approach presumes a social visibility – whether via self-identification, state-sponsored classification, or both – that the state failed to grant African-descended Mexicans until 2015. Thus, the descendants of enslaved Africans as well as more recent African-

[27] Carlos Paredes Martínez and Blanca Lara Tenorio, "La población negra en los valles centrales de Puebla: Orígenes y desarrollo hasta 1681," in Martínez Montiel, *Presencia africana en México*, 21; and Ben Vinson III, "The Racial Profile of a Rural Mexican Province in the 'Costa Chica': Igualapa in 1791," *The Americas* 57, no. 2 (2000): 269–82.

[28] Loveman, *National Colors*, 22, 135–37, 208, 233, and 241; and Mara Loveman, "The Modern State and the Primitive Accumulation of Symbolic Power," *American Journal of Sociology* 110, no. 6 (2005): 1651–83.

[29] For an overview of these debates, see Alan Knight, "The Mexican Revolution: Bourgeois? Nationalist? Or Just a 'Great Rebellion'?" *Bulletin of Latin American Research* 4, no. 2 (1985): 1–37; Gilbert M. Joseph and Daniel Nugent, eds., *Everyday Forms of State Formation: Revolution and the Negotiation of Rule in Modern Mexico* (Durham, NC: Duke University Press, 1994); and Paul Gillingham and Benjamin T. Smith, eds., *Dictablanda: Politics, Work, and Culture in Mexico, 1938–1968* (Durham, NC: Duke University Press, 2014).

descended migrants from the Caribbean, many of whom fled Cuba's wars of independence (1868–98), were incapable of using their ancestry to shape the political and social boundaries of nation-state formation; they could not enter the historical annals as racially conscious political actors in the same way that indigenous communities could.

To place the history of Mexican blackness, in all its political, social, and symbolic incarnations, in conversation with these examinations of democracy and authoritarianism, I contend that we must give primacy to the interplay between cultural expressions and intellectual currents. Of course, we cannot ignore local histories of community formation. Afro-diasporic organizations, such as Peñaloza Pérez's Black Mexico, were instrumental in giving African-descended individuals state recognition for the first time since independence.[30] Understanding how Mexican intellectuals, cultural producers, and eventually local activists recovered the nation's African heritage expands our understanding of the state's racial policies, especially those focused on indigenous integration after the Second World War, when historians and anthropologists traditionally describe assimilationist and developmentalist policies as supplanting the postrevolutionary state's pluralist agenda.[31] As such, I reframe questions about nation-state formation by examining the ways in which the Mexican state, if it wanted to be democratic or at least have the trappings of democracy, had to continuously refashion existing identities, like indigeneity, and introduce new ones, like blackness, into the nation's social fabric.[32]

[30] Community formation, of course, is also a transnational process, as historian Fredy González examines in *Paisanos Chinos: Transpacific Politics among Chinese Immigrants in Mexico* (Oakland: University of California Press, 2017). There is a large literature discussing the transnationality of post-revolutionary nation-state formation; for example, see Helen Delpar, *The Enormous Vogue of Things Mexican: Cultural Relations between the United States and Mexico, 1920–1935* (Tuscaloosa: University of Alabama Press, 1992); López, *Crafting Mexico*; and Karin Alejandra Rosemblatt, *The Science and Politics of Race in Mexico and the United States, 1910–1950* (Chapel Hill: University of North Carolina Press, 2018).

[31] The literature on the post-1940 transitions in Mexican indigenist policy is vast and rapidly expanding; for example, see Alexander S. Dawson, *Indian and Nation in Revolutionary Mexico* (Tucson: University of Arizona Press, 2004); López, *Crafting Mexico*; and Stephen E. Lewis, *Rethinking Mexican Indigenismo: The INI's Coordinating Center in Highland Chiapas and the Fate of a Utopian Project* (Albuquerque: University of New Mexico Press, 2018).

[32] Ernesto Laclau and Chantal Mouffe, *Hegemony and Socialist Strategy: Towards a Radical Democratic Politics* (London: Verso, 1985), 93–148; and Judith Butler, "Restaging the Universal: Hegemony and the Limits of Formalism," in *Contingency, Hegemony, Universality, Contemporary Dialogues on the Left*, by Judith Butler, Ernesto Laclau, and Slavoj Žižek (London: Verso, 2000), 11–43.

MEXICO IN THE AFRICAN DIASPORA

Afro-diasporic methodologies have similarly sidelined modern Mexico's cultural and spatial visions of blackness. Postcolonial Mexican history forces us to consider a diasporic politics framed more by liberal racelessness than by the maintenance of a racial consciousness rooted in specific histories of migration and political exclusion.[33] After all, African-descended individuals, including independence-era leaders like José María Morelos and Vicente Guerrero, embraced assimilationist rhetoric and, in the name of egalitarianism, promoted homogenizing acts such as the abolition of caste categories.[34] The possibility of a politically charged racial consciousness, the lynchpin of Afro-diasporic methods, manifested itself more acutely within the social anxieties of the nineteenth-century liberals and conservatives who wanted to whiten the nation than with the political motivations of the African-descended peoples who wanted rid themselves of slavery's stigmas. The liberal ideologies Mexico's founding fathers articulated were not seen, either at the time or subsequently, as some variation on W. E. B. Du Bois's "talented tenth" or as a south-of-the-border version of Uncle-Tom-ism looking to curry favor with the lighter-skinned elite.[35] Rather they were an alternative vision of

[33] For an overview of these definitions of diaspora, see James Clifford, "Diasporas," *Cultural Anthropology* 9, no. 3 (1994): 302–38; Colin Palmer, "Defining and Studying the Modern African Diaspora," *Perspectives on History*, September 1998, www.historians.org/publications-and-directories/perspectives-on-history/september-1998/defining-and-studying-the-modern-african-diaspora; and Kim D. Butler, "Defining Diaspora, Refining a Discourse," *Diaspora: A Journal of Transnational Studies* 10, no. 2 (2001): 189–219.

[34] Lowell Gudmundson and Justin Wolfe make a similar argument for Central America; see their introduction to *Blacks and Blackness in Central America: Between Race and Place*, ed. Lowell Gudmundson and Justin Wolfe (Durham, NC: Duke University Press, 2010), 2 and 16. For a discussion of why African-descended Mexicans rejected racial categories after abolition, see John Radley Milstead, "Afro-Mexicans and the Making of Modern Mexico: Citizenship, Race, and Capitalism in Jamiltepec, Oaxaca (1821–1910)" (PhD diss., Michigan State University, 2019). As historian Timo H. Schaefer explains, in the decades following independence, many different sectors of society, including indigenous communities, mestizos, and communities living on haciendas, selectively embraced aspects of liberalism; see *Liberalism as Utopia: The Rise and Fall of Legal Rule in Post-Colonial Mexico, 1820–1900* (New York: Cambridge University Press, 2017).

[35] Literary scholar Henry Louis Gates Jr. analyzes African American assimilation, the talented tenth, and Uncle Tom-ism in "Parable of the Talents," in *The Future of the Race*, by Henry Louis Gates Jr. and Cornell West (New York: Vintage Books, 1996), 50. In regard to these questions in Mexico, see Joel A. Rogers, "The Negro Who Freed Mexico," *Negro World*, January 4, 1930; and Ted Vincent, "The Blacks Who Freed Mexico," *Journal of Negro History* 79, no. 3 (1994): 257–76. Peter Guardino argues that

postemancipation society, one built on the political equality theoretically bestowed when vice and virtue unseated race and caste.

The mapping of blackness in Latin American nations points to the methodological limitations cast by a political fixation on social visibility. Historian George Reid Andrews deconstructs the time-honored practice to divide Latin America into its African-descended regions, which are etched into Afro-diasporic geographies, and its predominately indigenous areas, which are not. Demography grounds his approach: at least 5 percent of the nation's populace must identify or be classified as African-descended to be part of Afro-Latin America. Accordingly, he includes Mexico in 1800, when it was a colony with race-based census data. The liberal rejection of racial categories forced him to state that there was "No data" in 1900. In 2000, there was an insufficient number of visible African-descended people to be included.[36] The tacit assumption that certain communities, regions, or nations can leave and even reenter the African Diaspora hovers over the history of blackness in nineteenth- and twentieth-century Mexico just as it does throughout Indo-Latin America.[37] This is especially apparent when we consider that colonial Mexico's place in the Afro-diasporic world goes unquestioned but post-revolutionary Mexico's is open to debate.

To query "Who is black?" is to be at odds with Mexican racial formations throughout most of the twentieth century.[38] However, black social and demographic invisibility neither suggests that Mexicans were unaware of diasporic movements in other American nations nor assumes thatAfrican-descended identities were antithetical to postrevolutionary nation-state formation. *Finding Afro-Mexico* shows that Mexican

racial discourses persisted more frequently among elites who claimed Spanish descent and who were concerned that the abolition of caste could lay the groundwork for a racial revolution akin to the Haitian Revolution; see *The Dead March: A History of the Mexican-American War* (Cambridge, MA: Harvard University Press, 2017), 27–28.

[36] George Reid Andrews, *Afro-Latin America, 1800–2000* (Oxford: Oxford University Press, 2004), 4 and maps 1, 2, and 3. Stuart B. Schwartz questions the validity of these longstanding distinctions between Indo- and Afro-Latin America in "Black Latin America: Legacies of Slavery, Race, and African, Culture," *Hispanic American Historical Review* 82, no. 3 (2002): 430.

[37] Kim D. Butler discusses the possibility for people to exit and to return to a diaspora in "Defining Diaspora," 207.

[38] The political pressures leading to the INEGI's inclusion of African-descended peoples in the 2015 census show that the question "who is black?" has become more acceptable; also see María Elisa Velázquez and Gabriela Iturralde Nieto, *Afrodescendientes en México: Una historia de silencio y discriminación*, 2nd ed. (Mexico City: Consejo Nacional para Prevenir la Discriminación, 2016), 36–38.

constructions of blackness were in constant dialogue with cultural and political projects such as the New Negro Movement and Black Nationalism in the United States, Afro-Cubanism, Haitian negrism, and Brazilian modernism.[39] The multiple disciplinary registers and cultural genres that rendered black identities socially visible in other countries also invigorated the postrevolutionary ethnographic mapping of African-descended cultures and then African-descended peoples.[40]

Mexico's unique relationship to slavery in the United States helps us understand the nation's steadfast adherence to black social and demographic invisibility. When cotton producers in Texas declared their independence in 1836 and subsequently sought annexation to the United States, the contrast between Mexican abolition, on the one hand, and US slavery and racial discrimination, on the other, hardened.[41] This hallmark of Mexican nationalism diverged slightly from the rest of mainland Spanish America, where the leaders of independence and the liberal intellectuals and statesmen who followed them affixed their respective claims of racial harmony more to the condemnation of the Spanish caste system than to US westward expansion. In this regard, Mexico's mid-century racial comparisons foreshadowed the more well-known rhetorical flourishes condemning US segregation articulated by Cuba's José Martí in the 1880s and 1890s, Mexico's

[39] For a discussion of these transnational conversations, see Kevin A. Yelvington, "The Invention of Africa in Latin America and the Caribbean: Political Discourse and Anthropological Praxis, 1920–1940," in *Afro-Atlantic Dialogues: Anthropology in the Diaspora*, ed. Kevin A. Yelvington (Santa Fe, NM: School of American Research Press, 2006), 35–82; Micol Seigel, *Uneven Encounters: Making Race and Nation in Brazil and the United States* (Durham, NC: Duke University Press, 2009); and Frank Andre Guridy, *Forging Diaspora: Afro-Cubans and African Americans in a World of Empire and Jim Crow* (Chapel Hill: University of North Carolina Press, 2010).

[40] Among the many exemplary scholarly accounts of these interdisciplinary ethnographic methodologies, see Daphne Lamothe, *Inventing the New Negro: Narrative, Culture, and Ethnography* (Philadelphia: University of Pennsylvania Press, 2008); David Luis-Brown, *Waves of Decolonization: Discourses of Race and Hemispheric Citizenship in Cuba, Mexico, and the United States* (Durham, NC: Duke University Press, 2008); and Emily A. Maguire, *Racial Experiments in Cuban Literature and Ethnography* (Gainesville: University Press of Florida, 2011).

[41] There has been a growing in historical interest in the intertwined histories of Mexican republicanism, Texan independence, and the Mexican–American War; see James E. Sanders, *The Vanguard of the Atlantic World: Creating Modernity, Nation, and Democracy in Nineteenth-Century Latin America* (Durham, NC: Duke University Press, 2014), 64–80; and Andrew J. Torget, *Seeds of Empire: Cotton, Slavery, and the Transformation of the Texas Borderlands, 1800–1850* (Chapel Hill: University of North Carolina Press, 2015).

José Vasconcelos in 1925, and Brazil's Gilberto Freyre and Arthur Ramos in the 1930s and 1940s.[42]

The perceptibility of blackness in Mexico had a different foil than in nations, like the United States, Cuba, and Brazil, where black bodies have been a point of departure for scholars, activists, and policy makers. In regions where black social visibility has gone unquestioned, its opposite has been invisibility: exclusion from politics, history, and culture. As African American novelist Ralph Ellison proclaimed in his prologue to *Invisible Man* in 1952, "I am invisible, understand, simply, because people refuse to see me ... When they approach me they only see my surroundings, themselves, or figments of their imagination – indeed, everything and anything except me."[43] Drawing on Ellison, philosopher Charles W. Mills defines African American history and society in relation to the invisibility – in other words, the dehumanization – that has been thrust onto the black body. "For blacks," he writes, "the body thus necessarily becomes central in a way it does not for whites, since this is the visible marker of black invisibility." In Mexico, the opposite was true until 2015. The Mexicans who grappled with the legacies of slavery described blackness in a manner more akin to what Mills calls "invisibly visible": its social and demographic absence facilitated its transformation into a culturally visible, universalized symbol of racial egalitarianism, social justice, and national modernity.[44]

HISTORICIZING MEXICAN BLACKNESS

To understand contemporary Mexican constructions of blackness in all their vicissitudes, the intellectual and cultural histories of black identity need to be told. Mexico's unique vision of its African heritage, however,

[42] Marixa Lasso, *Myths of Harmony: Race and Republicanism during the Age of Revolution, Colombia, 1795–1831* (Pittsburgh, PA: University of Pittsburgh Press, 2007); and Paulina L. Alberto and Jesse Hoffnung-Garskof, "'Racial Democracy' and Racial Inclusion: Hemispheric Histories," in *Afro-Latin American Studies: An Introduction*, ed. Alejandro de la Fuente and George Reid Andrews (New York: Cambridge University Press, 2018), 264–316.

[43] Ralph Ellison, *Invisible Man* (New York: Vintage International, 1995), 3.

[44] Charles W. Mills, *Blackness Visible: Essays on Philosophy and Race* (Ithaca, NY: Cornell University Press, 1998), 16. Mills is not alone in drawing on Ralph Ellison to think about the ways in which both racial universality and racial exclusion give birth to invisibility; for example, see Michele Wallace, "Modernism, Postmodernism, and the Problem of the Visual in Afro-American Culture," in *Dark Designs and Visual Culture* (Durham, NC: Duke University Press, 2004), 369–70.

makes this narrative more difficult to recount without imposing racial vocabularies, politics, and ontologies from elsewhere in the diaspora onto Mexico's past, present, and future. As such, Mexicans concerned with tropes of diasporic authenticity have selectively embraced and rejected *negro* for its emphasis on phenotype not ancestry.[45] For some scholars and activists, the term Afro-descendant has the potential not only to overcome the pernicious nomenclatures of Spanish colonialism but also to unite communities of African descent through their common history of exploitation and exclusion.[46] In certain communities, especially in the states of Guerrero, Oaxaca, and Veracruz, terms like mulatto, *moreno* (dark-skinned, brown, or indigenous), and *jarocho* (a colloquialism in the region surrounding the city of Veracruz) are used in daily conversations to reference blackness in racial, cultural, or spatial terms.[47] Neologisms – such as *afromestizo*, which signifies a racially mixed person or culture predominantly of African descent – have gained academic appeal in Mexico and, to a lesser degree, the United States. Moreover, Mexico lacks a clear genealogy of racial vocabularies that, for instance, mirrors the linear progression from Negro to Black to African American in the United States. Even the increasingly common fusion of blackness and nationality – African American, Afro-Cuban, Afro-Brazilian, etc. – has not acquired the grassroots support seen elsewhere in the Western Hemisphere.[48]

For the sake of clarity, I use the racial vocabularies found in my sources, along with their contexts and connotations, as accurately as possible. The frequency with which Mexican scholars, cultural producers, and policy makers looked abroad, especially to the United States and Cuba, to corroborate their empirical observations further complicates matters. These polyglot dialogues bridged national mythologies, political ideologies, and cultural imaginaries. The racial terminologies used by Mexicans

[45] Bobby Vaughn, "My Blackness and Theirs: Viewing Mexican Blackness Up Close," in *Black Mexico: Race and Society from Colonial to Modern Times*, ed. Ben Vinson III and Matthew Restall (Albuquerque: University of New Mexico Press, 2009), 215.

[46] Alejandro Campos García, introduction to *Identidades políticas en tiempos de afrodescendencia: Auto-identificación, ancestralidad, visibilidad y derechos*, ed. Silvia Valero and Alejandro Campos García (Buenos Aires: Corregidor, 2015), 15–21.

[47] For a discussion of some of these popular vocabularies, see Alfredo Martínez Maranto, "Dios pinto como quiere: Identidad y cultura en un pueblo afromestizo de Veracruz," in Martínez Montiel, *Presencia africana en México*, 556–60.

[48] Michael Hanchard, "Identity, Meaning and the African-American," *Social Text*, no. 24 (1990): 35–36; and Gates, "Parable of the Talents," 50. Regarding some Mexicans' aversion to the term Afro-Mexico, see Vaughn, "My Blackness and Theirs," 210–15.

and foreigners concerned with blackness in Mexico were palimpsests reflecting the diasporic visions and perceived daily realities of nations where African-descended identities were socially identifiable as well as the dictums of Mexican nationalism that nourished black cultural and spatial visibility alongside black social and demographic invisibility.[49] In this context, the term African American is especially problematic, since Mexicans, like almost all Latin Americans, consider themselves to be Americans. Without an alternative elegant way to distinguish African-descended peoples in the United States from those in Mexico or other parts of the Western Hemisphere, I use African American solely to describe African-descended US citizens.[50]

Because the intellectuals and cultural producers I analyze moved between disciplines and across multiple regional and national spaces, so do my sources. Anthropological, musical, historical, and literary texts written by a small but influential group of Mexicans and their colleagues provide the most extended discussions of blackness in Mexico. Newspaper and magazine articles as well as archival repositories dedicated to specific institutions and individuals provide me with the intellectual genealogies, transnational networks, and disciplinary debates necessary to enliven these published documents. Of course, Mexico's relationship to the African Diaspora was not one-sided; it was part of the nation's intellectual and artistic engagement with political and cultural movements on both sides of the Atlantic. In particular, archives dedicated to prominent African Americans – like W. E. B. Du Bois, Langston Hughes, and Katherine Dunham – help explain the cultural and political convergences and divergences between Mexico and the African Diaspora.

My sources, their authors and intended audiences, and their spatial orientations are exceptionally varied. I found no archival folders or boxes dedicated specifically to blackness in twentieth-century Mexico, let alone a national archive tasked with the singular purpose of preserving it. I had to trace the intellectual and cultural networks found in letters, footnotes, and institutions to connect these disparate ideational threads. A few

[49] Similarly, in his analysis of racial vocabularies and translation, literary scholar Brent Hayes Edwards brilliantly argues that the inability to translate racial connotation sits at the root of diasporic identity; see *The Practice of Diaspora: Literature, Translation, and the Rise of Black Internationalism* (Cambridge, MA: Harvard University Press, 2003).

[50] In her ethnographic work, Laura A. Lewis explores these linguistic conflicts between African-descended Mexicans and African Americans; see *Chocolate and Corn Flour: History, Race, and Place in the Making of "Black" Mexico* (Durham, NC: Duke University Press, 2012), esp. 314–18.

Mexicans, all of whom were men and none of whom were of African descent, stand out for their devotion to the subject. Most of them arrived at the subject through other pursuits. Artist Miguel Covarrubias (1904–57) participated in the New Negro Movement and in archeological expeditions to determine whether the cultural expressions he investigated were indigenous, African-descended, or some combination thereof. Composers Carlos Chávez (1899–1978) and Gerónimo Baqueiro Foster (1898–1967) moved between modernist and indigenist networks as they used jazz to recognize and modernize the nation's African-descended melodies, harmonies, and rhythms. Marxist José Mancisidor (1894–1956) moved effortlessly between fiction and nonfiction to craft a national narrative that celebrated slave revolts and venerated the abolition of slavery and caste. Only two of the individuals I analyze in *Finding Afro-Mexico* consciously set out to integrate blackness into the nation's historical narrative and cultural landscape: Gonzalo Aguirre Beltrán (1908–96), an anthropologist who scholars and activists universally consider to be the founder of Afro-Mexican studies, and poet Francisco Rivera (1908–94), the official chronicler of the city of Veracruz.

Aguirre Beltrán, Baqueiro Foster, Chávez, Covarrubias, Mancisidor, and Rivera are at the center of *Finding Afro-Mexico*, because they constructed blackness as Mexican more coherently than their colleagues, who only referenced it while they researched other aspects of the histories and cultures of Mexico or the African Diaspora. As members of the generation born just before the 1910 Revolution, these six intellectuals and cultural producers came of age in the 1920s and 1930s, when modernist ethnographers and artists across the Atlantic world rejected the nineteenth-century racial hierarchies that justified the colonization of Africa and Asia and that proclaimed the absolute superiority of Western civilization.[51] Accordingly they shared a steadfast belief that the study of Mexico's African heritage would make the postrevolutionary state socially just, culturally pluralist, and politically inclusive. With the exception of Rivera, all of them also worked with major state institutions, ranging from the INBA to the INI, as they undertook their respective projects to refashion blackness, indigeneity, and mestizaje. Most

[51] Anthropologist George W. Stocking Jr. provides an overview of modernism's contribution to the history of anthropology in "The Ethnographic Sensibility of the 1920s and the Dualism of the Anthropological Tradition," in *Romantic Motives: Essays on Anthropological Sensibility*, vol. 6 of History of Anthropology, ed. George W. Stocking Jr. (Madison: University of Wisconsin Press, 1989), 208–76.

importantly, they embodied Mexico's cultural conception of race. Blackness, they argued from their disparate spatial and disciplinary positions, had its roots in a history of cultural production and consumption, not a history of biological race; it could be enjoyed, studied, and constructed by anyone, even individuals like themselves who did not claim to possess any African ancestry.[52]

The first part of *Finding Afro-Mexico* traces the historical, cultural, and ethnographic visions of blackness from independence to the early 1940s. It culminates with the state's selective embrace of black cultural and symbolic visibility during the socialist policies of the Lázaro Cárdenas presidency (1934–40). Chapter 1 describes the historical, archeological, and cultural currents that rendered blackness socially and demographically invisible after independence. A hallmark of nineteenth-century liberalism, the trope of black disappearance left Mexican nationalists without a coherent ideology on which to construct blackness prior to, during, and immediately after the 1910 Revolution. In sum, this chapter establishes a political and historiographic foundation for the evolution of Mexican blackness after the 1910 Revolution. In the 1930s, as the next two chapters detail, Marxism, modernism, and antifascism provided new political and aesthetic platforms to render blackness Mexican. Chapter 2 treats the Marxist historians who placed enslaved Africans and their descendants in the national pantheon. Black insurgency, Mancisidor and his compatriots claimed, helped lay the foundation for Mexican independence, postcolonial racial egalitarianism, and the Mexican Revolution. Chapter 3 turns to cultural sources – many of which had direct ties to Mancisidor, Covarrubias, or Chávez – to show the transnational manifestations of this black radical tradition.

The second part of *Finding Afro-Mexico* examines how the racialization of culture in specific local and regional spaces set the stage for blackness to become socially and demographically visible after the Second

[52] For a similar historical study of Afro-diasporic consumption and performance by people without African ancestry, see George Reid Andrews, *Blackness in the White Nation: A History of Afro-Uruguay* (Chapel Hill: University of North Carolina Press, 2010). While African-descended intellectuals, such as José María Morelos, Vicente Guerrero, and Vicente Riva Palacio, participated in nineteenth-century political and intellectual life, there has been a notable absence of self-identified or subsequently classified African-descended intellectuals in twentieth-century Mexico. For an excellent analysis of the history and politics of African-descended thought in Latin America, see Frank A. Guridy and Juliet Hooker, "Currents in Afro-Latin American Political Thought," in *Afro-Latin American Studies: An Introduction*, ed. Alejandro de la Fuente and George Reid Andrews (New York: Cambridge University Press, 2018), 179–221.

World War. Chapters 4 and 5 highlight the innovations in anthropology and ethnomusicology that provided the theoretical and methodological rigor necessary for Mexicans to find African cultural retentions in contemporary society.[53] Chapter 4 traces Mexico's entrance into Afro-diasporic cultural politics. Mexican, Afro-Cubanist, and African American interests converged during the Second World War, when Mexico transformed into an ideal site for the inter-American study of indigenous and African-descended peoples and cultures. These antifascist conversations inspired Aguirre Beltrán and Covarrubias to construct the nation's African heritage for the first time. To examine the ascription of race and culture to space, Chapter 5 turns to Baqueiro Foster's investigations into the music of Veracruz, especially the musical genres encompassing "La bamba." This case study reveals how Mexican composers and Afro-diasporic performers, namely, Katherine Dunham, defined Veracruz's soundscapes as Afro-Caribbean.

After the Second World War, social visibility slowly began to define blackness in Mexico. In this context, Chapters 6 and 7 and the Conclusion foreground the multiple relationships between Mexican nationalism and Afro-diasporic methodologies in Cuba and the United States. Chapter 6 discusses popular culture, especially Rivera's poetry in the 1950s, 1960s, and 1970s. His local response to the everyday forms of nation-state formation demonstrates how little the elite constructions of blackness detailed in previous chapters permeated the public sphere. Reading the same Afro-Cubanist ethnographers and writers who helped Baqueiro Foster and Dunham Africanize "La bamba," Rivera adopted an Afro-Cuban vernacular to denounce the pace of postrevolutionary progress and assert the port city's musical and historical relationship to the African

[53] Regarding these disciplinary histories, see Clara Meierovich, *Vicente T. Mendoza: Artista y primer folclorólogo musical* (Mexico City: Universidad Nacional Autónoma de México, 1995); and Mechthild Rutsch, *Entre el campo y el gabinete: Nacionales y extranjeros en la profesionalización de la antropología mexicana (1877–1920)* (Mexico City: INAH, 2007). The question of whether African cultures survived the Middle Passage and New World slavery has been at the center of debates about African American anthropology since the 1920s. Until the 1940s, it was widely assumed that these cultures had not survived and that the black cultures found in the Americas were, in fact, native to the Western Hemisphere. For a discussion of these ideas and the research required to prove that African cultures did indeed survive the horrors of the slave trade and slavery, see Melville J. Herskovits, *The Myth of the Negro Past* (New York: Harper, 1941); Roger Bastide, *Les Amériques noires: Les civilisations africaines dans le nouveau monde* (Paris: Payot, 1967), esp. 214; and Marcus Wood, *Blind Memory: Visual Representations of Slavery in England and America* (New York: Routledge, 2000), 21–23.

Diaspora. While music of Veracruz detailed in Chapters 5 and 6 tied regional cultural expressions to what is now called the Black Atlantic, the ethnographic and artistic constructions of blackness examined in Chapter 7 consider the political stakes surrounding the black body in Mexican nation-state formation and the global dimensions of African American activism. In part by focusing on the intellectual and cultural networks surrounding Aguirre Beltrán and Covarrubias, Chapter 7 explains how African Americans and Mexicans looking to make blackness socially visible articulated two disparate definitions of what and who was authentically African-descended. Finally, the Conclusion traces the evolution of blackness in Mexico – its spatial orientations, histories, and relationships to culture, society, and the black body – in the years leading up to the 2015 intercensal survey. It uses the transnational histories detailed throughout *Finding Afro-Mexico* to examine recent debates about the legacies of the long 1960s, post-racial societies, Afro-diasporic methodologies, and the politics of racial comparison.

PART I

MAKING BLACKNESS MEXICAN, 1810–1940s

1

Black Disappearance

Histories of indigeneity, blackness, and mestizaje after the 1910 Revolution usually begin with Manuel Gamio and José Vasconcelos. Frequently anointed as the "father of Mexican anthropology," Gamio established the terms of debate for postrevolutionary indigenous policies when he declared in 1916, "To incorporate the Indian we should not attempt to 'Europeanize' him suddenly; on the contrary, we must 'Indianize' ourselves a little in order to present to him our civilization, already diluted by his, which will make ours no longer appear exotic, cruel, bitter, and incomprehensible to him."[1] These words, as well as his position directing the Bureau of Anthropology, set in motion a modern ethnographic project to study all the nation's peoples and cultures. In short, he concluded, the Mexican state could only govern justly and democratically once ethnographers charted the nation's indigenous and mestizo culture areas. There was one notable absence: in the 1910s and 1920s, he failed to see blackness as part of the national mosaic.[2]

[1] Gamio, *Forjando patria*, 172. Regarding Gamio's place as the father of Mexican anthropology, see Gonzalo Aguirre Beltrán, "Manuel Gamio," in *Crítica antropológica: Hombres e ideas. Contribuciones al estudio del pensamiento social en México*, vol. 15 of *Obra antropológica* (Mexico City: Fondo de Cultura Económica, 1990), 270; and Claudio Lomnitz, "Bordering on Anthropology: Dialectics of a National Tradition," in *Deep Mexico, Silent Mexico: An Anthropology of Nationalism* (Minneapolis: University of Minnesota Press, 2001), 250.

[2] Gamio eventually realized the value of studying Mexico's African heritage. As Chapter 4 explains, he asked anthropologist Gonzalo Aguirre Beltrán to study the nation's African heritage in 1942. However, the origin of this request is unclear. As I argue in this chapter, Gamio's suggestion was a substantial deviation from his historical and ethnographic

In 1925, after the Revolution's violence had subsided, José Vasconcelos conceived of an alternative vision of national unity, one that paid homage to the history of African slavery. He fancifully predicted in *La raza cósmica* that Mexico and Latin America more generally would soon climb to the pinnacle of human progress, as the first civilization to combine all the races of the world – black, Indian, Mongol, and white – into one biological and cultural type. This version of postrevolutionary mestizaje, which he honed while running the SEP, acknowledged the presence of African-descended peoples in Mexican history and implied that their cultural and biological footprints pervaded Latin America's racial superman.

Accordingly, Vasconcelos's polemic has often been the point of departure, particularly among US academics, for the study of black identity in twentieth-century Mexico. Claiming he sought to make blackness disappear, and therefore whiten the nation, they have lambasted his utopian prediction as a racist reformulation of the nineteenth-century racial models honed by historians, archeologists, and armchair ethnographers.[3] While this criticism is correct, it is not sufficient; such scholarly reprobation takes Vasconcelos out of his Mexican context, where most nationalists, like Gamio, assumed black disappearance and failed to broach the subject at all.[4] Moreover, to view blackness only through Vasconcelos's cosmic formulation reduces postrevolutionary notions of race, culture, and nation to the musings of an individual whose influence would wane and who would soon be a reactionary at the margins of nation-state formation.

Indeed, in the 1920s, there was no singular theoretical basis for the integration of African-descended peoples and cultures into Mexico's historical narrative and its cultural landscape. The myriad constructions of

discussions of African-descended peoples and cultures in Mexican and world history in the 1910s and 1920s.

[3] For example, see Marco Polo Hernández Cuevas, *African Mexicans and the Discourse on Modern Nation* (Lanham, MD: University Press of America, 2004), 1–30; and Alva Moore Stevenson, ed., "Africans in México: History, Race, and Place," special issue, *Journal of Pan African Studies* 6, no. 1 (July 2013). Despite Vasconcelos's radical embrace of racial mixture, Alan Knight has described his ideas as a form of reverse racism; see "Racism, Revolution, and *Indigenismo*: Mexico, 1910–1940," in *The Idea of Race in Latin America, 1870–1940*, ed. Richard Graham (Austin: University of Texas Press, 1990), 86–88.

[4] Regarding the importance of understanding Vasconcelos's context with more historical nuance, see Juliet Hooker, *Theorizing Race in the Americas: Douglass, Sarmiento, Du Bois, and Vasconcelos* (New York: Oxford University Press, 2017), 164.

blackness immediately following the 1910 Revolution were the unintended byproducts of the prerevolutionary conceptions of race and world history that Gamio, Vasconcelos, and others of their ilk selectively embraced and rejected. Since independence, nineteenth-century liberals championed equality under the law and venerated the abolition of slavery and caste, even when they glorified European civilization as the apex of human achievement. These doctrines left emancipated slaves and their descendants without the ability to use race to negotiate with the state. African-descended peoples either had disappeared (as some decreed) or would disappear (as others hoped) amid the inexorable course of mestizaje. Whether these historical and ethnographic accounts were assumptions or prophecies of racial assimilation, they nonetheless rendered blackness socially invisible, left to be historical emblems of a bygone era, a civilizational model, or a cultural identity, either regional or foreign, but never to be a pillar of modern Mexican nationalism. This was the political, cultural, and historiographic context for Vasconcelos's musings on blackness and for Gamio's mapping of the nation's indigenous and mestizo communities. With the trope of black disappearance permeating Mexican social science, any discussion of blackness as Mexican in the 1920s was a radical act sitting on the fringes of postrevolutionary racial formations.

LIBERALISM, ABOLITION, AND BLACK DISAPPEARANCE

Declaring the abolition of slavery and caste was a hallmark of liberal nation-state formation during and immediately after the wars of independence. Father Miguel Hidalgo y Castillo, the Catholic priest whose September 16, 1810, cry for independence initiated the war against Spain, advocated for almost immediate emancipation in addition to the abolition of Indian tribute. The following year, fellow insurgent Ignacio López Rayón decreed that "slavery will remain completely proscribed" and that all Mexican citizens "will not be hindered by anything but personal fault."[5] These credos reemerged in 1813, when another priest, the African-descended José María Morelos y Pavón, abolished slavery and the caste system in his famous *Sentiments of a Nation* in Chilpancingo.

[5] Ignacio López Rayón, "Elementos constitucionales circulados por el Sr. Rayón," in *Leyes fundamentales de México, 1808–1994*, coord. Felipe Tena Ramírez (Mexico City: Editorial Porrúa, 1994), 26; and Ben Vinson III, *Flight: The Story of Virgil Richardson, a Tuskegee Airman in Mexico* (New York: Palgrave Macmillan, 2004), 140.

Finally, on September 15, 1829, in commemoration of Hidalgo's declaration of independence, the African-descended President and General Vicente Guerrero abolished slavery.

In between, politicians announced more moderate laws accelerating the pace of emancipation. In the 1821 Plan of Iguala, Emperor Agustín de Iturbide explained that caste identities would be forbidden, even though his vision for the new Mexican state was dominated by creoles (Spaniards born in the Americas) rather than the multiracial troops Hidalgo and Morelos had led into battle. Debates about abolition continued when the Atlantic slave trade ended in 1824.[6] To continue the process of gradual abolition in 1825, Guadeloupe Victoria, Iturbide's successor, emancipated the slaves who had fought for Mexican independence and gave others the right to buy their freedom. In this spirit, and until Guerrero abolished slavery, national leaders annually freed a few slaves in honor of Hidalgo's 1810 declaration.[7]

The frequency with which liberals celebrated the abolition of slavery points to the ideological weight the founding fathers ascribed to it. Blackness, which the Spanish introduced to the New World as enslaved labor to replace the dwindling indigenous population, was fundamentally at odds with the basic tenets of the new nation. In outlining his vision for a Mexican constitution in 1813, Morelos decreed, after abolishing slavery and caste in the fifteenth point of his *Sentiments of the Nation*, "that the only distinction between one American and another shall be that between vice and virtue."[8] By affixing the abolition of slavery to the reformulation of social categories, he and his fellow insurgents rejected the Spanish caste system, an ad hoc assemblage of geographic, religious, biological, phenotypical, and occupational terms used to denote ancestry, purity of blood, and social status. Usually described in sets of sixteen, the caste system often began with the following five iterations:

> The child of a Spaniard and Indian is called *Mestizo*.
> Of Mestizo and Spaniard, *Castizo*.

[6] For a discussion of national debates about abolition in 1821, see Salvador Méndez Reyes, "Hacia la abolición de la esclavitud en México: El dictamen de la comisión de esclavos de 1821," in *De la libertad y la abolición: Africanos y afrodescendientes en Iberoamérica*, coord. Juan Manuel de la Serna (Mexico City: Instituto Nacional de Antropología e Historia, 2010), 179–93.

[7] Torget, *Seeds of Empire*, 144.

[8] José María Morelos, "Sentiments of the Nation, or Points Outlined by Morelos for the Constitution," in *The Mexico Reader: History, Culture, Politics*, ed. Gilbert M. Joseph and Timothy J. Henderson (Durham, NC: Duke University Press, 2002), 190.

Of Castizo and Spaniard, *Spaniard.*
Of Spaniard and Black, *Mulatto*
Of Mulatto and Spaniard, *Moorish.*[9]

As racial exogamy continued, an array of nonsensical terms, like Chinese and Wolf, permeated this genealogical wordplay, even if they did not make their way into colonial society with any uniformity. According to Mexico's founding fathers, these odious, divisive terms needed to disappear and be replaced by the egalitarian and homogenizing futures that mestizaje made possible.[10]

In the decades following independence, the memory of the abolition of slavery and caste did not wane. The lettered elite often quoted these foundational emancipatory proclamations. It was as if their mere inclusion in the national narrative verified the ideological bona fides of the author and the state itself. In 1871, lawyer, politician, and archeologist Alfredo Chavero placed Mexico's independence-era heroes within a global history of slavery from prehistoric man to the transatlantic slave trade. After referencing the abolitionist spirit in Pennsylvania and the British Empire, which abolished the Atlantic slave trade in 1808, he quoted Father Hidalgo's emancipatory proclamation. Morelos continued the fight, but, for Chavero, his words needed to be more than repeated. A facsimile of his "vulgar but expressive" denunciation of slavery from October 5, 1813, accompanied the text. The nation's history of abolitionist statements carried more weight in the abstractions of ideology than in the everyday realities of Mexican society. After all, the demographic peculiarities of Mexican slavery minimized the social and economic reverberations of these pronouncements. In Chavero's estimation, the soon-to-be independent country was a society with slaves, not one dependent on them: in 1805, only 10,000 individuals were still in chains.[11]

[9] This version of the caste system is adapted from Vicente Riva Palacio, *El Virreinato*, vol. 2 of *México a través de los siglos: Historia general y completa* [...], ed. Vicente Riva Palacio (Mexico City: Ballescá, 1888–89), 472. For a discussion of the various social, cultural, and biological identities that permeated the Spanish caste system, see María Elena Martínez, "The Black Blood of New Spain: Limpieza de Sangre, Racial Violence, and Gendered Power in Early Colonial Mexico," *William and Mary Quarterly* 61, no. 3 (July 2004): 479–520; and Kathryn Burns, "Unfixing Race," in *Histories of Race and Racism: The Andes and Mesoamerica from Colonial Times to the Present*, ed. Laura Gotkowitz (Durham, NC: Duke University Press, 2011), 57–71.

[10] Ben Vinson expertly discusses the ambiguities within the caste system and their legacies after independence in *Before Mestizaje*.

[11] Alfredo Chavero, "Decreto del Sr. Morelos aboliendo la esclavitud," in *Boletín de la Sociedad Mexicana de Geografía y Estadística*, second series, vol. 3 (Mexico City:

This egalitarian narrative continued during the dictatorship of Porfirio Díaz (1876–1910). In the 1880s, Vicente Riva Palacio, the grandson of Vicente Guerrero, took up the daunting task of compiling an official national history to justify the political stability Díaz brought to Mexico. Previously, civil wars and foreign interventions by the United States, France, Britain, and Spain had left the country in political and economic ruins. Completed in five volumes in 1889, *México a través de los siglos* quoted, cited, and reproduced these abolitionist decrees as well as other canonical historical and visual artifacts. In doing so, it set the terms for Mexican historiography for decades.[12] Writing the history of Mexican independence, Julio Zárate noted that a few African-descended peoples along the coasts joined Morelos and Guerrero in fighting against the Spanish. These insurgents, the individuals who benefited most directly from abolition, however, were such a small segment of the population that there was no need to discuss them once they had been freed. An excerpt of Hidalgo's decree in Guadalajara on November 29, 1811, abolishing slavery, tribute, and corporate rights, paved the way. Zárate elevated Hidalgo's goals to the lofty ideological sphere of "human liberty," particularly since slavery was, for Zárate, "the shame of history." References to the abolition of slavery and caste continued with Morelos, who wanted to replace the caste system and its slanderous depiction of Americans, Asians, and Africans with race-blind signifiers. Reinforcing the symbolic value liberals gave to independence, Zárate included the same facsimile that Chavero had reproduced in 1871.[13]

Throughout the nineteenth century, fantasies about indigenous and black disappearance lurked beneath the egalitarian veneer of abolition. Although military generals and liberal theoreticians frequently paid homage to leaders like Cuauhtémoc, who valiantly fought against Hernán Cortés, they cast creole elites as the patriots who founded the

Imprenta del Gobierno, 1871), 49–57. Ira Berlin distinguishes societies with slaves, which he defines as those using slavery, with slave societies, or those dependent on slave labor, in *Many Thousands Gone: The First Two Centuries of Slavery in North America* (Cambridge, MA: Harvard University Press, 1998), 8–9.

[12] Historian Enrique Florescano effectively explains that the approximately 2,000 images accompanying *México a través de los siglos* forged a visual and archival narrative that anchored Diaz's dictatorship; see *National Narratives in Mexico: A History*, trans. Nancy Hancock (Norman: University of Oklahoma Press, 2006), 292–309. Also see José Ortiz Monasterio, *México eternamente: Vicente Riva Palacio ante la escritura de la historia* (Mexico City: Fondo de Cultura Económica, 2004).

[13] D. Julio Zárate, *La guerra de la independencia*, vol. 3 of Riva Palacio, *México a través de los siglos*, 18, 185, 287, 406–11, and 468.

Mexican nation. Pre-Columbian indigenous empires were at best historical and cultural symbols of national greatness. Their grandeur, symbolized by ancient artifacts housed at the National Museum, had little to no relationship to what, in 1836, the liberal historian José María Luis Mora called the "state of wretchedness, dejection, and stupidity" that characterized contemporary indigenous communities. Indigenous legal, political, and social visibility had to disappear, for its endurance could only signify the Mexican state's inability to forge "equality under the law for all castes and races."[14] These social yearnings also sanctioned black disappearance. Liberals eager to overcome Spanish racial policies and conservatives fearful of caste insurgencies hoped African-descended citizens would also assimilate into a new mestizo populace.[15] Just pages after Mora blamed the Spanish for the indigenous population's lamentable conditions, he declared that the black population "had almost completely disappeared." Because of their demographic scarcity and geographic isolation, the few who remained along the Atlantic and Pacific coasts were "entirely insignificant."[16]

The continuation of caste categories in states with larger black populations, such as Guerrero, Oaxaca, and Michoacán, confounded liberals throughout the century.[17] The evaporation of black and indigenous

[14] José María Luis Mora, *Méjico y sus revoluciones*, vol. 1 (Paris: Librería de Rosa, 1836), 66–67. For more detailed discussions of the representation of the indigenous after independence, see Enrique Florescano, *Etnia, Estado y Nación* (Mexico City: Taurus, 2002); Rebecca Earle, *The Return of the Native: Indians and Myth-Making in Spanish America, 1810–1930* (Durham, NC: Duke University Press, 2007); and Christina Bueno, *The Pursuit of Ruins: Archaeology, History, and the Making of Modern Mexico* (Albuquerque: University of New Mexico Press, 2016).

[15] Mora, *Méjico y sus revoluciones*, 4:165. Ben Vinson explores the relationship between Mexican mestizaje and whitening in *Before Mestizaje*, 61–62. As Enrique Florescano explains, fears of caste wars had crystallized in Mexican social thought and history by the middle of the nineteenth century; see *Etnia, Estado y Nación*, 352–57.

[16] Mora, *Méjico y sus revoluciones*, 1:73–74.

[17] For examples of how caste categories continued after independence, see "1921 Secretaría de Gobierno del Estado libre y soberano de Veracruz – Llave, Departamento de Fomento, Trabajo y Agricultura," no. 39, Letra D. Datos Estadísticos, expediente 54, caja 251, Fomento, AGEV. Scholars have begun to draw on these examples; see Ma. Luisa Herrera Casasús, "Raíces africanas en la población de Tamaulipas," in Martínez Montiel, *Presencia africana en México*, 513; J. Arturo Mota Sánchez, "El censo de 1890 del estado de Oaxaca," in *El rostro colectivo de la nación mexicana*, coord. María Guadalupe Chávez Carbajal (Mexico City: Instituto de Investigaciones Históricas, 1997), 127–41; and Milstead, "Afro-Mexicans and the Making of Modern Mexico," esp. 62–63 and 80. As Frank "Trey" Proctor III explains, intermarriage among the first generations of Africans in colonial Mexico was not as extensive as commonly thought in postindependence Mexican thought; see "African Diasporic Ethnicity in Mexico City to 1650," in *Africans to Spanish*

populations always seemed to be a demographic ideal that was on the horizon.[18] It was on the tips of the pens of liberals, such as German immigrant and Veracruz plantation owner Carl Sartorius. Conforming to nineteenth-century conceptions of biological race in 1859, he wrote, "The African race, which is but slightly in Mexico, has such very marked characteristics, that it may be recognized in spite of every intermarriage, by the woolly hair, thick lips, and compressed nose." Recent migrations from Louisiana, Cuba, and other slaveholding regions of the Caribbean rendered blackness more visible in port cities. Yet, mestizaje would eventually overwhelm this black social visibility, particularly because African-descended peoples were, in his opinion, not suitable for Mexico's more temperate climate. "In time," he predicted, "the black race will disappear altogether."[19] In 1892, Enrique Herrera Moreno similarly explained that in Córdoba, Veracruz, "the pure black race, vestige of the slaves of the colonial period, is prone to disappear through its crossing with the other races."[20] While Mexicans gave various justifications for black disappearance – chiefly demographic insignificance, climate, and mestizaje – they nonetheless assumed the inevitability of black social invisibility.

Once policy makers and intellectuals determined that blackness had disappeared, slavery's social and demographic footprints no longer needed to be discussed. For example, in 1858, the renowned mapmaker Antonio García Cubas noted that there were 201 purely African people and another 10,000 with some African heritage in the state of Tamaulipas. Oaxaca was home to another 4,500 people who descended from slavery.[21] By 1884, his sociological categories lacked these racial scripts.

America: Expanding the Diaspora, ed. Sherwin K. Bryant, Rachel Sarah O'Toole, and Ben Vinson III (Urbana: University of Illinois Press, 2012), 50–72.

[18] Regarding the liberal desire to make indigeneity disappear, particularly through the disentailment of communal lands, see Emilio H. Kourí, "Interpreting the Expropriation of Indian Pueblo Lands in Porfirian Mexico: The Unexamined Legacies of Andrés Molina Enríquez," *Hispanic American Historical Review* 82, no. 1 (February 2002): 84–87.

[19] Carl Sartorius, *Mexico, Landscapes and Popular Sketches*, ed. Dr. Gaspey (London: Trübner, 1859), 48 and 82; qtd. 50–51. Ben Vinson outlines the concept of disappearance in "La historia del estudio de los negros en México," in *Afroméxico: El pulso de la población negra en México. Una historia recordada, olvidada y vuelta a recordar*, by Ben Vinson III and Bobby Vaughn, trans. Clara García Ayluardo (Mexico City: Fondo de Cultura Económica, 2004), 38.

[20] Enrique Herrera Moreno, *El cantón de Córdoba: Apuntes de geografía, estadística, historia, etc.* (Cordoba: Tip. "La Prensa" de R. Valdecilla, 1892), 27.

[21] Antonio García Cubas, *Atlas geográfico, estadístico e histórico de la República Mexicana* (Mexico City: Imprenta de José Mariano Fernández de Lara, 1858). For a discussion of the origins of the *Atlas* and its significance, see Raymond B. Craib, *Cartographic Mexico:*

Data about the size of the country's largest cities better served liberal projects to industrialize the country. With race absent, the countryside receded into the background of a nationalist history represented by the deeds of great men: the Catholic priests, Spanish viceroys, and heroes of independence, who predictably were of Spanish ancestry.[22] Blackness vanished – and, since its disappearance was foreordained, no explanation was required.

By the turn of the century, policy makers and academics had assumed black social and demographic invisibility. Scientific theories of race – defined through some combination of biology, environment, and behavior – hardened under Díaz's dictatorship. Society itself was a living organism, and Díaz's policy makers, nicknamed "the scientists," believed they could increase the pace of national evolution by improving public education, teaching all Mexican citizens about modern hygiene and nutrition, and curtailing the immigration of undesirable racial communities, such as those of African or Chinese origin. Mexican historians, archeologists, and armchair anthropologists plotted world history as a series of great civilizations that began with ancient Egypt; continued with Greece, Rome, and India; and culminated with Europe.[23] Biological homogeneity, these late nineteenth-century social scientists presumed, begat national unity, and whiteness signified national progress.

After 1882, Díaz decided it was necessary to use state coffers to study the national populace and chart the most expedient path toward European modernity. The 1895 and 1900 censuses therefore counted

A History of State Fixations and Fugitive Landscapes (Durham, NC: Duke University Press, 2004), 27–34.

[22] Antonio García Cubas, *Cuadro geográfico, estadístico, descriptivo é histórico de los Estados Unidos Mexicanos* (Mexico City: Oficina Tip. de la Secretaría de Fomento, 1884), 11–12 and 391–470. This narrative omission is also present in volumes 3, 4, and 5 of Riva Palacio, *México a través de los siglos*. However, in his volume on the colonial period, Riva Palacio noted that African-descended peoples were still visible "among the mestizos of the Gulf and Pacific, and in the interior lands we call hot." See Riva Palacio, *El Virreinato*, 480. As María Dolores Ballesteros Páez explains as she recounts foreign observers' discussions of African-descended Mexicans in the decades after independence, there was no consensus on how many people were black; see "La visión de viajeros europeos de la primera mitad del XIX de los afromexicanos," *Cuicuilco Revista de Ciencias Antropológicas*, no. 69 (2017): 191–93.

[23] For example, see N. León, *La enseñanza de etnología en el Museo Nacional de México* (Mexico City: Imprenta del Museo Nacional, 1906), C8–19, UDLAP-SACE-FMQ; Justo Sierra, *Historia general*, vol. 11 of *Obras completas* (Mexico City: Universidad Nacional Autónoma de México, 1948). For a broader context regarding this global history of human civilizations, see Patrick Manning, *Navigating World History: Historians Create a Global Past* (New York: Palgrave Macmillan, 2003), 30.

how many individuals spoke indigenous languages, Spanish, and twenty-two foreign languages. Assuming linguistic assimilation, the state failed to provide a category for its African-descended peoples.[24] Similarly, in 1898, Eduardo Noriega placed African-descended peoples outside the nation's demographic parameters, which consisted of indigenous, racially mixed, and foreign peoples.[25] By 1902, liberal historian Justo Sierra had eschewed blackness entirely. In synthesizing Riva Palacio's *México a través de los siglos*, he characterized Mexico as mestizo, the exclusive mixture of the Spanish and the indigenous.[26] Taking cues from imperialist paradigms of civilization in 1904, he placed Europeans at the pinnacle of human development. Africans were extraneous to world history. They, he implied, belonged to the category of savage people who "are material for sociological anthropology, not that of history."[27]

Finally, writing about Mexico's agrarian problems in 1909, on the eve of the Mexican Revolution that overthrew Díaz, lawyer and sociologist Andrés Molina Enríquez cast blackness as irrelevant to society. In his seminal book, *Los grandes problemas nacionales*, he deconstructed the liberal racial scripts that anticipated black and indigenous disappearance. Although indigenous and African-descended peoples were less evolved than the mestizo citizenry who would carry the nation toward modernity, only indigenous communities needed to be studied; their social and demographic presence – in other words, their inability to disappear – demanded that the government protect them. Contemporary Mexico consisted of "the indigenous, the creole, and the mestizo." Conversely, people of African descent were "insignificant," only needing to be addressed "when it would be opportune." This perspective carried over into his analysis of world politics. Africa and Oceania, he opined, were only relevant as abstractions, "because, in international politics, these two continents do not signify anything now, and they will not signify anything for many centuries."[28]

[24] Loveman, *National Colors*, 103, 109, and 135–37. There were exceptions, of course. For example, Antonio Peñafiel noted that in the Municipality of Mexico, there were three people, two men and one woman, who had been born in Africa; see *Estadística general de la República Mexicana* (Mexico City: Ministerio de Fomento, 1890), esp. 890.

[25] Eduardo Noriega, *Geografía de la República Mexicana* (Mexico City: Librería de la Viuda de Ch. Bouret, 1898), 225.

[26] Justo Sierra, *Evolución política del pueblo mexicano* (Mexico City: Editorial Porrúa, 1986), 67.

[27] Sierra, *Historia general*, 23–24.

[28] Molina Enríquez, *Los grandes problemas nacionales*, 292 and 348. For analyses of Molina Enríquez's indigenous policies, see Kourí, "Interpreting the Expropriation of

RACIAL COMPARISON AND THE MEXICAN–AMERICAN WAR

Liberal claims of black disappearance were often comparative. In the decades immediately after independence, mestizaje sat in contrast to the Spanish caste system. However, by the 1840s, the United States blossomed as the foil to Mexican claims of racial harmony. Texan independence set this pillar of Mexican racial formation in motion. Since 1819, and at the behest of the Spanish empire and then the Mexican state, Anglo settlers like Stephen F. Austin and Sam Houston migrated to Texas to establish a modern cotton economy and to protect this sparsely populated region from Comanche raids. After Vicente Guerrero abolished slavery in 1829, many colonists protested, claiming that the Mexican government violated their constitutional rights to property – in other words, to own slaves – before declaring their independence in 1836. For many Mexicans, abolitionists in the United States, and African Americans, this conflict was more question of slavery and abolition than it was of federalism and centralism. As such, in Mexico, national pride was at stake. For instance, National Guard units in what would eventually become the state of Guerrero placed Afro-Mexican and indigenous federalists alongside mestizos and Afro-Mexicans in favor of a more centralized state. When Mexico lost the northern half of its country following the Mexican–American War (1846–48), the comparison between Mexico's claims of racial harmony and the hardening color line in the United States proved inescapable.[29]

During the war, Mexican newspapers published articles wondering whether a victorious United States would enslave African-descended Mexicans and possibly other nonwhite citizens. At the most extreme, some feared that the United States would incite a race war. The belief

Indian Pueblo Lands in Porfirian Mexico," 93–103; Rosemblatt, *The Science and Politics of Race in Mexico and the United States*, 35; and Rutsch, *Entre el campo y el gabinete*, 154–55. At the turn of the century, it was common for intellectuals to use race as a basis for their understanding of international relations; see Robert Vitalis, *White World Order, Black Power Politics: The Birth of American International Relations* (Ithaca, NY: Cornell University Press, 2015).

[29] In *Seeds of Empire*, Andrew J. Torget examines the role of these two competing rationales for the conflict in Texas. Also see María del Rosario Rodríguez Díaz, "Mexico's Vision of Manifest Destiny during the 1847 War," *Journal of Popular Culture* 35, no. 2 (2001): 41–50; and Florescano, *National Narrative in Mexico*, 276–81. For a discussion of National Guard units in Guerrero, see Peter Guardino, *The Dead March*, 162–63. Paul Ortiz explores the perspectives of abolitionists and African Americans in the United States in *An African American and Latinx History of the United States* (Boston, MA: Beacon Press, 2018), 39–53.

that Mexico was morally correct to resist US expansion encouraged some to keep fighting once Mexico City fell in 1847 and defeat appeared inevitable.[30] Conservative historian Lucas Alamán hyperbolically argued that Mexico's geopolitical position adjacent to slaveholding states placed the nation strategically at the center of global politics about slavery, abolition, and social justice. "Do not think," he exclaimed, "that the consequences of the future fate of Mexico are limited only to this republic; they include territorial and commercial interests of the highest importance for the European powers and for the maintenance of a principle that England has been so determined to establish, that all other nations have adopted with ardor, and to the observance of which they have been tied by the most solemn treaties: the abolition of slavery." A strong state able to rebuff US expansion would preserve the race-blind freedoms granted to all African-descended, indigenous, and mestizo citizens. Internationally, a sovereign Mexico would be the primary bulwark against slavery's expansion.[31] Writing positively about Mexican racial formations in 1852, the abolitionist historian José María Tornel y Mendivil noted that the liberal project aimed "to establish a barrier between Mexico and the United States, where slavery was maintained in open contradiction to the principles solemnly proclaimed in its Declaration of Independence in 1776."[32] In the wake of this embarrassing defeat, Mexican liberals under the leadership of Benito Juárez, a Zapotec Indian, reaffirmed Mexico's devotion to abolition in the Constitution of 1857: the first article asserted Mexico's belief in the rights of man, and the second proclaimed the state's dedication to the abolition of slavery.[33]

[30] Sanders, *The Vanguard of the Atlantic World*, 71–72; and Guardino, *The Dead March*, 216–19 and 324.

[31] Lucas Alamán, *Historia de México*, vol. 5 (Mexico City: Victoriano Agüeros, 1885), 700–702. For the translation, see Lucas Alamán, "The History of Mexico (1849–1852) (selection)," in *Nineteenth-Century Nation Building and the Latin American Intellectual Tradition: A Reader*, ed. and trans. Janet Burke and Ted Humphrey (Indianapolis, IN: Hackett, 2007), 187.

[32] José María Tornel y Mendivil, *Breve reseña histórica de los acontecimientos más notables de la nación mexicana desde el año de 1821 hasta nuestros días* (Mexico City: Imprenta de Cumplido, 1852), 85. On Tornel's attempts to abolish slavery in 1824, see Torget, *Seeds of Empire*, 144.

[33] Historian Karl Jacoby examines the Constitution of 1857 from this transnational perspective in *The Strange Career of William Ellis: The Texas Slave Who Became a Mexican Millionaire* (New York: W. W. Norton, 2016), 17–18. Liberal Mexicans continued to compare slavery in the United States and Mexican abolition for decades after the Mexican–American War, even after the Thirteenth Amendment abolished slavery in the United States; for example, see D. Enrique Olavarría y Ferrari, *México independiente*,

After the US Civil War, Jim Crow segregation replaced the expansion of slavery as the rhetorical foil to Mexican racial formations. While blackness had theoretically disappeared from Mexican society, it remained visible in legal statutes and could be found scrawled on signs across the United States. For Justo Sierra, the infamous slogan "*for whites*, para blancos" broadcast the country's racial problems and ideological inconsistencies. Traveling through the United States on the eve of the *Plessy v. Ferguson* Supreme Court decision that legalized segregation, he simultaneously sympathized with the oppression African Americans encountered daily and used his firsthand observations to buttress nineteenth-century racial tropes about their inferiority. The United States' egalitarian credos rang hollow. In practice, democratic government, he commented, "is a dream; a democracy is an aristocracy constantly assaulted by those who want to enter it." However, racial tolerance did not accompany his disdain for the color line. He cast pure-blooded African Americans working in Washington, DC, hotels as "dirty and ugly like a low class devil," whereas New York City's racially mixed mulattoes were "clean, elegant, and nice." As both a critique of the United States and a reference to stereotypes of black incivility, he went as far as to exclaim that African Americans would enslave the white population if they ever were to take control of the nation's capital.[34]

Despite its claim to racial egalitarianism, Mexican society was not free of racism. Alberto María Carreño best illustrates this racial chauvinism. Shortly before the 1910 Revolution, he spoke to the Mexican Geographic and Statistic Society about a proposal to bring 20,000 African Americans from the United States. For forty years, Mexican policy makers had debated whether African American laborers with knowledge of cotton production could help northern Mexico develop a capitalist economy, prevent Indian attacks, and deter further US territorial acquisition.[35] These claims did not convince Carreño, who inveighed against what he called a *black threat*. Like many

vol. 4 of Riva Palacio, *México a través de los siglos*, 289n1–90, 372, and 652. As part of this comparison, Mexico claimed to be a place of refuge for runaway slaves; see Sarah E. Cornell, "Citizens of Nowhere: Fugitive Slaves and Free African Americans in Mexico, 1833–1857," *Journal of American History* 100, no. 2 (2013): 351–74.

[34] Justo Sierra, *En tierra yankee (Notas á todo vapor)* (Mexico City: Tipografía de la Oficina Impresora del Timbre, 1898), 20, 21, and 122.

[35] Vinson, "La historia del estudio de los negros en México," 38–40; Jacoby, *The Strange Career of William Ellis*, 77–117; and Todd W. Wahlstrom, *The Southern Exodus to Mexico: Migration across the Borderlands after the American Civil War* (Lincoln: University of Nebraska Press, 2015), 25–47.

intellectuals across the Atlantic, he disregarded slavery's pernicious structural legacies and the racist assumptions that diffused throughout postemancipation societies. Freed slaves and their descendants in the United States and Cuba, he argued, were "lazy and indolent" laborers prone to criminality and race war. He echoed the historical philosophies espoused throughout the nineteenth century that minimized the agency of Africans and their descendants across the globe. African Americans and Afro-Cubans, he concluded, "lack history" and "intellectual development," and therefore "descend into barbarism." Deprived of any positive traits, African-descended migrants could only hinder the social and cultural advancement of the Mexican nation.[36]

AFRICA, AFRICANS, AND MEXICO'S FIRST SETTLERS

The certainty of black disappearance fueled all branches of Mexican social science. In 1862, José María Melgar y Serrano unwittingly entered these debates when he visited the rural village of San Andrés Tuxtla, Veracruz, in search of indigenous antiquities to sell to collectors or to display in the National Museum. When a farmer showed him a partially disinterred artifact, what archeologists would eventually call an Olmec head, he stumbled upon a sculpture that catapulted blackness into liberal histories of pre-Columbian Mexico. With large lips and a flat nose, the immense head conjured stereotyped images of African phenotypes ubiquitous in physical anthropology texts and ethnographic accounts (See Figure 1.1). The nineteenth-century conflation of race, place, and biology verified the head's African pedigree. Melgar had limited information about Mexico's pre-Columbian roots and even less about the sculptors of this half-buried object.[37] He did little with the artifact, which itself was too large to move, even though it kept his attention for years. "As a piece of art," he explained

[36] Alberto María Carreño, *El peligro negro* (Mexico City: Sociedad Mexicana de Geografía y Estadística, 1910), 4 and 8. Also see Alberto María Carreño, *México y los Estados Unidos de América: Apuntaciones para la historia* [...], prologue by Francisco Sosa (Mexico City: Imprenta Victoria, 1922), 45–49. There is a large literature about the nineteenth-century belief that African civilizations lacked historical agency; see Herman L. Bennett, "The Subject in the Plot: National Boundaries and the 'History' of the Black Atlantic," *African Studies Review* 43, no. 1 (2000): 101–24; and Susan Buck-Morss, *Hegel, Haiti, and Universal History* (Pittsburgh, PA: University of Pittsburgh Press, 2009).

[37] Christopher A. Pool, *Olmec Archeology and Early Mesoamerica* (New York: Cambridge University Press, 2007), 35.

FIGURE 1.1 Colossal head, no. 1, "El Rey," 1200–900 BC, San Lorenzo Tenochtitlán, Veracruz. Museo de Antropología de Xalapa/Catálogo digital, Universidad Veracruzana.

in 1869, "it is without exaggeration a magnificent sculpture." "But what amazed me the most," he continued, "was the Ethiopic type it represented; I thought that undoubtedly there had been blacks in this country, and this had been at the beginning of the world: this head was not only important for Mexican archeology, but also for the world in general, since it revealed a fact whose consequences were already evident."[38]

The giant head forced archeologists and historians to retell the history of the first Mesoamericans and thus the first inhabitants of Mexico. For decades, archeologists had been unearthing pre-Columbian artifacts to examine the racial, cultural, and historical contours of indigeneity and

[38] J. M. Melgar, "Antigüedades mexicanas," *Boletín de la Sociedad Mexicana de Geografía y Estadística*, second series, vol. 1 (Mexico City: Imprenta del Gobierno, 1869): 292–97. After excavating two additional artifacts, he slightly expanded his findings; see José M. Melgar, "Estudio sobre la antigüedad y el origen de la cabeza colosal de tipo etiópico que existe en Hueyápam del Canton de los Tuxtlas," *Boletín de la Sociedad Mexicana de Geografía y Estadística*, second series, vol. 3 (Mexico City: Imprenta del Gobierno, 1871): 104–9.

mestizaje.[39] They had considered the Mayans to be the mother civilization for all of Mesoamerica. Every known ancient indigenous society – like the Aztec, Zapotec, and Maya – lacked anything resembling the head's unique, ostensibly African facial features. Without a viable explanation for its genesis within Mesoamerica, the Western Tradition, or Asia, archeologists assumed the facial features they interpreted as Ethiopic proved the migration of Africans to Mexico long before Christopher Columbus arrived in the Caribbean.[40] In 1880, historian Manuel Orozco y Berra thought these discoveries underscored "the problem of the origin of the American population." At the heart of the issue was the question: "Were there blacks in America?" Citing Melgar's work, he established a historiography built on the assumption that the colossal head was "exactly the black type," sculpted with "the deliberate intention to represent the Ethiopian race." He was not so kind to these African migrants once they crossed the Atlantic by way of Atlantis. Their presence was neither a feat of human ingenuity nor proof of a grand African civilization; rather, it was the product of the wind and water currents that transported the unsuspecting travelers to Mexico.[41]

Alfredo Chavero also used the head to discuss the historical and mythological origins of human civilizations in the Western Hemisphere. Archeologists needed to discard most of the theories, what he called "absurd hypotheses," that enlivened previous accounts of the first indigenous inhabitants. Previously migration across the Bering Strait, Carthaginian voyages, wandering Jews, and the mythical land of Fusang founded by Buddhist monk Hoei Shin had captivated those fascinated with Mexico's first settlers. The union of two or more continents, whether via land bridges from Asia and Oceania or Atlantis, was possible. The

[39] Magali M. Carrera, *Traveling from New Spain to Mexico: Mapping Practices of Nineteenth-Century Mexico* (Durham, NC: Duke University Press, 2011), 108–43; and Laura Cházaro, "From Anatomical Collection to National Museum, circa 1895: How Skulls and Female Pelvises Began to Speak the Language of Mexican National History," trans. Lucía Cirianni and Benjamín de Buen, in López Caballero and Acevedo-Rodrigo, *Beyond Alterity*, 178–79.

[40] Khristaan D. Villela, "Miguel Covarrubias and Twenty Centuries of Pre-Columbian Latin American Art, from the Olmec to the Inka," in *Miguel Covarrubias: Drawing a Cosmopolitan Line*, ed. Carolyn Kastner (Austin: University of Texas Press, 2014), 51. On the likening of indigenous artifacts to Western and Asian aesthetics, see Bueno, *The Pursuit of Ruins*, 44–46 and 69.

[41] Manuel Orozco y Berra, *Historia antigua y de la conquista de México*, vol. 1 (Mexico City: Tipografía de Gonzalo A. Esteva, 1880), 105–11; and Manuel Orozco y Berra, *Historia antigua y de la conquista de México*, vol. 2 (Mexico City: Tipografía de Gonzalo A. Esteva, 1880), 443–46.

question was not whether Africans had made it to the Americas – for that was already confirmed – but whether they had arrived before the first indigenous communities. Archeological digs at Teotihuacán, the head from San Andrés Tuxtla, and the research done by scholars like Orozco y Berra provided all the evidence Chavero needed. He determined, "*the swollen and flat nose and the protruding lips*" on these artifacts "could not apply to any individuals except those of the black race." His analysis of the African head and the people who carved it concludes with a discussion of disappearance. In language often utilized to explain how nomadic, seemingly more evolved indigenous societies, like the Aztecs, conquered other civilizations in central Mexico, he stated that this first society in the Americas "presents themselves to us as an expelled race," which left no clear imprint on national identity.[42] Theories about the irrelevance of Africans in world history and about black disappearance distanced contemporary Mexico from these pre-Columbian African settlers, thereby leaving mestizaje safely affixed to the nation's indigenous past and European future.

BLACKNESS AND REVOLUTIONARY MEXICO: AT HOME AND ABROAD

When, in 1910, Francisco Madero led a political revolution to overthrow Porfirio Díaz and reinstate democratic elections, no one presumed that blackness would capture the attention of those in search of a more inclusive nation-state. Taking up arms in search of political power, land reform, community autonomy, or socio-economic mobility, many local and regional elites across the country followed Madero's lead. Insurgents came from all sectors of society, from wealthy landowners to middle-class businessmen and impoverished rural communities; they were male and female, indigenous and mestizo. There was also a much smaller group of African-descended revolutionaries, including a few African Americans who joined Francisco "Pancho" Villa, a popular leader in northern Mexico who, some believed, possessed African ancestry.[43] In the 1920s,

[42] D. Alfredo Chavero, *Historia antigua y de la conquista*, vol. 1 of Riva Palacio, *México a través de los siglos*, 63–64. For a discussion of many of these myths, see Justin Winsor, ed., *Narrative and Critical History of America*, vol. 1 (Boston: Houghton, Mifflin, 1889).

[43] Regarding the African American soldiers from the United States who joined the Mexican Revolution, see Vinson, *Flight*, 156–67; and Gerald Horne, *Black and Brown: African Americans and the Mexican Revolution, 1910–1920* (New York: New York University Press, 2005). For a discussion of African-descended revolutionaries, see Lewis, *Chocolate*

the revolutionary violence subsided, and a new state apparatus emerged under Adolfo de la Huerta, Álvaro Obregón, and Plutarco Elías Calles, three Sonorans who rose to national prominence as a result of the previous decade's political factionalism and who, in succession, occupied the President's chair from May 1920 to November 1928. They assassinated some regional and national leaders like Villa and either exiled or, when it was suitable, integrated others into the state bureaucracy to institutionalize the 1910 Revolution's aims as expressed in the Constitution of 1917. At the same time, intellectuals like Manuel Gamio and José Vasconcelos maneuvered the growing, albeit underfunded, state infrastructure while they shaped the racial and cultural parameters of postrevolutionary indigeneity, mestizaje, and blackness.[44]

The relationship between the countryside and Mexican modernity established itself not only as a fundamental issue for the making of a mestizo nation but also as one of the most nettlesome. Questions about how to integrate indigenous communities into the nation were bandied about and have remained touchstones of Mexican social science and policymaking ever since. At one extreme were ideas like those expressed by Vasconcelos, who wanted the state to assimilate indigenous peoples into a homogenous mestizo nation whose aesthetic expressions would mirror the Western Tradition.[45] Others, like Gamio, embraced a more pluralist vision of contemporary society. Which indigenous cultures, they asked, should the state preserve? Setting the terms of debate for indigenous integration, Gamio famously declared in 1916, "To incorporate the Indian we should not attempt to 'Europeanize' suddenly; on the contrary, we must 'Indianize' ourselves a little in order to present to him

and Corn Flour, 34–43; Arce, *Mexico's Nobodies*, 138–42; and Milstead, "Afro-Mexicans and the Making of Modern Mexico," 1 and 306–8.

[44] On the weakness of the Mexican state in the 1920s and the inconsistent institutional support it provided intellectuals like Vasconcelos and Gamio, see Vaughan, *The State, Education, and Social Class in Mexico* (DeKalb: Northern Illinois University Press, 1982), 127–64; and López, *Crafting Mexico*, 127–37. Historian Sarah Osten explains how, in the 1920s, the postrevolutionary state became more stable, ultimately falling under the control of the PNR; see *The Mexican Revolution's Wake: The Making of a Political System, 1920–1929* (New York: Cambridge University Press, 2018).

[45] José Joaquín Blanco discusses Vasconcelos's fascination with the Western Tradition and especially ancient Greece; see *Se llama Vasconcelos: Una evocación crítica* (Mexico City: Fondo de Cultura Económica, 1979), 68–75 and 104–5. Regarding Vasconcelos's desire to utilize Spanish-only language instruction with the nation's indigenous peoples and his pedagogical differences with Gamio, see Claude Fell, *José Vasconcelos: Los años del águila (1920–1925). Educación, cultura e iberoamericanismo en el México postrevolucionario* (Mexico City: Universidad Autónoma de México, 1989), 203–16.

our civilization already diluted by his, which will make ours no longer appear exotic, cruel, bitter, and incomprehensible to him."[46]

The national preoccupation with indigeneity did not have an obvious parallel with blackness. At best, there were fears that any reference to a so-called black problem would manufacture one that endangered the nation's claim to racial egalitarianism.[47] In fact, no one was critiqued for failing to mention African slavery or its cultural footprints. Its absence was the point of departure for any inquiry into the postrevolutionary recognition of Mexico's African heritage. To discuss blackness therefore was a conscious act, a choice for intellectuals like Vasconcelos to describe a history and to reintroduce communities that liberal scripts had erased from the national landscape. Of course, the same can be said for others, like Gamio, when they chose to ignore blackness. As these scholars and policy makers established the racial, cultural, and political contours of mestizaje, they had to decide which tenets of nineteenth-century social science were valid and which needed to be replaced with new ethnographic theories, historical narratives, and aesthetic judgments. In other words, they had to decide which pillars of black disappearance were relevant to postrevolutionary nation-state formation and which they needed to discard as pseudo-science.

Almost all research into Mexico's relationship to the African Diaspora begins with José Vasconcelos's 1925 *La raza cósmica*, a polemic based primarily on his travels through South America in 1922. While his description of blackness in Mexico was the most literal reincarnation of prerevolutionary racial fantasies, his spiritual conception of humanity uniquely brought the cultural dynamics of mestizaje to the forefront of postrevolutionary statecraft. As the first Director of the SEP between 1921 and 1924, he shaped the ideological and aesthetic parameters of nation-state formation. He founded rural schools to give isolated indigenous communities a sense of national pride, commissioned murals to detail the nation's history on the walls of government buildings, and gave composers the institutional support to combine indigenous, popular, and classical inspirations into a transcendent auditory experience.[48] Like his liberal predecessors, Vasconcelos cast his policies in contrast to US segregation, which he had experienced as a child living in Eagle Pass, Texas. Fearing

[46] Gamio, *Forjando patria*, 172. [47] Jacoby, *The Strange Career of William Ellis*, 196.

[48] For an overview of Vasconcelos's policies at the SEP, see Fell, *José Vasconcelos*; and Vaughan, *The State, Education, and Social Class in Mexico*, 134–40 and 251–56. Regarding his vision of mestizaje, see Basave Benítez, *México mestizo*, 130–36.

that bilingual education, for instance, would create a nation filled with indigenous reservations akin to those in the United States, he embraced assimilation as a cornerstone of nation-state formation.[49] In *La raza cósmica*, he divided humanity into "four stages and four trunks: black, Indian, Mongol, and white." Conceiving of race at the intersection of international relations and human evolution, he declared that each group had dominated global affairs at one time in history, with Caucasians, particularly Anglo-Saxons, being the most advanced and currently enjoying a global preeminence buttressed by racial segregation. In the next and last stage of historical development, the cosmic race – the fusion of these four racial groups – would replace Britain and the United States as the global hegemon. All four races, he predicted, would supply their best cultural traits and liberate themselves from their worst. In sum, racial mixture would bring humanity into its golden age.[50]

A philosopher moored to nineteenth-century pseudo-scientific ideas that described racial progress in relation to environmental factors, Vasconcelos echoed the prerevolutionary intellectuals who envisioned black disappearance as a fait accompli. As he explained in *La raza cósmica*, black blood was "eager for sensual happiness, drunk with dance and unbridled lust." African-descended peoples in Latin America would eventually disappear through a "voluntary extinction," first whitening themselves by becoming mulattoes, then blossoming into a racially mixed cosmic superman. Abolition advanced this assimilationist project; it symbolized "a universal human sentiment" capable of overcoming racial division. "Hidalgo, Morelos, Bolívar, Pétion the Haitian, the Argentines in Tucumán, Sucre," Vasconcelos averred in a distinctly liberal fashion, "all were concerned with liberating the slaves, with declaring by natural right the equality of all people, the social and civic equality of whites, blacks and Indians."[51] However, liberals failed to enshrine these lofty goals, for

[49] Despite holding particular contempt for US racial formations, Vasconcelos placed the blame on the English colonial ventures that established the social and legal foundations for segregation across the British empire; see José Vasconcelos, *A Mexican Ulysses: An Autobiography*, trans. W. Rex Crawford (Bloomington: Indiana University Press, 1963), 23–26, 132, and 169. For a discussion of his ideas as anticolonial, see Hooker, *Theorizing Race in the Americas*, 155–94. Finally, regarding assimilation and bilingual education, see Fell, *José Vasconcelos*, 203–6.

[50] Vasconcelos, *La raza cósmica*, vigesimoquinta ed. (Mexico City: Colección Austral, 2002), 16.

[51] Ibid., 28, 31, and 43. It is not surprising that Vasconcelos echoed many nineteenth-century tropes about black disappearance. He read many of the intellectuals, such as

blackness had not yet disappeared, as he lamented during his Norman Wait Harris Memorial Foundation lectures at University of Chicago in 1926. Blackness was still present in tropical regions, including along the coasts of Mexico, which were "largely mulatto, a mixture of the Spanish and the Negro." Its survival was "probably the most vital problem for the future of our whole continent – perhaps even the most vital for the future of humanity at large."[52]

Anthropologist Manuel Gamio accompanied Vasconcelos to the University of Chicago. In contrast to his colleague, Gamio failed to reference Mexico's history of African slavery and its legacies in contemporary society. The modern ethnographic methods that he introduced to Mexico have likely obscured this omission. Numerous historians and anthropologists have pointed out that he wanted modern anthropology, as an applied science, to integrate the indigenous into a united mestizo nation more than his mentor anthropologist Franz Boas did.[53] In 1916, at the peak of the revolutionary violence, Gamio penned that a well-functioning government needs "to know the characteristics of individuals and groups in order to attend consciously to their needs and improve them."[54]

Despite Gamio's unwillingness to address blackness as Mexican, his project to document and integrate the nation's peoples and cultures – and the intellectual networks that surrounded it – elucidate the myriad constructions of blackness that wove in and out postrevolutionary social science just before, during, and immediately after the 1910 Revolution. As such, his ethnographic project sat at the confluence of prerevolutionary paradigms rooted in black inferiority, biological evolution, and national homogeneity, on the one hand, and the modern ethnographic methods

Antonio García Cubas and Vicente Riva Palacio, who established this national narrative; see Blanco, *Se llama Vasconcelos*, 22.

[52] José Vasconcelos, "The Latin-American Basis of Mexican Civilization," in *Aspects of Mexican Civilization*, by José Vasconcelos and Manuel Gamio (Chicago, IL: University of Chicago Press, 1926), 12–13 and 88. Political scientist Juliet Hooker explains that he made similar albeit more positive claims about African-descended peoples in Latin America when he gave lectures in Puerto Rico and the Dominican Republic; see *Theorizing Race in the Americas*, 174–79.

[53] For example, see Guillermo de la Peña, "Nacionales y extranjeros en la historia de la antropología mexicana," in *La historia de la antropología en México: Fuentes y transmisión*, comp. Mechthild Rutsch (Mexico City: Plaza y Valdés, 1996), 41–81; Lomnitz, "Bordering on Anthropology," 228–62; and Rosemblatt, *The Science and Politics of Race in Mexico and the United States*, 29–59.

[54] Gamio, *Forjando patria*, 45–46.

that inveighed against such cultural and racial assumptions, on the other.[55] He gave primacy to Mexico's indigenous heritage and its subsequent fusion with European cultures: Mexican culture emerged from "pre-Hispanic" and "foreign" elements. Because of their "important influences" on Mexican society, the people of Central America, the United States, South America, Spain, and France merited special recognition. Africans were absent from his version of Mexican history and were invisible in contemporary society. Defined by European colonialism, slavery, passivity, and social instability, they only deserved mention as part of "the history of the other countries in general, no matter how remote or close, because all peoples are influenced by each other."[56]

Gamio's opaque references to Africa did not align with the conclusions about African civilizations espoused by Boas and other modernists in New York City in the first decades of the twentieth century, when the New Negro Movement caught the eye of some of the intellectuals, artists, and writers of Gamio's generation. Boas famously divorced culture from biology, thereby transforming the nineteenth-century paradigms that used physiology and ancestry to rank cultures into pseudo-scientific musings not representative of the human condition. Each race, Boas stated and Gamio restated, possessed the same natural abilities as every other. For Boas, European communities on both sides of the Atlantic were not the most evolved, and African societies, whether in the Americas or Africa were not, in any absolute terms, the least. Anthropologists needed to evaluate every community on its own terms. "To those unfamiliar with the products of native African art and industry," Boas explained in 1911, "a walk through one of the large museums of Europe would be a revelation." Turning to the African craftsmen that armchair anthropologists had disregarded, he continued, "The blacksmith, the wood-carver, the weaver, the potter, – these all produce ware original in form, executed with great care, and exhibiting that love of labor, and interest in the results of work, which are apparently so often lacking among the negroes in our

[55] For a discussion of Gamio's selective embrace of prerevolutionary social scientific thought, see David A. Brading, "Manuel Gamio and Official Indigenismo in Mexico," *Bulletin of Latin American Research* 7, no. 1 (1988): 75–89; and Rosemblatt, *The Science and Politics of Race in Mexico and the United States*, 34–45.

[56] Gamio, *Forjando patria*, 13, 61–68, and 112–13. Many scholars in the United States echoed Gamio's racial schema; for example, see Philip Ainsworth Means, "Race-Appreciation in Latin America," *Science* 48, no. 1237 (1918): 257; and Frederick Starr, "The Mexican Situation: Manuel Gamio's Program," *American Journal of Sociology* 24, no. 2 (1918): 128–38.

American surroundings ... All the different kinds of activities that we consider valuable in the citizens of our country may be found in aboriginal Africa."[57]

Boas's celebration of African plastic arts illustrates the broader social and cultural transformations that Gamio likely encountered during his sojourns to New York City. With African Americans migrating from the rural south, and with thousands of Afro-Caribbean migrants arriving annually, New York City blossomed as a space for African-descended cultural expressions to flourish and to inspire cultural producers and ethnographers thirsty to transcend nineteenth-century racial models.[58] Although Harlem's transformation into a thriving Afro-diasporic community and downtown's modernist reinterpretation of African American life did not captivate Gamio, it did catch the attention of other Mexicans, including caricaturist and expatriate Marius de Zayas. Having already embraced the Parisian art scene that Boas referenced, de Zayas was the first curator to display African sculptures for Manhattan's cosmopolitan elite in December 1915.[59] Similar to Boas, modernist artists like Pablo Picasso, Henri Matisse, and de Zayas presumed African primitiveness, even while they refashioned it as something capable of enlivening Western aesthetics. For de Zayas, Africans had "no history." A continuation of nineteenth-century racial tracts, his civilizational model separated Egypt and North Africa – the regions that historically had been in contact with the great empires of Greece, Rome, and the Middle East – from the rest of the continent, which despite having slight variations in its spiritual practices and aesthetics was made up of the psychologically homogenous "Negro Race." Accordingly, he used European colonial boundaries, not African politics or cultural expressions, to map sub-Saharan Africa (See Map 1.2). In modernist terms, his exhibits helped recast the African

[57] Franz Boas, *The Mind of Primitive Man* (New York: Macmillan, 1911), 270. Despite embracing Boas's assertion that all races had the same capabilities, Gamio also stated, in language typical of turn-of-the-century Latin American social science, that environmental factors allow people in certain parts of the world to be more advanced than those living in other regions; see *Forjando patria*, 37–38.

[58] Regarding the influence of these migrations to New York City, see Winston James, *Holding Aloft the Banner of Ethiopia: Caribbean Radicalism in Early Twentieth-Century America* (London: Verso, 1998); and Marcy S. Sacks, *Before Harlem: The Black Experience in New York City before World War I* (Philadelphia: University of Pennsylvania Press, 2006).

[59] For information about de Zayas's exhibitions and their reception, see Marius de Zayas, *How, When, and Why Modern Art Came to New York*, ed. Francis M. Naumann (Cambridge, MA: MIT Press, 1996).

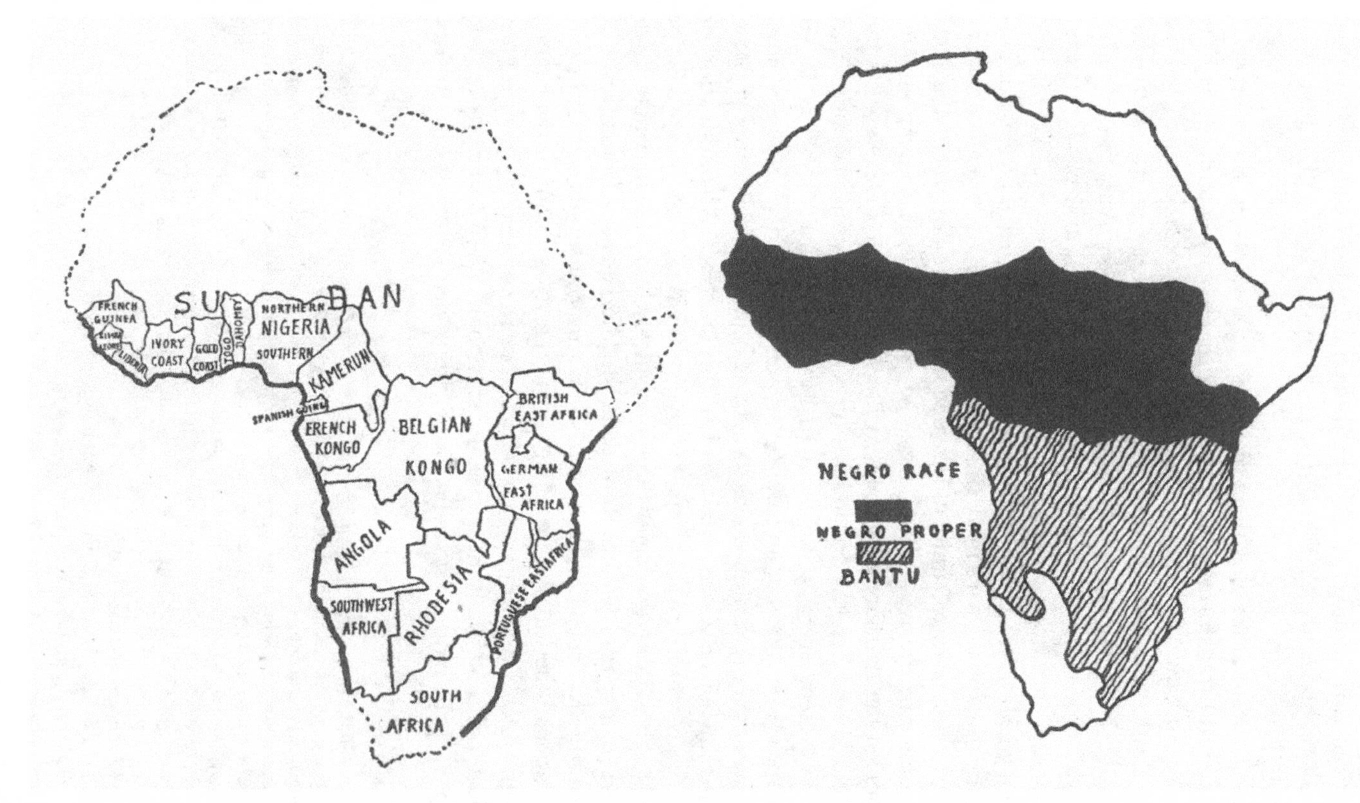

MAP 1.2 Political and racial maps of Africa, 1916. From de Zayas, *African Negro Art*, np.

reliquary masks and other plastic arts frequently assumed to be ethnographic objects as inspirations for new artistic forms. These artifacts captured during imperial adventures became pieces of art in their own right, ready to share the spotlight with Western masters like Édouard Manet, Paul Cézanne, and Vincent Van Gogh.[60]

When Gamio arrived at Columbia University in November 1909, he too was versed in the social scientific paradigms that relegated African-descended peoples to obscurity. But, unlike de Zayas, Gamio did not escape these tenets of Porfirian social science. He had studied archeology at Mexico's National Museum of Archaeology, History, and Ethnology, where he was part of the first cohort to take classes in ethnology in 1906. Because he and his fellow students were beginning to undertake fieldwork unearthing pre-Columbian artifacts and observing contemporary indigenous communities, Nicolás León, one of Gamio's professors, rewrote the curriculum to highlight ancient history. African civilizations found a place on the syllabus in 1907, when León added a unit on the "Black or Ethiopic trunk," which itself consisted of several ethnic groups: the Sudanese, Bantus, Negritos, Bushmen, and Hottentots. Although these culture areas pushed back against homogenizing assumptions of a single African biological, historical, and cultural type, they also provided greater credence to the nineteenth-century assumptions that specific indigenous civilizations, like the one Melgar unearthed in the 1860s, had their origins in Africa. Accordingly, Gamio's introduction to the peoples and cultures of Africa was nothing more than a rehashing of nineteenth-century armchair anthropology. It was certainly neither a modernist reevaluation of African historical agency nor a relativist introduction to ethnographic methods.[61]

[60] Marius de Zayas, *African Negro Art: Its Influence on Modern Art* (New York: Modern Gallery, 1916), esp. 7, 10–13, and 36. Regarding de Zayas's understanding of Egypt and the Western Tradition, see Marius de Zayas and Paul B. Haviland, *A Study of the Modern Evolution of Plastic Expression* (New York: "291," 1913), 31–35. De Zayas took many of these ideas about human evolution from his father, Rafael, who discussed the racial foundations of world history in R. de Zayas Enríquez, *La redención de una raza: Estudio sociológico* (Veracruz: Tip. de R. de Zayas, 1887). There is a voluminous literature discussing the influence of African visual culture on modern art, including Petrine Archer-Straw, *Negrophilia: Avant-Garde Paris and Black Culture in the 1920s* (New York: Thames and Hudson, 2000); and John Warne Monroe, "Surface Tensions: Empire, Parisian Modernism, and 'Authenticity' in African Sculpture, 1917–1939," *American Historical Review* 117, no. 2 (2012): 445–75.

[61] "Programa del curso de etología del Museo Nacional de México: Segundo año" (1907) (C8–21), Obras de Dr. N. León #14, UDLAP-SACE-FMQ. Regarding León's discussion of pre-Columbian Africans among the Tarascan peoples of west central Mexico, see

Upon Gamio's arrival to New York City, Boas quickly recognized that his protégé lacked a sufficient foundation in modern ethnographic techniques.[62] Unsurprisingly, their perspectives on African-descended peoples and cultures differed dramatically. Whether or not Boas and Gamio discussed the NAACP or the contributions of Africans to humanity is unclear.[63] Gamio only defended African-descended peoples and cultures within broader condemnations of racial hierarchies. Absolute conceptions of racial inferiority and superiority could not permeate the ethnographic mapping of Mexico's peoples and cultures, as Gamio explained when he lashed out against Porfirian Secretary of Foreign Affairs Francisco Bulnes in the pages of *El Universal* in 1921, the year he received his PhD in anthropology from Columbia. In articles published on March 1 and 3, Bulnes described the deficient work habits of African-descended and indigenous peoples to explain the poor social, economic, and political conditions found in Mexico and other Latin American nations. However, he reserved the most scorn for people of African descent, who were the least evolved and whose work habits, he believed, had only declined after emancipation.[64] Within days, Gamio responded, condemning Bulnes for adhering to "the old and unsustainable postulate that there are irredeemable inferior races fatally condemned to disappear." Modern social science had concluded that "all races are equally capable of assimilating into modern civilization."[65]

Nicolás León, *Compendio de la historia general de México: Desde los tiempos prehistóricos hasta el año de 1900* (Mexico City: Herrero Hermanos, 1902), 30–31. For a discussion of the National Museum's pedagogies as well as León's intellectual trajectory, see Cházaro, "From Anatomical Collection to National Museum"; Rutsch, *Entre el campo y el gabinete*, 103–9 and 144; and Vinson, "La historia del estudio de los negros en México," 42–43. Ángeles González Gamio examines Gamio's relationship with León in *Manuel Gamio: Una lucha sin final*, 2nd ed. (Mexico City: Universidad Nacional Autónoma de México, 2003), 33–34.

[62] Rutsch, *Entre el campo y el gabinete*, 245–46.

[63] Lee D. Baker explores Boas's political activism with the NAACP in *From Savage to Negro: Anthropology and the Construction of Race, 1896–1954* (Berkeley: University of California Press, 1998), 120–25.

[64] Francisco Bulnes, "Las razas inferiores son funestas en el trabajo libre," *El Universal*, 1 de marzo de 1921, Record ID: 737276, ICAA-MFAH; and Francisco Bulnes, "Las razas indígenas mexicanas y sus estadistas ante el problema de la existencia de la patria," *El Universal*, 3 de marzo de 1921, Record ID: 737263, ICAA-MFAH. Also see Natalia Priego, *Positivism, Science, and "The Scientists" in Porfirian Mexico: A Reappraisal* (Liverpool: Liverpool University Press, 2016), 97.

[65] Manuel Gamio, "Las pretendidas razas inferiores de México," *El Universal*, 4 de marzo de 1921, Record ID: 737290, ICAA-MFAH.

By the 1920s, Gamio's application of Boasian thought created a theoretical and methodological space for Mexican social scientists to discuss African-descended peoples and cultures. In 1924, he made his most direct statement about the discrimination African Americans faced in an issue of *Survey Graphic* dedicated to postrevolutionary Mexican society and culture. Despite focusing on indigeneity, Gamio equated the social and political inequalities encountered by African Americans in the US South with those endangering indigenous communities throughout Latin America. Although he failed to give African Americans any cultural ingenuity or historical agency, he rejected invectives that used racial hierarchies to justify socio-economic stratification. Instead, Gamio held colonialism liable, explaining, for instance, that Europeans "cheated the Indian of his material good and tried to erase his nationality and civilization."[66]

More importantly, blackness appeared briefly in Gamio's ethnographic project to describe the entire national populace. Founded in 1917 under his directorship, the Bureau of Anthropology undertook a qualitative study of Mexico's "regional physio-biology": its physical types, languages, cultures, and environment.[67] Its mouthpiece *Ethnos* provided social scientists with the opportunity to disseminate information about indigenous cultural areas.[68] In 1921, Alfonso Toro published a short article "Influencia de la raza negra en la formación del pueblo mexicano." It was the decade's most deliberate attempt to situate blackness in national identity.[69] He analyzed the demographic presence of colonial-era slaves to understand their influence on contemporary society. Because African-descended peoples outnumbered Spanish settlers in the mid-sixteenth century, they contributed as much as, if not more than, Europeans to the biological roots of the national populace. Mestizaje, however, hid these contributions. It reduced black visibility to such a degree that "black physical characteristics have disappeared" across most of the nation.

[66] Manuel Gamio, "The New Conquest," *Survey Graphic*, May 1, 1924, 143.

[67] Anónimo, "Reglamento interior de la Dirección de Antropología" (1440.–12), pp. 1–3, tomo CLXXXII: Leyes y estudios para formular la "Ley sobre protección y conservación de monumentos arqueológicos e históricos y su reglamento," 1896–1926, INAH-AT-CNA.

[68] Manuel Gamio, "El conocimiento de la población mexicana y el problema indígena," *Ethnos* 1, no. 4 (1920): 81; and González Gamio, *Manuel Gamio*, 84.

[69] Vinson, "La historia del estudio de los negros en México," 47. Ben Vinson astutely notes that Alfonso Toro was more concerned with presence of blackness in Mexican society than José Vasconcelos was; see "Introduction: African (Black) Diaspora History, Latin American History," *The Americas* 63, no. 1 (2006): 10n30.

For Toro, black biological invisibility was a statement of fact, not an aspirational plea to whiten the nation's history and racial landscape. The cultural vestiges of the black body only remained regionally. "The persistence of the ethnographic traits of the African race," he noted, "is demonstrated among many of the mestizos of the Gulf and Pacific and in the regions called *tierra caliente.*" Colonial-era stereotypes about black primitiveness informed his conclusions as well. Black cultural behaviors, such as a propensity to rebel, still resided in contemporary society. Refusing to fall for the supposition that black bellicosity was mere criminality, he wondered whether "the unwillingness of the Mexican people to subject themselves to their ruler and their tendency to incite revolution comes from their black blood."[70]

At the University of Chicago in 1926, Gamio continued to avoid discussing blackness, even while Vasconcelos articulated what might have been his most coherent statement about Mexico's black predicament. The indigenous and the European still defined Gamio's conception of postrevolutionary history and society. Mexico's struggle for independence and the 1910 Revolution could find parallels, if not their origins, in the "incessant wars and bloody ceremonies" that defined pre-Columbian societies. Toro's references to the indelible stamp black insurgencies left on the national spirit went unmentioned. So too did any discussion of Mexico's African heritage. Taking black disappearance as a historical truism, Gamio embraced an alternative strand of prerevolutionary historicism: Spanish colonial atrocities exploited and impoverished indigenous communities. However, the abolition of race, caste, and slavery no longer defined independence. Independence now marked the consolidation of racial inequality and social hierarchy:

> Mexico achieved her independence from Spain in 1821, but it was a movement which favored only the white minorities, for the indigenous masses remained in the same miserable situation, or perhaps worse, as during the colonial period. By the new constitution they lost the only support they had, the weak Laws of the Indies. This constitution proclaimed equal rights for all inhabitants, but it did not establish any means of making these rights effective or beneficial to the Indian. All

[70] Lic. Alfonso Toro, "Influencia de la raza negra en la formación del pueblo mexicano," *Ethnos* 1, nos. 8–12 (1920–21): 215–18 (emphasis in original). On the association between blackness and criminology in the Americas, see Alejandra Bronfman, *Measures of Equality: Social Science, Citizenship, and Race in Cuba, 1902–1940* (Chapel Hill: University of North Carolina Press, 2004); and Khalil Gibran Muhammad, *The Condemnation of Blackness: Race, Crime, and the Making of Modern Urban America* (Cambridge, MA: Harvard University Press, 2010).

relationships between the two ethnic groups continued under the same evil auspices begun after the Conquest.[71]

CONCLUSION

The 1926 Norman Wait Harris Memorial lectures tell a tale of two intellectuals and two conceptions of black invisibility. Of course there were similarities between Gamio and Vasconcelos. They both came of age when nineteenth-century educational systems decreed the insignificance of African-descended peoples on the world's stage. By 1925, they were so disillusioned with the pace of postrevolutionary progress that they went into self-imposed exile. Yet, these two faces of Mexican nation-state formation embraced two distinct visions of black disappearance by the time they set foot on the University of Chicago's hallowed grounds. Gamio recited what is, in retrospect, the more common history of Mexico, a history of indigenous exploitation that required the eventual formation of a mestizo citizenry erected on the nation's pre-Columbian and European ancestries. Vasconcelos conversely articulated his most detailed account of contemporary blackness: it was present regionally, along the country's tropical coasts. While Gamio conceived of blackness as irrelevant to the exigencies of postrevolutionary nation-state formation, Vasconcelos still yearned for that future moment when it would melt into obscurity. By the 1920s, liberal theories about racial disappearance had defined blackness negatively as foreign, regional, dangerous, and invisible. This definition left Gamio, Vasconcelos, and the intellectuals and cultural producers who followed them without a coherent platform for constructing blackness as Mexican. It would take intellectuals, cultural producers, and policy makers from Mexico, the United States, and other parts of the Americas decades to reintroduce blackness into Mexican history, culture, and society.

[71] Manuel Gamio, "The Indian Basis of Mexican Civilization," in *Aspects of Mexican Civilization*, by José Vasconcelos and Manuel Gamio (Chicago, IL: University of Chicago Press, 1926), 117 and 119. Gamio criticized nineteenth-century intellectuals and policy makers for exacerbating the social and cultural tensions left by the Spanish. He argued that prerevolutionary liberals had "almost entirely forgotten" the needs of indigenous communities; see Manuel Gamio, *Introduction, Synthesis and Conclusions of the Work the Population of the Valley of Teotihuacan* (Mexico City: Talleres Gráficos de la Nación, 1922), xviii.

2

Marxism and Colonial Blackness

In 1936, Andrés Molina Enríquez described Emiliano Zapata as "far from a classic leader, orator, or polemicist." This is hardly a mythologizing proclamation for an indigenous leader in the midst of becoming a martyred icon. Continuing to describe the revolutionary from Morelos, he pushed the racial boundaries of the national pantheon beyond the Eurocentrism of the previous century. Zapata was a "triple mestizo, because he had fifteen percent black blood; of little instruction, but of great sensibility, he was serious and reflexive, almost always dressed like a cowboy, with a notable simplicity: of good stature, strong physique and pleasant appearance, moreno, with black eyes, profound and serious."[1] To describe Zapata as sensible and serious was common in 1930s historical texts. No longer a bandit or the instigator of an irrational popular insurgency, he had blossomed into the symbol of the Revolution of 1910.[2] He was worthy of Diego Rivera's graceful brushstrokes on the walls of the Hernán Cortés Palace in Cuernavaca, Morelos, and of Mexico City's National Palace.

To ascribe black blood to Zapata and to contemporary Mexican society, however, transcended the racial boundaries of postrevolutionary society. When Molina Enríquez completed the first volume of his agrarian history *Esbozo de la historia de los primeros diez años de la revolución*

[1] Andrés Molina Enríquez, *Esbozo de la historia de los primeros diez años de la revolución agraria de México (de 1910 a 1920)*, vol. 5 (Mexico City: Talleres Gráficos del Museo Nacional de Arqueología, Historia y Etnografía, 1936), 147.

[2] Samuel Brunk, *The Posthumous Career of Emiliano Zapata: Myth, Memory, and Mexico's Twentieth Century* (Austin: University of Texas Press, 2008), 59–118.

agraria de México (de 1910 a 1920) in 1932, Marxist historians had only begun to revise the national narrative. Prerevolutionary historicism, with its celebration of political order and its evolutionary ranking of world civilizations by race and nation, fell out of favor. Fearing the specter of communism, dissidents on the right, such as José Vasconcelos, rejected the materialist undercurrents of this new narrative.[3] Amid the radicalization of national politics, visible social groups – indigenous and mestizo, rural and urban, male and female – brokered deals with the state and helped forge the political boundaries for the ruling party that Plutarco Elías Calles founded in 1929 and that would become the PRI in 1946. For those on the left eager to see socialism nurture postrevolutionary progress, the election of Lázaro Cárdenas in 1934 signaled the triumph of the nation's democratic possibilities. For them, the barriers to citizenship and political participation appeared to be shattering.[4]

Retelling the national narrative was as much a political act as it was a historiographic one. Historians and historically minded intellectuals like Andrés Molina Enríquez, Rafael Ramos Pedrueza, Alfonso Teja Zabre, and José Mancisidor reexamined slave resistance by situating African-descended peoples within broader debates about Mexican independence and the development of a modern Mexican society.[5] Creole patriotism no longer symbolized Mexican modernity. Instead, Marxism, which fastened the abolition of slavery and caste to the ascendancy of a bourgeois state, provided them with an ideological scaffolding to construct blackness as Mexican for the first time since independence. Unlike the prerevolutionary

[3] On this historiographic shift, see Mary Kay Vaughan, *Cultural Politics in Revolution: Teachers, Peasants, and Schools in Mexico, 1930–1940* (Tucson: University of Arizona Press, 1997), 38–40; and Stephen E. Lewis, *Ambivalent Revolution: Forging State and Nation in Chiapas, 1910–1945* (Albuquerque: University of New Mexico Press, 2005), 84–85.

[4] For example, see Jocelyn Olcott, *Revolutionary Women in Postrevolutionary Mexico* (Durham, NC: Duke University Press, 2005); Kevin J. Middlebrook, *The Paradox of the Revolution: Labor, the State, and Authoritarianism in Mexico* (Baltimore, MD: Johns Hopkins University Press, 1995); and Dawson, *Indian and Nation in Revolutionary Mexico*.

[5] Dominick LaCapra effectively shows the ways history and historiography are written dialogically in *Rethinking Intellectual History: Texts, Contexts, Language* (Ithaca, NY: Cornell University Press, 1983). While there is ample discussion surrounding the historiography of colonial Mexico and the wars of independence, these Marxist interventions have not garnered the attention they deserve. For example, see Vinson, "La historia del estudio de los negros en México," 45–73; and Eric Van Young, "No Human Power to Impede the Impenetrable Order of Providence: The Historiography of Mexican Independence," in *Writing Mexican History* (Stanford, CA: Stanford University Press, 2012), 127–63.

liberals who defined the demographic, social, and cultural legacies of slavery negatively, as something the laws of science ordained to disappear, Marxist historians depicted African-descended peoples as heroes emblematic of the spirit of 1910 Revolution and, in a few cases, as political theorists who set the stage for socialism in the not too distant future.[6]

MARXISM AND POSTREVOLUTIONARY SOCIAL JUSTICE

Marxism was not new to Mexico in the 1930s, but its centrality in postrevolutionary nation-state formation was. Since the outbreak of the revolutionary violence, socialist programs in the states of Yucatán, Jalisco, Michoacán, Tabasco, Tamaulipas, and Veracruz had a touch-and-go relationship with the federal state. Soviet attempts to export Marxist-Leninist revolution through the Communist International, or Comintern, failed to adapt to Mexico's local realities. In Mexico City, the preoccupation with the study and incorporation of rural communities – the crafting of a mestizo nationality – stressed ethnicity and culture, which according to orthodox Marxists were of secondary importance to questions about the modes of production, class exploitation, and proletarian consciousness-raising.[7] Many of the Mexican intellectuals swept up in the excitement surrounding Vladimir Lenin's 1917 seizure of power in Russia believed that these two social revolutions, the first and second of the twentieth century, were inextricably bound.[8] By the 1930s, federal policy makers, artists, and academics adopted many of the reforms, such as land redistribution, the expansion of workers' rights, and socialist public education, that governors had enacted regionally. This was not a full-fledged embrace of socialist

[6] This materialist description of African-descended Mexicans as conspirators, rebels, and political theorists places them not only in Mexico's revolutionary teleology but also in a black radical tradition similar to what Gregory Childs explores in "Conspiracies, Seditions, Rebellions: Concepts and Categories in the Study of Slave Resistance," in *New Perspectives on the Black Intellectual Tradition*, ed. Keisha N. Blain, Christopher Cameron, and Ashley D. Farmer (Evanston, IL: Northwestern University Press, 2018), 217–31.

[7] Barry Carr, *Marxism and Communism in Twentieth-Century Mexico* (Lincoln: University of Nebraska Press, 1992); and Daniela Spenser, *Stumbling Its Way through Mexico: The Early Years of the Communist International*, trans. Peter Gellert (Tuscaloosa: University of Alabama Press, 2011).

[8] Rafael Ramos Pedrueza, *Rusia soviet y México revolucionario: Vicente Guerrero, precursor del socialismo* (Mexico City: Secretaría de Educación Pública, 1922), 3–17.

dogma but rather was an attempt to consolidate the Revolution and to soften the capitalist economic structures that had led to its outbreak.[9]

In the 1930s, these populist exhortations were global in their revolutionary spirit, democratic aspirations, and rejection of class exploitation, imperialism, and racial inequality.[10] Inspired by Lenin's conception of a Communist vanguard, Alfonso Teja Zabre believed that popular movements could best be understood through "great men" who "are indices of the spontaneous thrust of the people."[11] The most theoretically inclined but the least dogmatic of this generation of Marxist historians, he considered social relations and cultural production in tandem. A modern relativist perspective, he affirmed, would begat "a new humanism" that engendered agrarian reform, economic liberation, and social equality.[12] In 1936, Stalinist writer and historian José Mancisidor cast heroes, like José María Morelos and Emiliano Zapata, as revolutionary symbols for all of the world's colonized peoples.[13] Completed in 1931, José Clemente Orozco's five frescos at the New School for Social Research in Manhattan – *Science, Labor, and Art*; *Homecoming of the Worker of the New Day*; *Struggle in the Orient*; *Struggle in the Occident*; and *Table*

[9] Sarah Osten explains how Plutarco Elías Calles's embrace of these regional socialist movements established the political foundation for the single-party state that emerged under the PNR and then became the PRM in 1938 and the PRI in 1946; see *The Mexican Revolution's Wake*, 234–59. Some of these reforms took inspiration from abroad, looking for example to Soviet agricultural and industrial projects; see Friedrich E. Schuler, *Mexico between Hitler and Roosevelt: Mexican Foreign Relations in the Age of Lázaro Cárdenas, 1934–1940* (Albuquerque: University of New Mexico Press, 1998), 54–55.

[10] For an example of this anti-imperialist politics, see Rafael Ramos Pedrueza to Señor Lic. Don Emilio Portes Gil, 5 de septiembre de 1933, 518.3/1, AGN-FAR. Strongly resembling the arguments in this chapter, historian Jessica Lynn Graham explains that communists in Brazil and the United States in the 1930s saw racism as a signpost for the failures of democracy; they envisioned multiracial movements as a means to foment racial equality and democracy; see *Shifting the Meaning of Democracy: Race, Politics, and Culture in the United States and Brazil* (Berkeley: University of California Press, 2019), 28–68.

[11] Alfonso Teja Zabre, "Las raíces de la Revolución Mexicana," 15, 433/26, AGN-FLCA.

[12] Alfonso Teja Zabre, *Teoría de la revolución* (Mexico City: Ediciones Botas, 1936), esp. 56–57. Teja Zabre discussed modernism and culture in relation to the politics of historical writing in *Biografía de México: Introducción y sinopsis* (Mexico City: Universidad Nacional de México Autónoma, 1931), 11–20. For a discussion of his less orthodox version of Marxism, see Luis F. Ruiz, "Where Have All the Marxists Gone? Marxism and the Historiography of the Mexican Revolution," *A Contra corriente* 5, no. 2 (2008): 203. Also see Arturo Arnáiz y Freg, "Alfonso Teja Zabre (1888–1962): El historiador," *Revista de Historia de América*, nos. 53/54 (1962): 229.

[13] José Mancisidor, "Índice de la decoración mural de la Escuela Normal Veracruzana," in vol. 4 of *Obras completas de José Mancisidor* (Xalapa: Gobierno del Estado de Veracruz, 1980), 142.

of Universal Brotherhood – associated the 1910 Revolution with Lenin's anticolonial sentiments and Mahatma Gandhi's quest for Indian independence. This kindred revolutionary spirit was not confined to past events and current uprisings, for Orozco extended the brotherhood to include the would-be revolutionaries of all races: the colonized people of the Americas, Africa, and Asia.[14] Reflecting on the relationship between race and social justice during Mexico's struggle for independence, but with obvious implications for postrevolutionary indigenism and for the hatred spread by fascism, he stated in 1945, "To achieve unity, peace, and progress, it would be enough, perhaps, to dismiss the racial question for good and all."[15]

President of Mexico from 1934 to 1940, Lázaro Cárdenas personified the euphoria surrounding the socialist turn in Mexican politics. He redistributed more land than all of his predecessors combined, nationalized the petroleum industry, and presided over the expansion of socialist education in the countryside. In 1939, Ángel M. Corzo of the Socialist Party of Chiapas extolled the virtues of the decade's radicalism. A member of the Department of Indian Affairs that Cárdenas founded in 1936, he wanted indigenous communities to participate, whether through surveys or at congresses, in their transformation into a mestizo citizenry.[16] In favor of the materialist focus on class, Corzo announced that Cárdenas established, "for the first time in the History of our country, a campaign in favor of the liberation of the Indian, an attitude eminently revolutionary that, by embodying the highest postulate of social justice in favor of the oppressed classes, has merited the unanimous applause of the Mexican people and of all the Indo-American nations."[17]

The radicalization of national politics provided a pretext to rewrite the nation's history and, in a vanguardist manner, to spread class consciousness among the rural and industrial workers.[18] This desire was not new. For years, the historians who came of age during the revolutionary violence had clamored for an opportunity to put their stamp on Mexico's

[14] Desmond Rochfort, *Mexican Muralists: Orozco, Rivera, Siqueiros* (San Francisco, CA: Chronicle Books, 1998), 137–38.

[15] José Clemente Orozco, *An Autobiography*, trans. Robert C. Stephenson (Austin: University of Texas Press, 2014), 108.

[16] Dawson, *Indian and Nation in Revolutionary Mexico*, 88 and 108.

[17] Statement by Ángel M. Corzo, Genaro V. Vázquez, Amador Coutiño, Ranulfo Calderón, Anastasio García Toledo, Blanca de la Vega, Ismael Corzo Blanco and Jorge H. Marín, 29 de agosto de 1939, 533.4/1, AGN-FLCA.

[18] Luis G. Monzón, *Detalles de la educación socialista implantables en México* (Mexico City: Talleres Gráficas de la Nación, 1936), 9–15 and 327–28.

past.[19] In 1921, communist teacher, congressional representative, and historian Rafael Ramos Pedrueza foreshadowed the political stakes of this historiographic revision. "The independence of a people," he penned, explaining how historical narration sets the stage for social justice, "is compensation for their conquest; consequently the names of the liberators are loved; those of the conquistadores, loathed."[20] By 1934, his hopes were coming true, since a materialist national history "gave children and adults the ability to achieve their mission of social emancipation."[21] Teja Zabre echoed these sentiments in *Historia de México: Una moderna interpretación*, one of the decade's most frequently read texts. "The history of Mexico," he lamented in 1935, "is perhaps one of the branches of universal history in greatest need of rewriting."[22]

FROM SLAVE RESISTANCE TO THE 1910 REVOLUTION

Marxist historians reconsidered the historical importance of independence when they retold the national narrative. In overthrowing Spanish feudalism, heroes like Father Hidalgo, José María Morelos, and Vicente Guerrero set Mexico on its revolutionary path toward the socialist overtures of the 1930s. Their abolitionist decrees not only gave currency to postcolonial claims of racial harmony but, in this new political climate, also pointed to the historical agency of enslaved Africans and their descendants. Before the 1910 Revolution, pseudo-scientific racial assumptions had rendered all black peoples historical objects only capable of elucidating the horrors of Spanish colonialism. For example, according to Vicente Riva Palacio, the introduction of African slaves artificially divided colonial society into castes, what he called "the odious distinction among Spaniards and Indians, mestizos, blacks, mulattoes and zambaigos." Anxieties about racial degeneration speckled his reflections on colonial blackness. The caste moniker going backward, *salta atrás*, signified a person who "has black characteristics" but was "born of a white

[19] Thomas Benjamin, *La Revolución: Mexico's Great Revolution as Memory, Myth, and History* (Austin: University of Texas Press, 2000), 141.

[20] Ramos Pedrueza, *Rusia soviet y México revolucionario*, 24.

[21] Rafael Ramos Pedrueza, *La lucha de las clases a través de la historia de México* (Mexico City: Ediciones Revista LUX, 1934), 10.

[22] Alfonso Teja Zabre, *Historia de México: Una moderna interpretación* (Mexico City: Secretaría de Relaciones Exteriores, 1935), vii. Translation from Alfonso Teja Zabre, *Guide to the History of Mexico: A Modern Interpretation*, trans. P. M. del Campo (Mexico City: Press of the Ministry of Foreign Affairs, 1935), vii.

family." The term represented an "atavistic phenomenon," a reduction in the family's whiteness because of the presence of "a black grandmother." Nearly all mulattoes, he maintained, shared this regressive trait, whereas mixed-race people who only descended from European and indigenous lines never possessed it. Despite his distinctly nineteenth-century orientations, Riva Palacio's conclusions had their roots in centuries-old Spanish theories about purity of blood, which cast indigenous peoples as pure and Africans as permanently stained for having resisted Catholic conversion in the Old World.[23] Porfirian intellectuals, like Nicolás León, sustained these racial conceits into the 1920s. The presence of African-descended peoples, he purported, had not only forged the discriminatory caste system but also lowered the social standing of indigenous and other mixed-race people. "Fortunately," he penned, "not all of the regions of Mexico were invaded by them, since they were almost only found in the territories of Veracruz, Oaxaca, Cuernavaca and Guerrero."[24]

In the 1930s, Marxism fed a historiographic revision that situated enslaved Africans, indigenous communities, and their mixed-race descendants as the forerunners to a revolutionary teleology that began with the wars of independence, continued with the mid-century triumph of liberalism, and culminated with the 1910 Revolution. In 1932, Rafael Ramos Pedrueza provided public school students with a straightforward economic platform to anchor Mexico's history of resistance, rebellion, and race. His narrative interpretation pays homage to "the production achieved by slaves." Fundamentally a class relation, slavery acquired distinctly racial overtones once the Spanish forbade indigenous slavery and turned exclusively, in theory, to Africans for forced labor. Yet, for him, historians should not understand slavery in isolation, as the history of one racial group exploiting another. It was one piece of a larger socio-economic system that allowed the Spanish to exploit all of their colonial subjects, "the castes, mestizos, blacks, mulattoes and their multiple subdivisions."[25]

[23] Riva Palacio, *El Virreinato*, viii and 471–72. Regarding the centrality of black blood in Spanish definitions of purity of blood, see Martínez, "The Black Blood of New Spain," 479–520.

[24] Nicolás León, *Las castas del México colonial o Nueva España: Noticias etno-antropológicas* (Mexico City: Talleres Gráficos del Museo Nacional de Arqueología y Etnografía, 1924), 20.

[25] Rafael Ramos Pedrueza, *Sugerencias revolucionarias para la enseñanza de la historia* (Mexico City: Universidad Nacional de México Autónomo, 1932), 10 and 15.

Mestizaje therefore suggested more than racial mixture. As the foundation for cross-racial alliances and eventually national unity, it transcended the oppression and atomization inherent to the caste system. Accordingly, slave resistance was part of Mexico's revolutionary spirit. More than any other historical figure, Gaspar Yanga represented this political and historiographic transformation in the study of colonial blackness.[26] An Angolan-born slave who worked in the sugar plantations of Córdoba, Veracruz, he revolted against his master in the last decades of the sixteenth century and subsequently established the first maroon society to gain recognition as a free black town in the Americas in 1609. Prior to the 1930s, Riva Palacio had written the most comprehensive history of Yanga and his followers. Following the liberal narrative that reduced African slavery to a symbol of Spanish injustice, he explained in 1870 that African-born slaves "thought about liberty, not only because the love of liberty is innate in the heart, but also in order to flee from the barbaric treatments that they were exposed to every day and all day."[27] With Porfirio Díaz's emphasis on law and order, the glorification of subaltern insurgency became a distant memory by the time Riva Palacio compiled *México a través de los siglos* in 1889. Despite the runaway community's success in establishing the town of San Lorenzo de Cerralvo (or San Lorenzo de los Negros as it was also called), Riva Palacio focused on Yanga's mistakes and poor relations with the Spanish. No longer lovers of liberty, runaway slaves were intransigent violent insurrectionaries who robbed nearby estates, burned plantations, and raped women.[28]

In the 1930s, the glorification of subaltern resistance led to a decree on November 5, 1932, renaming the town of San Lorenzo de Cerralvo eponymously after its early seventeenth-century leader. As a historical icon and a now community, Yanga was consecrated in the state's geography. National historians also embraced his symbolism. Rafael Ramos Pedrueza placed Yanga's military successes in a long line of colonial rebellions that also included indigenous revolts and the 1692 Mexico

[26] García de León, *Tierra adentro*, 557.

[27] Vicente Riva Palacio, "Los treinta y tres negros," in vol. 1 of *El libro rojo, 1520–1867*, by Vicente Riva Palacio et al. (Mexico City: A. Pola, 1905), 353.

[28] Riva Palacio, *El Virreinato*, 549–50. For a discussion of political order in Porfirian historical thought, see Sierra, *Evolución política del pueblo mexicano*; and Herrera Moreno, *El cantón de Córdoba*, 83–103. For a discussion of nineteenth-century constructions of African-descended peoples, especially soldiers, as brutal and violent, see Milstead, "Afro-Mexicans and the Making of Modern Mexico," 33–40.

City grain riot. Runaway slaves, like those who followed Yanga into Veracruz's mountains, voluntarily chose "the dangerous life of the wild animals" to what Ramos Pedrueza sarcastically called "the peace of tyranny." In broader terms, he defined the entire American-born population – free and enslaved Africans, Spanish creoles, indigenous communities, and mixed-race peoples – by their dissatisfaction with Spanish colonialism. Centuries later, as popular grievances escalated, all of these caste groups came together to fight for independence. Accordingly, the cross-race populations that composed the lowest rungs of the Spanish caste system – not just the creole elites who nineteenth-century liberals had fêted – founded the Mexican nation.[29]

Historian José Mancisidor communicated the decade's regional and national embrace of African-descended peoples even more directly than other Marxist historians did. Born to a family on the edge of poverty in the city of Veracruz on April 20, 1894, he was acutely aware of the difficulties that the poor encountered daily. These experiences eventually pushed him toward an uncritical view of Marxism-Leninism.[30] From 1930 to 1936, he taught at the Normal School of Xalapa, which socialist circles revered for its innovative pedagogies, and participated in the state's progressive literary and artistic circles. With anthropologist Julio de la Fuente, a fellow native of the state, he established the literary magazine *Ruta* in 1933 and continued to direct it until he left for Mexico City in 1937.[31]

Mancisidor first tied the nation's revolutionary ethos to blackness in his 1931 novel *La asonada*. Set in Veracruz, *La asonada* is what he called a "realist novel in that the reader will encounter familiar places, events, characters." Blackness is present through the words of the unnamed narrator, a soldier in the revolutionary army who contrasts his Marxist yearnings with the current political scene, where generals and politicians break their ties to the people and become arms of the exploitative national and foreign bourgeoisie. To show that the 1910 Revolution's tragic

[29] Ramos Pedrueza, *Sugerencias*, 16–24. Historian R. Douglas Cope explores the relationship between the caste system and the 1692 grain riot in *The Limits of Racial Domination: Plebeian Society in Colonial Mexico City, 1660–1720* (Madison: University of Wisconsin Press, 1994).

[30] For a discussion of Mancisidor's early years, including his involvement in 1910 Revolution, see Alfonso Berrios, "Vida y Obras de José Mancisidor," in vol. 1 of *Obras Completas de José Mancisidor* (Xalapa: Gobierno del Estado de Veracruz, 1978), 17–27.

[31] Berrios, "Vida y Obras de José Mancisidor," 27–33; and Miguel Bustos Cerecedo, "José Mancisidor: El Hombre," in vol. 1 of *Obras Completas de José Mancisidor* (Xalapa: Gobierno del Estado de Veracruz, 1978), 252–64. Regarding the Normal School of Veracruz, see Monzón, *Detalles de la educación socialista implantables en México*, 257.

demise is not inevitable, Mancisidor introduced Cleofas, a poor black woman from Veracruz, who the narrator encounters when he and his unit trek from Xalapa to the port of Veracruz. Famished, they seek assistance from this "good black woman." Although she is impoverished, she gives beans and tortillas to them. As the narrator tells her story, readers learn that she had been an orphan dependent public assistance. She only knows that her father had gladly joined the revolutionaries when the war broke out. Her ignorance tugs at the narrator's heartstrings and points to the dangers of being a member of a racial group whose history has been silenced. Universalizing blackness, the narrator notes his sympathy toward her and the entire black race: "It is the race. The race numbed for having suffered so much, suffers stoically, as it always has." This history of misery and the revolutionary spirit that emanates from it transforms Cleofas into an avatar of the narrator's revolutionary consciousness. As his comrades tramp through the countryside enjoying themselves, oblivious of the war's larger social stakes, he remains troubled by her story and begins to reconsider the ideologies driving the nation into chaos. Bugles blaring in the distance end the narrator's brief respite into a spiritual world built on the revolutionary ideals Cleofas personifies.[32]

For Mancisidor, the fulfillment of the 1910 Revolution required communism. His adherence to Marxism-Leninism solidified after he visited the Soviet Union in 1936.[33] He understood history through the actions of the lettered elite: the writers, theoreticians, and politicians who advocated for the poor were often his intellectual muses.[34] His theatrical works include *Juárez* and *Yanga*, and his historical publications venerate national heroes like Father Hidalgo, José María Morelos, and Vicente Guerrero. In 1934, he equated Vladimir Lenin with none other than Emiliano Zapata, whose legacy, he hoped, would mirror that of the founder of the Soviet Union.[35] Mancisidor's vision of Mexican history

[32] José Mancisidor, *La asonada: Novela mexicana*, 1st ed. (Jalapa, Veracruz: Editorial Integrales, 1931), esp. "Explicación" and 46–52.

[33] José Mancisidor, "Stalin: El hombre de acero," in vol. 5 of *Obras completas de José Mancisidor* (Xalapa: Gobierno del Estado de Veracruz, 1980), esp. 581–82. Regarding Stalin's popularity in Mexico, see Tobias Rupprecht, *Soviet Internationalism after Stalin: Interaction and Exchange between the USSR and Latin America during the Cold War* (Cambridge: Cambridge University Press, 2015), 148.

[34] José Mancisidor, "Lenin (Conferencia)," in vol. 5 of *Obras completas de José Mancisidor* (Xalapa: Gobierno del Estado de Veracruz, 1980), 509–27.

[35] José Mancisidor, "Lenin en el corazón del pueblo," in *Imágenes de mi tiempo*, in vol. 5 of *Obras completas de José Mancisidor* (Xalapa: Gobierno del Estado de Veracruz, 1980), 654.

and its socialist future came to fruition with murals he outlined and the SEP financed for the Normal School in Xalapa. He explicitly fêted Gaspar Yanga, José María Morelos, Benito Juárez, and Emiliano Zapata. To contextualize the portraits, José Chávez Morado and Feliciano Peña painted additional murals telling the history of capitalism in Mexico and globally. Collectively, the panels illustrate the social and political bonds between the people and their leaders. One depicts a community protecting the body of a schoolteacher, who reactionary forces funded by imperial powers and their Mexican allies had killed. Others represent somber images from Mexican history, like the foreign exploitation of natural resources and a rural family yearning to escape poverty.[36]

Completed in 1936, the murals, the first ones displayed in the state capital, were commissioned by Gonzalo Vázquez Vela, a SEP official who had previously been the Governor of Veracruz. The collaboration between Vázquez Vela and Mancisidor reveals the manner in which the Cárdenas regime integrated socialist projects and the materialist glorification of blackness at the regional level into postrevolutionary nation-state formation. For Mancisidor, the four main panels illustrate the "four people representative of the four states of our history." Yanga, as runaway slave, represents popular discontent with Spanish rule and the origins of Mexican rebelliousness. Morelos extends this revolutionary trajectory by advocating for the nation's political and economic liberation. In overthrowing the French in the 1860s, Juárez is an anti-imperialist who cemented liberalism in national politics. Finally, Zapata personifies the Mexican Revolution and its "program of social vindication."[37]

Of all the portraits painted by Francisco A. Gutiérrez and described by Mancisidor, Yanga is the outlier. Morelos, Juárez, and Zapata stand within their respective historical contexts, the national events most often associated with Mexico's revolutionary tradition: the wars of independence, the rise of liberalism, and the 1910 Revolution. In contrast, Yanga stands with no historical markers behind him and with his image blending almost seamlessly into the background, which appears to be the state's major geographic features: a dark, dense jungle and the Gulf of Mexico. His hands hidden, he appears passive, shirtless, shoeless, unarmed, and alone. Gutiérrez sanitized his image, at least when compared to the paintings of Morelos and Zapata, both of whom possess weapons. The specter

[36] Mancisidor, "Índice de la decoración mural de la Escuela Normal Veracruzana," 142–43 and 147.

[37] Ibid., 139–42.

of a race war is absent, and Yanga's association with Mexico's revolutionary teleology is at best implied. Conversely, Mancisidor highlighted Yanga's bellicosity and celebrated the freedoms his actions bestowed. Yanga alone was able "to embody this stage of the liberation of a people who, in their battle program, would eventually register the abolition of slavery."[38] Clarifying these ideas in an undated play or screenplay *Yanga*, Mancisidor explained that he was "the symbol of life and of liberty" who signified "the love of life. Hope in the future. The belief in a better tomorrow. The pain of living and the joy of rebirth."[39]

BLACKNESS AND JOSÉ MARÍA MORELOS

To associate abolition with the independence-era heroes who proclaimed it was just as common in the 1930s as it had been in the decades before historical materialism entered the national narrative. Yet this newfound emphasis on class brought the structural aspects of abolition to the forefront. In particular, José María Morelos's economic policies caught the eye of this postrevolutionary generation. In 1929, Rafael Ramos Pedrueza argued that his predecessors had ignored these ideas, thereby belying the impact of "the first soldier of our contemporary history." In historiographic terms, Ramos Pedrueza bemoaned the prerevolutionary proclivity to highlight his military triumphs without any reference to the ideological roots of independence that most closely aligned with the Mexican Revolution's goal of "economic emancipation," as he called it. His fifteen-page biography outlines, often quoting at length, Morelos's plans for wealth redistribution, which of course included the fifteenth point from his famous 1813 address at Chilpancingo that abolished slavery and caste. Abolition was of paramount importance, since it symbolized Morelos's dedication to the most humble of citizens. Ramos Pedrueza celebrated how he "insisted tenaciously and vehemently on the need to 'abolish slavery and all that smells of it.'" To weigh in on the significance of these few words, Ramos Pedrueza clarified, "that is to say, all that constitutes injustice, tyranny, exploitation."[40]

[38] Ibid., 141.

[39] José Mancisidor, *Yanga*, in vol. 7 of *Obras Completas de José Mancisidor* (Xalapa: Gobierno del Estado de Veracruz, 1982), 150 and 160.

[40] Rafael Ramos Pedrueza, *José María Morelos y Pavón: Precursor del socialismo en México* (Mexico City: Dirección General de Acción Educativa Recreativa, 1930), 9 and 11.

Ramos Pedrueza's brief biography bespoke another political and historiographic shift in the 1930s. Because of Morelos's lower-class origins, his life story became a point of interest for scholars interested in improving the lot of the oppressed classes. One question was implicit in countless biographies: how did this man, born of poverty and arguably of African descent, become not only a national hero but also, as Ramos Pedrueza explained, the "herald of Socialism in Mexico?"[41] In 1936, Rubén Salazar Mallén attempted to determine when and how Morelos became a national icon from a more conservative perspective than most of his colleagues. Three key moments shaped Morelos's life: his decision to enter the priesthood in 1798, Father Hidalgo's call for independence, and his 1813 outline of the Mexican Constitution, which in all its brilliance "greatly overtook his age and radiates toward ours." Morelos's social mobility and intellectual prowess – not his race – characterized his greatness, and his unassuming upbringing undergirded his social consciousness.[42]

There was debate about Morelos's ancestry. Immediately after the Mexican–American War, conservative historian Lucas Alamán noted that Morelos's baptism record stated he had two creole parents, even though he was "from one of the castes with indigenous and black origins."[43] In the third volume of *México a través de los siglos*, Julio Zárate recounted Morelos's unpretentious childhood; Morelos was "of medium height, a robust build and moreno color." Using the term moreno, an often used euphemism for someone with black and possibly indigenous ancestry, he highlighted Morelos's African heritage when, during the apex of prerevolutionary liberalism, blackness was thought to be the bugbear of degeneracy.[44] Implying that Morelos was of Spanish descent, other historians did not reference any potential African bloodlines. Justo Sierra went as far as to call him "a donkey-driver," who having acquired "great popularity among the mountain people, had resolved, no doubt, to attain a position that would serve as a shield against the contemptuous despotism of the Creole and the Spaniard."[45]

[41] Ibid., 3.

[42] Rubén Salazar Mallén, *Morelos* (Ediciones de la Universidad Nacional, 1936), 22.

[43] Lucas Alamán, *Historia de México*, vol. 2 (Mexico City: Victoriano Agüeros, 1884), 241.

[44] Zárate, *La guerra de la independencia*, 183.

[45] Justo Sierra, *The Political Evolution of the Mexican People*, trans. Charles Ramsdell (Austin: University of Texas Press, 1969), 156. Ramsdell translated *arriero* as "donkey-driver," but others translate it as "mule driver" or "muleteer." For the original, see Sierra, *Evolución política del pueblo mexicano*, 106. As historian Beau Dayeon Jovan Gaitors explains, arrieros were key economic intermediaries in the colonial and early nineteenth-century Mexican economies who were frequently of indigenous and/or African descent;

The uncertainty surrounding Morelos's racial heritage continued after the 1910 Revolution. Concerned with class, not race, Ramos Pedrueza described him as "a proletarian."[46] In 1934, José R. Benítez was tasked with preserving Morelos's residence. Eventually with the INAH's financial support, he wrote a biography that examined Morelos's family and, in theory, everyone who was of his caste. Despite his careful archival research, Benítez concluded that he could not determine the hero's racial lineage. No postrevolutionary historian explicitly referenced Morelos's African heritage to explain his abolitionist aims at Chilpancingo, even though historians often cited his childhood as the reason why he advocated for the downtrodden. Benítez came the closest. Based on his research between 1934 and 1947, he used increasingly outdated pseudo-scientific methodologies like craniometry to claim that Morelos's caste identity helped explain his actions during the wars of independence.[47] In 1947, Marxist historian and indigenist Luis Chávez Orozco assumed that Morelos turned toward revolution after he concluded that "his personal condition as a mestizo or mulatto distanced himself from the ecclesiastic status to which he aspired."[48]

Alfonso Teja Zabre explicitly engaged in this genealogical minefield. Morelos fascinated him. Beginning in 1917, he wrote five biographies of the priest-turned-insurgent.[49] In the 1934 biography *Morelos: Caudillo de la independencia mexicana*, he stated that baptism records classified this independence hero as "a creole of the lower class." Acknowledging this controversy in historiographic terms, Teja Zabre continued:

> Historians did not acquiesce in recognizing the pure Spanish blood in the man who later was the most formidable enemy of Spanish domination in America ... Perhaps because of physical traits or unknown verbal testimonies, [Lucas] Alamán affirmed that both of Morelos's parents were of the caste that had a mixture of indigenous and black lineage.[50]

see "Traders, Vendors, and Society in Early-Independence Veracruz, 1821–1850" (PhD diss., Tulane University, 2017), esp. 158–59.

[46] Ramos Pedrueza, *José María Morelos y Pavón*, 12.

[47] José R. Benítez, *Morelos, su casta y su casa en Valladolid (Morelia)* (Guadalajara: 1947), 9 and 70–71.

[48] Luis Chávez Orozco, *Historia de México (1808–1836)* (Mexico City: Instituto Nacional de Estudios Históricos de la Revolución Mexicana, 1985), 78.

[49] Arnáiz y Freg, "Alfonso Teja Zabre (1888–1962)," 230.

[50] Alfonso Teja Zabre, *Morelos: Caudillo de la independencia mexicana*, 1st ed. (Madrid: España-Calpe, 1934), 24–25.

Before the 1910 Revolution, the political stakes of giving Morelos an indigenous or African heritage were not always clear, for they had no obvious political affiliations: some nineteenth-century liberals and conservatives had ascribed these bloodlines to him while others had not. If anything, the prerevolutionary acknowledgment of his blackness pushed back on nineteenth-century theories of black disappearance and rejected the creole patriotism that many espoused. The Marxist glorification of a class-based, cross-racial revolutionary tradition, however, signified that, while Morelos did not have to be of African descent for this new national narrative to be coherent, he certainly could be.

Recognition of Morelos's caste ancestry affixed the decade's historiographic revisions about black agency in the colonial period to Mexico's revolutionary pantheon: people of African descent could be at the vanguard of the nation's narrative, and more importantly they could be symbols of Mexico's political future. Writing for schoolchildren, Teja Zabre understood independence through its leaders, regardless of their racial backgrounds: Father Hidalgo forged the national spirit, José María Morelos radicalized it, Vicente Guerrero won it on the battlefield, and Agustín de Iturbide entrenched it in politics. Regarding people of mixed racial ancestries, he devoted most of his attention to indigenous communities and even called the struggle against Spain "almost a counter-blow to the Conquest that gave the indigenous nation its usurped sovereignty." He explained Hidalgo's abolitionist decrees and extolled Morelos's egalitarian political doctrines, including the need "to order or confirm legally the regulations relative to the distribution of property, the suppression of slavery and the castes, and the allocation of taxes." Accordingly, Morelos "came close to the fundamental rule of the modern social revolution" when he attempted create an economically just society.[51] And, in *Morelos*, he extended this interpretation for more advanced readers: Morelos's ideology should inspire "the contemporary generations [who] still have much to destroy and reconstitute in accordance with the immense projects of the great fighter."[52]

[51] Alfonso Teja Zabre, *Breve historia de México* (Mexico City: Talleres Gráficos de la Nación, 1934), 122, 126, 133, and 134. For a discussion of the text's place in public education in the 1930s, see Manuel Carrera Stampa, "Alfonso Teja Zabre (1888–1962): El Hombre," *Revista de Historia de América*, nos. 53/54 (1962): 233.

[52] Teja Zabre, *Morelos*, 202.

RESPONSES TO HISTORICAL MATERIALISM

The socialist aspirations represented by this new revolutionary pantheon did not fulfill the goals of many on the left and most on the right, where the materialist refashioning of blackness was particularly troubling. By end of his six-year term, Lázaro Cárdenas had backed away from the socio-economic reforms that had galvanized the nation's Marxist intellectuals and cultural producers. Socialist education, the redistribution of land, and the nationalization of the petroleum industry lost some of their luster as single-party rule loomed over national politics. Yet, because of the Comintern's Popular Front ideology that sought alliances with the bourgeoisie to defeat global fascism, the Mexican Communist Party requested representation within the state. The 1910 Revolution's democratic aims, it and other less radical groups argued, needed to be reinvigorated and the electoral farces that allowed each President to pick his successor needed to end.[53] For example, anthropologist Manuel Gamio took what he saw as the best aspects of these materialist perspectives while he inveighed against the worst. In particular, isolated indigenous communities and the urban proletariat, he feared, would face an economic crisis if there were not some buffers between them and unfettered capitalism.[54]

In Jalisco, where the state government had constantly supported the muralist movement for more than a decade, the conservative Governor Everardo Topete commissioned José Clemente Orozco to paint a series of murals at the University of Guadalajara and the Governor's Palace. Not surprisingly, Mexican heroes anchor Orozco's political commentaries. Contrasting the emaciated rebellious poor with their wealthy rotund leaders, these frescos criticize the global politics of the 1920s and 1930s, particularly the disjuncture between revolutionary theory and praxis. In the stairwell of the Governor's Palace, a monumental image of Father Hidalgo stands above a bloody, almost apocalyptic clash among Christianity, communism, and fascism, the three demagogic ideologies

[53] While Cárdenas established the PRM as the successor to the PNR in 1938, members of the Mexican Communist Party wrote telegrams to him requesting representation in the government; see 544.61/103, AGN-FLCA. There is a voluminous literature on the political transformations in the second half of the Cárdenas presidency; for example see Nora Hamilton, *The Limits of State Autonomy: Post-Revolutionary Mexico* (Princeton, NJ: Princeton University Press, 1982); and Gillingham and Smith, *Dictablanda*.

[54] Manuel Gamio, *Hacia un México nuevo: Problemas sociales* (Mexico City, 1935), 80–84 and 229–35. As historian Rick A. López explains, the Mexican state made a concerted effort to narrow the scope of social scientific research by 1938; see *Crafting Mexico*, 127–50.

that, according to Orozco, exacerbated social tensions rather than resolved them. Wielding a fiery, rolled-up parchment, Hidalgo represents a utopian alternative built on social equality: the ideology that these false leaders had never implemented.[55]

Conservatives were even more disenchanted with the course of postrevolutionary progress than their progressive counterparts were. A particular sore spot was the December 1934 amendment to Article 3 of the 1917 Constitution that required public education be socialist and free of religious dogma.[56] Former Director of the SEP, José Vasconcelos was the most visible spokesperson of this reactionary movement and its racial anxieties. After living in the United States as a sociology professor at the University of Chicago and the University of California between 1926 and 1928, he returned to Mexico to run unsuccessfully for president in 1929. Hostile toward to the anticlerical reforms introduced by Plutarco Elías Calles and Lázaro Cárdenas, Vasconcelos was no longer the innovative father of Mexican public education and the patron of public muralism. He remade himself as a figurehead for the Catholic right that in 1934 took up arms against the secularism of socialist education.[57]

Vasconcelos's antipathy toward postrevolutionary nation-state formation came to the forefront during the Spanish Civil War. The battle between Spain's Second Republic and Francisco Franco caught the attention of Mexicans on both sides of the political aisle, especially once Cárdenas sent military assistance to the Republic. Anticlerical laws in both countries mobilized Catholics already unseasy with Mexico's educational policies and revised national pantheon. As such, the Spanish Civil War operated as a parable of the dangers of communism in Mexico and throughout the world, even when, after 1936, Lázaro Cárdenas softened the state's anticlerical programs to expand his popular support. Since the Soviet Union was the only other country to send military aid to the

[55] Luis Cardoza y Aragón, *José Clemente Orozco: Pinturas murales; en la Universidad de Guadalajara, Jalisco* (Mexico City: Imprenta Mundial, 1937), Record ID: 733088, ICAA-MFAH. For an excellent analysis of these murals, see Rochfort, *Mexican Muralists*, 139–43; also see Dawn Ades, *Art in Latin America: The Modern Era, 1820–1980* (New Haven, CT: Yale University Press, 1989), 165–67.

[56] For example, see Benjamin T. Smith, *The Roots of Conservatism in Mexico: Catholicism, Society, and Politics in the Mixteca Baja, 1750–1962* (Albuquerque: University of New Mexico Press, 2012), 203–45. Historian Mary Kay Vaughan provides a broader discussion of socialist education and state formation in the 1930s; see *Cultural Politics in Revolution.*

[57] Marilyn Grace Miller, *Rise and Fall of the Cosmic Race: The Cult of* Mestizaje *in Latin America* (Austin: University of Texas Press, 2004), 40–44.

Republicans, Vasconcelos equated "the extremism of Moscow" to that of Mexico. Both states, he claimed, required allegiance to a single party that determined which politicians would ascend the political ladder and which would be thrown off it.[58] Condemnations of the Soviet-driven international communist movement framed his critique of the materialist turn in Mexican intellectual circles. They also inspired him to rewrite Mexican history. In his anything-but-short 1937 *Breve historia de México*, he commented that recent political conflicts, especially Calles's attack on Christianity in the mid-1920s, was the result of "hot air" propped up by "the dummy front-men with nicknames taken from the Russian Revolution or from masonic leftism: liberalism, socialism, revolutionism, foreignisms." Indigenist demands for land distribution, he decried, were nothing more than hollow echoes of communist ideologies. Such policies were superfluous and only thought to be legitimate because "vulgar patriotic lies" had bogged down true progress.[59]

From this position, Vasconcelos grappled with the role of Africans in Mexican and world history. He compared Spanish colonialism to expansionist endeavors in North America and Africa. In accordance with nineteenth-century screeds justifying the European colonization of Africa, he counterfactually explained that the Western Hemisphere would be in disarray if it had been "discovered and conquered by Muslims" rather than by Catholic Spaniards. "The interior regions of present-day Africa," he offered as proof, "can give us an idea of the misery and slavery, the degradation in which we would find ourselves." Similar to his prerevolutionary predecessors' veneration of the nation's creole heritage, Vasconcelos cast African historical agency as dangerous to colonial and modern Mexico. He vaguely analyzed a failed revolt of African slaves, which was likely the 1537 plot to kill Viceroy Antonio de Mendoza and establish an African kingdom in the colony. The Spanish executed the rebels in what Vasconcelos called "a general slaughter of blacks" that was "among the sorrows of Mendoza's career." Turning to Mexican independence, Vasconcelos penned what might be his most inconsistent

[58] José Vasconcelos, *Qué es el comunismo: Por qué se pelea en España* (Mexico City: Ediciones Botas, 1936), 49; also see 67–68. On the broader context for Mexico's involvement in the Spanish Civil War and how international debates about communism and fascism shaped Mexican society in the second half of the Cárdenas presidency, see Schuler, *Mexico between Hitler and Roosevelt*. Regarding Cárdenas's rejection of extreme anticlericalism, see Lewis, *Ambivalent Revolution*, 142.

[59] José Vasconcelos, *Breve historia de México*, 1st ed. (Mexico City: Acción Moderna Mercantil, 1937), 17, 20, and 26; on Calles's anti-religiosity, see 604 and 613.

statements about Mexico's black population. At the beginning of the nineteenth century, there were 6 million people living in the colony: 1 million creoles, 40,000 Spaniards, 3.5 million Indians, and 1.5 million mestizos, but no blacks or mulattoes. Despite their apparent demographic invisibility, African-descended individuals along the Pacific Coast, he acknowledged, briefly joined Morelos's band of insurrectionaries. This motley crew of castes was incapable of contributing to national independence and eventually rebelled "against the Mexicans." Like the slaves who revolved in the sixteenth century, these insurgents had to be killed in the name of political expediency and social control. Hidalgo's call for independence – to arm those with African heritage and to rid Mexico of its Spanish past – was, for Vasconcelos, analogous to the maxim "'kill the bourgeoisie' of the contemporary pseudo-revolutionary-ism."[60]

MOLINA ENRÍQUEZ AND MEXICO'S BLACK PANTHEON

Unlike Vasconcelos, Andrés Molina Enríquez adapted to the radicalism of the 1930s and bequeathed African-descended people a greater role in Mexican and world history than he previously had. Although Molina Enríquez did not embrace the Marxist dictum that the people needed to overthrow those in control of the means of production to enjoy the fruits of their labor, he acknowledged that revolutions needed to transform the economic structures that underpin all aspects of society.[61] Since the publication of *Los grandes problemas nacionales* in 1909, his ideas about agrarian reform had influenced state-building policies, including the celebrated Article 27 of the 1917 Constitution that established a legal precedent for land redistribution. They also helped lay the foundation for many populist histories of the 1910 Revolution.[62] With the radicalization of Mexican politics, he returned to the agrarian question in his five volume *Esbozo de la historia de los primeros diez años de la revolución agraria de México*, which he published between 1932 and 1936. Although

[60] Ibid., 10, 11, 221, 270, and 334. Ben Vinson examines the 1537 slave revolt in "Fading from Memory: Historiographical Reflections on the Afro-Mexican Presence," *Review of Black Political Economy* 33, no. 1 (2005): 59.

[61] Andrés Molina Enríquez, *Esbozo de la historia de los primeros diez años de la revolución agraria de México (de 1910 a 1920)*, vol. 2 (Mexico City: Talleres Gráficos del Museo Nacional de Arqueología, Historia y Etnografía, 1932), 43.

[62] Kourí, "Interpreting the Expropriation of Indian Pueblo Lands in Porfirian Mexico," 104–15.

he never completely abandoned his prerevolutionary evolutionary beliefs, he began to recast them in the less rigid framework of cultural relativism, a theoretical paradigm that he likely encountered at the Seventeenth Annual Congress of Americanists in Mexico City in 1910.[63]

By 1932, Molina Enríquez echoed the refrains of other modernist historians, Marxist and not, condemning the antiquated belief that there was only one linear path to modernity. He cast history as a clash between two cultures: an Eastern culture defined by its "memory of seeing," where language and writing is visual and denoted by characters, and a Western one characterized by a "memory of hearing," which associates a specific sound with each letter. The lone exception to his bifurcated world-system was Africa, which "remains between the one and the other as an always indecisive camp."[64] In Mexico, blackness was more important than it was on the world's stage. In some regions, like Morelos and the city of Veracruz, the mestizo population, he noted, had a higher percentage of black ancestry, which he explained in two maps. The first illustrates the "distribution of black blood," a hereditary category that he primarily situated along the coasts (See Map 2.1). The second identifies various iterations of Mexico's mestizo population, thereby proving that mestizaje was not a singular historical process destined to birth the homogenous national populace that nineteenth-century liberals had wanted. Central Mexico was predominately of indigenous and European heritage, the variation of racial and cultural mixture that pre- and postrevolutionary nationalists most often analyzed. The north-central region was chiefly of European origin. Finally, and mirroring the distribution of black blood he had already mapped, the Gulf Coast and parts of central

[63] See several essays in Emilio Kourí, coord., *En busca de Andrés Molina Enríquez: Cien años de Los grandes problemas nacionales* (Mexico City: El Colegio de México, 2009).

[64] Andrés Molina Enríquez, *Esbozo de la historia de los primeros diez años de la revolución agraria de México (de 1910 a 1920)*, vol. 1 (Mexico City: Talleres Gráficos del Museo Nacional de Arqueología, Historia y Etnografía, 1932), 12–23 and 74; and Basave Benítez, *México mestizo*, 73. Molina Enríquez was not alone in making these dualistic assertions about human civilizations. The juxtaposition between West and East – material and spiritual, modern and natural, colonizer and colonized – circulated within Mexican thought and around the world in the first decades of the twentieth century; see Mauricio Tenorio-Trillo, *I Speak of the City: Mexico City at the Turn of the Twentieth Century* (Chicago: University of Chicago Press, 2012), 211–79, esp. 212–14; and Erez Manela, "Imagining Woodrow Wilson in Asia: Dreams of East–West Harmony and the Revolt against Empire in 1919," *American Historical Review* 111, no. 5 (2006): 1340–44.

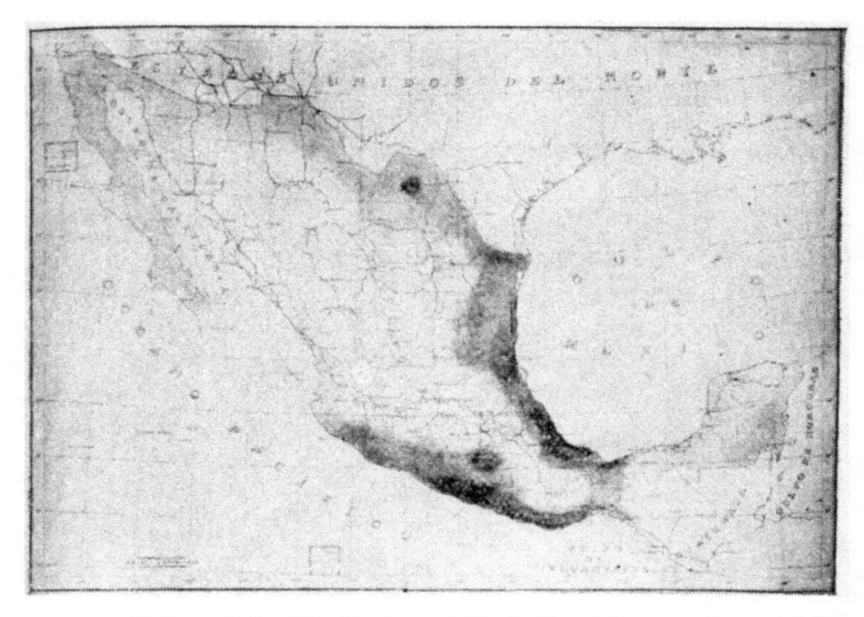

MAP 2.1 “Map of the Distribution of Black Blood,” 1932. From Molina Enríquez, *Esbozo de la historia de los primeros diez años de la revolución agraria de México (de 1910 a 1920)*, vol. 1. Grupo Editorial Miguel Ángel Porrúa.

and southern Mexico were a mixture of “European, indigenous, and black blood.”[65] (See Map 2.2.)

To discuss mestizaje historically, Molina Enríquez invoked a pillar of black disappearance. With independence and abolition, he stated, “the number of blacks has been diminishing” to such a degree that they were hardly ever seen.[66] Instead of being a social problem akin to the indigenous population, African-descended Mexicans enjoyed “full liberty” and lived “in conditions of relative wellbeing.”[67] While there were still people with African ancestry in contemporary society, they melted into the broadly defined mestizo population. The black and mestizo populations “appear muddled between one and another,” he explained. To distinguish

[65] Molina Enríquez, *Esbozo de la historia de los primeros diez años de la revolución agraria de México (de 1910 a 1920)*, 1:113–21. For a discussion of where Molina Enríquez’s deconstruction of mestizaje fits in his oeuvre, see Basave Benítez, *México mestizo*, 78.

[66] Molina Enríquez, *Esbozo de la historia de los primeros diez años de la revolución agraria de México (de 1910 a 1920)*, 1:116.

[67] Molina Enríquez, *Esbozo de la historia de los primeros diez años de la revolución agraria de México (de 1910 a 1920)*, 2:64.

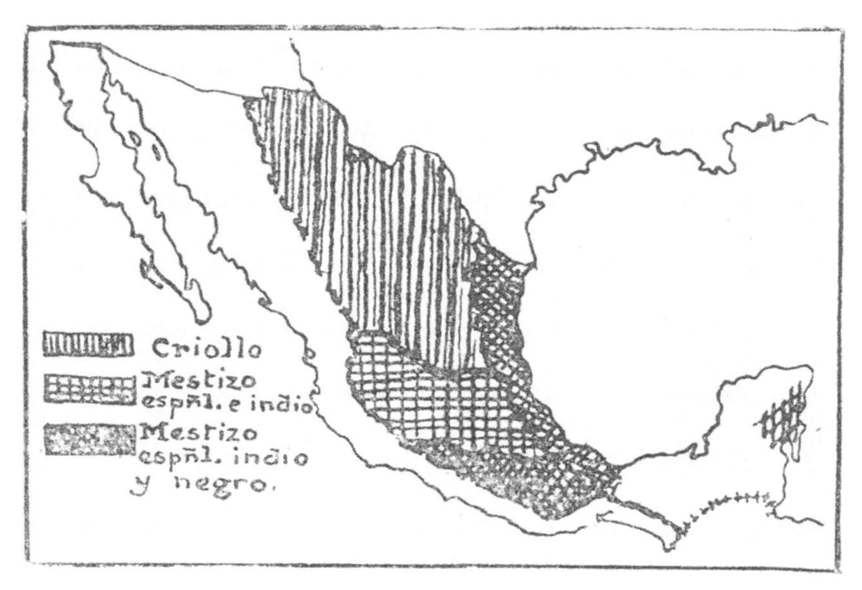

MAP 2.2 "Map of the Distribution of Mestizajes," 1932. From Molina Enríquez, *Esbozo de la historia de los primeros diez años de la revolución agraria de México (de 1910 a 1920)*, vol. 1. Grupo Editorial Miguel Ángel Porrúa.

this African-descended population, he coined the term "triple mestizo" to signify Mexicans with indigenous, Spanish, and African ancestries.[68]

By 1933, Molina Enríquez rejected the insidious credo that African-descended people were incapable of contributing to the nation's history. He lauded two independence-era leaders with African ancestry: José María Morelos and Vicente Guerrero. A "mestizo of three bloods," Morelos embodied Mexican independence. Implicit in his analysis was the supposition that Morelos, as a triple mestizo, could effectively advocate for the economic equality and social justice of all the oppressed peoples of Mexico.[69] Molina Enríquez's celebration of Morelos's ideas

[68] Molina Enríquez, *Esbozo de la historia de los primeros diez años de la revolución agraria de México (de 1910 a 1920)*, 1:116–17; and Basave Benítez, *México mestizo*, 75–76.

[69] Regarding Morelos's racial ancestry, see Andrés Molina Enríquez, *Esbozo de la historia de los primeros diez años de la revolución agraria de México (de 1910 a 1920)*, vol. 3 (Mexico City: Talleres Gráficos del Museo Nacional de Arqueología, Historia y Etnografía, 1933), 55. For a longer analysis of Morelos's political and economic plans, see Molina Enríquez, *Esbozo de la historia de los primeros diez años de la revolución agraria de México (de 1910 a 1920)*, 2:38–45.

and his racial heritage resembled many of the panegyrics written by Marxist historians in the 1930s. However, he extended this history when he characterized Vicente Guerrero as a triple mestizo. This rejected the longstanding assumption that Guerrero was of indigenous descent. More importantly, it centered him uniquely in a national narrative that often appended him to an already lengthy list of independence-era heroes. Nineteenth-century liberals had grappled with the need to reconcile his military feats with the political chaos that his presidency unleashed. In contrast, Molina Enríquez was in awe of Guerrero's career. His brief tenure as President in 1829 illustrated the rapid social, economic, and ideological transformations that the new nation had witnessed. "Twenty years after the outbreak of the movements for Independence, a triple mestizo, of Spanish, indigenous and black [descent], arrived at the Presidency of the Republic in time to found its nationality," Molina Enríquez exclaimed, "and to save it from its first foreign threat." His political ascension was "so unexpected and so surprising." Because of the damming legacies of liberal histories and their veneration of whiteness, Guerrero's political achievements and racial ancestry had remained hidden, only to be exhumed in 1933. "Even today," Molina Enríquez noted about the African heritage of one of the nation's first presidents, "it appears unbelievable to us."[70]

In 1936, Molina Enríquez reintroduced the concept of the triple mestizo and again associated it with a major figure in Mexican history: Emiliano Zapata. By the mid-to-late 1930s, Zapata was no longer a social bandit or merely a regional icon. Placing him on par with the heroes who fought for Mexican independence, Alfonso Teja Zabre described him as a radical social reformer whose Plan of Ayala was "the proletarian basis of the distribution of land."[71] Rafael Ramos Pedrueza asserted that the revolutionary hero was not only versed in the history of the Russian Revolution but also saw socialism as a pillar of social justice.[72] For Molina Enríquez, Zapata was a triple mestizo with 15 percent black ancestry. How he came to this conclusion can only be inferred.

[70] Molina Enríquez, *Esbozo de la historia de los primeros diez años de la revolución agraria de México (de 1910 a 1920)*, 3:52–53. For other views of Guerrero's life, including references to his indigenous heritage, see Olavarría y Ferrari, *México independiente*, 177–83, 210, and 215; Ramos Pedrueza, *Rusia soviet y México revolucionario*, 21–32; and Teja Zabre, *Historia de México*, 281 and 309–13.

[71] Teja Zabre, *Guide to the History of Mexico*, 339.

[72] Brunk, *The Posthumous Career of Emiliano Zapata*, 99–100 and 106; and Spenser, *Stumbling Its Way through Mexico*, 36.

Zapata's birthplace – the sugar producing state of Morelos that Molina Enríquez had already noted was inhabited by people of Spanish, indigenous, and black blood – was the only evidence that he provided.[73] Molina Enríquez described Zapata without the traditional stereotypes of black sensuality or passivity. Rather, Zapata was "of little instruction, but of great sensibility ... serious and reflexive ... of good stature, strong physique and pleasant appearance, moreno, with black eyes, profound and serious."[74]

INDIGENEITY AND THE LIMITS OF MARXIST BLACKNESS

While historical materialism became a foundation for integrating blackness into the national narrative in the 1930s, Mexican social scientists rarely saw it as a constitutive element of contemporary society. Despite writing blackness into Mexico's hall of heroes and the history of the Mexican Revolution, Molina Enríquez failed to translate this analysis into concrete policy proposals. As his last volume of *Esbozo de la historia de los primeros diez años de la revolución agraria de México* came off the presses, he and Eulogio R. Valdivieso penned a memorandum to Lázaro Cárdenas asking him to address land redistribution, indigenous education, and the representation of indigenous history in national institutions. They divided society into indigenous, mestizo, and white communities.[75] The triple mestizo was absent, cast off by the more pressing need to assist the indigenous peoples who had taken up arms en masse during the Mexican Revolution.

As a result, Carlos Basauri's three-volume *La población indígena de México*, the most complete ethnographic research undertaken during the Cárdenas presidency, stands out for recognizing the presence

[73] Molina Enríquez, *Esbozo de la historia de los primeros diez años de la revolución agraria de México (de 1910 a 1920)*, 5:147. For a discussion of the African-descended population in Morelos, see Cheryl English Martin, *Rural Society in Colonial Morelos* (Albuquerque: University of New Mexico Press, 1985), esp. 151–52.

[74] Molina Enríquez, *Esbozo de la historia de los primeros diez años de la revolución agraria de México (de 1910 a 1920)*, 5:147.

[75] Eulogio R. Valdivieso and Andrés Molina Enríquez, "Memorándum de lo que 'La Organización de los Indios de la República,' pide respetuosamente al Señor Presidente de la República, 11 de febrero de 1936," 533.4/1, AGN-FLCA. They were not alone in ignoring black communities in contemporary society. Working for the PNR, Gilberto Loyo explicitly stated that that African-descended peoples were not present in post-revolutionary Mexico; see "Población de América – Cifras absolutas," in *La política demográfica de México* (Mexico City: Secretaría de Prensa y Propaganda, 1935), between pp. 482 and 483.

of African-descended peoples in postrevolutionary society. Based on a questionnaire written by Ángel Corzo, Basauri set out to study every indigenous community that had not yet disappeared.[76] *La población indígena de México*'s last chapter details Mexico's black population, which he claimed still lived along the Pacific and Gulf coasts, particularly in the states of Veracruz, Guerrero, and Quintana Roo. Between 10,000 and 14,000 rural laborers who descended from enslaved Africans resided along the Costa Chica of Guerrero and Oaxaca. Focusing on Oaxaca, he employed ethnographic tools and anthropometric data to describe these communities and their cultural behaviors. He believed they were racially mixed, because their physical features – the size of their noses and lips and the color of their hair and skin – did not correspond to "the anthropological type of the classic black person." In comparative terms, he determined these citizens maintained social statuses on par with those of nearby indigenous groups. But, as a result of mestizo and indigenous racial discrimination, these black communities generally remained isolated, without any allegiance to the nation and with only a nominal affinity to Oaxaca. "The black influence," he concluded, "is one of the fundamental problems of Mexican racial integration."[77]

By 1940, the postrevolutionary state's project of indigenous liberation and integration had gained an international audience.[78] From April 14 to 24, indigenists from nineteen American nations, including many of the historians who ascribed blackness to Mexico's historical pantheon, descended on the lakeside town of Pátzcuaro, Michoacán, for the First Inter-American Conference on Indian Life. Initially the Conference was to be held in La Paz, Bolivia, in August 1939, but in what can be seen as a coup for Cárdenas and his legacy, it moved to Mexico. Critical of the theory of assimilation, participants discussed various nationalist projects to preserve and to integrate indigenous communities across the Western Hemisphere and, in the process, laid the groundwork for the III to be

[76] Carlos Basauri, *La población indígena de México*, vol. 1 (Mexico City: Secretaría de Educación Pública, 1940), 8. For a discussion of this quantitative project, see Dawson, *Indian and Nation in Revolutionary Mexico*, 87–93.

[77] To corroborate his claims about African-descended peoples in Mexico, Basauri drew on research by Vicente Riva Palacio and Andrés Molina Enríquez, among others; see Carlos Basauri, *La población indígena de México*, 3:670 and 674–78.

[78] Cárdenas used the language of indigenous liberation; see Lázaro Cárdenas to Los C.C. Gobernadores de los 8 Pueblos de la Tribu Yaqui, 10 de junio de 1939, 533.11/1, AGN-FLCA.

founded in Mexico City.[79] Mexico sent a large delegation, including Manuel Gamio and Luis Chávez Orozco, who as Director of the Department of Indian Affairs convened the Conference.[80] With the US Commissioner of Indian Affairs John Collier, Chávez Orozco envisioned indigenist projects that did not divide communities by race, "since no scientific evidence exists showing innate differences either biological or mental between the Indian and other racial groups."[81] Andrés Molina Enríquez submitted reports on indigenous languages, educational and penal reforms, and social justice initiatives. He continued to filter Mexican history through the interactions between indigenous and European peoples, cultures, and economies: the complex analyses of the triple mestizo he marshaled a few years earlier were missing.[82]

In contrast, Alfonso Teja Zabre submitted a short paper "Tata Vasco: En honor de Don Vasco de Quiroga – Tierra india – Cultura criolla" that bridged these hemispheric discussions with Mexico's historiographic revision of slavery and abolition. In broad terms, he presented an account of the Americas' long history of indigenous redemption. Its origins, he claimed, dated back to Bartolomé de las Casas's and Vasco de Quiroga's religious criticisms of the Spanish Conquest and their attempts to convert and protect Mexico's indigenous peoples. Teja Zabre drew a direct line from Quiroga's utopian ideals about indigenous salvation to the socialism of 1930s Mexico and the indigenist initiatives espoused at Pátzcuaro. The abolition of slavery was a watershed moment in this religious-cum-social agenda since it dealt a major blow to feudalism in Mexico. "In 1810, the spirit of Quiroga was not with [Manuel] Abad y Queipo who excommunicated Don Miguel Hidalgo," he wrote, "but with Don Miguel Hidalgo who ordered the abolition of slavery and captivated the Indians in the utopian and premature business of independence."[83]

[79] For a hemispheric perspective on the First Inter-American Conference on Indian Life, see Laura Giraudo, "Neither 'Scientific' nor 'Colonialist': The Ambiguous Course of Inter-American Indigenismo in the 1940s," trans. Victoria J. Furio, *Latin American Perspectives* 39, no. 186 (2012): 13–15.

[80] Dawson, *Indian and Nation in Revolutionary Mexico*, 83.

[81] Luis Chávez Orozco and John Collier, "Agenda for the First Inter-American Institute for Mexico and the United States," 533.4/1, AGN-FLCA.

[82] Andrés Molina Enríquez, "La necesidad de facilitar la acción de la justica en beneficio de los indios," in *Reunión/Conferencia Congreso Indigenista Interamericano*, vol. 2 (Pátzcuaro, Michoacán: Primer Congreso Indigenista Interamericano, 1940), 173–77, FD AI/0001, CDI-CDJR.

[83] Alfonso Teja Zabre, "Tata Vasco: En honor de Don Vasco de Quiroga – Tierra india – Cultura criolla," in *Reunión/Conferencia Congreso Indigenista Interamericano*, 2:74–75.

CONCLUSION

Teja Zabre's passing reference to Hidalgo's abolitionist decree in the transcripts of the First Inter-American Conference on Indian Life can easily be skipped over among the four volumes of proceedings. Yet, when placed within the decade's Marxist histories and socialist aspirations, it points to the historical and political symbolism that he and other Marxist and Marxist-inspired scholars attributed to blackness, slavery, and abolition: enslaved Africans and their descendants helped forge an independent Mexico and helped propel the nation's revolutionary spirit forward. Because of Hidalgo's, Morelos's, and Guerrero's liberal ideologies and abolitionist decrees, this multiracial insurrectionary pastime blossomed into a bourgeois revolution in the first decades of the nineteenth century and, after 1910, a socialist revolution. By the time Alfonso Teja Zabre and Andrés Molina Enríquez stepped foot in Pátzcuaro in April 1940, African-descended leaders – Yanga, Morelos, Guerrero, and even Zapata – had already found their place on the national pedestal.

Amid the historiographic interventions of the 1930s, Mexican independence symbolized either the foundation for Mexico's utopian future or, as José Vasconcelos begrudged, its demise. With the notable exception of Molina Enríquez's representation of Zapata as a triple mestizo and Basauri's discussion of the Costa Chica, African-descended peoples were not visible in postrevolutionary society. Unlike indigeneity, blackness did not require immediate social, economic, and political policy proposals. The materialist revision of prerevolutionary blackness was national in scope yet almost exclusively entombed in the annals of Spanish colonialism and the struggle for independence. Like prerevolutionary intellectuals, these Marxist historians failed to look back to Africa or to any systematic analysis of the social legacies of the slave trade in Mexico. The transnationality of blackness was not part of their historical narratives or their predictions for the nation's future. As the next chapter shows, like-minded cultural producers expanded the geographic boundaries of these materialist constructions of blackness in the 1930s and 1940s. Concerned about the spread of fascism, artists, writers, and composers placed musical and visual representations of Mexican history and contemporary life in conversation with initiatives to rehabilitate African-descended identities in other American nations.

3

Making Blackness Transnational

At the end of his undated play or screenplay titled *Yanga*, Marxist historian José Mancisidor provided a single performance note: "African, Afro-American and Afro-Cuban musical background and songs." Other than a script published in his complete works, little is known about this text. Resembling many of the materialist histories of the 1930s, it mythologizes Gaspar Yanga as a revolutionary who runs away from a sugar plantation in Veracruz to establish a maroon community and then the first legally recognized free black community in the Americas in 1609. Throughout *Yanga*, a foreboding chant proclaims:

> Forests, dark forests
> Mountains, dark mountains
> Shelter of wolves and serpents
> Shelter also for liberty.

As the refrain rhythmically spreads "over the surface of the land like a promise," it strikes fear into the Spanish settlers who feverishly but unsuccessfully search for the omnipresent voice. The performance note references the fact that this chant was, according to the unnamed narrator, "reminiscent of Africa."[1]

Mancisidor's musical reference points to the transnational Marxist and antifascist ideologies that Mexican cultural producers used to attach blackness to postrevolutionary nation-state formation in the 1930s and 1940s. This complex political and geographic matrix was more visible in the interdisciplinary threads of culture than the dense footnotes of

[1] Mancisidor, *Yanga*, 134, 139, 140, and 176.

historicism. Music – jazz, in particular – came to symbolize the simultaneous reformulation of Mexican nationalism and blackness by the end of the 1930s. In conversation with New Negro and Afro-Cubanist intellectuals across the Atlantic world, artist Miguel Covarrubias, composer Carlos Chávez, and writer José Mancisidor situated themselves at the center of the cultural networks that exploded the geographic boundaries and political resonances of black cultures in Mexico.

JAZZ, MIGUEL COVARRUBIAS, AND 1920S MEXICAN MUSIC

The postrevolutionary embrace of jazz and, more broadly, of a transnational blackness was not a forgone conclusion after the 1910 Revolution. At the turn of the century, Mexican composers found greater inspiration in European romanticism and the piano music performed in Parisian salons than in indigenous and African-descended melodies, harmonies, and rhythms.[2] Mexican music had typically been defined by some combination of indigenous and European musicological traits, which Alba Herrera y Ogazón described in 1917 as the fusion of "the sadness of the Indian" and "the vivacity of the Spanish."[3] Inspired by the Revolution's popular mobilizations, composer Manuel M. Ponce championed the integration of vernacular, often indigenous, songs into classical compositions. It was the composer's job to enliven vernacular music – what he called in 1919 "the loyal expression of the people" – so that it could remain a vital component of everyday society.[4]

Composers and musicologists thought that black melodies, harmonies, and rhythms were dangerous to the national soundscape. After revolutionary factionalism encouraged Ponce to seek voluntary exile in Cuba from 1915 to 1917, he explicitly disassociated Afro-Cuban music and other foreign influences from his bounded notion of national identity. For instance, popular musical genres along the Gulf Coast of Veracruz, such as Cuba's "voluptuous *danzones*," could not be Mexican, since they did not originate during the colonial-era fusion of indigenous and Spanish cultures. While these songs had been

[2] Yolanda Moreno Rivas, *Rostros del nacionalismo en la música mexicana: Un ensayo de interpretación* (Mexico City: Fondo de Cultura Económica, 1989), 68–72.

[3] Alba Herrera y Ogazón, *El arte musical en México* (Mexico City: Departamento Editorial de la Dirección General de las Bellas Artes, 1917), 21.

[4] Manuel M. Ponce, "Cultura: Escritos y composiciones musicales," *Cultura* 4, no. 1–6: 7 and 41–43; and "El folk-lore musical mexicano: Lo que se ha hecho. Lo que puede hacerse," *Revista musical de México* 1, no. 5 (1919): 5.

created in Mexico and became extremely popular, we should consider them as true imitations of Cuban music ... They are genuinely of Cuban origin and while composed in our country, they are not freed from the peculiar musical styles of the Antillean pearls. While modifying them and converting them into national dances, I conclude that they should not be considered important parts of Mexico's folkloric nationalism.[5]

These historical and cultural boundaries continued into the 1920s, but with the modernist trappings of ethnography providing a new methodological departure.[6] In 1928, Rubén M. Campos cast musical expressions as fluid, not something that could be exhumed as an archeological artifact. Mexico's sonic tradition had clearly defined roots in Spanish, indigenous, and, to a lesser extent, Arab aesthetics. Other inspirations – such as polka, foxtrot, jazz, and various Cuban dances – endangered these musical pillars, particularly the indigenous rhythms that exemplified the nation's musical landscape but that were on the brink of disappearing. No matter how popular, these foreign genres could not be part of "the memory of our people." Since Cuban music shared many rhythmic structures with Mexican songs, it was particularly dangerous for indigenous communities that could easily integrate its African-descended musical traits into their own expressions.[7]

It was in this context that jazz captivated Mexicans interested in forging a new national culture. Performed live, it was a modern spectacle ready to be enjoyed by moviegoers eager to watch the newest Hollywood films and by the cosmopolitan intellectuals who visited trendy urban nightspots across the Atlantic. While F. Scott Fitzgerald announced that the 1920s were "the Jazz Age," classical composers in Mexico, just like in France and the United States, wondered if and how jazz – as an urban, black, and quintessentially modern sound – could enter the national soundscape.[8] Among Mexicans, jazz's first proponents came

[5] Ponce, "Cultura," 11 and 16.

[6] On beginning of the ethnographic turn in Mexican musicology, see Dr. Jesús C. Romero, *La historia crítica de la música en México* (Mexico City: Tall. Linotip, 1927), 21, expediente 1527, INBA/CENIDIM-ABF; and Francisco Domínguez, "Nuevas orientaciones sobre el folk-lore mexicano: Tesis presentada en el Primer Congreso Nacional de Música en México, el día 5 de septiembre de 1926," 3–5, expediente 1527, INBA/CENIDIM-ABF.

[7] Rubén M. Campos, *El folklore y la música mexicana: Investigación acerca de la cultura musical en México (1525–1925)* (Mexico City: Secretaría de Educación Pública, 1928), 7, 27–38, 53–56, 74, and 160–61.

[8] Regarding the relationship between jazz and Mexico's first cinemas, see Laura Isabel Serna, *Making Cinelandia: American Films and Mexican Film Culture before the Golden Age* (Durham, NC: Duke University Press, 2014), 60 and 65–66.

from the up-and-coming artists and composers who made their way to New York City to escape the institutional chaos and inconsistent cultural patronage left in the wake of the 1910 Revolution. For example, muralist José Clemente Orozco basked in African Americans' physical and aesthetic magnificence. "Girls of vibrant features, strong, firm bodies, and an incredible beauty," he noted as he described Harlem's dance floors and stages. They were "like no others in the world."[9] His lithograph *Vaudeville in Harlem* (1928) gives viewers this impression by placing them in the audience, watching African Americans dance and brilliantly contort their bodies on stage.

Most notably illustrator and caricaturist Miguel Covarrubias entrenched himself in Manhattan's jazz scene. He arrived in New York City in 1923, as a nineteen-year old caricaturist. Nicknamed "el chamaco," or "the kid," because of his youthful exuberance and artistic talents, he had already made a name for himself drawing caricatures of celebrities at Los Montes, a bohemian café in Mexico City owned by Orozco's brother. One of its patrons, José Juan Tablada, who Adolfo de la Huerta had exiled in 1920, turned to his friends in the Álvaro Obregón administration to acquire the funds to allow Covarrubias travel to Manhattan for six months. Already in New York City, Tablada wrote newspaper articles celebrating Mexican artists and rejecting US stereotypes of Mexicans on both sides of the Rio Grande. For instance, in January 1919, he praised Marius de Zayas's curatorial endeavors (See Chapter 1) for having presented "an eloquent history of contemporary art from Negro-African sculpture and the primitives of Asia and Europe to the modernist 'Cubists' Derain, Picabia, or the Mexican Diego Rivera."[10]

This was the New York that Covarrubias entered with Tablada as his guide. No one could have predicted that this artistic prodigy and autodidact would become de Zayas's unofficial cultural heir.[11] A keen eye for cultural nuance gave Covarrubias the tools to create caricatures that were sometimes spartan in their color palate, occasionally modernist in their

Historian Jeffrey H. Jackson analyzes jazz's influence in France in *Making Jazz French: Music and Modern Life in Interwar Paris* (Durham, NC: Duke University Press, 2003).

9 Orozco, *An Autobiography*, 124.

10 José Juan Tablada, "Tres artistas mexicanos en Nueva York: Marius de Zayas, Pal-Omar, Juan Olaguíbel," *El Universal Ilustrado*, 17 de enero de 1919.

11 By 1938, Covarrubias described de Zayas's *African Negro Art* as a fundamental text for the study of African and African-descended art; see "Bibliografía: Arte negro africano," 7/32085, expediente 7, UDLAP-SACE-AMC. Also see various documents in expediente 255, UDLAP-SACE-AMC.

geometry, and always in the spirit of the subject. His entrance into the metropolis's avant-garde circles put him in conversation with New Negro intellectuals like W. E. B. Du Bois, Alain Locke, Langston Hughes, W. C. Handy, and Zora Neale Hurston. With like-minded artists and intellectuals, both white and black, he visited Harlem's dance clubs to listen to jazz bands improvise and to watch locals dance the Charleston, the lindy hop, and, in the 1930s, the jitterbug. Cultural magnate Carl Van Vechten served as a key intermediary; he placed Covarrubias in contact with Alfred and Mary Knopf and *Vanity Fair*'s Frank Crowninshield. Covarrubias's vivid renditions of black Harlemites immediately enthralled all of them. In 1924, *Vanity Fair* published his caricatures for the first time under the banner "Enter, The New Negro, a Distinctive Type Recently Created by the Jazz Spirit of Their Own Invention." Covarrubias discarded the stereotypical Old Negro – such as the "Coloured Crooner of Lullabys, the Cotton-Picker, the Mammy-Singer, and the Darky Banjo-Players" – and extolled the New Negro who frequented upscale nightclubs in fashionable garb: men dressed in bow ties and suit jackets, and women with bob haircuts, in pearls and boyish dresses.[12] The following year, Locke included Covarrubias's drawing *Blues Singer* in what quickly became his seminal anthology *The New Negro*. Covarrubias's image sits alongside poems written by Hughes, essays by Locke, and countless other pieces written by New Negro luminaries.[13] Recalling their social engagements in nightclubs and at the homes of patrons like Charlotte Osgood Mason, Hurston wrote to Covarrubias in 1935, "I still feel the golden glow of those days when we were all here in New York playing around so carefree."[14]

Music defined Covarrubias's visual record book of black life in the United States and abroad. He decorated the cover of Handy's *Blues: An Anthology* as well as Hughes's first poetry collection *The Weary Blues*, which Van Vechten introduced. His caricatures conjured the essence of the peoples and cultures he observed: the joy of jazz musicians playing

[12] "Enter, The New Negro, a Distinctive Type Recently," 3/30229, expediente 571, UDLAP-SACE-AMC; and Archer-Straw, *Negrophilia*, 17.

[13] Mary Kay Vaughan and Theodore Cohen, "Brown, Black, and Blues: Miguel Covarrubias and Carlos Chávez in the United States and Mexico," in *Open Borders to a Revolution: Culture, Politics, and Migration*, ed. Jaime Marroquín, Adela Pineda Franco, and Magdalena Mieri (Washington, DC: Smithsonian Institution Scholarly Press, May 2013), 68–70; and Miguel Covarrubias, *Blues Singer*, in *The New Negro: Voices of the Harlem Renaissance*, ed. Alain Locke (New York: Touchstone, 1992), 227.

[14] Zora [Neale Hurston] to Miguel and Rose, May 21, 1935, 11/9651, expediente 179, UDLAP-SACE-AMC.

FIGURE 3.1 Miguel Covarrubias, "The Lindy Hop," c. 1936. María Elena Covarrubias/Archivo Miguel Covarrubias. Sala de Archivo y Colecciones Especiales. Dirección de Bibliotecas, Universidad de las Américas Puebla.

pianos, saxophones, and banjos; the grace of African American singers; African sculptures found in museums; and the black body, nude or clothed, posed or in motion. His image of Harlemites dancing the Lindy Hop at the Savoy Ballroom, as one commentator explained, illustrates the choreography in exquisite detail; in one still image, couples simultaneously depict "in a more or less complete fashion, the various steps and gestures of the dance" (See Figure 3.1.)[15] In addition to Covarrubias's observations, photographs and newspaper clippings provided him with veritable representations of daily life across the Black Atlantic. In contrast to the standard narratives of black inferiority and disappearance found in Mexico, Covarrubias's images extol black cultural innovation and historical agency.

Visits to Cuba and North Africa expanded Covarrubias's Afro-diasporic worldview. In 1926, his trip to Cuba complemented his gaze into Harlem's sights and sounds. Afro-Cuban music, especially rumba, and the secret practices of Afro-Cuban religious brotherhoods caught his attention. Ethnographic and visual references to Africa only appear in his works after this trip to the island nation, whose vital

[15] Image of the Lind Hop, 8/23556; and "Miguel Covarrubias," 8/23557, expediente 454, UDLAP-SACE-AMC.

rhythms "really come from the innermost recesses of darkest Africa." Of course, these cultural traits, like "all things – the exotic, barbaric, mystic, secret – sooner or later come to cosmopolitan New York," where he thought they would tragically lose some of their authenticity. The African-descended cultural expressions found in Harlem and Cuba nonetheless shared common tropes, most notably the raising and shaking of one's arms and hands above the head in a manner he thought mirrored epileptic tremors. For Covarrubias, this bodily performance symbolized all incarnations of African-descended culture. It was both the physical embodiment of a "jazz-bound life" and a quintessential aspect of Afro-Cuban ritual.[16]

Covarrubias's first book *Negro Drawings* (1927) compiled many of his initial drawings of African American and Afro-Cuban bodies. A pamphlet advertising the book describes Covarrubias's art as a window into American culture, particularly the aspects of it he had not encountered prior to coming to New York. Harlem was "the scene which has afforded him the widest scope for the exercise of his particular powers." As a foreigner not moored to US racial stereotypes, he arguably represented the unblemished black body in its truest sense, a talent that Alfred A. Knopf, Inc., called "the simplest statement of the artist's achievement."[17] Describing these caricatures as bona fide ethnographies, Ralph Barton wrote in the preface to *Negro Drawings* that they "need merely to be looked at to be understood."[18] *Vanity Fair* editor and negrophile Frank Crowninshield celebrated Covarrubias's innate ability to capture "three-dimensional form" in two. He crafted an "'aliveness,' a feeling of actuality, plus a rhythmic, almost sensuous movement." Images of performers and everyday people from the United States and Cuba showed that he had mastered, as Crowninshield noted, the "Negro types."[19]

[16] Miguel Covarrubias, "Voodoo Blackens the Night-Spots," 3/30026, expediente 570, UDLAP-SACE-AMC. On his visit to Africa, see "A Tour of North Africa" (February 1928)," 4/30051, expediente 570, UDLAP-SACE-AMC; and "Studies of North African Negroes Brought Back By Covarrubias," 21227, expediente 427, UDLAP-SACE-AMC. Photos of African communities, art, and artifacts are scattered throughout the Miguel Covarrubias Papers housed at UDLAP.

[17] "*Negro Drawings* by Miguel Covarrubias," 1/6429, expediente 125, UDLAP-SACE-AMC.

[18] Ralph Barton, preface to *Negro Drawings*, by Miguel Covarrubias (New York: Alfred A. Knopf, 1927).

[19] Frank Crowninshield, introduction to *Negro Drawings*, by Miguel Covarrubias (New York: Alfred A. Knopf, 1927).

In Mexico, the black body and its cultural expressions continued to be antithetical to the musical and visual contours of national identity. When *El Universal Ilustrado* published excerpts of composer George Gershwin's 1926 "Jazz is the Voice of the American Soul," the page appeared more like a tribute to Covarrubias than a tribute to one of the first US classical composers to embrace African American music. Editors strategically placed Gershwin's history of jazz around five of Covarrubias's caricatures (See Figure 3.2). Unsure of what to make of Gershwin's aesthetic, they christened his essay the brash statements of "the young vanity of an American composer, who relentlessly rallies against everything old, exalting at the same time his composition . . . and jazz, which he considers to be nothing less than representative of the artistic life of North America." Covarrubias's caricatures depict black women dancing with their arms, legs, and hips contorted to fit different dance styles. In the center of the page, and accompanying an image of a woman dancing in garb resembling the stars and stripes of the American flag, is the inscription: "Jazz, spirit of Yanquilandia, personified in a black woman, according to our 'chamaco.'"[20]

Covarrubias received less praise in Mexico than in the United States. While magazines like *Vanity Fair* published his caricatures, and while New York City reviewers admired them, the few Mexicans aware of his illustrations fêted their creator, not his representation of African-descended cultural expressions. As the decade came to a close, *Tiempo* recognized him in nationalist terms as "one of the best cartoonists of Mexico's newest generation."[21] José Juan Tablada anointed him as the scion of Abraham Lincoln and "the man who discovered blacks in the United States," an idea that Diego Rivera would echo years later.[22] However, in evaluating the place of Mexican art in the United States for Mexico's *El Universal* on March 7, 1929, Tablada highlighted the muralists, particularly José Clemente Orozco, whose art adorned government buildings, universities, and other private and public venues across Mexico

[20] "El jazz es la expresión del alma americana," 6676, expediente 128, UDLAP-SACE-AMC; see also Alain Derbez, *El jazz en México: Datos para una historia* (Mexico City: Fondo de Cultura Económica, 2001), 57 and 110–11.

[21] "Covarrubias y Montenegro han llegado," *Tiempo*, 18 de septiembre de 1929, 1/21033, expediente 425, UDLAP-SACE-AMC.

[22] José Juan Tablada, "New York de día y de noche: Miguel Covarrubias; El hombre que descubrió a los negros en los Estados Unidos; La belleza en donde nadie la había visto," *El Universal*, 30 de noviembre de 1924, Record Number 771677, ICAA-MFAH. Also see Diego Rivera's biographical statement about Miguel Covarrubias, 20849–20850, expediente 423, UDLAP-SACE-AMC.

FIGURE 3.2 Miguel Covarrubias, drawings accompanying George Gershwin, "El jazz es la expresión del alma americana," *El Universal Ilustrado*, 31 de marzo de 1927. María Elena Covarrubias/Archivo Miguel Covarrubias. Sala de Archivo y Colecciones Especiales. Dirección de Bibliotecas, Universidad de las Américas Puebla.

and the United States. Covarrubias's caricatures, with their ethnographic awareness and sharp wit were outside the scope of Tablada's conception of Mexican nationalism. Inverting the nineteenth-century racial paradigms that dismissed blackness in all its forms, Tablada recognized their importance on the world's stage, where everyone could celebrate Covarrubias's drawings of black Harlemites and Afro-Cubans as "human and universal," but where they were certainly not Mexican.[23]

MAKING JAZZ MEXICAN, 1928–40

The inspiration to integrate black musical genres, especially jazz, into the national soundscape came from abroad, brought to Mexico primarily by Covarrubias's good friend, composer Carlos Chávez. During a four-month trip to Manhattan in December 1923 and a more extended visit between September 1926 and June 1928, Chávez entered the interdisciplinary avant-garde circles that looked to define a New World modernity in contrast to the horrors Western civilization produced during the First World War. He was not alone – other Mexican musicians, notably Manuel M. Ponce and Julián Carrillo – also interacted with like-minded US and Cuban composers in the International Composers' Guild, the Copland-Sessions Concerts, and the Pan-American Association of Composers.[24] Working with musicians such as Edgard Varèse, Henry Cowell, and Aaron Copland, Chávez entered these preeminent cosmopolitan circles, where he quickly rose to prominence. Writing about Chávez's time in New York City in 1928, music critic Paul Rosenfeld considered his compositions to be not only the revival of the Aztec spirit but what surely had been the goal of many modernists in Manhattan: the consummation of a truly American aesthetic.[25]

In the 1920s, it was in vogue for composers to include jazzy motifs in their classical compositions, just as Gershwin had in his groundbreaking 1924 composition *Rhapsody in Blue*. Accordingly, Chávez's fascination with indigeneity blossomed into a one for all the vernacular music of the

[23] José Juan Tablada, "Arte y revolución," *El Universal*, 7 de marzo de 1929.

[24] Christina Taylor Gibson, "The Music of Manuel M. Ponce, Julián Carrillo, and Carlos Chávez" (PhD diss., University of Maryland, 2008).

[25] Paul Rosenfeld, *By Way of Art: Criticisms of Music, Literature, Painting, Sculpture, and the Dance* (New York: Coward-McCann, 1928), 273–83. Also see Leonora Saavedra, "Carlos Chávez and the Myth of the Aztec Renaissance," in *Carlos Chávez and His World*, ed. Leonora Saavedra (Princeton, NJ: Princeton University Press, 2015), 134–64.

Americas.[26] While some of his colleagues were skeptical of the value of black musical genres for modern art music, he embraced them. Jazz was modern and urban, tied directly to the art deco motifs that adorned Manhattan's skyscrapers. In 1928, he composed *Blues* and *Fox*. Orchestrated between 1926 and 1932, his ballet *Horse Power*, or *H.P.*, references Mexican vernacular genres, such as the *huapango* from the state of Veracruz, in addition to jazz.[27]

Chávez's penchant for African American music placed him alongside other Mexican cultural ambassadors – including Tablada, Covarrubias, and Orozco – who used the sights and sounds of black Harlemites as their muses. It also situated him within broader musical and political networks across the Atlantic world. Like his Manhattan brethren, composers in Paris envisioned a new wave of classical art music that sought inspiration from jazz and other African-derived musical genres, like the Brazilian sambas utilized by France's Darius Milhaud.[28] For colonial subjects, jazz came to be a musical expression that united Caribbean port cities, such as Kingston, Jamaica, and Panama City, Panama, with European metropolises.[29] A product of its diasporic origins, jazz was truly an Atlantic expression capable of bridging multiple musical genres, from Western art music to the Brazilian samba, the Cuban danzón, and the Argentine tango.[30]

For modernist composers across the globe, jazz's improvisation, syncopation, and dissonance represented the primitiveness of Africa and modern compositional forms. Copland condescendingly argued that the genre's musicological techniques and compositional styles were more important for classical composers than its "spirit, whatever it symbolized." "It seems safe to suppose," he quipped, "that it began long ago on

[26] Chávez was already receiving attention for his transposition of indigenous music into modern music. In 1924, Pedro Henríquez Ureña saw him, following in Ponce's footsteps, as one of the next composers to invigorate the national soundscape; see "The Revolution in Intellectual Life," *Survey Graphic*, May 1, 1924, 166.

[27] Carol J. Oja, *Making Modern Music: New York in the 1920s* (Oxford: Oxford University Press, 2000), 313–60; Delpar, *The Enormous Vogue of Things Mexican*, 185; and Stephanie N. Stallings, "The Pan/American Modernisms of Carlos Chávez and Henry Cowell," in *Carlos Chávez and His World*, ed. Leonora Saavedra (Princeton, NJ: Princeton University Press, 2015), 29–39.

[28] Jackson, *Making Jazz French*, 71–103.

[29] Lara Putnam, *Radical Moves: Caribbean Migrants and the Politics of Race in the Jazz Age* (Chapel Hill: University of North Carolina Press, 2013), 153–95; and Marc Matera, *Black London: The Imperial Metropolis and Decolonization in the Twentieth Century* (Oakland: University of California Press, 2015), 145–99.

[30] Seigel, *Uneven Encounters*, 67–94.

some Negro's dull tom-tom in deepest Africa." After outlining this stereotyped sketch of African cultural regions, he turned to the Atlantic slave trade. "In the slave ships of the early traders it came to America, and then, in a new environment, took on different but distinctly related forms in Cuba, in Brazil, and in the United States." Despite its origins on the other side of the Atlantic, jazz matured in the Western Hemisphere. As a quintessentially American composer, Chávez took inspiration from it, much to Copland's delight. Reflecting in 1941 on his friend's career, Copland complimented him on his innate ability to transform disparate rural and urban motifs into classical forms. *Blues* and *Fox* were inspired by "the peoples of the Dark Continent"; industrial sounds flourished in *H.P.*; and Aztec music came to the forefront in *Xochipilli-Macuilxochitl.*[31]

Returning to Mexico in 1928, and outfitted with international acclaim, Chávez instituted a new musical agenda for the nation, one that rendered black music, especially jazz, a lynchpin of the postrevolutionary musical canon. To make music not only inspired by but also for the people, he founded the OSM. As its conductor, he meticulously designed its program with two goals in mind: to celebrate Mexican music and to introduce modern compositions by Varèse, Milhaud, Dmitri Shostakovich, and Paul Hindemith, among others, to Mexican audiences.[32] To train the next generation, he also directed the National School of Music, which became the National Conservatory of Music, and the SEP's Department of Fine Arts.[33]

Jazz helped free Mexico from the prerevolutionary aesthetics that looked to Europe for inspiration. Instead of fostering musical nationalism, such crudely mechanical imitations of European music stifled, if not endangered, Mexico's postrevolutionary rejuvenation of vernacular

[31] Aaron Copland, *Our New Music* (New York: McGraw-Hill, 1941), 88–89, 99–100, and 207–8.

[32] Francisco Agea, *21 años de la Orquesta Sinfónica de México, 1928–1948* (Mexico City: Nuevo Mundo, 1948); and Ricardo Miranda, "'*The heartbeat of an intense life*': Mexican Music and Carlos Chávez's Orquesta Sinfónica de México, 1928–1948," in *Carlos Chávez and His World*, ed. Leonora Saavedra (Princeton, NJ: Princeton University Press, 2015), 46–61.

[33] Leonora Saavedra, "Of Selves and Others: Historiography, Ideology, and the Politics of Modern Mexican Music" (PhD diss., University of Pittsburgh, 2001), 219–33; and Alberto Rodríguez, "Nacionalismo y folklore en la Escuela Nacional de Música," in *Preludio y fuga: Historias trashumantes de la Escuela Nacional de Música de la UNAM*, coord. María Esther Aguirre Lora (Mexico City: Universidad Nacional Autónoma de México, 2008), 391–98.

soundscapes. Good music, Chávez concluded, needed to be uniquely Mexican, indigenous in its inspiration and musical origins, yet modern in its compositional style.[34] He wanted composers to adopt the more sophisticated discordant chords commonplace in avant-garde music. Although jazz was not yet Mexican, it was quintessentially modern, and therefore it could enter the national soundscape.[35]

This new musical canon pushed the technical and aesthetic limits of the country's best musicians. In 1928, the National Symphony was in shambles, and the Musician's Union was severely divided between classically trained and jazz instrumentalists. Chávez aligned with the jazz community. He trained them to perform art music so that they could perform with the OSM.[36] In 1937, Gerónimo Baqueiro Foster, a friend of Chávez's and a professor at the National Conservatory, reaffirmed these aesthetic divisions. Hailing Chávez's musical programming, he recalled the labor dispute between the "Jazzistas," who wanted a more ambitious musical repertoire, and the more traditional "Snobistas." The irony, for Baqueiro Foster, was that these two groups collectively "had become, without dispute, the soul of the nation's musical movement."[37] In this sarcastic juxtaposition, jazz signified more than black music – it conveyed a modern repertoire that harnessed the best attributes of classical, vernacular, and popular music. Similarly, for Chávez, jazz was just one element in his global fascination with all things primitive. He celebrated the explosion of studies about this musical genre and marveled at African art and music.[38] He assigned branches of the National Conservatory to study vernacular traditions in Mexico as well as to summarize the work done on these traditions in Asia and Africa.[39]

Mexico's indigenous music continued to seduce Chávez, his colleagues at the National Conservatory, and his students. Although a few

[34] Carlos Chávez, "Sexto Editorial de Música," expediente 5 (Artículos Periodísticos, 1924–1934), vol. 1, caja 1, sección escritos, AGN-FCC.

[35] Carlos Chávez, "Armonía y Melodía," *El Universal*, 21 de diciembre de 1924. Chávez cast Mexican aesthetics as part of a hemispherically American modernism; see Vaughan and Cohen, "Brown, Black, and Blues," 67–90.

[36] Armando Ramón Torres Chibrás, "José Pablo Moncayo, Mexican Composer and Conductor: A Survey of His Life with a Historical Perspective of his Time" (DMA, University of Missouri–Kansas City, 2002), 75–76 and 98–101.

[37] J. Baqueiro Foster, "Gallarda labor de la Orquesta Sinfónica," *Jueves de Excélsior*, 2 de septiembre de 1937, expediente 12 (OSM – "Jueves de Excélsior" – J. Baqueiro Foster – 1937), vol. 5, caja 1, serie prensa, sección Orquesta Sinfónica de México, AGN-FCC.

[38] Carlos Chávez, "El Arte Popular y el no Popular," 7 de julio de 1929, expediente 5 (Artículos Periodísticos, 1924–1934) vol. 1, caja 1, sección escritos, AGN-FCC.

[39] Saavedra, "Of Selves and Others," 231.

composers and musicologists had begun to map Mexico's musical regions in the 1920s, this ethnographic project still needed to be completed when the decade came to an end.[40] Conceiving of ethnography as a foundation for modern Mexican music, Chávez expanded the study of the nation's regional vernacular and popular genres. A historical account of all rural communities, particularly their musical exchanges with Spanish colonists, provided indispensable context for anyone truly interested in authentic Mexican music. If musicologists did not study indigenous harmonies, then these traits would be lost, and composers would be unable to transcribe them, let alone adorn them with modernist accoutrements. The cautious mixture of historical, ethnographic, and musical methods, he hoped, would provide composers with the tools to reveal "a musical intellectual expression that presents and typifies the characteristic features of its nationality."[41]

Amid the materialist cultural politics of the 1930s, Mexican musical nationalism began to utilize class as a means to extoll the entire populace, whether urban or rural, indigenous or mestizo, Spanish, or even at time African-descended. The nationalist repertoire had to bridge elite theories and popular tastes. According to critic Salomón Kahan, it needed to be understood sociologically in addition to aesthetically.[42] In a 1934 article entitled "Arte proletario," Chávez explained that he founded the OSM as a way to give music to the workers.[43] He similarly wanted the concert program *Mexican Music*, which he performed at New York City's MoMA in 1940, to be "interesting not only for specialists but for everybody."[44] To clarify the relationship between Mexican nation formation and his artistic agenda, Chávez cited Karl Marx. Artistic movements, he concluded, helped create a revolutionary class consciousness that would overthrow bourgeois musical palates and unveil the nation's true spirit.[45] As such, the Mexican Revolution was a "liberating movement"

[40] Carlos Chávez to David H. Stevens, September 14, 1940, expediente 104 (Rockefeller Foundation), vol. 4, caja 10, sección correspondencia, AGN-FCC.

[41] Expediente 9 (Nacionalismo en Latino América), vol. 1, caja 1, sección escritos, AGN-FCC.

[42] Salomón Kahan, "La Música y el Marxismo," *El Nacional*, 30 de septiembre, RP-MF 06091, cuaderno julio 1934 a diciembre 1935, CNA-BA-FE-AGBF.

[43] Carlos Chávez, "Arte proletario," expediente 69 (Arte proletario), vol. 5, caja 5, sección escritos, AGN-FCC.

[44] Carlos Chávez to Irving Leonard, September 14, 1940, expediente 104 (Rockefeller Foundation), vol. 4, caja 10, sección correspondencia, AGN-FCC.

[45] Carlos Chávez, "La Arte en la Sociedad," expediente 69 (Arte proletario), vol. 5, caja 5, sección escritos, AGN-FCC.

that stressed "the fight for the redemption of the oppressed classes and the fight against imperialist foreigners." Chávez's music gave a voice to these often-unnamed groups. *Sinfonía proletaria* (1934) was for the workers and *Sinfonía india* (1935), for the Indians. Marxist historian Alfonso Teja Zabre reiterated this perspective. He venerated Chávez for depicting Mexico's "popular roots" – pre-Columbian instruments as well as musical motifs crafted by the Huichol of Nayarit, the Yaqui of Sonora, and the Seri of Baja California – in *Sinfonía india*.[46]

Mexico's fascination with African-descended music also helped affix postrevolutionary cultural politics to African American music. Langston Hughes and W. C. Handy came to believe that blues standards, like the latter's "St. Louis Blues," could be found in almost any Mexican dance hall.[47] The NAACP's the *Crisis* exclaimed in 1935 that jazz orchestras had become one of the most common ways for Mexicans to experience African American life.[48] A defender of jazz on both sides of the border, Chávez often served an interlocutor, both literally in his compositions and programming as well as symbolically as the figurehead of Mexican music most often seen in the United States. In 1937, he expressed his admiration for Handy's bluesy compositions.[49] On February 2, 1940, the *Washington Star* proclaimed that swing music might be more popular in Mexico than in the United States. "Mr. Chávez," it continued, "says that American dance music has become so familiar and popular in Mexico through radio programs, movies and records that its influence is even to be seen in the writing of modern popular Mexican music."[50]

Not all Mexicans enjoyed this fad. Acknowledging the popularity of African American musical genres in 1930, folklorist Rubén Campos explained that jazz "is the sonorous expression of a happy people." Despite this tepid embrace, he was skeptical of its value south of the Rio Grande. The jazz craze, he hoped, would pass quickly.[51] In 1935, José Vasconcelos lamented jazz's influence on Mexican nationality. "Our

[46] Alfonso Teja Zabre, *Panorama histórico de la Revolución Mexicana* (Mexico City: Ediciones Botas, 1939), 198.

[47] Verna Arvey, *In One Lifetime* (Fayetteville: University of Arkansas Press, 1984), 125.

[48] Sue Baily Thurman, "How Far from Here to Mexico?," *Crisis*, September 1935, 267.

[49] "Dynamic Chávez Arrives as Symphony Conductor," *Pittsburgh Post-Gazette*, November 8, 1937, in *Carlos Chávez: North American Press, 1936–1950* (Mexico City: Ediciones Mexicanas de Música, 1951), 31.

[50] "Chávez, Mexican Composer, Sees Promise in Swing," *Washington Star*, February 2, 1940, in *Carlos Chávez: North American Press, 1936–1950*, 50.

[51] Rubén M. Campos, *El folklore musical de las ciudades: Investigación acerca de la música mexicana para bailar y cantar* (Mexico City: Publicaciones de la Secretaría de Educación

immigrants to Yankeeland lose their civilization, for all the refinement they may have acquired in cultivated cities like Guadalajara or Mexico City," he complained, "is exchanged for jazz rhythms and negroid dance movements as soon as they have spent a couple of months in the dance halls of California."[52] Similarly, on March 3, 1937, Fernando Urdanivia penned the editorial "La era del jazz" condemning modern society for having replaced idealism with practicality and materialism. Bewilderment, frenzy, emptiness, helplessness – these terms characterized Mexico and global politics after the First World War. Jazz, "a loyal echo of the current world," as he described it, was equally appalling. It "imitated the trot of beasts, the howling of wolves, the moaning of suffering."[53]

By the time Urdanivia published his polemic against modern aesthetics, transnational debates about jazz had entered the public sphere. Many Mexicans had learned to love African-descended musical genres, like jazz, ragtime, and danzón, at movie theaters and in dance halls.[54] A spate of newspaper articles, including one by French composer Darius Milhaud, traced the origins of jazz back to Negro Spirituals in the United States. A product of slavery, jazz was inherently the music of black misery – and, for Milhaud, it had its roots in Africa, an idea that most Mexicans did not yet fathom.[55] In *El Nacional*, France's M. Gérard Bauer traced its origins to "the street," among the working poor, rather than to the stuffier cabarets where it was a popular spectacle for urban cosmopolitans.[56] During a trip to Mexico in 1938, African American tenor Roland Hayes reinforced the idea that jazz, as an inherently somber but raucous genre,

Pública, 1930), 5–6 and 185–93, qtd. 188. Also see Rodríguez, "Nacionalismo y folklore," 389.

[52] Vasconcelos, *A Mexican Ulysses*, 142.

[53] Fernando D. Urdanivia, "La era del jazz," 3 de marzo de 1937, RP-MF 06897, cuaderno 1 de enero hasta el 22 de octubre de 1937, CNA-BA-FE-AGBF.

[54] Mary Kay Vaughan, *Portrait of a Young Painter: Pepe Zúñiga and Mexico City's Rebel Generation* (Durham, NC: Duke University Press, 2015), 78; and Alejandro L. Madrid and Robin D. Moore, *Danzón: Circum-Caribbean Dialogues in Music and Dance* (Oxford: Oxford University Press, 2013). Alain Derbez traces these debates about jazz in Mexico back to 1921; see *El jazz en México*, 35–42, 106–9, and 112–13.

[55] Darius Milhaud, "La música de los negros de Norteamérica," *El Nacional*, 23 de diciembre de 1934, RP-MF 06157, cuaderno julio 1934 a diciembre 1935, CNA-BA-FE-AGBF. Also see various articles in cuaderno *El Nacional*, enero 1936 a 6 de junio de 1937, CNA-BA-FE-AGBF.

[56] M. Gerard Bauer, "El Origen del Jazz," *El Nacional*, 10 de julio de 1938, RP-MF 09174, cuaderno 11 de julio 1937 al 11 de diciembre de 1938 – continuación de 1937 *El Nacional*, CNA-BA-FE-AGBF.

gave the racially oppressed descendants of slaves the means to express their discontent.[57] Even more aligned with the decade's materialist rhetoric, José Pomar deemed black music in the United States to be as revolutionary as the popular songs of the Mexican Revolution, like "La Adelita," and those of the Russian Revolution.[58]

As Director of the Department of Music within the Department of Fine Arts, composer Luis Sandi best grafted the class-based symbolism of jazz onto the postrevolutionary quest to transpose and modernize indigenous music. Under Chávez's direction, he glorified indigenous communities, especially the Yaqui of Sonora, who possessed a well-known history of political resistance. Their quest for autonomy preserved local musical cultures. It also allowed composers and musicologists, like Chávez and Sandi, to study and recreate their authentic melodies, harmonies, and rhythms. Sandi took inspiration from Yaqui cultural conservativism in his arrangement *Yaqui Music*, which Chávez performed in 1940 at New York City's MoMA as part of the national quest to map all of the country's vernacular music.[59]

Sandi aspired to create a truly modern national culture. It should emerge, he proclaimed, organically from the contemporary period but also take cues from "those of analogous epochs" with kindred virtues, aesthetics, and politics. Any music that paralleled the Yaqui spirit and Mexico's revolutionary tradition would enhance this new musical aesthetic. This included jazz. In the cross-racial language typical of 1930s Mexican nationalism, he envisioned a common bond among the musical expressions of all subjugated peoples. "Regarding today's music," he poetically waxed, "it has descended from the heights of the unreal to the everyday reality of everyone; it has moved away from gavottes and minuets of a refined and faraway aristocracy to move closer to the Jazz of the black slaves of all countries and to the dances of the enslaved Indians of America; ... it has become the spokesperson for the humble in contrast to the public announcements of the

[57] Ana Salado Álvarez, "Roland Hayes, el eminente tenor negro, nos habla del triste canto de su pueblo," *Excélsior*, 14 de enero de 1938, RP-MF 09745, cuaderno música (arte en general) – del 23 de octubre 1937 al 24 de febrero de 1938, CNA-BA-FE-AGBF.

[58] José Pomar, "¿Qué significan los cantos de lucha del proletariado?," 8 de noviembre, RP-MF 06647, cuaderno *El Nacional*, enero 1936 a 6 de junio de 1937, CNA-BA-FE-AGBF.

[59] Luis Sandi, "Música yaqui," expediente 169 (Luis Sandi), vol. 6, caja 10, sección correspondencia, AGN-FCC; and Herbert Weinstock, *Mexican Music: Notes by Herbert Weinstock for Concerts Arranged by Carlos Chávez* (New York: Museum of Modern Art, 1940), 23–27.

splendors of the dominant castes."[60] As an expression of subaltern resistance born in the Americas, jazz was part of the Marxist historical flourishes that contextualized and modernized Mexican music.

REVOLUTIONARY BLACKNESS IN REDES

In his 1936 film *Redes*, translated as *The Wave* in the United States, US photographer Paul Strand located the nameless oppressed peoples symbolized by jazz in Alvarado, Veracruz, a coastal community just south of the port city of Veracruz. The film gives these abstractions about black bellicosity and Mexico's revolutionary teleology a face to be seen, if not recognized, in a historically and culturally specific locale. Growing up in New York, Strand came of age while Alfred Stieglitz pioneered modern photography and while Mexicans, like Chávez, flocked to Manhattan to hone their craft. Strand met with Chávez there, and their paths crossed again in 1931 in Taos, New Mexico. Strand arrived in Mexico the next year. South of the border, he gained a Marxist perspective on social justice and, with Chávez's assistance, contributed to postrevolutionary nation-state formation as a teacher, photographer, and filmmaker.[61]

Presented by the SEP's Department of Fine Arts, *Redes* details the struggles of Alvarado's poor fishing community. The film juxtaposes the local moneyed elite – merchants and government officials – with fishermen, especially Miro, a revolutionary who brings a class consciousness to the workers. In perhaps the most direct critique of Mexican politics, Miro proclaims in front of his fellow workers, "We are tired of voting for strawmen."[62] Later, after Miro publicly advocates for unity against the slavery and unjust poverty caused by bourgeois exploitation, Juan García Sánchez, a local politician, responds by invoking the language of democracy to quell the rabble-rousers in a hollow, hastily improvised speech. Mindful of the exploitation they encounter daily, the fishermen rebel

[60] Luis Sandi, "La música y las épocas," expediente 169 (Luis Sandi), vol. 6, caja 10, sección correspondencia, AGN-FCC. Also see Luis Sandi, "La música proletaria y la proletarización de la música," 6 de septiembre, RP-MF 06604, cuaderno *El Nacional*, enero 1936 a 6 de junio de 1937, CNA-BA-FE-AGBF.

[61] For an overview of Strand's work in Mexico, see James Krippner, *Paul Strand in Mexico* (New York: Aperture Foundation, 2010).

[62] Paul Strand, *Redes* (The Wave), digitally restored edition by World Cinema Foundation and Universidad Nacional Autónoma de México, DVD authoring by Full Circle Post (2009), DVD to accompany *Paul Strand in Mexico*, by James Krippner, 28:15.

against the town's leadership, most notably Don Anselmo, the local fish distributer. During one skirmish, Sánchez shoots and kills Miro. The film then crescendos toward the inevitable revolution that will soon transform class relations in Alvarado.

Redes was part of a SEP project to teach the Mexican people about economic inequality, or, in other words, to instill a materialist consciousness in them. To add regional character, and to facilitate the pluralist tendencies of the postrevolutionary ethnographic project, Alvarado's residents – not professional actors – were hired for most roles. As the SEP noted, the locals selected for the film were "genuine and characteristic in their aesthetic sense" and representative of the "characteristic types of the racial mixes of [Mexico's] East Coast."[63] Recognition of the region's African-descended population pushed back against cinematic tropes that depicted blackness as foreign, immoral, and dangerous.[64] In *Redes*, audiences saw African-descended peoples who not only represented the nation's revolutionary spirit but also the essence of humanity itself.[65]

Conceived in 1933, *Redes* presented a revolutionary message that was well known within the SEP. Already fluent in historical materialism, Chávez was initially chosen to provide the film's sound track. When Lázaro Cárdenas assumed the presidency in 1934, the job of composing the score went to Silvestre Revueltas, Chávez's former student.[66] According to Aaron Copland, Revueltas "does not write symphonies and sonatas so much as vivid tone pictures." His music depicts "the more usual everyday side of Mexican life."[67] Revueltas's aesthetic dovetailed nicely with Strand's photographic sensibility, which gave primacy more to the static picturesque than to the dynamism of cinematic motion. Of course, Revueltas visited Alvarado to compose the music. To add a local flavor, he included the huapango, an African-descended musical genre from Veracruz, in the background during celebratory moments, such as when the fishermen have an

[63] Krippner, *Paul Strand in Mexico*, 75–77 and 79, translation and parenthetical addition provided by James Krippner.

[64] Madrid and Moore, *Danzón*, 108–9.

[65] On the film's universal spirit, see Brian Neve, "A Past Master of His Craft: An Interview with Fred Zinnemann," in *Fred Zinnemann: Interviews*, ed. Gabriel Miller (Jackson: University Press of Mississippi, 2005), 146.

[66] Krippner, *Paul Strand in Mexico*, 84–86.

[67] Aaron Copland, "Mexican Composer," *New York Times*, May 9, 1937. Also see Nicolas Slonimsky, *Music of Latin America* (New York: Thomas Y. Crowell, 1945), 224 and 248.

especially good catch.[68] His use of more foreboding dissonance during the less triumphal but equally poignant scenes of the fishermen toiling, suffering, and plotting revolution enhances *Redes*'s romanticism and ties the ethnomusicological specificity of the huapango to the postrevolutionary musical canon.

A mix of modernist ethnography, revolutionary didacticism, and utopian yearning, *Redes* weds Chávez's musical project to the Marxist celebration of Alvarado's African ancestry. Strand did not trumpet revolutionary blackness but rather implied it in the phenotypes of the actors and in the film's locale. The same can be said for Revueltas's music. The fusion of social justice, Marxist politics, and popular culture, however, was explicit. Copland went as far as to declare, "The Mexican Government, choosing Revueltas to supply the music for 'The Wave,' is very much like the U.S.S.R. asking Shostakovich to supply sound for its best pictures."[69] Other commentaries reduced *Redes* to state propaganda about unionization and economic exploitation.[70] Nonetheless, Chávez had assembled a cultural project that, with state support, voiced the decade's materialist themes for audiences in Mexico and in the United States. In *Redes*, Strand anointed a small fishing village, with its indigenous and African-descended peoples, the vanguard of a Mexico's revolutionary tradition.

JOSÉ MANCISIDOR, LEAR, AND BLACK RADICALISM

In April 1935, José Mancisidor traveled to New York City for the First American Writers Congress. Like many other Mexicans who had visited the metropolis since the outbreak of the Mexican Revolution, he drew inspiration from the New Negro Movement and its historical, social, and cultural reformulation of the African American experience. He arrived with the financial help of LEAR, a revolutionary cultural association that latched onto the leftward turn in Mexican politics and the Comintern's Popular Front ideology. LEAR's members embraced socialist education and wanted to extend these pedagogies into music, dance, and literature, among other cultural mediums. In Marxist-Leninist terms, they wanted to

[68] For a musicological analysis of Revueltas's compositions for *Redes*, see Roberto Kolb-Neuhaus, "Silvestre Revueltas's *Redes*: Composing for Film or Filming for Music?," *Journal of Film Music* 2, nos. 2–4 (2009): 127–44.

[69] Copland, "Mexican Composer."

[70] "An American Photographer Does Propaganda Movie for Mexico," 3/30942, expediente 572, UDLAP-SACE-AMC.

be "the vanguard of Mexican intellectualism" who protected workers domestically and abroad.[71] Given its cultural breadth, LEAR attracted intellectuals from a wide range of fields: Mancisidor in literature and history, composers Luis Sandi and Silvestre Revueltas, anthropologist Julio de la Fuente, painters Leopoldo Méndez and Pablo O'Higgins, and photographer Manuel Álvarez Bravo, among others.

Considering the history of radicalism associated with the state of Veracruz and celebrated in *Redes*, it is not surprising that many of the state's artists and scholars, like Mancisidor, joined LEAR. However, after the assassination of Governor-Elect Manlio Fabio Altamirano on June 25, 1936, Miguel Alemán Valdés was elected to the position. He introduced a conservative ideology that forced many of the state's left-leaning intellectuals to leave Xalapa for Mexico City. During Alemán's campaign, Mancisidor lost his job at the Normal School. His unemployment interfered with, as LEAR's Executive Committee explained, "the three books Mancisidor is writing about revolutionary themes that honor our national literature and mass orientation." Pointing to the overlapping political interests between the postrevolutionary state and LEAR, the Committee asserted that this issue merited the attention of President Lázaro Cárdenas, who subsequently named Mancisidor Director of Secondary Education for the SEP in 1939.[72]

New York City was a focal point of LEAR's cultural networks, just as it had been for New Negro intellectuals. The First American Writers Congress caught the attention of the League as well as other radicals from the Americas and Europe. The connection between progressive circles in Manhattan and Mexico City continued the intellectual and cultural dialogues previously honed by modernist artists and ethnographers in the 1910s and 1920s.[73] Congress-goers proposed the creation of two continental magazines, *Sin Fronteras* and *All America*, to unite the hemisphere's cultural left. They wanted Mancisidor, who had already founded *Ruta* in Veracruz, to coordinate them.[74] LEAR's Executive Committee reinforced these

[71] "Resumen del Congreso Nacional de Escritores y Artistas convocado por la LEAR," *Frente a Frente*, no. 8 (1937): 22–23. Also see Patrick Iber, *Neither Peace nor Freedom: The Cultural Cold War in Latin America* (Cambridge, MA: Harvard University Press, 2015), 33; and John Lear, *Picturing the Proletariat: Artists and Labor in Revolutionary Mexico, 1908–1940* (Austin: University of Texas Press, 2017), 160–65.

[72] Luis I. Rodríguez to Presidente Cárdenas, 3 de octubre de 1936, 703.2/174, AGN-FLCA; and Bustos Cerecedo, "José Mancisidor," 273.

[73] Ben Ossa to Luis Arenal, 8 de noviembre de 1935, Record ID: 801606, ICAA-MFAH.

[74] Luis Arenal to Ángel Flores, 14 de junio de 1935, Record ID: 801551, ICAA-MFAH. For a discussion of *Ruta*, see Berrios, "Vida y Obras de José Mancisidor," 49.

transnational aspirations. Hoping to expand the circulation of its magazine *Frente a Frente*, the League inquired about the possibility of exchanging it for issues of *New Masses*, the mouthpiece of the Communist Party of the United States.[75] As part of this leftist cultural brotherhood, LEAR occasionally republished articles from *New Masses*, and *New Masses* published Mancisidor's short story "The Lecture" in its issue from April 30, 1935.[76]

In New York City, Mancisidor found refuge in the communist and antifascist circles that celebrated black cultural expressions alongside black political protest. He noticed the growing popularity of African American writers within these communist-backed cultural outlets. New Negro poet and *New Masses* contributor Langston Hughes stood out. In Mexico to dispose of his father's estate, Hughes did not attend the First American Writers Congress but instead sent the statement "To Negro Writers" that was published in the May 7, 1935, issue of *New Masses*.[77] He also translated Mancisidor's short story "Home" for the fashionable *Partisan Review*, a magazine whose pro-Soviet and anticapitalist politics resembled LEAR's.[78] This intellectual dialogism made its way back to Mexico. In 1935, Mancisidor examined Hughes's cultural and political activism on behalf of "millions of subjected blacks." He referenced several of Hughes's poems, including "I, Too" from Alain Locke's 1925 anthology *The New Negro* and "Good Morning Revolution" that *New Masses* published in 1932. Hughes's rhythmic grace, particularly his ability to channel music in verse, impressed Mancisidor. However, class – not race – was Mancisidor's focus. Hughes, he noted, "speaks of blacks not by the pigmentation of their skin, but through their social condition."[79]

[75] Juan de la Cabada and Luis Arenal to Bernabé Barrios, 6 de junio de 1935, Private Archive, Mexico City, Record ID: 801000, ICAA-MFAH; Comité Ejecutivo de la Liga de Escritores y Artistas Revolucionarios to Joseph Freeman, National Secretary of the John Reed Club, 22 de enero de 1935, Record ID: 800989, ICAA-MFAH; and Secretario del Comité Ejecutivo de la Liga de Escritores y Artistas Revolucionarios to *New Masses* Magazine, 6 de julio de 1935, Record ID: 801041, ICAA-MFAH.

[76] Alicia Azuela, "*El Machete* and *Frente a Frente*: Art Committed to Social Justice in Mexico," *Art Journal* 52, no. 1 (1993): 86.

[77] Lawrence P. Jackson, *The Indignant Generation: A Narrative History of African American Writers and Critics, 1934–1960* (Princeton, NJ: Princeton University Press, 2011), 27–45; and Ann George and Jack Selzer, "What Happened at the First American Writers Congress? Kenneth Burke's 'Revolutionary Symbolism in America,'" *Rhetoric Society Quarterly* 33, no. 2 (2003): 47.

[78] "Editorial Statement," *Partisan Review* 1, no. 1 (1934): np.

[79] José Mancisidor, "La risa de Langston Hughes," in *Imágenes de mi tiempo*, in vol. 5 of *Obras Completas de José Mancisidor* (Xalapa: Veracruz: Gobierno del Estado de Veracruz, 1980), 645–49.

Others echoed Mancisidor's repugnance toward the treatment of African Americans. Reflecting in 1945 on his time in Harlem, muralist José Clemente Orozco noted the slave-like dependency African Americans had on white Americans for survival. The alternative, he lamented, was to abandon one's blackness, to whiten one's skin or to straighten one's hair.[80] Likely inspired by Orozco's lithograph *Hanging Blacks*, Julio de la Fuente included images of lynched African Americans on the cover of the May 1933 issue of *Ruta*.[81] Mancisidor's biographer and fellow LEAR member, Miguel Bustos Cerecedo painted an equally gloomy picture of the daily lives of black Harlemites in his 1939 poem "Carta a Nueva York." He described the city as cold, epitomized by what he called the "inflexible" and "crude" realities of democracy in the city's neglected neighborhoods. The exploitation inherent to a city defined by empire contradicted its image as a beacon of light for the world's tired, poor, huddled masses. Bustos Cerecedo included a racial dynamic to his observations about the city's paradoxes. While white New Yorkers enjoy jazz and watch Joe Louis fight, there is a "relentless scorn" for black Harlemites.[82]

New York similarly inspired Mancisidor. In 1935, he published *Nueva York revolucionario*. Written in a journalistic style, the novel is part travelogue, part Marxist musing on the city's past, present, and future. As he explained on the interior cover page, "I dedicate this book to everyone who, like me, experiences the need for social revolution." An unnamed narrator arriving in New York for the Writers' Congress examines the city as a metonym for modern society. New York City is divided by class and race, imbued with jazz, and in need of communist revolution. People take to the streets lined with skyscrapers, and African Americans march down the metropolis's main thoroughfares listening to "Foreign music. Melodies that speak of an old slavery." Protesters of all races garner support among the residents of Harlem who begin to see Marxism as the only remedy for their poverty, social ostracism, and political marginalization. Their class consciousness offsets the bourgeoisie's stifling racial vocabulary that, at its best, "tries to feign consideration and humanitarianism for

[80] Orozco, *An Autobiography*, 124. [81] Lear, *Picturing the Proletariat*, 173–74.

[82] Miguel Bustos Cerecedo, "Carta a Nueva York," in vol. 2 of *Veracruz: Dos siglos de poesía (XIX y XX)*, ed. Esther Hernández Palacio and Ángel José Fernández (Mexico City: Consejo Nacional para la Cultura y las Artes, 1991), 77–82.

blacks." *Nueva York revolucionario* climaxes when a race riot overtakes Harlem, home to "the most important black population in the world."[83] Mancisidor did not invent this conflagration. He alluded to a two-day riot that began on March 19, 1935, after sixteen-year-old black Puerto Rican Lino Rivera was caught stealing a penknife and was rumored to have been arrested, beaten, and killed. This was no small event that caught Mancisidor's eye. It has come to signal the end of the period "when the Negro was in vogue," as Langston Hughes called the New Negro Movement in 1940.[84]

The Communist Party of the United States – and the entire international communist movement – debated the role of race in social protest, just as it does in *Nueva York revolucionario*, where the racial and national diversity of international communism is on full display alongside José Clemente Orozco's murals at the New School for Social Research.[85] There were multiple questions as stake: Were African Americans part of the revolutionary leadership? In the United States, would the revolution begin in the rural south, where most blacks lived? Or, would it take place in the industrial north, where a proletarian revolution was possible and where black Harlemites could act as the vanguard? In essence, Mancisidor and his colleagues debated whether orthodox Marxist theory could coexist with racial mobilization and even black statehood.[86] The Harlem riot pointed to some of the radical racial possibilities radiating out from Harlem, particularly since African American membership in the Communist Party spiked after March 19, 1935.[87]

Mexico's hallowed place as the first social revolution of the twentieth century made it an exciting place for revolutionaries to debate Marxist polemics, especially once the Second World War made travel to the Soviet Union impossible. The waves of reporters and refugees, who came in the 1910 Revolution's wake and again with Republican losses during the

[83] José Mancisidor, *Nueva York revolucionario* (Xalapa: Editorial "Integrales," 1935), 87, 88, and 147.

[84] Langston Hughes, *The Big Sea* (New York: Hill and Wang, 1993), 223. Historian David Levering Lewis explains that these protests in March 1935 marked the end of the New Negro Movement; see *When Harlem Was in Vogue* (New York: Penguin Books, 1997), 306–7.

[85] Mancisidor, *Nueva York revolucionario*, 55–61 and 91.

[86] Robin D. G. Kelley, *Race Rebels: Culture, Politics, and the Black Working Class* (New York: The Free Press, 1996), 104–20; and Glenda Elizabeth Gilmore, *Defying Dixie: The Radical Roots of Civil Rights, 1919–1950* (New York: W. W. Norton, 2008), 29–66.

[87] Jackson, *The Indignant Generation*, 43–44.

Spanish Civil War, turned the country into a safe haven for Communist dissidents and African Americans alike.[88] In 1939, Trinidad's C. L. R. James came to Mexico to bask in its socialist projects. Concerned with the same issues as Mancisidor, he spoke with Leon Trotsky, the Soviet theoretician who found political asylum in Mexico after Joseph Stalin exiled him for continuing to champion global revolution.[89] Framed by Nazi Germany's ethnic chauvinism, they discussed the relationship between black political protest and Marxism's theoretically race-blind practices. James envisioned revolutionary theory and praxis within the parameters of a black radical tradition that commenced with Haitian independence, continued with the American Civil War and contemporary antifascist politics, and would culminate eventually with decolonization. He saw Mexico not as a hotbed of black politics but as an intellectual and cultural paradise where such revolutionary imaginings could flourish.[90] Accordingly, he penned in 1940, "Trotsky could not rest anywhere. No country wanted him until Mexico added lustre to its history by giving him a home."[91]

ANTIFASCISM AND THE TRANSNATIONALITY OF BLACKNESS

Polemics about Marxist revolution were as much about culture as they were about race – and, in theory, both were of secondary importance to class. Marxism therefore provided an ideal bridge between the biological and cultural constructions of blackness in the Atlantic world. After all, questions about whether African-descended peoples could be at the forefront of Marxist revolution in the United States developed in parallel with inquiries into the revolutionary nature of Mexico's indigenous communities. Most famously in Mexico, these diatribes circled around muralist David Alfaro Siqueiros's condemnation of Diego Rivera, a Trotskyite who Siqueiros claimed had exchanged a proletarian aesthetic for his

[88] Hazel Rowley, *Richard Wright: The Life and Times* (Chicago: University of Chicago Press, 2001), 138 and 165; Iber, *Neither Peace nor Freedom*, 21–28 and 34; and Margaret Stevens, *Red International and Black Caribbean: Communists in New York City, Mexico and the West Indies, 1919–1939* (London: Pluto Press, 2017), esp. 213–18.

[89] Stephanie J. Smith, *The Power and Politics of Art in Postrevolutionary Mexico* (Chapel Hill: University of North Carolina Press, 2017), 90–95.

[90] J. R. Johnson [C. L. R. James], "The Negro Question," *Internal Bulletin: Socialist Workers Party*, no. 9 (1939): 23.

[91] J. R. Johnson [C. L. R. James], "Trotsky's Place in History," *New International* 6, no. 8 (1940): 165.

patrons' bourgeois tastes.[92] The fascist threat in Spain softened these ideological divides, particularly within LEAR. The League sent some members to Spain to support the Republicans fighting against General Francisco Franco. The Spanish Civil War, Mancisidor contended, was a fight over human dignity, with Mexico, the Soviet Union, and Republican Spain leading the charge against hatred, slander, and indecency.[93] Internationally, the Comintern directed the International Brigades that brought Republican sympathizers, including some African Americans who fought in the Abraham Lincoln Brigades, to the battlefield.

The international correspondents and cultural producers who fought against fascism and traveled to Spain helped Mexicans envision black cultures transnationally. Among African Americans, an incipient black internationalism developed when fascist Italy invaded Ethiopia in 1935 and then when people from across the African Diaspora arrived in Spain to combat fascism. "And now, in Madrid, Spain's besieged capital," Langston Hughes wrote on September 13, 1937, "I've met wide-awake Negroes from various parts of the world – New York, our Middle West, the French West Indies, Cuba, Africa – some stationed here, others on leave from their battalions – all of them here because they know that if fascism creeps across Spain, across Europe, and then across the world, there will be no place left for intelligent young Negroes at all."[94] Mexicans were also aware of fascism's ethnocentrism, but they did not conceptualize the war in Spain as one fundamentally about the global rights of Africans. In 1936, Mancisidor noted that fascism was not only an "enemy of culture" but also "in reality, the clearest expression of the most reactionary forces in capitalist society." He only affixed fascism to the violation of Ethiopian sovereignty in 1947, a decade after African Americans made the same racial and political association.[95]

[92] Azuela, "*El Machete* and *Frente a Frente*," 87.

[93] José Mancisidor, *Ciento veinte días* (Editorial México Nuevo, 1937), 3–4.

[94] Langston Hughes, "Negroes in Spain," in *Volunteer for Liberty* 1, no. 14, September 13, 1937, reprinted in *African Americans in the Spanish Civil War: "This Ain't Ethiopia, but It'll Do,"* ed. Danny Duncan Collum (New York: G. K. Hall, 1992), 103. Also see Brenda Gayle Plummer, *Black Americans and US Foreign Affairs, 1935–1960* (Chapel Hill: University of North Carolina Press, 1996), 37–81; Kelley, *Race Rebels*, 123–58; and James H. Meriwether, *Proudly We Can Be Africans: Black Americans and Africa, 1935–1961* (Chapel Hill: University of North Carolina Press, 2002), 27–56.

[95] José Mancisidor discussed his sympathy toward Ethiopia in 1947, when he interviewed Pablo Picasso and agreed that Italy's invasion was "the assassination of defenseless

For Mexicans, the Spanish Civil War represented a broader battle between fascism and democracy. For example, with composer Silvestre Reveultas appointed President of LEAR, the League organized a Congress of National Writers, Artists, Scientists, and Intellectuals in Guadalajara, Jalisco, from January 17 to 24, 1937. Looking to continue the intellectual comradery and political activism of the American Writers' Congress, this gathering was part of the global effort to fight "against fascism and in favor of democracy and liberty." Mancisidor took a prominent role, particularly as a member of the Congress's Permanent Commission. LEAR appointed honorary chairs from Spain, Germany, the Soviet Union, and other countries in the Western Hemisphere. Although Hughes did not attend, he was one of these esteemed guests. Afro-Cubanist poet and Communist Party member Nicolás Guillén, one of Hughes's close friends and a central figure in the North-South conversations about blackness in the United States and Cuba, helped convene the Cuban delegation.[96]

Six months later, intellectuals from Mexico, Cuba, the United States, and Europe traveled to the Republican stronghold of Valencia to participate in the Second International Congress of Anti-Fascist Writers. Led by Mancisidor, several LEAR members left Mexico on June 14, 1937, for New York City, where they stayed for five days before traveling to France, then Spain. In Republican-controlled Valencia, the International Brigades enjoyed performances of Revueltas's music, and, in Barcelona, he conducted the score to *Redes*.[97] While LEAR members fought against fascism, they were in contact with New Negro and Afro-Cubanist intellectuals like Langston Hughes, Nicolás Guillén, and Alejo Carpentier.[98] These

blacks"; see "30 minutos con Picasso," in *Imágenes de mi tiempo*, in vol. 5 of *Obras completas de José Mancisidor* (Xalapa: Gobierno del Estado de Veracruz, 1980), 743.

96 "Resumen del Congreso Nacional de Escritores y Artistas convocado por la LEAR," 22 and 24. LEAR member Luis Cardoza y Aragón called Hughes "the poet of his race"; see "Langston Hughes: el poeta de los negros," *El Nacional*, 17 de marzo de 1935, folder A1, box 1, reel 1, NYPL-SCRBC-LM-LHC. For a discussion of the Nicolás Guillén's collaboration with Langston Hughes, see Keith Ellis, "Nicolás Guillén and Langston Hughes: Convergences and Divergences," in *Between Race and Empire: African-Americans and Cubans before the Cuban Revolution*, ed. Lisa Brock and Digna Castañeda Fuertes (Philadelphia: Temple University Press, 1998), 129–67; and Guridy, *Forging Diaspora*, 107–50. Regarding the relationship between antifascist cultural production in the United States and Mexico, see Smith, *The Power and Politics of Art in Postrevolutionary Mexico*, 153–60.

97 Eduardo Contreras Soto, *Silvestre Revueltas: Baile, duelo y son* (Mexico City: CONACULTA, 2000), 55–57.

98 For example, see Langston Hughes, "Paris-Spain 1937 Notes," folder 12442, box 492, YU-BRBML-JWJCYCAL-LHP.

dialogues brought Afro-diasporic artistic expressions common to the United States and Cuba to Mexico's musical scene, just as they brought devastating images of fascism home to Mexican audiences.[99]

Silvestre Revueltas best illustrates the integration of postrevolutionary cultural politics into the world of black internationalism. He most likely encountered black music, chiefly blues, for the first time when he enrolled at Saint Edward's College in Austin, Texas, in 1917. His appreciation of these musical genres continued a few years later when Chávez introduced him to New York City's musical circles. In the 1930s, Afro-Cubanist composers Amadeo Roldán and Alejandro García Caturla promoted Revuetlas's and Chávez's compositions. The admiration was mutual, for Revueltas reveled in their classical renditions of Afro-Cuban vernacular music.[100] These racial dialogues helped him expand the black musical geographies he had honed in *Redes*. At some point, either in Guadalajara or in Spain, Revueltas heard Guillén read the poem "Sensemayá." Its African-derived rhythmic chants inspired him to transform the verses into a classical composition of the same name.[101] Fondly recounting his time in Spain, Hughes exclaimed that Revueltas "set my 'Song for a Dark Girl' to music." Revueltas finished this composition as well as *Sensemayá* in 1938, after a lack of funding prevented LEAR's cultural ambassadors from continuing their travels abroad.[102] Mancisidor hailed *Sensemayá* for its ability "to strengthen and harness the bitterness of the enslaved 'ñáñigo,'" a member of a secret Afro-Cuban brotherhood. Revueltas's genius was in his ability to give voice to all dimensions of the human condition, including "the suffering of blacks oppressed by centuries of misery."[103]

Although Carlos Chávez never joined LEAR, he brought these cultural networks full circle. At the end of the 1930s, his modernist sensibilities blossomed into a hemispheric antifascism. With Miguel Covarrubias and Anita Brenner, he wanted to produce a film to discredit the dictatorships

[99] For a discussion of Mexican images of the Spanish Civil War, see Lear, *Picturing the Proletariat*, 240–60.

[100] Contreras Soto, *Silvestre Revueltas*, 18–19, 29, and 38.

[101] Eugenia Revueltas, "La Liga de Escritores y Artistas Revolucionarios y Silvestre Revueltas," in *Diálogo de resplandores: Carlos Chávez y Silvestre Revueltas*, ed. Yael Bitrán and Ricardo Miranda (Mexico City: Consejo Nacional para la Cultura y las Artes, 2002), 179.

[102] Langston Hughes, *Autobiography:* I Wonder as I Wander, vol. 14 of *The Collected Works of Langston Hughes*, ed. Joseph McLaren (Columbia: University of Missouri Press, 2003), 372.

[103] José Mancisidor, "Perfil de Silvestre Revueltas," *El Nacional*, 20 de agosto de 1939, RP-MF 00055 and 29324, expediente enero-noviembre 1939, CNA-BA-FE-AGBF.

making waves across Europe and Asia. Vernacular sounds, animation, and the history of the Americas, they thought, best elucidated the dangers of fascism and the democratic potential of historical empathy and ethnographic objectivity.[104] Racial tolerance was implicit in their conversations but explicit in Chávez's performance of African American composer William Grant Still's cantata *And They Lynched Him on a Tree* in 1944. Recruited by Alain Locke to put music to Katherine Garrison Chapin's poem of the same name in 1939, Still composed the cantata to elucidate the dangers of racialized violence. Built around two choral groups – one white and one black – and a contralto soloist, the mother of a lynching victim, the twenty-minute piece traces the aftermath of a lynching and concludes when the two choruses come together to celebrate a racially unified future.[105]

And They Lynched Him on a Tree, with its dissonance and jazzy motifs, continued the intellectual networks and cultural appropriations Chávez first embraced in Manhattan, where he, Covarrubias, and Still became friends. In 1926, the International Composers' Guild performed Still's *Darker America* alongside an early version of Chávez's *H.P.* Their paths continued to cross, first through the Pan-American Association of Composers in the late 1920s and then in Mexico in the 1930s and early 1940s. Their mutual admiration continued after Verna Arvey, a composer who met Chávez in 1933, became Still's publicist and then, in 1939, his wife. Chávez took to Still's willingness to apply black vernacular melodies, harmonies, and rhythms to art music. In 1944, he became the only Latin American conductor – and the OSM, the only Latin American orchestra – to perform *And They Lynched Him on a Tree*.[106] He took an active role in the bringing cantata to Mexico City. Still's compositions symbolized Chávez's continued fascination with black music in the mid-to-late 1930s, long after he had left Manhattan's musical scene for Mexico's.[107] Chávez even helped translate the lyrics into

[104] See documents in expediente 82 (Anita Brenner), caja 2, vol. 5; and expediente 42 (Walt Disney), caja 4, vol. 2, sección correspondencia, AGN-FCC.

[105] Wayne D. Shirley, "William Grant Still's Choral Ballad *And They Lynched Him on a Tree*," *American Music* 12, no. 4 (1994): 425–61.

[106] See several letters from Carlos Chávez in the folder "Chávez, Carlos, November 29, 1935–September 6, 1944," box 8, UAL-SC-WGSVAP.

[107] Regarding Chávez's desire to study *Darker America* in 1935, see Carlos Chávez to Mr. William Grant Still, November 29, 1935, folder "Chávez, Carlos, November 29, 1935–September 6, 1944," box 8, UAL-SC-WGSVAP.

Spanish.[108] After several rehearsals, he wrote to Chapin, "the Orchestra is just as pleased as I am to present it to the Mexican public."[109]

Performed from July 21 to 23, 1944, the OSM program describes Still as a "noted black composer," the first in the history of the United States to have his work performed by a major symphony. It follows Mexico's proclivity to universalize blackness, its history of suffering, and its cultural expressions. As such, *And They Lynched Him on a Tree* is "impressive in its drama and its profoundly human qualities."[110] The narrator was Chávez's friend Carlos Pellicer, who despite not being a member of LEAR had traveled as part of the League's delegation to Spain in 1937.[111] Reflecting on the performances and the potential historical, linguistic, and cultural disconnect between African American history and postrevolutionary Mexican society, Arvey commented that the program should have included the lyrics to help the audience follow along. "I don't know how much was understood of what was going on," she wrote, "but the public definitely seemed to like the work and applauded with enthusiasm."[112]

Whether or not Mexican audiences understood the nuances of *And They Lynched Him on a Tree*, they, like African Americans, thought lynching cast a dark shadow on the United States and, by the Second World War, the democratic potential of the Western Hemisphere. Alain Locke wrote that the calls for justice found in *And They Lynched Him on a Tree* made it "*the* ballad for democracy."[113] While in the United States, Miguel Covarrubias observed the violence of Jim Crow legislation. Newspaper reports of African American lynching victims and Ku Klux Klan activities caught his attention and inspired some of his most somber illustrations not only of US

[108] William Grant Still to Katherine Garrison Chapin, June 18, 1944, folder 40, box 20, GUL-BFCSC-PKB. Also see several letters in folder 29, box 56, GUL-BFCSC-PKB.

[109] Carlos Chávez to Katherine Garrison Chapin, 2 de agosto de 1944, folder 29, box 56, GUL-BFCSC-PKB.

[110] Orquesta Sinfónica de México, Programa XVII Temporada 1944, folder 16, box 42, GUL-BFCSC-PKB. Still received similar praise in Gertrude Duby's pamphlet *¿Hay Razas Inferiores?* (Mexico City: Secretaría de Educación Pública, 1946), 73–74.

[111] Lear, *Picturing the Proletariat*, 239–40.

[112] Excerpts from Verna Still (July 31, 1944), folder 29, box 56, GUL-BFCSC-PKB.

[113] Alain Locke, "Ballad for Democracy," *Opportunity*, August 1940, 228–29; and Shirley, "William Grant Still's Choral Ballad *And They Lynched Him on a Tree*," 427–35.

society but also of the dangers of ethnocentrism.[114] Chávez also took to this crusade. In addition to performing Still's cantata, he composed *North Carolina Blues* in 1942. His bluesy piano score accompanied Xavier Villaurrutia's 1938 antilynching poem "North Carolina Blues: A Langston Hughes."[115] The OSM program places *And They Lynched Him on a Tree* in this political context. "Inspired by the old tragedy caused by the illegality of the crowds who claim to take justice into their own hands, and with particular reference to the racial problem in the United States," it states, "Chapin's poem expresses her profound conviction that 'lynching' is a serious social defect, and her belief that the majority of sensible people hold this conviction."[116]

These transnational conversations and the cultural expressions they produced destroyed the remaining prerevolutionary conventions that Mexican blackness needed to be surveilled in the name of social control. At odds with postrevolutionary social justice initiatives, these stereotypical assumptions about black criminality only begat racial hostilities, just as lynching in the United States so gruesomely illustrated. Accordingly, one of the most entrenched legends about the perils of blackness gained new life when Xavier Villaurrutia wrote the screenplay *La mulata de Córdoba* in 1939. Conceived around 1839, the legend drew on the trope of black disappearance born in the decades after independence. Typically told in the context of the Spanish Inquisition in the sixteenth or seventeenth centuries, it is a story about a mulatta accused of witchcraft who escapes from jail when she draws a boat and then takes it out to sea to regain her freedom.[117] Turning the tale into one about two families feuding over a lovers' quarrel surrounding Sara, the mulatta of Córdoba, during the Mexican Revolution, Villarrutia brought the symbolism surrounding blackness to the revolutionary present. Black identity nonetheless remains imprecise, for Sara's mother, whose name always goes unmentioned, "was thought to be black." As society's "invisible enemy," Sara uses magic to kill the individuals who marginalize her or

[114] See expediente 255, UDLAP-SACE-AMC; and Miguel Covarrubias, *Untitled Lithograph*, in *Uncle Tom's Cabin; or, Life among the Lowly*, by Harriet Beecher Stowe (New York: The Heritage Press, 1938), between 236 and 237.

[115] Stallings, "The Pan/American Modernisms of Carlos Chávez and Henry Cowell," 39–41.

[116] Orquesta Sinfónica de México, Programa XVII Temporada 1944, folder 16, box 42, GUL-BFCSC-PKB.

[117] Marisela Jiménez Ramos, "Black Mexico: Nineteenth-Century Discourses of Race and Nation" (PhD diss., Brown University, 2009), 164–85.

to make them go insane.[118] In other words, her bellicosity was born from racial prejudice rather than her blackness.

By 1948, and with the help of writer Agustín Lazo and composer José Pablo Moncayo, Villaurrutia transformed the mulatta of Córdoba legend into a modern opera for Chávez to conduct. Moncayo emphasized the opera's Atlantic geography when he included vernacular sounds, like the *son jarocho*, from the state of Veracruz.[119] Unlike the screenplay, it is set during the struggle for independence and the mulatta is Soledad, or Solitude. Following nineteenth-century stereotypes of black exoticism, men lust for her and women believe she is an evil sorcerer. Unsure of where Soledad was born or when she arrived in the region, the xenophobic chorus sings that she does not belong "in our land." Aware of her social isolation, Soledad responds in kind:

> I don't know if I should, if I can
> stay in this city.[120]

A Mexican everyman, she is everywhere and nowhere, of no specific historical epoch but all of them.[121] At the climax of the opera, she goes to the Inquisition needing only to name her father to be saved. Instead, she chooses to rebel; she returns to the sea, where she can be free, rather than submit to a society that, in rejecting her, compels everyone to be violent.

CONCLUSION

In the 1930s, jazz flourished as the lynchpin that connected Mexican, African American, and Afro-Cuban music. As the symbol of all oppressed peoples, this musical genre introduced the transnational potentialities of blackness to Mexico's musical canon and the cultural worldview of the Mexican left. No longer a threat to indigenous music or Mexican identity,

[118] Xavier Villaurrutia, "La mulata de Córdoba: Escenario cinematográfico," in *Obras: Poesía/Teatro/Prosas varias/Crítica*, 2nd ed., comp. Miguel Capistrán, Alí Chumacero y Luis Mario Schneider (Mexico City: Fondo de Cultura Económica, 1966), 192 and 226.

[119] Leonora Saavedra, "Staging the Nation: Race, Religion, and History in Mexican Opera of the 1940s," *The Opera Quarterly* 23, no. 1 (2007): 7.

[120] Xavier Villaurrutia, "La mulata de Córdoba: Ópera en un acto y tres cuadros [en colaboración con Agustín Lazo, Música de J. Pablo Moncayo]," in *Obras: Poesía/Teatro/Prosas varias/Crítica*, 2nd ed., comp. Miguel Capistrán, Alí Chumacero y Luis Mario Schneider (Mexico City: Fondo de Cultura Económica, 1966), 241.

[121] Ramos, "Black Mexico," 190–91.

black melodies, harmonies, and rhythms from across the Americas elucidated the radical spirit that animated the nation's new historical pantheon, New World modernism, and global antifascism. As Mexican writers, artists, and composers traveled to New York City and Spain, they began to envision the shared structural, historical, and cultural experiences of African-descended peoples in the Western Hemisphere. In other words, they constructed a revolutionary community that made the black radical tradition, chiefly New Negro and Afro-Cubanist artistic expressions, compatible with postrevolutionary nation-state formation. Their conceptions of blackness, no matter how transnational, were still native to the Americas, devoid of any specific ties to Africa. As the next two chapters detail, Mexican social science expanded these cultural geographies during and immediately after the Second World War. When antifascist networks concerned with the Spanish Civil War transformed into inter-American dialogues about the fate of democracy and racial egalitarianism, ethnographically trained Mexicans began to notice Mexico's African heritage.

PART II

FINDING AFRO-MEXICO, 1940s–2015

4

Looking Back to Africa

In 1943, W. E. B. Du Bois's research associate and *Pittsburgh Courier* columnist Irene Diggs proclaimed that Mexico was "the cradle for Afro-American studies not only in America, nor on a scale inter-American, but in the world."[1] Mexico City's International Institute of Afro-American Studies inspired her laudatory remark. The International Institute's founder and Director, Cuban lawyer and ethnographer Fernando Ortiz chose this location because Mexico lacked "prejudice to the degree of other nations." The sprawling capital city, he contended, was an ideal place to discuss "all these racial problems" unleashed first by slavery and colonialism and more recently by segregation and imperialism.[2] In this transnational context – the North-South conversations that propelled twentieth-century histories and historiographies about African history, New World slavery, and postemancipation societies – Afro-diasporic intellectual and cultural debates entered Mexican nation-state formation and Mexico entered the cultural politics of the African Diaspora.

The Second World War cast a shadow over the International Institute. National myths about Latin American racial benevolence, which had encouraged African Americans to look south of the Rio Grande for a temporary or permanent respite from US racial policies, suddenly

[1] Irene Diggs, "Cuban Leader Helped to Found Negro Study Center," *Pittsburgh Courier*, December 4, 1943.

[2] Fernando Ortiz to Melville J. Herskovits, 26 de enero de 1944, folder 24 (International Institute of Afro-American Studies, 1943–1944), box 28, NULA-MJHP. These discussions about blackness and racial formations, as Jessica Graham argues, were part of global debates about the relationship between racial inclusion and democracy in the 1930s and 1940s; see *Shifting the Meaning of Democracy*.

acquired global political currency. The Old World represented ethnocentrism, racism, and fascism – and the New World, cultural pluralism, racial tolerance, and democracy. With its long history of avoiding racial categories and favoring cultural ones, Mexico offered the rest of the Americas an alternative window into the hemisphere's white, indigenous, African-descended, and racially mixed communities.

An extraordinary collective of artists, writers, and government officials interested in African-descended peoples and cultures coalesced in Mexico City for the International Institute. Taking inspiration from them, Mexican intellectuals, most notably anthropologist Gonzalo Aguirre Beltrán and caricaturist Miguel Covarrubias, adopted the ethnographic theories and methods used in other countries to recognize the presence of African cultural retentions, or Africanisms, in the Western Hemisphere. For the first time, ethnographic data and archival research about enslaved Africans and their descendants in the United States, Cuba, and Brazil were relevant to Mexican history and ethnography. In other words, Mexicans began to recognize the nation's African heritage.

AFRICAN AMERICANS LOOK SOUTH

In the nineteenth and early twentieth centuries, Mexico's liberal silencing of race captivated the attention of African Americans. Because Mexico abolished slavery decades before the United States, African Americans depicted it along with Canada and parts of the Caribbean as a haven for slaves in search of a temporary respite or a permanent home away from their master. After Reconstruction, African Americans disenchanted with Jim Crow laws continued to contrast US racial policies with Mexico's ostensible racelessness. As much a loyal account of slavery as a commentary on life under Jim Crow, slave narratives recorded by the Works Progress Administration in the 1930s described Mexico as a place of refuge. Felix Haywood of Texas commented to an interviewer, "In Mexico you could be free. They didn't care what color you was, black, white, yellow or blue."[3]

By the twentieth century, African Americans had recast comparisons between slavery and abolition within the more malleable trappings of postemancipation race relations. Writing to government officials,

[3] Spencer R. Crew, Lonnie G. Bunch, and Clement A. Price, eds., *Memories of the Enslaved: Voices from the Slave Narratives* (Santa Barbara, CA: ABC-CLIO, LLC, 2015), 174, 241, and 243.

including President Álvaro Obregón, they frequently referenced their work ethic as well as the racial atrocities they encountered north of the Rio Grande.[4] In 1919, world-famous boxer Jack Johnson crossed the border after his relationship with Lucille Cameron, a white woman, led to the accusation that he violated the Mann Act by taking her across state lines. For him, Latin America was "a land that has never known racial prejudice." Mexico stood out since it was "willing not only to give us the privileges of Mexican citizenship, but will champion our cause."[5] That same year, Langston Hughes, a high school student who had not yet blossomed into a New Negro poet, traveled to Mexico for the first time to visit his father, James. Like other African Americans, James Hughes had moved to Latin America, first Cuba, then Mexico, to escape the racism pervasive in US society. While in Mexico, Langston began to sympathize with the nation's oppressed indigenous peoples, like the revolutionary Zapatistas, and began a lifelong fascination with Latin America.[6] After graduating the next year, he returned to Mexico and stayed there until he enrolled at Columbia University in 1921. He became fluent in Spanish, a skill that helped him maintain friendships across the region and that transformed him into a key figure in the transnational dialogues about the African Diaspora in the interwar period. Reflecting on his own travels in 1940, he praised Mexican racial practices. In Mexico, as in Europe, "one can sleep or eat anywhere, no matter what one's complexion." The absence of institutional racism made US segregation "seem doubly stupid."[7]

By the mid-1930s, when fascism in Europe was on the ascent, African Americans set their sights on Mexico.[8] In particular, Hughes's visits south of the border brought greater attention to the legacies of the colonial caste system. In 1935, he returned to Mexico City for one year to secure his late father's estate. Upon his arrival, the

[4] Julian Lim, *Porous Borders: Multiracial Migrations and the Law in the U.S.–Mexico Borderlands* (Chapel Hill: University of North Carolina Press, 2017), 175–78.

[5] Horne, *Black and Brown*, 21–22 and 28; and Theresa Runstedtler, *Jack Johnson, Rebel Sojourner: Boxing in the Shadow of the Global Color Line* (Berkeley: University of California Press, 2012), 219–30.

[6] Hughes, *The Big Sea*, 39–40. Regarding his interest in indigeneity, see Nicolás Guillén, "Conversación con Langston Hughes," in vol. 1 of *Prosa de prisa, 1929–1972*, comp. Ángel Augier (Havana: Editorial Arte y Literatura, 1975), 17.

[7] Hughes, *The Big Sea*, 53–69, 79, and 301. Richard Wright made a similar statement regarding the segregation he encountered on a train once he crossed the border from Mexico to the United States; see Rowley, *Richard Wright*, 208–9.

[8] Thurman, "How Far from Here to Mexico?," 274.

Mexico City newspaper *El Nacional* published a series of editorials that introduced the esteemed New Negro poet to the Mexican public.[9] As Cuban journalist, diplomat, and Afro-Cubanist patron José Antonio Fernández de Castro expressed,

> Now that L[angston] H[ughes] – an upright man and artist – is in Mexico, I do not doubt that he will devote part of his efforts to knowing how African elements, which have not yet been incorporated into Mexican mestizaje, unfold in this country, which is admirable in so many ways.

Shifting his attention to Hughes, Fernández de Castro contrasted US and Mexican constructions of blackness: "Do not forget, dear Langston, that colonial Mexico divided its black population into no fewer than 18 classes, according to what the experts tell us."[10] These ideas were not lost on Hughes. Reflecting on the biological foundations of black identity from a hemispheric perspective that made the one-drop rule appear constraining, Hughes asked, "What constitutes Negro blood?" He too recognized that the social construction of race in the United States and Latin America created confusion when a person of color traveled internationally.[11]

The relationship between race and law was of paramount importance when Mexican and US citizens crossed the border. In 1932, W. E. B. Du Bois received a letter from the Royal Schools of Mexico wondering whether Mexicans of African descent would encounter discrimination in Texas.[12] The history of race in Mexico had piqued his interest since at least 1924.[13] On November 16, 1926, he wrote a letter to President Plutarco Elías Calles regarding his concern about traveling to Mexico. In legal-cum-racial terms, Du Bois asked, "Is there any reason in law or practice which would hinder an American citizen from visiting Mexico because of his race, color or descent?" Turning to the malleability of racial

[9] Arnold Rampersad, *The Life of Langston Hughes: I, Too, Sing America*, vol. 1, *1902–1941* (Oxford: Oxford University Press, 1986), 302–3.

[10] J. A. Fernández de Castro, "Impresión personal," *El Nacional*, 3 de marzo de 1935, folder A1, box 1, reel 1, NYPL-SCRBC-LM-LHC.

[11] Langston Hughes, "What Constitutes Negro Blood?" and "Negro, Negro Prieto – Black," c1930, folder 12436, YU-BRBML-JWJCYCAL-LHP.

[12] Royal Schools of Mexico to W. E. B. Du Bois, February 9, 1932, UMAL-SCUA-WDP.

[13] Du Bois's knowledge of Mexican history, however, was limited. In 1924, he incorrectly described Simón Bolívar, the liberator of Spanish South America, as the leader of Mexican and Central American independence; see W. E. Burghardt Du Bois, *The Gift of Black Folk: The Negroes in the Making of America* (Boston, MA: Stratford, 1924), 155.

identification, he continued, "If there is discrimination as to color or race, just what is the definition of Negro in Mexican law?"[14]

In 1937, Du Bois again considered travel to Mexico. The nation returned to his diasporic purview as a result of his *Encyclopedia of the Negro*, a project to amass information about African-descended peoples across the world. After the apparent collapse of Western civilization during the First World War, African Americans such as Carter G. Woodson, Joel Augustus Rogers, and Du Bois began to inquire into the historical agency of Africans in the United States and globally. As the members of the first generation of trained African American historians, they redeemed the history of African-descended peoples from the racist civilizational musings that loomed over nineteenth-century historicism.[15] Writing about Mexico, Rodgers went as far as to describe the African-descended independence hero and abolitionist President Vicente Guerrero as "the George Washington and the Lincoln combined of Mexico."[16] Accordingly, Du Bois hoped to include information from "the West Indies, Mexico, South America ... Italy, Spain and Portugal" in the *Encyclopedia*.[17]

This immensely global vision of Afro-diasporic history forced Du Bois, his research assistant the African American historian Rayford W. Logan,

[14] W. E. B. Du Bois to the President of the Republic of Mexico, November 16, 1926, UMAL-SCUA-WDP. These concerns were not confined to Mexico. He sent a nearly identical copy of this letter to the President of Brazil; see W. E. B. Du Bois to the President of the Republic of Brazil, November 16, 1926, UMAL-SCUA-WDP. As Teresa Meade, Gregory Alonso Pirio, and Jeff H. Lesser explain in relation to African American migration to Brazil and, to a lesser extent, Mexico, European imperialism in Africa forced African Americans to look toward Latin America when they attempted, rather unsuccessfully, to create self-sustaining black communities; see Meade and Pirio, "In Search of the Afro-American 'Eldorado': Attempts by North American Blacks to Enter Brazil in the 1920s," *Luso-Brazilian Review* 25, no. 1 (1988): 85–110; and Lesser, "Are African-Americans African or American? Brazilian Immigration Policy in the 1920s," *Review of Latin American Studies* 4, no. 1 (1991): 115–37.

[15] For example, see Carter G. Woodson, *The Negro in Our History*, 7th ed., further revised and enlarged (Washington, DC: Associated Publishers, 1941); and J. A. Rogers, *Sex and Race: A History of White, Negro, and Indian Miscegenation in the Two Americas*, 2 vols. (St. Petersburg, FL: Helga M. Rogers, 1970). On these historical and historiographic contributions, see Earl Lewis, "To Turn as on a Pivot: Writing African Americans into a History of Overlapping Diasporas," *American Historical Review* 100, no. 3 (1995): 765–67; and Robin D. G. Kelley, "'But a Local Phase of a World Problem': Black History's Global Vision, 1883–1950," *Journal of American History* 86, no. 3 (1999): 1047–60.

[16] Rodgers, "The Negro Who Freed Mexico."

[17] W. E. B. Du Bois to Rayford W. Logan, June 26, 1937, UMAL-SCUA-WDP. Also see Anson Phelps Stokes, "Summary of Important Material Prepared for the *Encyclopedia of the Negro*," December 9, 1939, UMAL-SCUA-WDP.

and others to determine which famous Mexicans were of African descent and which aspects of the national narrative were most relevant to their project. José María Morelos, who in the 1930s captivated Marxist historians like Alfonso Teja Zabre (See Chapter 2), caught their attention.[18] Logan was well aware of the debates in Mexico about Morelos's potential African ancestry and the methodological difficulties inherent to the *Encyclopedia*'s project to identify people in Latin America as black. "We realize that in some instances, as in that of Jose Maria Morelos, for example," he wrote to Rafael Heliodoro Valle on January 19, 1937, "it will be difficult to determine the exact racial classification of an individual especially since racial classifications in the United States differ considerably from those in Latin-America."[19]

The Mexico of 1937, however, was not identical to the one that captivated Du Bois eleven years earlier. As early as 1924, there had been attempts within the Ministry of the Interior to limit immigration. This process was generally arbitrary and dependent on the economic status of each individual. In 1930, migration laws tightened to soften the blow of the Great Depression. The state could deny visas to undesirable people, such as prostitutes and cripples. Concerned with the specter of national degeneration, xenophobic officials deemed it necessary to encourage migrants with good morality and beneficial racial stocks.[20] By 1936, race – like sex, age, civil status, and occupation – were explicitly part of the postrevolutionary fashioning of a modern unified national populace.[21] In September 1935, the *Crisis*, the official mouthpiece of the

[18] Du Bois used Alfonso Teja Zabre's 1934 biography *Morelos* as his primary source for this independence-era hero; see W. E. B. Du Bois "*Encyclopedia of the Negro* subject listing, ca. 1936," 71–72, UMAL-SCUA-WDP. Also see W. E. B. Du Bois to Rafael Heliodoro Valle, March 16, 1937, UMAL-SCUA-WDP.

[19] Rayford W. Logan to Rafael Heliodoro Valle, January 19, 1937, UMAL-SCUA-WDP.

[20] Instituto Nacional de Migración, "Ley de Migración de 1926" and "Ley de Migración de 1930," *Compilación histórica de la legislación migratoria en México, 1821–2002*, 3rd ed., corrected and expanded (Mexico City: Secretaría de Gobernación, 2002), 121–45 and 162–63. To contextualize these laws, see Moisés González Navarro, *Los extranjeros en México y los mexicanos en el extranjero, 1821–1970*, vol. 3 (Mexico City: El Colegio de México, 1994), 34; and Pablo Yankelevich, "Explotadores, truhanes, agitadores y negros: Deportaciones y restricciones a estadounidenses en el México revolucionario," *Historia Mexicana* 57, no. 4 (2008): 1186–89.

[21] Instituto Nacional de Migración, "Ley General de Población de 1936," in *Compilación histórica de la legislación migratoria en México*, 184; and Alexandra Minna Stern, "From Mestizophilia to Biotypology: Racialization and Science in Mexico, 1920–1960," in *Race and Nation in Modern Latin America*, ed. Nancy P. Appelbaum, Anne S. Macpherson, and Karin Alejandra Rosemblatt (Chapel Hill: University of North Carolina Press, 2003), 194–95.

NAACP, shed light on the difficulties African Americans encountered when they attempted to obtain tourist visas.[22] The following year, Logan had a tough time acquiring the necessary paperwork to visit Mexico. Writing to the progressive journalist Carleton Beals on June 5, 1937, Du Bois asked whether this problem could be resolved. He strategically rebranded the question of Mexican race relations as an issue of liberalism: "it seems to me an extraordinary bit of tyranny for the liberals of Mexico to refuse me and other American Negroes the right of temporary visit to Mexico and to discriminate purely on racial lines."[23]

Beals was a logical person for Du Bois to contact. Since 1918, he had completed extensive research in Mexico and befriended intellectuals and artists on both sides of the border who supported the 1910 Revolution's populist goals.[24] He had a vested interest in social justice in both countries and was one of the few scholars aware of an African-descended population in Mexico. Beals's ethnographic account of Mexican regional life *Mexican Maze* (1931) includes a chapter on Oaxaca's African-descended community Valerio Trujano. In the 1930s, it was such an unprecedented window into blackness in contemporary Mexico that Fernández de Castro referenced it in his 1935 apostrophe to Hughes.[25] Edited by Du Bois, the *Crisis* also published an excerpt of Beals's research with the following prefatory note:

> Here is a charming discription [*sic*] of a Negro-Mexican village. Most writers and travellers in Central and South America and the West Indies very carefully omit all mention of Negro blood. They seem desperately afraid that the Negroes of all the Americas should become acquainted with each other. But Carleton Beals, one of our best authorities, has no such inhibitions and sends us this most interesting story.[26]

Beals had established personal ties to Mexican elites who Du Bois thought could remedy Logan's problem. In July 1937, Beals responded to Du Bois's inquiry. He had talked with the Consul General of Mexico,

[22] Thurman, "How Far from Here to Mexico?," 267. This critique of the Mexican state's policies toward visas for African Americans was possibly in response to a letter Langston Hughes wrote to the NAACP on May 15, 1935; for part of this letter, see Lim, *Porous Borders*, 158.

[23] W. E. B. Du Bois to Carleton Beals, June 5, 1937, UMAL-SCUA-WDP.

[24] For a discussion of Beals's political interests in Mexico and across Latin America, see John A. Britton, *Carleton Beals: A Radical Journalist in Latin America* (Albuquerque: University of New Mexico Press, 1987).

[25] Carleton Beals, *Mexican Maze* (Philadelphia: J. B. Lippincott, 1931); and Fernández de Castro, "Impresión personal."

[26] Prefatory note, ca. May 1931, UMAL-SCUA-WDP.

Dr. Rafael de la Colina, about Logan's troubles visiting Mexico and had warned the diplomat that any future racial discrimination would result in an article "on the stupidities of the Mexican immigration laws in relation to their claims of being a liberal and progressive government." In November, Beals told Du Bois that he had "been led to understand" that those problematic laws had been changed – and, by May 1939, the NAACP reported that "there exists in Mexico now no distinction or discrimination with regard to Negro Americans visiting Mexico for pleasure purposes."[27]

It is unclear what changed or why. It could have been Beals's threat to dismantle Mexican claims of racial egalitarianism. Du Bois had also contacted Frank Tannenbaum, another progressive with ties to the Mexican state; Tannenbaum took Du Bois's complaint to the Mexican ambassador and to his friend President Lázaro Cárdenas.[28] Incidents about discriminatory visa policies and Du Bois's subsequent exchanges about them point to the allure of Mexican racial paradigms for African Americans, even when they encountered evidence to the contrary.[29] They also illustrate the state's intentions to project its nationalist policies as a foil to the color line found in the United States and therefore to remain a global beacon of racial tolerance. When called racist, the Mexican government did whatever was necessary to alleviate, if not solve, the problem. Even if it was not always true, Mexico's claim to be free of racial discrimination was a lynchpin in postrevolutionary nation building and a key point of reference for African Americans in search of alternatives to Jim Crow segregation.

ORIGINS OF THE INTERNATIONAL INSTITUTE OF AFRO-AMERICAN STUDIES

During the Second World War, the rhetoric of Mexican racial egalitarianism expanded to include a hemispheric orientation that celebrated New World democracy. The absence of widespread racial categories in Mexico became less a critique of US Jim Crow policies, although this invective certainly continued in Mexico and across the hemisphere, and more

[27] Carleton Beals to W. E. B. Du Bois, July 7, 1937, and November 26, 1937, UMAL-SCUA-WDP; and "Mexico Now Open to Colored Tourists," *Crisis*, May 1939, 149.

[28] Frank Tannenbaum to W. E. B. Du Bois, February 16, 1937, UMAL-SCUA-WDP.

[29] David Hellwig makes the same argument regarding African American perceptions of Brazilian racial formations in *African-American Reflections on Brazil's Racial Paradise* (Philadelphia, PA: Temple University Press, 1992).

a rejection of the ethnocentric violence seen in Europe and the Pacific.[30] Latin American racial mixture became an especially exciting alternative to Nazi Germany's veneration of racial purity.[31] With the specter of fascism looming over his racial imagination, African American novelist Richard Wright described Mexican racial formations as a potential solution to the black problem in the United States. While on his honeymoon in Mexico in 1940, he noted that, "people of all races and colors live in harmony and without racial prejudices or theories of racial superiority ... always resisting the attempts of Anglo-Saxon tourists and industrialists to introduce racial hate and discrimination."[32] Others contrasted the Western and Eastern hemispheres, with the Americas sharing a common history of European colonialism and cultural cross-pollination that laid the foundation for the New World's democratic proclivities.[33] For the *Journal of Negro Education* in 1941, Rayford Logan cast racist policies and class exploitation as global hindrances to democratic practices. "Those who envisage a united front of all workers as the essential prerequisite to the establishment of democracy in the Western Hemisphere," he reported, "must realistically analyze the historical causes of racial conflicts." Mexico embodied these egalitarian aspirations, since its government, in giving him a tourist visa, "has removed the humiliating requirements for Negroes who wish to visit the country."[34]

Not surprisingly other African Americans in the United States also saw Mexico as an exemplar of racial inclusion and a foundation for their own political aspirations during the Second World War. Since Satchel Paige first left the Negro Leagues for Mexico in 1938, many African American baseball players crossed the border. They marveled at Mexico's lack of

[30] Regarding the continued comparisons between Latin American and US racial formations, Paulina L. Alberto and Jesse Hoffnung-Garskof believe that anthropologist Arthur Ramos referred to the term "racial democracy" in 1941 for the first time in Brazilian social theory; see "'Racial Democracy' and Racial Inclusion," 277.

[31] Lewis Hanke, "The Incorporation of Indians and Negroes into Latin American Life," *Journal of Negro Education* 10, no. 3 (1941): 504–9.

[32] Richard Wright, "I Bite the Hand That Feeds Me," *Atlantic Monthly*, June 1940, 826. Also see Rowley, *Richard Wright*, esp. 174–78 and 197.

[33] For example, see Arthur P. Whitaker, "Cultural Interchange and the Teaching of History in the United States," in *Inter American Intellectual Exchange* (Institute of Latin American Studies of the University of Texas, 1943), 129–30; and Pan American Institute of Geography and History, Commission on History, *Press Notices: Creation and Program of the Pan American Commission on History* (Mexico City), folder Commission on History Meetings, Creation 1946, box 11, SI-NAA-PAIGH.

[34] Rayford W. Logan, "The Crisis of Democracy in the Western Hemisphere," *Journal of Negro Education* 10, no. 3 (1941): 340 and 348.

racial segregation and their comparatively good treatment, even if Mexicans who had never seen an African-descended person in the flesh followed them around town observing everything they did. In the language of the wartime era, Willie Wells commented to the prominent African American newspaper the *Pittsburgh Courier* in 1944, "I've found freedom and democracy here, something I never found in the United States."[35] Directly linking this rhetoric to Mexican policy in 1942, Esther Cooper of the Communist-affiliated Fifth All-Southern Negro Youth Conference asked President Manuel Ávila Camacho for support. She hoped his words would "give concrete evidence of unity of the democratic loving peoples of the world and particularly of the Americas."[36]

These ideas were not confined to African Americans. In October 1940, the progressive Council for Pan American Democracy compiled a pamphlet about "Negro immigration to Mexico." The pioneering scholar of African and African American anthropology Melville J. Herskovits contributed a brief note that placed Mexican racial formations at the vanguard of racially equality across the world. "It is good to learn," he penned, "that the Government of Mexico has reaffirmed its historic policy of refusing to discriminate against racial groups by insisting that its Consuls in the United States disregard the race of applicants in issuing tourist visas." These policies contrasted with those in the United States, where segregation continued to rear its ugly head. But, in the context of the Second World War, they signified even more: the possibility of democracy thriving across racial boundaries.[37]

Scholars from around the Americas – including Du Bois and Logan from the United States and Fernando Ortiz from Cuba – flocked to Mexico to found an institute devoted to the study of African-descended peoples and cultures in the Americas. Mexico City had a proud history of hosting international institutions, such as the International School of American Archeology and Ethnology that was founded in 1911, the Pan American Institute for Geography and History in 1928, the III in 1940, and the Smithsonian's Institute for Social Anthropology in 1943. It was

[35] Willie Wells qtd. in John Virtue, *South of the Color Barrier: How Jorge Pasquel and the Mexican League Pushed Baseball toward Racial Integration* (Jefferson, NC: McFarland, 1996), 90.

[36] Esther V. Cooper to Manuel Ávila Camacho, March 25, 1942, 161.1/58, AGN-FMAC.

[37] Melville J. Herskovits, "Statement," October 9, 1940; and David Efron to Dr. Herskovits, October 19, 1940, folder 14 (Council for Pan American Democracy, 1940–1941), box 6, NULA-MJHP.

not a coincidence that so many hemispheric institutions were located in the nation's capital. Most intellectuals in the United States and Latin America feared that such organizations would become, or at least be perceived to be, instruments of US imperialism and propaganda if they found a home in New York City, Washington, DC, or any other US city.[38] Because of Mexico's geographic centrality, its relative political stability, and its well-established academic institutions, Mexico City became a popular site for inter-American headquarters.[39]

The institutional groundwork for the International Institute of Afro-American Studies had its origins in intellectual networks devoted to the study of indigenous and African-descended populations. Within indigenist circles, the path commenced in 1938, when the Eighth Pan American Conference in Lima, Peru, established the methodological and ideological parameters for indigenous integration on a hemispheric scale, a project that would coalesce around the III in the 1940s.[40] In 1943, prominent intellectuals and statesmen traveled to Mexico City for the First Inter-American Demographic Congress. Participants recognized the urgent need to study all the peoples of the Americas to prevent their destruction in a manner akin to the Holocaust or Japanese annihilation campaigns. Questions about post-war migration and the future of democracy in the Americas framed the Congress. Mexico's Secretary of the Interior, Miguel Alemán set the tone in his opening speech. The meeting intended to establish an "international co-fraternity" among American nations. The attendees, he cautioned in quintessentially Mexican terms, needed to be careful when they studied demographics, since such statistics could foster racial hatred and hinder democratic inclusion.[41] From October 12 to 21, they discussed ethnography, eugenics, and demographic policies. The Congress emphasized the need to understand the racial and ethnic

[38] Ralph Beals to Dr. Steward, May 25, 1945, folder *Acta Americana*, 1944–1949, box 14, SI-NAA-ISA.

[39] For example, see Ralph Beals to Daniel Cosío Villegas, October 22, 1942, folder *Acta Americana*, Fondo de Cultura Económica, box 7, SI-NAA-RLBP; and W. E. B. Du Bois and Guy B. Johnson, *Encyclopedia of the Negro: Preparatory Volume with Reference Lists and Reports* (New York: The Phelps-Stokes Fund, 1945), 171.

[40] Regarding the early indigenist ideas that would become the III, see *Reunión/Conferencia Congreso Indigenista Interamericano*, vol. 1 (Pátzcuaro, Michoacán: Primer Congreso Indigenista Interamericano, 14–25 de abril de 1940), FD AI/0001, CDI-CDJR.

[41] Miguel Alemán, "Discurso del licenciado Miguel Alemán, Secretario de Gobernación, al inaugurarse el Congreso," in *Corresponde a las Américas: La forjación del mundo que ya llega* (Mexico City: Secretaría de Gobernación, 1943), 7–11.

foundations of the hemisphere's nations.[42] Following the lead of the III, the Congress wanted to "facilitate the incorporation of the indigenous population into the active life of the Nation." It even tasked the III with publishing an "Encyclopedia of the American Indian."[43]

Mexicans and Mexican nationalism, particularly the nation's cultural construction of race, figured prominently, setting the stage for the postwar rejection of biological race in censuses across Latin America.[44] Alemán presided over the Congress. Anthropologist Manuel Gamio attended simultaneously as Director of the Mexico's Demographic Department and the III. Marxist historian Luis Chávez Orozco participated in discussions about the assimilation of foreigners into American nations. Archeologist Alfonso Caso and doctor-turned-anthropologist Gonzalo Aguirre Beltrán participated in the Ortiz-led section "Ethnic composition of the American communities" that discussed indigeneity, blackness, and mestizaje.[45] The Congress encouraged all of the nations of the Western Hemisphere to follow Mexico's antiracist democratic example. Rather than biological classifications, cultural traits – like the linguistic and ethnographic ones employed in Mexican censuses – needed to be deployed to classify national populations. For example, Mexico's 1940 census defined indigeneity, mestizaje, and whiteness in relation to cultural behaviors, such as whether an individual ate wheat bread or not; wore shoes or sandals; and slept on beds, hammocks, or the floor.[46]

The successful indigenist meeting at Pátzcuaro and the founding of the III pointed to a lacuna in inter-American circles: the absence of any

[42] "Comisiones de estudio," ScGb430913c-1 and ScGb430913c-2, expediente Secretaría de Gobernación, III-AH-MAH.

[43] Primer Congreso Demográfico Interamericano, *Acta final del Primer Congreso Demográfico Interamericano: Celebrado en México, D.F. del 12 al 21 de octubre de 1943* (Mexico City: 1943), 14 and 34.

[44] For a discussion of the postwar shift from biological to cultural race in Latin American censuses, see Loveman, *National Colors*, 207–49.

[45] "Comisiones de estudio," ScGb430913c-2, expediente Secretaría de Gobernación, III-AH-MAH; and "Congreso Demográfico Interamericano (1943)," *Boletín Bibliográfico de Antropología Americana* 7, no. 1/3 (Enero 1943–Diciembre 1944): 54.

[46] See various documents about the Mexican census from 1941 and 1942 in expediente Censos, III-AH-MAH. Regarding the broader response to these policies in Mexico and at the Congress, see "Congreso Demográfico Interamericano (1943)," 53–55; and "First Inter-American Demographic Congress," *Population Index* 10, no. 1 (January 1944): 13–14. For an example of the Mexican census in 1940, see Dirección General de Estadística, "6° Censo general de población, 6 de marzo de 1940," www.beta.inegi.org.mx/programas/ccpv/1940/default.html.

institution dedicated to the study of African-descended peoples and cultures. The attendees of the First Inter-American Demographic Congress accordingly aspired "to stimulate the scientific study of black populations, their conditions, potentialities, cultures in general, and their contributions to the national and continental heritage."[47] Since the mid-1930s, there had been a concerted, albeit unsuccessful, effort to convene such a meeting. Du Bois led the charge. To amass a network of scholars for his *Encyclopedia of the Negro*, he attempted to organize a Conference on Negro Studies. Du Bois, Logan, and a somewhat begrudging Herskovits tried to hold the conference in Havana, Cuba, in 1941 or 1942 and then in Port-au-Prince, Haiti, in April 1942.[48] It was supposed to be a truly hemispheric gathering. However, many participants, including several from the United States had trouble finding flights to Port-au-Prince. The delegates from Puerto Rico, Mexico, and Venezuela had to cancel, as did sociologist Gilberto Freyre and anthropologist Arthur Ramos, two of the leading figures in the study of Afro-Brazilian history and culture.[49]

After the Conference on Negro Studies failed to meet, Herskovits turned to Ortiz to create a new organization. It would help him chart the relative survival of Africanisms in different New World locales, a project that had guided his research agenda since his first trip to Suriname in 1928.[50] In 1943, they outlined a grandiose project to study the African-descended populations of the Americas and publish a scholarly journal modeled after Ortiz's periodical *Estudios afrocubanos*. This new association would also contribute to the "furthering of Inter-American relations."[51] However, their collaboration fell apart during the First Inter-American Demographic Congress. Without consulting Herskovits, Ortiz founded and made himself Director of the International Institute of Afro-American Studies. According

[47] "Congreso Demográfico Interamericano (1943)," 54.

[48] Kenneth Robert Janken, *Rayford W. Logan and the Dilemma of the African-American Intellectual* (Amherst: University of Massachusetts Press, 1993), 137–43.

[49] D. H. Daugherty to W. E. B. Du Bois, March 12 and 25, 1942, UMAL-SCUA-WDP.

[50] Melville J. Herskovits to Ralph Linton, October 1, 1928, folder 31 (Linton, Ralph, 1928–1940), box 12, NULA-MJHP; and Melville J. Herskovits, "The Negro in the New World: The Statement of a Problem," *American Anthropologist* 32, no. 1 (January 1930): 145–55. Richard and Sally Price provide the historical context for Melville and Frances Herskovits's work in Suriname in *The Roots of Roots; or, How Afro-American Anthropology Got Its Start* (Chicago: Prickly Paradigm Press, 2003).

[51] Draft of letter to Dr. Joseph Willite, Rockefeller Foundation, November 27, 1943, folder 24 (International Institute of Afro-American Studies, 1943–1944), box 28, NULA-MJHP.

to Herskovits and his friend, the historian and State Department official Richard Pattee, Ortiz hijacked this initiative.[52]

Tensions between Ortiz and Herskovits intensified. On December 7, 1943, a slightly bewildered and clearly irritated Herskovits wrote to Ortiz:

> In this week's issue of the Pittsburgh Courier, one of our Negro newspapers, I ran across a story signed by Irene Diggs, telling of the formation in Mexico City of an International Institute of Afro-American Studies.
>
> As I have heard nothing of this development, I would appreciate learning something about it, particularly since, according to this story, I am a member of the Executive Committee.[53]

As Herskovits's eyes and ears in Mexico City, Pattee did not ameliorate the situation. In describing Ortiz's role in the International Institute, he wrote to Herskovits that Ortiz "has gone off the deep end."[54]

Despite this brewing personal conflict, the International Institute of Afro-American Studies was a product of a fetishized desire to study the demographics of all American nations and the zealous impulse to craft more inclusive national institutions. Although these conversations were grounded in the histories and cultures of indigenous, African-descended, and mixed-race peoples, they contributed to more ambitious intellectual projects to deconstruct the race-blind assumptions of liberal democracy across the Americas. Writing in 1943 for the III, Luis Chávez Orozco detailed Mexico's history of pre-Columbian democracy and the failings of the postindependence liberal state to protect the rights of indigenous peoples.[55] The next year, Swedish economist Gunnar Myrdal explained that the United States faced a moral crisis, what he called "the American dilemma," caused by the contradictions between the "Negro problem," as he described it, and the nation's founding principles.[56] For Chávez Orozco and Myrdal, these sociological conundrums could not be resolved in

[52] Melville J. Herskovits to Fernando Ortiz, December 7, 1943, and Richard Pattee to Melville J. Herskovits, March 2, 1944, folder 24 (International Institute of Afro-American Studies, 1943–1944), box 28, NULA-MJHP. Regarding the growing tension with Ortiz, see Richard Pattee to Melville J. Herskovits, December 29, 1944, folder 14 (Pattee, Richard, 1944–1946), box 35, NULA-MJHP.

[53] Melville J. Herskovits to Fernando Ortiz, December 7, 1943, folder 24 (International Institute of Afro-American Studies, 1943–1944), box 28, NULA-MJHP.

[54] Richard Pattee to Melville J. Herskovits, March 2, 1944, folder 24 (International Institute of Afro-American Studies, 1943–1944), box 28, NULA-MJHP.

[55] Luis Chávez Orozco, *Las instituciones democráticas de los indígenas mexicanos en la época colonial* (Mexico City: Ediciones del III, 1943).

[56] Gunnar Myrdal, *An American Dilemma: The Negro Problem and Modern Democracy* (New York: Harper, 1944).

isolation, as mere indigenous or black issues. They had to be part of a broader revision of the relationships among race, democracy, and society at large.

At the First Inter-American Demographic Congress, the delegates unanimously voted to establish the International Institute under Ortiz's watchful eye.[57] Not coincidentally, Ortiz selected Mexico City as its institutional hub, because Mexico lacked "prejudice to the degree of other nations." The capital city, he contended, was an ideal place to discuss "all these racial problems."[58] According to the *Baltimore Afro-American*, Mexico sat in contrast to the United States, where segregation would have cast a shadow over the proceedings.[59] Irene Diggs extended these compliments. Mexico was "the cradle for Afro-American studies not only in America, nor on a scale inter-American, but in the world."[60] An NAACP report coordinated by Diggs and Du Bois argued that the research made possible by organizations like the International Institute could resolve the enduring political and social tensions between liberal thought and racial inequality.[61] Having failed at establishing the Conference on Negro Studies, Du Bois praised Ortiz for successfully establishing the International Institute.[62] Aware of his global stature, the Institute's Executive Committee asked him to be a founding member and a contributor to its journal *Afroamérica*, a request that he accepted but never fulfilled.[63]

Following the agendas articulated at the First Inter-American Demographic Congress, the International Institute sought to enlighten

[57] "Instituto Internacional de Estudios Afroamericanos," *Boletín Bibliográfico de Antropología Americana* 7, no. 1/3 (Enero 1943–Diciembre 1944): 13.

[58] Fernando Ortiz to Melville J. Herskovits, 26 de enero de 1944, folder 24 (International Institute of Afro-American Studies, 1943–1944), box 28, NULA-MJHP. Questions about racial inequality emerged again in Mexico City the following year at the Inter-American Conference on Problems of War and Peace. As Paul Ortiz explains, Haiti and Mexico advocated for racial and gender equality, much to the delight of the African American press and to the chagrin of the US officials in attendance; see *An African American and Latinx History of the United States*, 143–47.

[59] "Cuban Heads New Racial Study Body," *Baltimore Afro-American*, December 4, 1943.

[60] Diggs, "Cuban Leader Helped to Found Negro Study Center."

[61] NAACP, "A Report on the Department of Special Research," October 4, 1944, UMAL-SCUA-WDP.

[62] W. E. B. Du Bois, "A Chronicle of Race Relations," *Phylon* 5, no. 1 (1944): 89.

[63] Regarding Du Bois's membership, see Comité ejecutivo, Instituto Internacional de Estudios Afroamericanos to W. E. B. Du Bois, 15 de febrero de 1944, UMAL-SCUA-WDP. On contributing to *Afroamérica*, see Instituto Internacional de Estudios Afroamericanos to W. E. B. Du Bois, 27 de octubre de 1944, and 15 de diciembre de 1944, UMAL-SCUA-WDP.

governments, private institutions, and individuals about the cultural and historical plight of African-descended peoples. It proposed "the study of the black populations of America, in their biological and cultural aspects, and of their influences in American communities."[64] Published in Mexico, *Afroamérica* transcended the linguistic boundaries of the Americas as it briefly placed English-, French-, Spanish-, and Portuguese-speaking intellectuals in conversation with each other. The impressive array of participating academics and artists included: Jean Price-Mars of Haiti; Gilberto Freyre and Arthur Ramos from Brazil; Cuba's Alejo Carpentier, Nicolás Guillén, and Fernando Ortiz; W. E. B. Du Bois, Melville and Frances Herskovits, Alain Locke, and Frank Tannenbaum of the United States; and Mexico's Gonzalo Aguirre Beltrán, Carlos Basauri, Luis Chávez Orozco, and Miguel Covarrubias.[65] Doomed by a lack of funding *Afroamérica* only published three issues in 1945 and 1946. The International Institute was defunct by 1948.[66]

MIGUEL COVARRUBIAS AND MEXICAN BLACKNESS

The International Institute of Afro-American Studies brought Mexico into Afro-diasporic dialogues just as it introduced ethnographic conversations about African cultural retentions to postrevolutionary nationalism. When the International Institute was founded in 1943, Mexico was the most politically significant Latin American nation without an established historiography and ethnographic tradition detailing its African-descended peoples and cultures.[67] Mexican scholars were beginning to ask whether the nation had an African heritage, even while some doubted the legitimacy of the field of study. In the spring of 1945, Rémy Bastien, a Haitian anthropology student in Mexico and later a contributor to *Afroamérica*,

[64] Fernando Ortiz to Alfonso Caso, 15 de febrero de 1944, folder 9: (Correspondencia de Caso con el Instituto Internacional de Estudios Afroamericanos), box 45, UNAM-IIA-FAC.

[65] "Resolución del Primer Congreso Demográfico Interamericano sobre la población negra," *Afroamérica* 1, no. 1–2 (1945): 147–66; and "Colaboradores," folder 29 (International Institute of Afro-American Studies, 1944–), box 33, NULA-MJHP.

[66] Regarding *Afroamérica*'s funding, see various letters in folder 17 (Beltrán, Gonzalo Aguirre, 1946–1948), box 37, NULA-MJHP. The November 1, 1947, to October 31, 1948, budget of the American Anthropological Association included an unused allocation of three dollars for a membership to the International Institute of Afro-American Studies; this implies that the Institute was no longer in operation; see "Report," *American Anthropologist* 51, no. 2 (1949): 354.

[67] For example, see Melville J. Herskovits, "Problem, Method and Theory in Afroamerican Studies," *Afroamérica* 1, no. 1–2 (1945): 14.

complained to Melville Herskovits that Mexican ethnography "is paralyzed by its total ignorance of Africology."[68] It was hard for Mexican social science to break out of the racially charged myths that relegated African-descended peoples to the past and that left ethnographic research relevant only for countries, like the United States, Brazil, and Cuba, where African-descended peoples were socially and demographically visible.[69]

By 1946, Gonzalo Aguirre Beltrán and Miguel Covarrubias began to fill this lacuna. In cultural and ethnographic circles, Covarrubias ushered in this new perspective. Although he was not a major figure in the International Institute, Covarrubias brought an awareness of African cultural retentions back to Mexico, a sensibility he refined drawing the New Negro Movement in the 1920s and 1930s. Already familiar with the relationship between African cultures and African-descended cultural productions in the United States and Cuba, he expanded his diasporic purview during the Second World War when he located the coastal state of Veracruz within Afro-Caribbean cultural exchanges. Echoing the language of wartime inter-Americanism, he used the study of racial formations as way to contrast cultural pluralism and ethnocentrism as well as democracy and fascism. Racial antagonism sat in contrast to his ideological crusade to study and depict the myriad cultures of humanity, from the music of black Harlemites and their white patrons to Balinese and Mexican dances, from Amerindian and African plastic arts to the cultural propaganda of political leaders, both good and evil. By the 1940s, he was concerned more with the imperialist ventures that exploited, discredited, and destroyed cultures not considered to be modern than with the juxtaposition of US and Mexican racial formations that historically preoccupied Latin American artists and intellectuals.

[68] Rémy Bastien to Melville J. Herskovits, 29 mars 1945, folder 11 (Bastien, Rémy, 1945–1946), box 32, NULA-MJHP; and Auguste Rémy Bastien, "Las características del negro americano," *Afroamérica* 2, no. 3 (1946): 38–41. Also see Joaquín Roncal, "The Negro Race in Mexico," *Hispanic American Historical Review* 24, no. 3 (1944): 530. Rafael Heliodoro Valle implied that there had been a little bit of research on blackness in Mexico by 1937, but he acknowledged that there was not yet a book on the subject; see his letter to Dr. Rayford W. Logan, January 27, 1937, UMAL-SCUA-WDP.

[69] For example, see Gertrude Duby's *¿Hay Razas Inferiores?*, which condemns all aspects of racial hierarchy, including the belief that Africans are the least evolved racial group. For proof, she referenced the research of prominent African-descended individuals from the United States, Cuba, and Haiti; she failed to reference Mexico. In 1945, W. E. B. Du Bois and Guy B. Johnson similarly ignored Mexico when they listed countries with research underway into their black populations; see *Encyclopedia of the Negro: Preparatory Volume with Reference Lists and Reports*, 169.

During the Second World War, Covarrubias gained an international acclaim that provided him with new venues to articulate his artistic point of view. Famed Soviet film director Sergei Eisenstein used caricatures from Covarrubias's *Negro Drawings* (1927) to understand the totemic worldview of non-Western peoples. In addition to reproducing several images, he provided the caption: "The drawings of Covarrubias (*Negro Drawings*). Remarkable!"[70] In 1938, Covarrubias's artistry caught the attention of Philip N. Youtz, the Consultant and Director of the 1939 Pacific Area of the Golden Gate International Exposition.[71] Because of the growing dangers of Japanese imperialism, Youtz hoped Covarrubias would paint a series of six murals to depict the diversity and interconnectedness of the Pacific world. Two thirteen-by-nine foot maps titled "Native Means of Transportation" and "Native Types of Dwellings" would introduce visitors to Covarrubias's style and acquaint them with the region's diverse cultural areas. Larger fifteen-by-twenty-four foot maps would depict the flora and fauna, people, economies, and cultural expressions found in the Pacific.

For these murals, Covarrubias read world histories in addition to historical and contemporary accounts of Asia, Oceania, and the Americas. Viewing humanity through a diffusionist lens, he emphasized cultural areas but rejected evolutionary concepts of race that classified human civilizations according to skin color. He described African cultural survivals in the Western Hemisphere through the exceptionalist rhetoric of inter-American inclusion. The descendants of African slaves were "thriving" in their current situation, having "developed into definite ethnic groups" that included African Americans, the African-descended peoples of the Caribbean, and Afro-Brazilians. In general, "they have more or less become assimilated to the local cultural life and often are good citizens, hard-working farmers, industrial workers and career men." The exception was the "the conservative Djukas, African Negroes who live today in the interior of Dutch Guiana since they mutinied and escaped to live a free jungle life, retaining the dress, habits and art of their West African ancestors."[72]

[70] Sergei Eisenstein, *Eisenstein on Disney*, ed. Jay Leyda, trans. Alan Upchurch (Calcutta: Seagull Books, 1986), 82–83.

[71] Philip N. Youtz to Alfred A. Knopf Publishers, June 23, 1938, 2/25147, expediente 475, UDLAP-SACE-AMC. For more information about Youtz, see *Time*, March 6, 1939, 4/25207, expediente 476, UDLAP-SACE-AMC.

[72] Miguel Covarrubias, "Pageant of the Pacific," 5/21358, expediente 429, UDLAP-SACE-AMC. Regarding slavery's role in destroying African cultures, see "On Herskovits," 5/2821, expediente 56, UDLAP-SACE-AMC.

The assumption that that the most visible African cultural retentions were found among the most rebellious slave communities was common within African American anthropology. This postulate also dovetailed nicely with the postrevolutionary materialist teleology that had taken hold of Mexican historiography in the 1930s. Covarrubias's continuum of New World Africanisms mirrored the work of Melville Herskovits, whose 1938 ethnography *Dahomey: An Ancient West African Kingdom* he considered a seminal study for all research on African and African-descended artistic production.[73] Following Herskovits's comparative work on New World Africanisms, he noted that the descendants of maroon communities in Suriname represent the purest survival of African behaviors in the Western Hemisphere. From this privileged ethnographic space, they were the only African-descended community in the Americas included on his maps of the Pacific.

As Covarrubias transitioned from being an artist to an ethnographer, he expanded his knowledge of African communities and their presence in the Americas. Mapping African cultural areas became a pillar of what he called his "hobby of anthropology – primitive peoples."[74] Nineteenth-century conventions that Africans, incapable of controlling their own destiny, lacked civilization disgusted him. Deficient in ethnographic rigor, these imperialist musings homogenized Africa's diverse peoples and cultures.[75] An accurate view of the continent's cultural behaviors was therefore vital to comprehend their vitality in the New World and to combat racism, fascism, and imperialism worldwide. He drew multiple maps of African societies that used regional customs and histories to counteract cartographic practices that divided the landmass according to European imperial possessions. His most sophisticated map divided Africa into nine regions according to "the hypothetical cultural areas by Herskovits": (1) the Hottentots, who he called "the most primitive of Africa"; (2) Bushmen; (3) eastern herders, with a western subarea (3a); (4) Congo and (4a) the subarea along the Gulf of Guinea; (5) eastern horn; (6) eastern Sudan; (7) western Sudan; (8) desert; and (9) Egypt.[76] (See Map 4.1.)

[73] Miguel Covarrubias, "Bibliografía: Arte negro africano," 7/32085, expediente 7, UDLAP-SACE-AMC.

[74] Alexander Fried, "Famous by Accident: Fair Will Add to Artist's Destiny," *San Francisco Examiner*, October 5, 1938, 4/25229, expediente 477, UDLAP-SACE-AMC.

[75] "TONYBEE, Arnold J." 5/2828, expediente 56; and "Africa" 14/32251, expediente 11, UDLAP-SACE-AMC.

[76] Untitled Map of African Cultural Areas, 14/32254, expediente 11, UDLAP-SACE-AMC. For other examples, see expedientes 1 and 7, UDLAP-SACE-AMC; and Alicia Inez Guzmán, "Miguel Covarrubias's World: Remaking Global Space at the 1939 Golden Gate International Exposition," in *Miguel Covarrubias: Drawing a Cosmopolitan Line*, ed. Carolyn Kastner (Austin: University of Texas Press, 2014), 24. Melville Herskovits

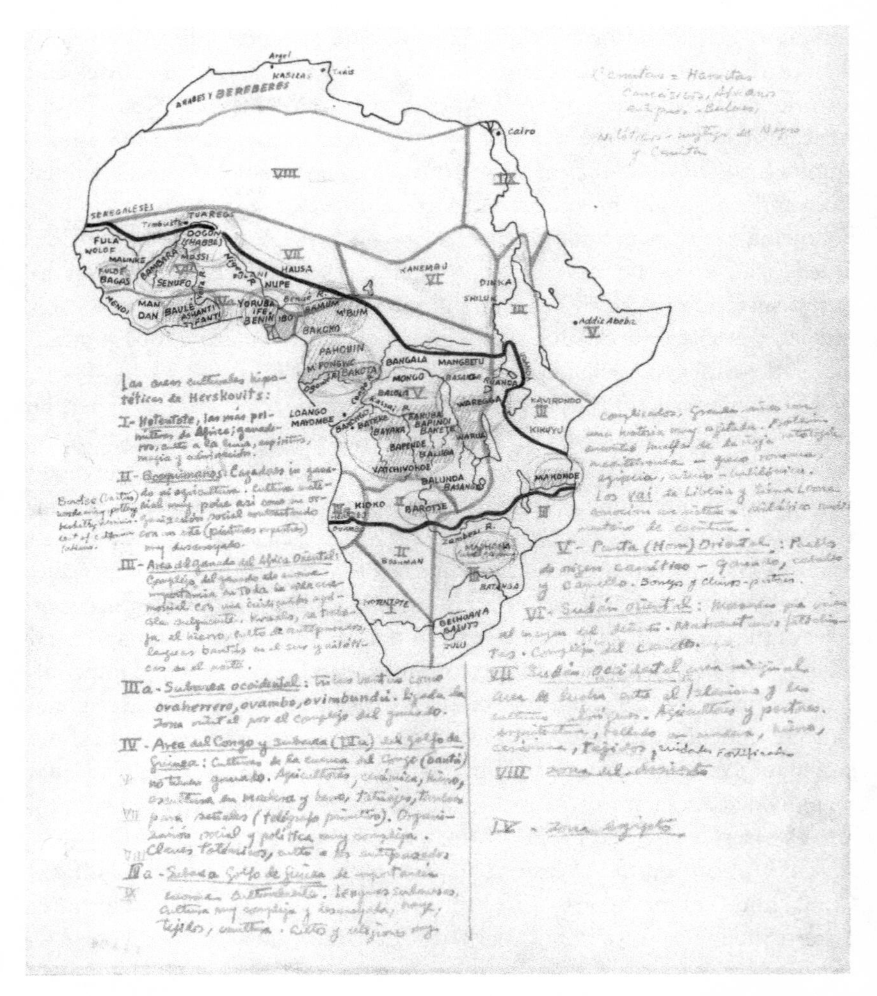

MAP 4.1 Miguel Covarrubias, map of African culture areas. María Elena Covarrubias/Archivo Miguel Covarrubias. Sala de Archivo y Colecciones Especiales. Dirección de Bibliotecas, Universidad de las Américas Puebla.

Lessening ethnic conflict and fostering cultural understanding were at the center of modern ethnographic sensibilities. This pluralist spirit placed Covarrubias in conversation with the International Institute of Afro-American Studies. He joined the International Institute and published an article about the Saramaka peoples of Suriname in *Afroamérica*. Like his mapping of African regions, he based his analysis on several ethnographies written by Melville Herskovits, his wife Frances, and their Brazilian colleague Arthur Ramos. In the essay, Covarrubias discussed the West African and Bantu origins of religion and art in Suriname.[77] Accordingly, the article points to his immersion in the hemisphere's ethnographic conversations about African-descended peoples and cultures by the end of the Second World War.

Covarrubias's recognition of African cultural survivals continued in his 1946 ethnography *Mexico South: The Isthmus of Tehuantepec*, his first book about Mexico. He researched and wrote it after returning to Mexico from the United States in 1937. Not surprisingly, it was a critique of undemocratic policies that destroyed vernacular cultures and forced nonwhite people into a state of servitude. Bernard Smith, his editor at Alfred A. Knopf, wondered about the relevance of these antifascist remarks in a tome about the peoples and cultures of southern Mexico. For Covarrubias, however, the relativist methods that undergirded true ethnographic research were inherently pluralist and therefore relevant to contemporary politics.[78] "Modern anthropology," he penned a few years after the Second World War, "was one of the principle levers used to demolish fascism" and, with it, the absurdities of racism, the ranking of human civilizations, and the romantic flourishes justifying imperialism in Africa, Asia, the Americas, and the Pacific.[79] Read from this perspective, *Mexico South* sits at the confluence of Mexican indigenism, global antifascism, and the Afro-Atlantic networks that, until the Second World War, had defined Covarrubias's career.

Resembling a modernist travelogue to pre-Columbian indigenous archeological sites, *Mexico South* commences in the port of Veracruz, the main

published several articles delimiting African cultural areas. His fascination with the topic began with his doctoral dissertation, which was published in four sections as "The Cattle Complex in East Africa," *American Anthropologist* 28, no. 1–4 (1926).

[77] Miguel Covarrubias, "Los djukas: 'Bush Negroes' de la Guayana Holandesa," *Afroamérica* 2, no. 3 (1946): 121–22.

[78] Miguel Covarrubias, *Mexico South: The Isthmus of Tehuantepec* (New York: Alfred A. Knopf, 1946), 406–8; and Bernard Smith to Miguel Covarrubias, September 20, 1945, 9379, expediente 169, UDLAP-SACE-AMC.

[79] "La antropología en la vida moderna," 5/2844–2845 and 2848, expediente 56, UDLAP-SACE-AMC.

point of entry for African slaves in the colonial period. There, Covarrubias noted the city's African-descended cultures. This cultural geography tied the inclusive spirit of New World democracy to postrevolutionary nation-state formation and the broader Black Atlantic. Focusing on music, he explained, "The *danzón*, the regional dance of Vera Cruz, is nationalized rather than native, for it came from Africa by way of Cuba, but it has acquired a strong local flavor – intense, self-confident, and full of erotic grandeur – that is wholly characteristic." And, the huapango, another popular musical genre, "is a direct descendant of the old Andalusian music transplanted to the jungle by its half-Indian, half-Negro interpreters."[80]

The visible black body was only a small part of this ethnographic vignette, for Covarrubias privileged African ancestry, which could be historically and ethnographically verified, more than contemporary demographics. The coastal peoples who enjoy danzón and improvise lyrics to the huapango "are a type in themselves, mostly a mixture of Spanish, Indian, and Negro bloods." At the end of *Mexico South*, he included a series of photographs of local plants, architecture, customs, and people; one photo was of "a handsome boy of Indian and Negro parentage." He did not deny the existence of African-descended Mexicans and made sure to note in his personal archive when others, like nineteenth-century cartographer Antonio García Cubas, acknowledged their presence. He also clipped photographs of African-descended Mexicans from newspapers to use as inspiration for future caricatures and ethnographies.[81]

Langston Hughes translated the Spanish musical verses that Covarrubias included into English.[82] The choice to use Hughes, a dear friend and New Negro collaborator, points to the transnational cultural networks that informed Covarrubias's construction of African-descended cultural expressions. The common history of enslavement and the shared African-descended cultural sensibilities Covarrubias saw in the United States, Cuba, and now Mexico justified his use of a New Negro intellectual as an interlocutor between Veracruz and the Black Atlantic. More importantly, the assertion that danzón had ties to Africa via Cuba singlehandedly brought

[80] Covarrubias, *Mexico South*, 6 and 18.
[81] Ibid., 11 and photo 69 after p. 408. For these references to black bodies and demographics in Covarrubias's personal papers, see "Tipo negroide de costa chica," 5/10678, expediente 210; and 8/14871, expediente 300, UDLAP-SACE-AMC.
[82] Langston Hughes to Miguel Covarrubias, undated, 10/9646–9650, expediente 179, UDLAP-SACE-AMC.

African cultural retentions into Covarrubias's vision of Mexican regionalism. Not only had African cultures survived the Middle Passage and processes of cultural transformation in Cuba – certain expressions withstood a second migration from Cuba to Mexico.[83]

Reviewers generally raved about *Mexico South*. Unlike Covarrubias's art in the 1920s, with its ambiguous ties to postrevolutionary nation-state formation, *Mexico South* aligned with the cultural and ethnographic initiatives unleashed after 1910. Founder of Catholic University of America's Institute for Ibero-American Studies James A. Magner trepidatiously observed that "Covarrubias generally bears the torch for the Mexican Revolutionary school of thought: anti-Spanish, contemptful and resentful of Catholicism, strongly anti-Diaz, and at least passively Marxian in sociological views and principles."[84] Anthropologist Ralph Beals praised Covarrubias for his innate ability to capture the essence of a person or a community. Focusing on indigeneity, not blackness, he incorrectly thought *Mexico South* failed to break new ground.[85] In contrast, Hubert Herring of the *New York Herald Tribune* stands out for noting that the region's inhabitants, with their indigenous and African ancestries, "turn a gay face toward the Atlantic."[86] After Covarrubias's sudden death in 1957, *México en la Cultura* noted the importance of the danzón in *Mexico South* but, dulling Veracruz's ties to the Atlantic world, failed to reference the genre's African heritage.[87] No one noted Langston Hughes's role as translator. As such, everyone placed *Mexico South* squarely within the intellectual confines of Mexican nation-state formation and outside the global dimensions of the Afro-diasporic politics in the postwar era.[88]

[83] Historian Ira Berlin calls these migratory patterns among African-descended peoples in the Americas "a second 'Middle Passage'"; see *The Making of African America: The Four Great Migrations* (New York: Viking, 2010), 31.

[84] James A. Magner, review of *Mexico South: The Isthmus of Tehuantepec* by Miguel Covarrubias, *The Americas* 3, no. 4 (1947): 561.

[85] Ralph L. Beals, review of *Mexico South: The Isthmus of Tehuantepec* by Miguel Covarrubias, *Pacific Historical Review* 16, no. 1 (1947): 84.

[86] Hubert Herring, "An Overflowing Book of Sheer Delight: Artist, Writer, Self-Made Scholar, Lover of His Land, Covarrubias Crowds Riches Here," *New York Herald Tribune*, November 3, 1946, 6664, expediente 128, UDLAP-SACE-AMC.

[87] *México en la Cultura*, 23 de abril de 1957, 5/2111, expediente 425, UDLAP-SACE-AMC.

[88] For an overview of postwar Afro-diasporic cultural politics, see Brent Hayes Edwards, "The Uses of *Diaspora*," *Social Text* 19, no. 1 (2001): 45–73.

GONZALO AGUIRRE BELTRÁN AND AFRO-MEXICAN STUDIES

After 1945, almost all discussions of Mexico's African heritage revolved around Gonzalo Aguirre Beltrán, not Covarrubias. The latter's stature in inter-American circles had already been established, but his cultural interests in the 1940s were moving toward indigeneity, which the reviewers of *Mexico South* noticed. Conversely, Aguirre Beltrán was an up-and-coming ethnographer who, as a result of his celebrity at the First Inter-American Demographic Congress, took charge of the underdeveloped field of Afro-Mexican studies. His position as Vice-Director of Ortiz's International Institute brought him into Herskovits's purview. Before the First Inter-American Demographic Congress, Herskovits did not know anything about Aguirre Beltrán, and it appears Aguirre Beltrán was unaware of Herskovits.

Born on January 20, 1908, Aguirre Beltrán came of age in a liberal family in Tlacotalpan, Veracruz, a small community about sixty miles southeast of the city of Veracruz. After earning a medical degree at the National Autonomous University of Mexico in 1931, he spent the early to mid-1930s working as a municipal doctor. Motivated by the radical reforms of the Cárdenas presidency, he studied the history of Huatusco, Veracruz, to advocate for land reform between 1938 and 1941.[89] Local histories, he contended, were essential to fulfilling the Mexican Revolution's goals. Because of this research, he published his first foray into ethnographic analysis *El señorío de Cuauhtochco* in 1940. Aguirre Beltrán narrated the history of indigenous landholding in Huatusco from pre-Columbian times to the present. He described indigenous land tenure in relation to the various historical antagonists who hindered it: Spanish colonists, local landholders, and postindependence liberal elites. The nineteenth-century liberal reforms that privatized communal lands, he argued, were the final blow to indigenous landholding. He also noted that runaway black slaves were equally deleterious. While other scholars in the 1930s venerated Mexico's black rebelliousness, he did not. These maroon societies, principally the free black community founded by Gaspar Yanga, endangered indigenous communities with their "violent and illegal actions," as Aguirre Beltrán called them.[90]

[89] Gonzalo Aguirre Beltrán, "Curriculum Vitae," August 3, 1944, folder 267 (Northwestern University – Beltrán, Gonzalo Aguirre (Visit, Anthropology), 1944–1952), box 19, series 216.S, record group 1.1, RAC-RFR.

[90] Gonzalo Aguirre Beltrán, *El señorío de Cuauhtochco: Luchas agrarias en México durante el Virreinato*, vol. 1 of *Obra antropológica* (Mexico City: Fondo de Cultura Económica, 1991), 48, 85, and 203–4.

Aguirre Beltrán's study of Huatusco gained the attention of indigenists like Manuel Gamio in Mexico City. In 1942, and after moving to the nation's capital, he began a career that was regularly bound to state projects and enmeshed in inter-American networks. As such, he not only affixed the study of African-descended peoples and cultures to the post-revolutionary project to document the entire populace but also used it to formulate new theories of state-sponsored indigenous integration after the Second World War. He was first a biologist within the Demographic Department, the agency Gamio directed within the Ministry of the Interior. At Gamio's request in 1942, he used the National Archives to document Mexico's colonial African slave population. When Gamio left to run the III in 1943, Aguirre Beltrán became the Department's Director.[91] That same year, he was selected to be part of Mexico's delegation to the First Inter-American Demographic Congress. Quickly making a name for himself, he became its Chief Clerk.[92]

The study of Mexico's African-descended population first entered the inter-American arena at the Demographic Congress. Two papers on Mexico's African-descended population gained widespread acclaim. The Ministry of the Interior published Carlos Basauri's *La población negroide mexicana* almost immediately. *Population Index* called it "one of the most interesting papers given at the Congress."[93] Basauri's work drew on his earlier research into Mexico's indigenous population, the three-volume *La población indígena de México* (1940) that concluded with a chapter on Mexico's black population. But, unlike his previous foray into Mexico's African-descended peoples, this short text was in dialogue with the explosion of research on African cultural retentions during the Second World War. Demography framed Basauri's and Aguirre Beltrán's research. While Mexico's lack of racial classification was a point of national pride and international acclaim, Basauri criticized it and the cultural forms of classification that were required as a result. Since independence, the census had not contained "any data on the black population." He continued, "That is to say: this sector is officially ignored in the Mexican population."

[91] Lewis, *Chocolate and Corn Flour*, 123; and Guillermo de la Peña, "Gonzalo Aguirre Beltrán," in vol. 9 of *La antropología en México: Panorama histórico*, coord. Lina Odena Güemes and Carlos García Mora (Mexico City: Instituto Nacional de Antropología e Historia, 1988), 65–66.

[92] Aguirre Beltrán, "Curriculum Vitae."

[93] "First Inter-American Demographic Congress," 14. For the Congress, Carlos Basauri also wrote *Breves notas etnográficas sobre la población negra del distrito de Jamiltepec, Oax.* (Mexico City: Primer Congreso Demográfico Interamericano, 1943).

Without any social or political benefit to self-identifying as African-descended, these citizens "prefer to declare themselves white or indigenous." Black physiological characteristics – like skin color, hair color and texture, and facial features – still remained visible in certain locales along the coast. Recalling nineteenth-century racial tracts, he noted that biology, not culture, was the most effective way to identify African-descended Mexicans, since their cultural behaviors lacked the evolutionary capacity to withstand generations of racial and cultural mixture. "The black and negroide population," he concluded, "has been assimilated into the Mexican population, principally into the Indian in rural regions."[94]

Although Basauri did not recognize any visible African-descended cultural practices, he made a passing reference to them in his discussion of Aguirre Beltrán's research on Mexico's colonial black population. Aguirre Beltrán's "magnificent and well-documented, unpublished book," he explained, discusses the Senegambian, Guinean, Congolese, and Angolan origins of Mexico's slave population. These conclusions bestowed a historical perspective upon Basauri's own ethnographic analyses. Not taking credit for this archival work, Basauri stated, "According to Aguirre Beltrán, many current dances like the huapango, the fandango, the bamba, etc. had their rhythmic origin in black music and dance."[95]

Perceiving Aguirre Beltrán's increasing importance in hemispheric circles, Melville Herskovits asked his acquaintances in Mexico for as much information about him as possible.[96] Once Herskovits was assured that Aguirre Beltrán was not only intelligent but also possessed an extremely assiduous work ethic, he invited the aspiring anthropologist to travel to Northwestern University for the 1944–45 academic year and even acquired a Rockefeller Foundation Grant to pay for the sabbatical.[97]

[94] Carlos Basauri, *La población negroide mexicana* (Mexico City: Secretaría de Gobernación/Primero Congreso Demográfico Interamericano, 1943), 5, 6, 7–17, and 19. Basauri was not the only scholar to note that the abolition of race in legal documents could engender black social and demographic invisibility; also see Harold Schoen, "The Free Negro in the Republic of Texas," *Southwestern Historical Quarterly* 39, no. 4 (1936): 293.

[95] Basauri, *La población negroide mexicana*, 7–17.

[96] Melville J. Herskovits to Dr. Richard Pattee, January 19, 1944; and Richard Pattee to Melville J. Herskovits, March 2, 1944, folder 24 (International Institute of Afro-American Studies, 1943–1944), box 28, NULA-MJHP. Also see Melville J. Herskovits to Richard Pattee, January 11, 1944, folder 5 (Pattee, Richard, 1943–1944), box 30, NULA-MJHP.

[97] Regarding Herskovits's interest in acquiring a Rockefeller Foundation Grant for Aguirre Beltrán, see Melville J. Herskovits to Richard Pattee, March 8, 1944, and April 10, 1944, folder 5 (Pattee, Richard, 1943–1944), box 30, NULA-MJH. By the 1970s, Aguirre

Bringing Aguirre Beltrán into Herskovits's ethnographic network was a calculated move to solidify his position as the preeminent anthropologist of African-descended peoples and cultures in the Western Hemisphere. Herskovits encouraged his students and mentees – including Katherine Dunham, Zora Neale Hurston, and Hugh Smythe – to conduct ethnographic research in unexplored regions of the Americas. Their observations helped him acquire the empirical data necessary to chart the relative survival of African cultural retentions.[98] Considering the tensions between Herskovits and Ortiz over the International Institute and Aguirre Beltrán's position as its Vice-Director, Aguirre Beltrán became a pawn in this power struggle. Moreover, his place at the forefront of Afro-Mexican studies made him the ideal person to bring Mexico into Herskovits's ethnographic pursuits.[99]

In the fall of 1944, Aguirre Beltrán arrived at Northwestern University with a completed draft of what would eventually become *La población negra de México*, the book that immediately established the historiographic baseline for the study of blackness in colonial Mexico.[100] He wanted only to tinker with his conclusions, but Herskovits had other plans. Reflecting on his protégé's manuscript, he told the Rockefeller Foundation that it was "a remarkable piece of work ... with findings that threw new and important light on the history of the Negro in the New World." However, he lamented, "Aguirre Beltrán lacked the knowledge of African backgrounds he should have, particularly as concerns tools with which to analyze tribal provenience, and second, that he was not in touch with the work of the men in the field of New World Negro studies."[101] Presumably Aguirre Beltrán's manuscript, like his earlier

Beltrán claimed that Alfred Métraux gave him the idea to study at Northwestern in 1944; see Gonzalo Aguirre Beltrán, *La población negra de México, 1519–1810: Estudio etnohistórico*, 2nd ed., corrected and expanded (Mexico City: Fondo de Cultura Económica, 1972), 10. However, Herskovits's correspondence with Métraux makes no mention of any such conversation.

[98] For a discussion of Herskovits's scholarly networks, see Yelvington, "The Invention of Africa in Latin America and the Caribbean," 35–82.

[99] Folder 351: "Some Next Steps in the Study of Negro Folklore," *The Journal of American Folklore*, January–March 1943, vol. 56, no. 219, box 38, NYPL-SCRBC-MA-MFHP.

[100] Gonzalo Aguirre Beltrán to Melville J. Herskovits, July 6, 1944; and Melville J. Herskovits to Mr. Roger F. Evans, April 4, 1944, folder 267 (Northwestern University – Beltrán, Gonzalo Aguirre (Visit, Anthropology), 1944–1952), box 19, series 216.S, record group 1.1, RAC-RFR.

[101] Melville J. Herskovits to Mr. Roger F. Evans, April 4, 1944, folder 267 (Northwestern University – Beltrán, Gonzalo Aguirre (Visit, Anthropology), 1944–1952), box 19, series 216.S, record group 1.1, RAC-RFR.

publications, failed to reference any of the historical or ethnographic studies of free and enslaved Africans published in other American countries.[102] To expand Aguirre Beltrán's knowledge about African-descended peoples in the Western Hemisphere, Herskovits proposed sending him for a few weeks to the East Coast to work with scholars at the Schomburg Center in Harlem, to visit historian Carter G. Woodson at Howard University, and to meet W. E. B. Du Bois in Atlanta. He also hoped that Aguirre Beltrán would go to the Deep South to "see something of Negro life there."[103] To his delight, Aguirre Beltrán postponed the book's publication so that he could learn African American ethnographic theories and methods from him, Du Bois, and Alain Locke.[104]

After Aguirre Beltrán returned to Mexico the following year, Woodson asked him to contribute several original essays about Mexico's slave population to the *Journal of Negro History*.[105] These three articles illustrate Herskovits's unmistakable impact on Aguirre Beltrán's research. In them, Aguirre Beltrán traced slavery in Mexico back, across the Atlantic, to African coastal regions like Guinea and São Tomé. Resembling Herskovits's comparative study of Africanisms, he stated that it was necessary "to fix exactly the origin of slaves, to know the base line" to determine their cultural footprints in the national landscape.[106] Unlike previous studies of black cultures in Mexico, he introduced African cultural behaviors to the postrevolutionary landscape and included maps of eight African cultural areas, such as those along the Rivers of Guinea and in Congo (See Maps 4.2 and 4.3). For instance, he noted that Mande slaves of West Africa, who were classified as Mandingos in colonial Inquisition records, "exercised the greatest influence in Mexico, during the entire 16th century."

[102] For example, see the citations in Aguirre Beltrán, *El señorío de Cuauhtochco*; and Gonzalo Aguirre Beltrán, "The Slave Trade in Mexico," *Hispanic American Historical Review* 24, no. 3 (1944): 412–31.

[103] Melville J. Herskovits to Roger F. Evans, April 4, 1944, and June 12, 1944; and Melville J. Herskovits to Gonzalo Aguirre Beltrán, June 27, 1944, folder 267 (Northwestern University – Beltrán, Gonzalo Aguirre (Visit, Anthropology), 1944–1952), box 19, series 216.S, record group 1.1, RAC-RFR.

[104] Melville J. Herskovits to Richard Pattee, February 14, 1945, folder 14 (Pattee, Richard, 1944–1946), box 35, NULA-MJHP.

[105] Gonzalo Aguirre Beltrán to Melville J. Herskovits, 7 de abril de 1946, folder 14 (Beltrán, Gonzalo Aguirre, 1944–1946), box 32, NULA-MJHP.

[106] Gonzalo Aguirre Beltrán, "Tribal Origins of Slaves in Mexico: Historical Background," *Journal of Negro History* 31, no. 3 (July 1946): 269–89. Also see Gonzalo Aguirre Beltrán, "Tribal Origins of Slaves in Mexico: The Rivers of Guinea," *Journal of Negro History* 31, no. 3 (1946): 290–316; and Gonzalo Aguirre Beltrán, "Tribal Origins of Slaves in Mexico: San Thome," *Journal of Negro History* 31, no. 3 (1946): 317–52.

MAP 4.2 Congo tribes, 1946. From Gonzalo Aguirre Beltrán, "Tribal Origins of Slaves in Mexico: San Thome," *Journal of Negro History*/University of Chicago Press. Copyright, 1946, by the Association for the Study of Negro Life and History.

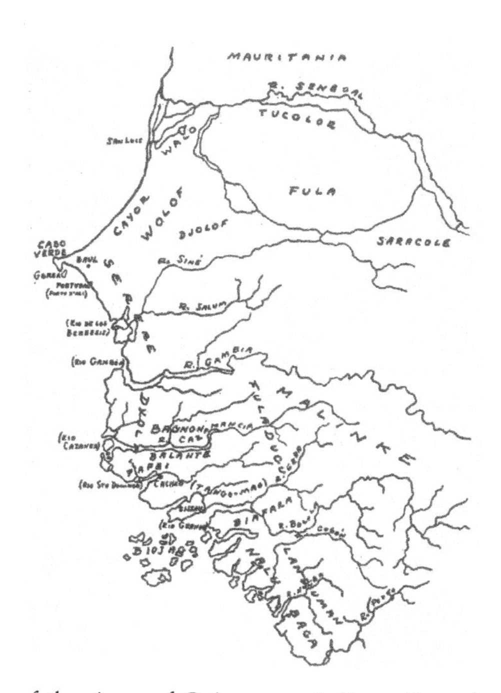

MAP 4.3 Tribes of the rivers of Guinea, 1946. From Gonzalo Aguirre Beltrán, "Tribal Origins of Slaves in Mexico: The Rivers of Guinea," *Journal of Negro History*/University of Chicago Press. Copyright, 1946, by the Association for the Study of Negro Life and History.

In presentist terms, he justified this statement by claiming that they "left as a souvenir of their presence in New Spain a number of geographical places which bear their name and the survival of the tribal name as a popular designation of the devil." In addition to using the archival research that he had completed at Mexico's National Archives, Aguirre Beltrán corroborated his discussions about the transfer of African cultures to Mexico with ethnographic data compiled by Cuba's Fernando Ortiz, Brazil's Nina Rodríguez, and Herskovits, among others.[107]

La población negra de México

Aguirre Beltrán's research had intellectual and institutional support from Mexican government officials as well as some of the most influential anthropologists in the Americas. Nonetheless, he feared that his study would not be published after completing the academic year at Northwestern. His cultural analysis of national society and social justice did not align with the new more conservative theories of economic development that influenced nationalist initiatives after fascism's defeat lessened the need to proclaim antiracist doctrines.[108] According to historian Daniel Cosío Villegas, editor of the Fondo de Cultura Económica, the monograph was "not economical," because it was too "specialized" to have a wide audience.[109] Aware of the groundbreaking nature of Aguirre Beltrán's research, Ediciones Fuente Cultural published it a few months later.

La población negra de México argues that African-descended peoples were part of Mexico's demographic past and, by association, its present. It documents the cultural survivals and transformations that accompanied African slaves as they crossed the Atlantic Ocean and entered colonial Mexican society. To make these claims, Aguirre Beltrán reproduced, albeit in Spanish, the same eight African cultural areas he had previously published in the *Journal of Negro History*. Drawing on other ethnographers' research, especially Ortiz's 1924 *Glosario de afronegrismos*, and using the archival records of the colonial officials and slave traders who adopted and invented tribal names to classify African ethnicities, he approximated the geographic origins of Mexico's enslaved Africans.

[107] Aguirre Beltrán, "Tribal Origins of Slaves in Mexico: Historical Background," 280.

[108] Gonzalo Aguirre Beltrán to Melville J. Herskovits, 30 de noviembre de 1945, folder 14 (Beltrán, Gonzalo Aguirre, 1944–1946), box 32, NULA-MJHP.

[109] Gonzalo Aguirre Beltrán to Melville J. Herskovits, 5 de marzo de 1946, folder 14 (Beltrán, Gonzalo Aguirre, 1944–1946), box 32, NULA-MJHP.

The postrevolutionary state's project to document all the nation's peoples and cultures framed his research. He argued that this information would give intellectuals and policy makers the tools to grasp the full range of physical and biological types that contributed to "the racial crucible that molded our population."[110]

Aguirre Beltrán surrounded his brief but innovative discussion of African cultural retentions in Mexico with social and demographic analyses of mestizaje. Considering his position in the Demographic Department and the inter-American fascination with demographics in the early 1940s, it is not surprising that he gave primacy to census data and racial classification. After all, African social and demographic visibility in the colonial period provided the historical context for any examination of African-descended cultural visibility in the twentieth century. Regarding culture, he noted that certain African cultural traits, most notably polygamy, survived the Middle Passage. This practice, he claimed in simplistic terms, illustrated the importance of women in Africa's informal family-based economies. Underestimating the ability of African-descended peoples to maintain kinship networks and traditional cultural beliefs after they adapted to their new surroundings, he declared that only maroon communities could maintain unadulterated African cultural behaviors. Most slaves integrated into colonial society to such a degree that, by 1600, there were African-born individuals who accepted the duties and customs of Spanish rule.[111]

Racial and cultural mixture dominated Aguirre Beltrán's conclusions. In demographic terms, the disproportionate presence of Spanish and African males engendered the complex caste system that propelled the postcolonial fascination with mestizaje. By the seventeenth century, the Spanish caste system identified individuals according to their percentage of Spanish, indigenous, and African blood. In this rubric, the most rudimentary

110 Gonzalo Aguirre Beltrán, *La población negra de México, 1519–1810: Estudio etnohistórico* (Mexico City: Ediciones Fuente Cultural, 1946), 95. Eight maps of African culture areas are located at the back of the monograph on unnumbered pages that follow the index.

111 Ibid., 160–61 and 254–55. A growing literature disputes Aguirre Beltrán's claim that only maroon communities could maintain African cultural practices and identities; see Bennett, *Colonial Blackness*, 58–85; and Joan C. Bristol, "Afro-Mexican Saintly Devotion in a Mexico City Alley," in *Africans to Spanish America: Expanding the Diaspora*, ed. Sherwin K. Bryant, Rachel Sarah O'Toole, and Ben Vinson III (Urbana: University of Illinois Press, 2012), 114–35. Laura A. Lewis discusses maroonage within a larger analysis of Aguirre Beltrán's intellectual history; see *Chocolate and Corn Flour*, esp. 127–28.

terms, such as mestizo (half-Spanish, half-indigenous) and mulatto, had precise meanings. But, these iterations continued, usually with colonial-era and nineteenth-century scholars providing sixteen derivations. Aguirre Beltrán concluded that this terminology became cumbersome, particularly because multiple variations of these caste nomenclatures permeated Spanish governance and colonial society. Depending on which version was referenced, the mixture of a Spaniard and a Moor (three-fourths Spanish, one-fourth black) could be Albino or Chinese. As racial exogamy became more complicated and society struggled to keep up with the lexicon necessary to classify it, terms deteriorated into ludicrous phrases like turning back, or *torna atrás*; suspended in mid-air, *tente en el aire*; and I do not understand you, *no te entiendo*. Such whimsical expressions, he resolved, were "were positively unintelligible."[112]

Because this complex system of classification was unsustainable, particularly in the wake of the egalitarian refrains of nineteenth-century liberalism, Aguirre Beltrán advocated for "a new vocabulary" that would prevent Mexico's African-descended population from being lost within the uncertainties of racial and cultural mixture. Through a cultural-cum-demographic matrix, he coined three new categories: *indomestizo*, *euromestizo*, and *afromestizo*. Indomestizos were mostly of indigenous descent. Euromestizos were predominately European. Afromestizos had a cultural heritage and biological roots that primarily descended from Africans. For him, these terms had a distinct advantage over the caste system's more taxonomic specifications; they allowed scholars and officials to classify racial mixture historically and ethnographically, without the degrees of inconsistency that inhered in colonial record keeping. Of course, the boundaries between categories were still fluid, reliant on cultural performance, social hierarchy, and political context. Similar to the 1930s Marxist historians who grouped indigenous, black, and mestizo resistance together while they examined class oppression, he declared that the indomestizo was "linked culturally to the afromestizo" through their shared colonial subjugation. Collectively, they were a foil to the more dominant euromestizo population.[113]

Using demographics from colonial-era censuses and statistical approximations of the lifespan of African slaves, Aguirre Beltrán noted the

[112] Aguirre Beltrán, *La población negra de México* (1946), 164–66, 177, and 249–53. Trey Proctor disproves the gendered dynamics of racial mixture that Aguirre Beltrán outlined; see "African Diasporic Ethnicity in Mexico City to 1650," 54–56.

[113] Aguirre Beltrán, *La población negra de México* (1946), 162 and 199–281.

relative population of Indians, Europeans, Africans, and afro-, indo-, and euromestizos between 1570 and 1810.[114] The number of people of pure African descent peaked at 2 percent of the population, or 35,089 people, a few years after the Atlantic slave trade was reoriented to other parts of the Americas in 1640. The afromestizo population, conversely, grew in absolute numbers throughout the colonial era. In 1570, there were 2,437 afromestizos; in 1810, there were 624,461.[115] By indicating that there was a substantial number of African-descended mixed-race peoples, just over 10 percent of the colony's population during the wars of independence, he demonstrated the African slave trade's undeniable demographic impact on Mexican mestizaje. His conclusions also implied that African-descended peoples did not disappear when the abolition of slavery and caste theoretically granted them demographic and social invisibility.

Aguirre Beltrán hoped that his research would make postrevolutionary mestizaje more culturally and demographically inclusive, an idea that harkened back to Manuel Gamio's 1916 ethnographic vision. To resolve contemporary social problems, Aguirre Beltrán declared that the state needed to expunge the remaining legacies of the caste system, which hindered racial uplift and national development. His neologisms were the solution, since assimilation was too homogenizing and destructive. Mexican mestizaje had to acknowledge the nation's African heritage without isolating it from the rest of colonial history and postindependence society; the act of quarantining peoples and cultures by race would reduce Mexican society to the segregationist policies of the United States. At the same time, postrevolutionary society needed to find avenues to protect these cultures so that national integration would not erase them. He advocated for a dialectical process defined by class mobility – not caste hierarchy – that would eventually conceal black social visibility in the ethnographic present but not rid the nation of its African cultural heritage.[116]

Aguirre Beltrán's emphasis on the demographic and cultural importance of Mexico's afromestizo population did not go unnoticed. While studying with Herskovits, he returned to Mexico City in February 1945 to give a lecture at the National Autonomous University of Mexico about

[114] Ibid., 199–237. Although other scholars have slightly adjusted Aguirre Beltrán's statistics, the general patterns he depicts are thought to be correct; see Vinson, "The Racial Profile of a Rural Mexican Province in the 'Costa Chica,'" 269n1.

[115] Aguirre Beltrán, *La población negra de México* (1946), 237.

[116] Ibid., 178, 270, and 278.

enslaved Africans in the sixteenth century.[117] Scholars from the United States, Mexico, and Cuba sang his praises. Melville Herskovits exclaimed to Mexican indigenist Jorge A. Vivó that the manner in which Aguirre Beltrán discussed how Mexico's African-descended people "contrived to lose himself in the preponderant Indian element in the Mexican population" was "described in masterly fashion."[118] Writing to Northwestern University President Franklin Snyder, he stated that *La población negra de México* "completely changes the accepted demographic picture" of Mexico.[119] In 1947, Manuel Gamio claimed that this monograph proved that the black population "was not destroyed, but assimilated." Similarly, Carter G. Woodson applauded the book's nuanced discussion of racial mixture and integration. Coming from two seemingly diverging political perspectives – Mexican indigenism and African American history – Gamio and Woodson both celebrated the advanced state of assimilation that, in their readings of *La población negra de México*, helped end racial prejudice in Mexico.[120] They utilized the nation's myth of racial egalitarianism to project a future Mexico defined by racial and cultural homogeneity, even if that was not Aguirre Beltrán's goal. Implicit in many of the book's reviews was a simplistic comparison between Mexico's lack of racial classification and discrimination and the United States' segregationist policies. The shadow of US racial formations permeated black identity politics in Mexico in 1946, just as it had for more than a century.

CONCLUSION

In 1946, Covarrubias and Aguirre Beltrán published meticulously researched tomes that detail Mexico's demographic and cultural roots in Africa. Before them, no Mexicans had related the nation's history of slavery or its Caribbean interludes back to Africa with any

[117] 13020 – Cursos de invierno, UNAM (1944), 10, expediente 244, UDLAP-SACE-AMC.

[118] Melville J. Herskovits to Jorge A. Vivó, September 24, 1946, folder 35 (International Institute of Afro-American Studies, 1946–1947), box 38, NULA-MJHP.

[119] Melville Herskovits to President Franklyn B. Snyder, October 29, 1946, folder 17 (Beltrán, Gonzalo Aguirre, 1946–1948), box 37, NULA-MJHP. Also see Manuel Moreno Fraginals, review of *La población negra de México, 1510–1810: Estudio etnohistórico* by Gonzalo Aguirre Beltrán, *Hispanic American Historical Review* 27, no. 1 (1947): 117–19.

[120] Manuel Gamio, review of *La población negra de México, 1510–1810* by Gonzalo Aguirre Beltrán, *América Indígena* 7, no. 1 (1947): 98; and Carter G. Woodson, review of *La población negra de México, 1510–1810: Estudio etnohistórico* by Gonzalo Aguirre Beltrán, *Journal of Negro History* 31, no. 4 (1946): 491–94.

methodological or theoretical rigor. Mexican blackness had been native to the Americas, birthed by the horrors of New World slavery and, by implication, devoid of any African heritage. These two ethnographies took inspiration from the inter-American rhetoric that celebrated the New World's vision of democracy, with its emphasis on cultural not biological race, as the antidote to fascism and ethnocentrism worldwide. Housing both the International Institute of Afro-American Studies and the III, Mexico City was at the center of this wartime inter-Americanism. Mexico's spirit of racial egalitarianism, which had historically captivated the attention of African Americans, set the stage for Mexico to become in Irene Diggs's words, "the cradle for Afro-American studies not only in America, nor on a scale inter-American, but in the world."

Moving among these national, hemispheric, and global intellectual currents, Covarrubias and Aguirre Beltrán rejected the nineteenth-century assumptions that minimized African cultural innovation and cast African societies as irrelevant to Mexican and world histories. Ethnographers, they asserted, needed to study the continent's cultural areas if blackness was to be examined with the social scientific precision that postrevolutionary nation-state formation demanded. Explicit in Covarrubias's *Mexico South* but buried in the footnotes of Aguirre Beltrán's *La población negra de México* was the hemispheric quest to connect all American peoples and cultures through the festooned language of democratic exceptionalism and cultural inclusion. By the end of the Second World War, two historical, ethnographic, and geographic conceptions of Mexico's African heritage had emerged: Covarrubias exclaimed Afro-Cuban cultures could be Mexican while Aguirre Beltrán traced these cultural roots directly back to Africa.

5

Africanizing "La bamba"

In the musical program guide for Mexico's 1940 exhibition *Twenty Centuries of Mexican Art*, book editor and music historian Herbert Weinstock took audiences at New York City's MoMA on a tour of Mexican music. They traveled across time, from the pre-Columbian epoch to the postrevolutionary present, and across the nation's many regions, from the northern states of Sonora and Durango to the cosmopolitan sounds of Mexico City and the coastal rhythms of Veracruz. The program signified the triumph of a new musical aesthetic based on the spirited reformulation of the vernacular melodies, harmonies, and rhythms that the 1910 Revolution made popular. Turning to the Gulf Coast, Weinstock parenthetically added that "La bamba" "has an unmistakable Negro tang."[1] Buried in a thirty-one-page pamphlet, this passing reference to blackness suggests that musicologists could not confine Mexico's soundscape to the exchanges between indigenous communities and Spanish settlers. It anchors his introduction to Gerónimo Baqueiro Foster's *Huapangos*, a classical composition that Carlos Chávez debuted at the MoMA. Any concertgoer only expecting to hear Spanish hymns and exotic Aztec instruments was undoubtedly shocked to read that Mexico was home to black melodies, harmonies, and rhythms. Previously, and like all Mexican music, "La bamba" had been depicted as the mixture of Spanish and indigenous cultures. However, in this transnational setting, Baqueiro Foster, Chávez, and Weinstock pushed back against the racialized cartography that had buttressed

[1] Weinstock, *Mexican Music*, 21.

Mexican musicology and composition before the Revolution and in its immediate aftermath.

Music scholars typically consider the program Chávez coordinated to be the culmination of Mexico's postrevolutionary musical nationalism: the historical, ethnographic, and musicological study of local and regional vernacular songs and their subsequent transposition into modern art music.[2] Regarding the African origins of Mexican music – the Negro tang, as Weinstock obliquely conceived it – the concert series did not mark the conclusion of the ethnographic program Chávez charted after his return to Mexico in 1928. The premier of *Huapangos* marked a moment of transition, tucked between the 1930s Marxist constructions of black cultures, which saw blackness devoid of an African past, and the postwar acknowledgment of the nation's African heritage.

Recognition of the African roots of "La bamba" was a spatial process built upon the simultaneous reformulation of race and culture in the state of Veracruz and the geographically overlapping *Huasteca*.[3] The democratic flourishes of postwar inter-Americanism as well as the consolidation of Mexican ethnomusicology as a social science set the stage for the "La bamba" to gain fame as a symbol of Veracruz and to lose its association with the more indigenous Huasteca. As such, composers, ethnomusicologists, and dancers, especially African American Katherine Dunham's Afro-diasporic dance troupe, brought it into the Caribbean world. The aesthetics that rendered the melodies, harmonies, and rhythms of Veracruz first black and then diasporic were quintessentially transnational, a product of the cultural cross-pollination of Mexican and African-descended musical sensibilities that took place when African Americans discontent with Jim Crow segregation traveled to Mexico.

THE HUAPANGO IN THE 1930S

The popular song "La bamba" dates back to colonial-era performances of the huapango (also called the *son huasteco*) and the son jarocho. These

[2] Dan Malmström, *Introduction to Twentieth Century Mexican Music* (Sweden: Institute of Musicology, Uppsala University, 1974), 98; Saavedra, "Of Selves and Others," 13 and 317–29; and Rodríguez, "Nacionalismo y folklore en la Escuela Nacional de Música," 415.

[3] Rolando A. Pérez Fernández explains that Blas Galindo's *Sones de Mariachi*, which also debuted at the MoMA, references blackness by including a variation of the song "La negra"; see *La música afromestiza mexicana* (Xalapa: Universidad Veracruzana, 1990), 175–76.

musical genres have geographic ties to the state of Veracruz. The huapango resides in the Huasteca, a multistate region that includes Veracruz's northernmost regions in addition to parts of San Luis Potosí, Puebla, Tamaulipas, Querétaro, and Hidalgo. In contrast, the son jarocho is located distinctly in the state of Veracruz and is most closely associated with the *Sotavento*, an area surrounding the city of Veracruz in the southern half of the state (See Map 5.1). Like all other varieties of the *son*, they shared and continue to share several musicological traits: a fast tempo, paired dancing, improvisational singing, a reliance on syncopated rhythms, and a 6/8 time signature not typical of indigenous music. One of the quintessential elements of "La bamba" is intricate footwork. Performed on a wood platform during festivities and social gatherings, the huapango and son jarocho provide a backdrop for dancers, especially males in search of female companionship, to impress onlookers. Courtship behaviors include the ability to tie and untie knots with one's feet as well as improvisational singing and dancing.[4] As such, there are no set lyrics for "La bamba," but performers typically begin with some variation of:

> To sing (or dance) La bamba
> One needs
> A little bit of flair

References to the Mexico's coastal traditions are ubiquitous. Singers often improvise verses about pirates and use variations of lines like "I am not a sailor" and "I am the captain."[5]

As part of Carlos Chávez's project to study and unite all the peoples of the nation, composers, musicologists, and ethnographers from Mexico and the United States traveled to the Huasteca and to Veracruz to study "La bamba" and the musical genres associated with it. In the 1920s, most considered the song to have some combination of indigenous and Spanish

[4] Daniel Edward Sheehy, "The 'Son Jarocho': The History, Style, and Repertory of a Changing Mexican Musical Tradition" (PhD diss., University of California, Los Angeles, 1979), esp. 64–101; and Lizette Alegre González, "Música, migración y cine: *Los Tres Huastecos*. Un ejemplo de entrecruzamiento cultural," in *Música sin fronteras: Ensayos sobre migración, música e identidad* (Mexico City: Consejo Nacional para la Cultura y las Artes, 2006), 238–44.

[5] For examples of the lyrics to "La bamba," see Randall Ch. Kohl S., *Ecos de "La Bamba": Una historia etnomusicológica sobre el son jarocho de Veracruz, 1946–1959* (Veracruz: Instituto Veracruzano de Cultura, 2007), 176–89; and Rafael Figueroa Hernández, *Son Jarocho: Guía histórico-musical* (Mexico City: CONACULTA, 2007), 49–50. For a discussion of this history of pirates, see Fernando Benítez and José Emilio Pacheco, *Crónica del Puerto de Veracruz* (Veracruz: Gobierno del Estado de Veracruz, 1986), 66–88 and 151–56.

MAP 5.1 Map of the Huasteca and the state of Veracruz.

origins. For the bilingual magazine *Mexican Folk-ways*, folklorist Francis Toor used Mexican vernacular cultures as a springboard to critique US stereotypes of Mexico and provide foreign audiences with an ethnographic window into Mexico's indigenous traditions.[6] An issue from October 1932 includes three articles on the huapango in addition to her introductory statement that situates the genre within "the European tradition." She failed to mention any black melodies, harmonies, or

[6] López, *Crafting Mexico*, 100–5.

rhythms.[7] In a more extended analysis, José de J. Núñez y Domínguez, a writer from Papantla, Veracruz, associated the "ethnical regional" genre's name with the pre-Columbian Nahuatl words for log (*cuahutil*), wood (*ipan*), and place (*co*). This etymology highlights the centrality of the large wood platforms utilized in all huapangos. In exotic terms, he characterized the genre as much as a spectacle as an art form. It was the product of "the rustic decoration of fantastic exuberance" that emerged from "the feverish temperature of the torrid zone which makes the blood boil in impetuous waves." Only locals, he continued, could "understand all the witchery of those melodies, born among the luxurious vegetation of the tropics, and at the same time of the still water blues that are like the tears of the woods."[8] Primitivist references to nature distanced the huapango from the Western cultures Toor highlighted. When read together, these essays characterize the genre as European and indigenous. With the exception of the linguistic connection to Nahuatl, the exact influence of either culture goes unmentioned if not undetermined.

Recognition of the African roots of the music of Veracruz began when Gerónimo Baqueiro Foster, a flutist of Mayan descent from the coastal state of Campeche, traveled to Veracruz. He arrived preoccupied with indigenous rhythms and hoping to write a book on the subject.[9] Indigeneity had long fascinated him and offered him a point of entry into the vernacular musics of the world, both past and present. Cutting his teeth on Julián Carrillo's theories of microtonality, or the subdivision of Western musical harmonics, he and a few other brash young musicologists, most notably Vicente T. Mendoza, believed that indigenous music did not align with the traditional twelve tones used in classical compositions. In 1926, he and his colleague Daniel Castañeda argued that Mexicans should use ninety-six instead. To provide composers with more tones, and therefore with smaller harmonic intervals between successive notes, would not only facilitate a more accurate transcription of indigenous melodies and harmonies but also improve classical arrangements of the non-Western genres found in Asia, the Middle East, Oceania, and Latin America.[10]

[7] Frances Toor, "Nota sobre los Huapangos/Note on Huapangos," *Mexican Folk-ways* 7, no. 4 (1932): 168.

[8] José de J. Núñez y Domínguez, "Los Huapangos/The Huapangos," *Mexican Folk-ways* 7, no. 4 (1932): 186.

[9] Gerónimo Baqueiro Foster to Carlos Chávez, 6 de noviembre de 1933, expediente 99 (Gerónimo Baqueiro Foster), vol. 4, caja 1, sección correspondencia, FCC-AGN.

[10] Gerónimo Baqueiro Foster and Daniel Castañeda, "Principios técnicos para el folk-lore en general, y en particular para el folk-lore mexicano," 7–8, expediente 1527, INBA/

In 1928, just before Chávez returned from the United States, Baqueiro Foster and Castañeda turned their attention to Mexico's regional soundscapes. The evolutionary assumption that vernacular harmonics mimicked the sounds of nature bolstered their inquiries into indigenous music.[11] To delineate the nation's musical regions, they embraced an idea attributed to Plato: the way people speak – and therefore sing – is emblematic of their environment.[12] In other words, regional dialects and colloquial expressions mirrored the harmonies found in nature and in vernacular music. This meant that Baqueiro Foster and Castañeda could use pre- and postrevolutionary linguistic and ethnographic research in addition to their own musical knowledge to map Mexico's indigenous musical landscape. They concluded that Mexico comprised seven regions. Veracruz occupied the majority of zone five, which included the Huasteca and stretched along the Gulf Coast from Texas to the southern edge of the state (See Map 5.2). Prefiguring Chávez's own ethnographic project to study indigenous melodies, harmonies, and rhythms, they proposed that 3 musicologists study each area to acquire 100 musical recordings, both a cappella and with instrumentation, as well as any other relevant ethnographic and musicological data.[13]

Baqueiro Foster and Castañeda failed to address the possible presence of African-descended melodies, harmonies, and rhythms. Delineating the world's major harmonic groups, they left out any references to sub-Saharan Africa or to the African-descended peoples of the Americas. Thinking about African musical areas in 1926, they only mentioned Egypt. Following nineteenth-century evolutionary theories, they separated this kingdom from the rest of the continent and placed it within the broader cultural histories of Western civilization. In 1928, they again reduced African music to Egypt, which they now lumped with the musical traditions of China, Assyria, Malaysia, Mexico, and Peru. Other valuable

CENIDIM-ABF. Also see other documents in this folder for a more holistic view of their musicological project, which drew inspiration from Julián Carrillo's concept of the thirteenth sound, the Sonido 13.

11 Saavedra, "Of Selves and Others," 234–37.

12 Gerónimo Baqueiro Foster y Daniel Castañeda, "Tonos y modos," 1, expediente 1528, INBA/CENIDIM-ABF.

13 Gerónimo Baqueiro Foster and Daniel Castañeda, "El folk-lore como fenómeno histórico," 6, expediente 1528, INBA/CENIDIM-ABF. Their linguistic mapping took inspiration from D. Francisco Pimentel, *Cuadro descriptivo y comparativo de las lenguas indígenas de México*, 2 vols. (Mexico City: Imprenta de Andrade y Escalante, 1862–65); Noriega, *Geografía de México*; and José María Bonilla, *La evolución del pueblo mexicano* (Mexico City: Herrero Hermanos Sucesores, 1922).

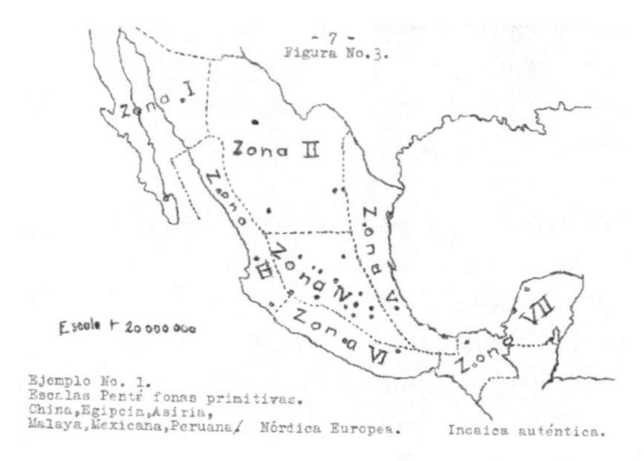

MAP 5.2 Map of Mexican musical zones, 1928. From Gerónimo Baqueiro Foster and Daniel Castañeda, "El folk-lore como fenómeno histórico," expediente 1528, CENIDIM/INBA.

musical expressions included those performed by Northern Europeans and the descendants of the Incas.[14]

Baqueiro Foster's assumptions about indigeneity and blackness fell apart in 1933. That year, he began to travel across the nation and began to perceive the musical footprints of African slaves. Between 1934 and 1942, he took numerous short trips to the state of Veracruz to study the huapango. Ethnographic observation proved to be more complex than he initially anticipated, because his conclusions did not align with either Western harmonics or the primacy that he and his Mexican compatriots had given to indigenous musical traits. Reflecting on his initial research in 1959, he explained that he had to listen to this music "to familiarize his Westernized ears with its exotic melodies."[15] Implicit in statements like this one is the belief that microtonality might be necessary for accurate ethnomusicological investigations of Mexico's black and indigenous harmonies. He determined that that he had to examine "the root of the SONES of the Huapango of Veracruz." In particular, and to not spread himself too thin, he decided to focus on "the music of the Sotavento, with its priceless traditional value and its fruitful instructions."[16]

In spatial terms, Baqueiro Foster reoriented the huapango – and thus "La bamba" – by focusing on the Sotavento of southern Veracruz and not

[14] Baqueiro Foster and Castañeda, "El folk-lore como fenómeno histórico," 7.

[15] Gerónimo Baqueiro Foster, "La música popular en el sotavento veracruzano. III," 1 de noviembre de 1959, expediente 0344 B0930, INBA/CENIDIM-ABF.

[16] Gerónimo Baqueiro Foster to Adolfo Ruiz Cortines, 29 de noviembre de 1945, expediente 2732 B0154, INBA/CENIDIM-ABF.

the multistate Huasteca. He concluded that the harmonics, rhythmic accents, and timber of traditional huapangos differed from other popular genres. Recalling his fascination with microtonality and his critique of equal temperament in the 1920s, he wrote in his 1942 article "El Huapango" that these vernacular harmonies resembled the primitive scales of Ancient Greek music more than classical art music. The encroachment of Western aesthetics, he feared, would endanger them. The adoption of the six-stringed guitar already threatened the huapango's harmonic vibrancy. Moreover, the quality of singing diminished when performers relied on the harmonies found in popular Italian operas. The Westernization of vernacular harmonics proved to him that the "La bamba" had to be defined by its rhythms, not its endangered melodies and harmonies.[17]

By 1942, Baqueiro Foster concluded that these harmonic and rhythmic observations forced composers to rethink the entire racial scaffolding on which national music was built. Blackness had to be introduced to the ethnomusicological study of Mexican regionality. Previously, only Gabriel Saldívar had referred to the huapango's origins among enslaved Africans. As trained doctor from the state of Tamaulipas, he penned a contradictory chapter on Mexico's African-descended music in his 1934 book *Historia de la música en México*. It was a critique of all those who preceded him: "Those who have dedicated themselves to writing about music have not given any importance – we do not know the reason why – to the influence that the African race has exerted in our musical production." Following the classist rhetoric of the 1930s, Saldívar asserted that black tunes were the most loyal expressions of African-descended slaves during the colonial period. Those who arrived at the port of Veracruz after 1766 introduced "African sentiments." Despite such seemingly concrete statements about the racial origins of the huapango, he was uncertain how much of this music originated in Africa and how much was a product of secondary cultural flows within the Western Hemisphere. African music "came to us with some modifications suffered during its time in the Caribbean." But, in more fatalistic and imprecise terms reminiscent of nineteenth-century epistemologies, he also declared that this music "did not conserve its old customs or remember them; slavery had killed all of the bad habits of their past, with the exception of their color."[18] In short,

[17] Gerónimo Baqueiro Foster, "El Huapango," *Revista Musical Mexicano*, no. 8 (1942): 175.

[18] Gabriel Saldívar, *Historia de la música en México (épocas precortesiana y colonial)* (Mexico City: Secretaría de Educación Pública, 1934), 219–25 and 290–92.

Saldívar did not explain the extent to which African and New World musical traits influenced the huapango, just as he left unanswered the question of whether unblemished African musical traits had disembarked in the port of Veracruz.

Expanding Saldívar's arguments, Baqueiro Foster cast himself as the preeminent historian of the music of Veracruz.[19] His predecessor, after all, was "for his erudition and interest in the topic, a forerunner."[20] They both shared the same methodological difficulties in ascertaining precisely which musicological aspects of the huapango were black, indigenous, and Spanish. Building on previous linguistic research, including his own, Baqueiro Foster highlighted the huapango's etymological roots in Nahuatl. In his most concrete analysis of its black harmonies, melodies, and rhythms, he declared that:

> "La Bamba" and "La Palomita," for example, were descendants of the songs of the black slaves of the Spanish conquerors.
>
> It would not be difficult to acknowledge this black ancestry in the harmonic, melodic, and rhythmic elements of "La Bamba."[21]

His historical imprecision was a result of the scarcity of colonial-era sources. The musical footprints of African slaves were perceptible, but not in discrete musicological traits that could be adumbrated, let alone associated with concrete cultural areas in Africa. Unfortunately, the recognition of blackness in the music of Veracruz raised, particularly in retrospect, a host of methodological questions about African cultural retentions that Baqueiro Foster did not think to ask – let alone answer – or that he believed were impossible to solve.

Baqueiro Foster began to present his research in August 1937.[22] Mexico's urban elite quickly grew fond of his version of "La bamba." Well aware of Mexico's jazz craze, he began to write a version of the song for a jazz orchestra the next year. This black musical genre became an ideal vehicle for him to translate his historical and ethnographic research into modern music – it amplified the black roots of "La bamba" by

[19] Regarding Baqueiro Foster's importance in Mexican music, see Arturo Sotomayor, "¡Cada Vez que te miro . . . !," *Prensa Gráfica*, 6 de marzo de 1946, 3/30928, expediente 572, UDLAP-SACE-AMC.

[20] Gerónimo Baqueiro Foster, "Historia de la música en México, de Gabriel Saldívar," *Suplemento de El Nacional*, 28 de diciembre de 1958, RP-MF 26235, cuaderno no. 14, 1 de abril de 1958 al 28 de febrero de 1959, CNA-BA-FE-AGBF.

[21] Baqueiro Foster, "El Huapango," 174 and 183.

[22] Advertisement for Departamento de Bellas Artes, Sección de divulgación de la alta cultura artística, expediente 2732 B0154, INBA/CENIDIM-ABF.

utilizing a comparable but more internationally recognizable musical genre. Before he completed the composition, Chávez invited him to compose a classical version for the 1940 concert series that would accompany Mexico's art exhibition *Twenty Centuries of Mexican Art* at the MoMA.[23] Funded by the Rockefeller Foundation, Baqueiro Foster arranged *Huapangos*, an orchestration that includes his renditions of "La bamba," "La morena," and "El balajú." Thinking about his musical aesthetic in October 1945, he explained that he wanted his arrangement of "El balajú" to be "of all times, but also modern, without damaging it with pretentious transpositions and modulations or inappropriate harmonies." In other words, it would represent the people who created it while simultaneously being universal.[24]

Twenty Centuries of Mexican Art traced the nation's visual and musical culture from its pre-Columbian roots, through European colonization, and finally to the contemporary period. Adhering to the modernist interest in vernacular culture, its organizers dedicated one section to the role of "Folk or Popular Art which runs through all periods."[25] In addition, the exhibit enriched the MoMA's interest in displaying vernacular art from around the world. In previous exhibitions – such as *American Folk Art* (1933–34), *African Negro Art* (1935–36), and *Three Mexican Artists* (1938–39) – the Museum provided patrons with a modernist gaze into rural white, African, and Mexican cultures.[26] To accompany the monumental art exhibition, Chávez formed an orchestra comprising musicians from the New York Philharmonic and the OSM that, according to *El Universal*, would give "an exact idea of our musical culture."[27] The concert program took the audience on a sonic tour of Mexican history and its contemporary vernacular traditions. Chávez and his friends, colleagues, and students contributed compositions that ranged from

[23] Gerónimo Baqueiro Foster to Sr. D. Martín Luis Guzmán, director de "TIEMPO," 2 de octubre de 1945, expediente 2732 B0154, INBA/CENIDIM-ABF. For a discussion of Baqueiro Foster's desire to make "La bamba" popular across the globe, see Sotomayor, "¡Cada Vez que te miro . . . !"

[24] Gerónimo Baqueiro Foster to Lic. Jorge Cerdán, 31 de octubre de 1945; and Gerónimo Baqueiro Foster to Adolfo Ruiz Cortines, gobernador del Estado de Veracruz, 29 de noviembre de 1945, expediente 2732 B0154, INBA/CENIDIM-ABF.

[25] "Twenty Centuries of Mexican Art Being Assembled for the Museum of Modern Art," February 21, 1940, 1, MoMA-PRA.

[26] "Current Exhibitions," *Bulletin of the Museum of Modern Art* 7, no. 5 (1940): 2–14.

[27] "La Exposición de Veinte Siglos de Arte Mexicano," *El Universal*, 8 de mayo de 1940, RP-MF 22057, cuaderno vol. 13, 22 de marzo 1940 a 21 de julio 1940, CNA-BA-FE-AGBF.

orchestral arrangements loyal to their vernacular inspirations to modernist tour-de-forces that employed similar musicological theories about natural music to those described by Baqueiro Foster and Castañeda in the 1920s. In addition to Baqueiro Foster's *Huapangos*, Chávez included orchestrations of pre-Columbian music and classical arrangements animated by Mexico's musical traditions in Mexico City as well as the states of Jalisco, Michoacán, Zacatecas, Durango, Chihuahua, and Sonora. In terms reminiscent of the vague historical narratives already attributed to "La bamba," the program locates the huapango in the eighteenth, nineteenth, and twentieth centuries: every other composition is marked as "traditional" or is situated in only one or two centuries.[28]

To introduce the concert, Chávez defined Mexican music as "the Indian music of the ancient Mexicans; the music of Spanish or other origin implanted in Mexico; and, finally, the production in Mexico of a mixture of these elements." Despite his emphasis on indigeneity and Spanishness, the 1940 debut of *Huapangos* located African-descended music within Mexico's nationalist soundscape. Just a few sentences after he sketched the cultural origins of Mexican music, he added that along "the entire coast of the Gulf of Mexico the music of Negro slaves from Africa has had an important influence."[29] To introduce the huapango, Herbert Weinstock selectively culled information from a draft of Baqueiro Foster's article "El Huapango."[30] In discussing "La bamba," Weinstock proclaimed that it had "an unmistakable Negro tang."[31] Geographically, he was inconsistent. Weinstock situated the huapango in the Huasteca but, when listing the program's contents, located it in the state of Veracruz. Whether its musicological attributes were born in Africa or the Americas was unclear. Like Baqueiro Foster, he too appeared ambivalent toward or unaware of the hemispheric debates about African cultural retentions.

Chávez recognized that the audience might have wanted a more scientific breakdown of Mexico's musical heritage. To justify his opaque definition of Mexican music, he preemptively proclaimed that it was difficult to note the precise ratios of a song's Spanish, indigenous, and perhaps African-descended origins:

[28] See Weinstock, *Mexican Music*. Regarding Chávez's rejection of microtonality, see Carlos Chávez, introduction to *Mexican Music: Notes by Herbert Weinstock for Concerts Arranged by Carlos Chávez* (New York: Museum of Modern Art, May 1940), 8; and Saavedra, "Of Selves and Others," 322–23.

[29] Chávez, introduction to *Mexican Music*, 9–10.

[30] Baqueiro Foster, "El Huapango," 175n1.

[31] Weinstock, *Mexican Music*, 21.

In what form and to what degree has a new music, characteristic of Mexico been produced from the sum of these elements? This is a question which cannot readily be answered. The best response is the program which the Museum of Modern Art is presenting, and the best answer will be that of the listeners.

By definition, musical mestizaje was inexact, needing to be placed in its historical context, understood in qualitative ethnographic terms that recognized ethnic and geographic specificities, and analyzed with modern musicological methods.[32] Music critics embraced Chávez's challenge to describe the amount to which indigenous, Spanish, and African-descended music permeated Mexico's soundscape. Presumably because of the elusive presence of black melodies, harmonies, and rhythms in the huapango, they came to very different conclusions about the racial roots of Baqueiro Foster's composition, at least in comparison to the more straightforward genealogies of compositions like Chávez's *Xochipilli-Macuilxochitl*, Luis Sandi's *Yaqui Music*, and Don José Aldana's *Mass*. *New York Times* music critic Howard Taubman explained that Baqueiro Foster's arrangement has "an earthly pace and vigor" that "sound[s] like blood brothers of 'le jazz hot.'"[33] Just as jazz helped inspire Baqueiro Foster to compose *Huapangos*, this distinctly American genre helped Taubman comprehend it.

Conversely, Olin Downes only praised Chávez for his valiant attempt to recuperate Mexico's pre-Columbian past. Evaluating Baqueiro Foster's orchestration, Downes was particularly satisfied with its "complete originality and [the] piquancy of the motives, the changing rhythmical designs, and the unique instrumentation, which employs, one would say the greater part of the battery of gourds, rattles, rasps, and percussive instruments of various sorts employed in Mexican folk-music." He continued, "This primitivism is fascinating by reason of its tone colors and rhythmical counterpoint and what one may call the truthfulness of its feeling."[34] Any reference to the huapango's African heritage was missing. *Huapangos* was based on a primitive indigenous song that presumably had some European ancestry. The absence of blackness, whether in Downes's review or in Mexican ethnomusicology, was not the result of any explicit desire within Mexican or US circles to rid the huapango of its black melodies, harmonies, or rhythms. Rather, it illustrates how

[32] Chávez, introduction to *Mexican Music*, 10.

[33] Howard Taubman, "Mexicans' Music Sung at Exhibition," *New York Times*, May 17, 1940.

[34] Olin Downes, "Perspective of Mexican Music," *New York Times*, June 2, 1940.

intellectuals in Mexico and the United States grappled with the ambiguous racial roots of Mexican musical mestizaje and the undefined cultural relationship between the Huasteca and the state of Veracruz. In particular, it illuminates how well-trained musical scholars could arrive at disparate conclusions about the vernacular sounds that were subsumed under the unwieldy labels of vernacular and racially mixed.

RACIAL GEOGRAPHIES OF "LA BAMBA" IN VERACRUZ IN THE 1940S

The blackening of the huapango was as much a spatial process as a musicological one. In 1938, Baqueiro Foster declared that all verses of the genre were "legitimately of Veracruz, with an original poetic expression."[35] He reaffirmed this cultural geography four years later when he declared that its melodies, harmonies, and rhythms were the "most pure" in the region surrounding the city of Veracruz.[36] This was a curious statement since the southern half of the state, including the port city, was typically associated with the son jarocho, not the huapango. Baqueiro Foster's conclusions therefore blurred the geographic distinction between these two vernacular genres, both famous for "La bamba," and brought the huapango closer to the port where most enslaved Africans disembarked during the colonial period.

These geographic and racial revisions made their way into Baqueiro Foster's *Huapangos* almost immediately after Chávez conducted it at the MoMA. In 1941, Baqueiro Foster's colleague and Chávez's disciple José Pablo Moncayo composed the similarly named *Huapango*, which Chávez premiered with the OSM. Moncayo's modernist composition aligned more with Chávez's emphasis on dissonance and the spirited reformulation of vernacular music than Baqueiro Foster's careful arrangement of "La bamba," "La morena," and "El balajú." Precisely for this reason, Baqueiro Foster disliked his colleague's brasher composition. "The 'Huapango,'" he stated in an interview in 1959, "is a brilliant and sensationalist piece, a bad translation. A potpourri. Moncayo failed to capture the spirit of the jarana. The work is shallow and fake."[37] Nonetheless, Moncayo's *Huapango* became a standard in the postrevolutionary canon,

[35] Gerónimo Baqueiro Foster to Inocencio y Nicolás Gutiérrez y Nicolás Sosa, 16 de junio de 1938, expediente 2722, INBA/CENIDIM-ABF.
[36] Baqueiro Foster, "El Huapango," 175.
[37] Expediente 0249-B0622, INBA/CENIDIM-ABF.

frequently performed by Chávez and the OSM, whereas Baqueiro Foster's *Huapangos* found a home with regional symphonies and on radio broadcasts.[38] Their similar titles, *Huapangos* and *Huapango*, undoubtedly created confusion. As the latter gained popularity, Baqueiro Foster rearranged and renamed his composition *Suite Veracruzana* no. 1 to distance it from the Huasteca and reorient it squarely in the state of Veracruz.[39]

Baqueiro Foster was not alone in associating blackness with the music of Veracruz. Two years after Baqueiro Foster published his ethnomusicological research, Walt Disney located black music in the cosmopolitan port city in his live-action animation film *The Three Caballeros* (1944). Sponsored by the Office of the Coordinator of Inter-American Affairs, the film was part of Disney's modernist project to play with artistic mediums and musical genres, just as he had in his fanciful animated film *Music Land* (1935), a short film that depicts the cultural majesty unleashed when art music and jazz are performed together.[40] The inter-American contrast between New World cultural inclusion and Old World ethnocentrism permeated *The Three Caballeros* and the intellectual networks that undergirded it. In 1939, Carlos Chávez and Miguel Covarrubias asked Disney to collaborate in a cinematic history of the Western Hemisphere that would be accompanied by avant-garde music. Disney declined, citing his

[38] Agea, *21 años de la Orquesta Sinfónica de México*, 58 and 100. Moncayo's *Huapango* had also replaced Baqueiro Foster's *Huapangos* abroad; see "Carlos Chávez leads National Symphony," *New York Times*, March 7, 1943. Of course, Baqueiro Foster's *Suite Veracruzana* no. 1 did not disappear from the national scene. Choreographer Ana Mérida danced to it, with scenery and costumes made by her father, Carlos, at the Palace of Fine Arts on June 18 and 20, 1952; see Antonio Luna Arroyo, *Ana Mérida en la historia de la danza mexicana moderna* (Mexico City: México Técnica Gráf., Abril 1959), 70 and 293–94.

[39] In 1947, Frances Toor also made a racial-spatial division between the indigenous Huasteca and the state of Veracruz. Although she stated that "La bamba" was popular in both regions, she only noted that there were black influences in Veracruz, where "the musicians and dancers are mestizos of native, Spanish, and Negro blood" and where there were "Negro dances" like "Los negritos"; see *A Treasury of Mexican Folkways* (New York: Crown, 1947), 354, 358–59, 366–68, and 375.

[40] Steven Watts, "Walt Disney: Art and Politics in the American Century," *Journal of American History* 82, no. 1 (1995): 92. However, scholars typically associate *The Three Caballeros* with Franklin Roosevelt's Good Neighbor Policy and US cultural imperialism during the Second World War. For example, see José Piedra "Pato Donald's Gender Ducking," in *Disney Discourse: Producing the Magic Kingdom*, ed. Eric Smoodin (New York: Routledge, 1994), 165; and Amy Spellacy, "Mapping the Metaphor of the Good Neighbor: Geography, Globalism, and Pan-Americanism during the 1940s," *American Studies* 47, no. 2 (2006): 57–58.

forthcoming film *Fantasia*, an animated feature that uses classical music and modernist storytelling to explore world history.[41] Yet, by 1941, Disney turned his attention southward to help combat the spread of fascism and to protect US interests in Latin America. Hoping to use existing contacts with artists and composers such as Covarrubias and Chávez, he wanted to make a series of short films, which included *Saludos Amigos* in 1942 and then *The Three Caballeros*.[42]

The Three Caballeros traces Donald Duck's fictional voyage through Brazil and Mexico. The film's aesthetics continue the innovative fusion of cultural observation and animation Disney had honed in *Saludos Amigos*. A playful collage detailing Disney's team of artists in South America, their drawings, and the animation they subsequently created, *Saludos Amigos* brings to life the ethnographic underpinnings – the marketplaces surrounding Lake Titicaca, the rough and tumble lives of Argentine gauchos, the sambas of Carnival in Rio de Janeiro – of their creative process. It was what the narrator quips, "can happen to a big city [Rio de Janeiro] when a crowd of cartoonists are turned loose."[43]

In *The Three Caballeros*, Panchito, a Mexican rooster, displays the country's regional diversity to Donald and José Carioca, a Brazilian parrot who the Disney team had introduced in *Saludos Amigos*. These scenes display an ethnographic mosaic of Mexico representative of postrevolutionary nation-state formation. After introducing Donald to a romanticized Mexico, Panchito takes his friends to Pátzcuaro, Michoacán; the city of Veracruz; and Acapulco, Guerrero. These choices were not accidental. Since the First Inter-American Conference on Indian Life met at Pátzcuaro in 1940, the town and its environs had become an internationally known site for the ethnographic study of indigeneity.[44] Similarly, Acapulco was rapidly modernizing, transforming into a tourist mecca that symbolized Mexican economic development in the 1940s.

After finishing their tour of Pátzcuaro, Panchito brings Donald and José to the city of Veracruz. To depict this voyage in ethnographic terms, the film fades to black before showing the three friends traveling on a flying blanket across a map of Mexico. Before they land, Panchito tells

[41] Vaughan and Cohen, "Brown, Black, and Blues," 79.

[42] Eric Smoodin, *Animating Culture: Hollywood Cartoons from the Sound Era* (New Brunswick, NJ: Rutgers University Press, 1993), 144.

[43] *Saludos Amigos*, 2-Movie Collection with *The Three Caballeros*, Walt Disney Classic Collection, DVD, 2008, esp. 32:00–32:04.

[44] Ruth Hellier-Tinoco, *Embodying Mexico: Tourism, Nationalism, and Performance* (Oxford: Oxford University Press, 2011), 126–27.

Donald, José, and the audience, "This is the way they dance in Veracruz." Surrounded by palm trees at dusk, they watch a local band, which includes a harpist, perform the song "Lilongo." Written by Felipe Gil in 1938, "Lilongo" talks about a man who wants to dance with Lilongo. She is a *negrita*, an affectionate but diminutive colloquial expression for a black woman. There are also nine light-skinned women dancing to the song on a large wood platform. After watching the women dance, Panchito and José encourage Donald to join them. Donald asks one woman, who he calls "Toots," if he can join her. However, he struggles to learn the steps and falls awkwardly to the floor with a decided thump. To redeem himself, he stomps his feet, switching the music to the jitterbug. Originating in Harlem in the 1910s, this improvised swing dance was, by the Second World War, associated with amateur dancers. Its popularity inspired Disney's animators and other cultural producers, like Miguel Covarrubias, who moved between the United States and Mexico.[45] With comparatively greater ease, Donald woos his dance partner. Pushing the limits of this improvised choreography, he dances – or, perhaps, as it is better stated, bounces – on one hand. Although his fanciful dance moves confuse the women, they hesitantly follow his lead. To reinforce Donald's comedic style, the women chuckle and the nearby children laugh at his jazzy creativity. By the end of the scene, the music returns to "Lilongo." While the women return to their traditional choreography, Donald still dances the jitterbug in the middle of the large wood stage.[46]

Donald's encounter with the son jarocho conflates distinct musical genres associated with blackness in the Americas in a modernist fashion. From an ethnographic perspective, the scene provides a thick description of the region's music and dance. There is a wood platform; the women dance in the correct style; the band uses appropriate instrumentation, including the genre's characteristic harp; and Donald tries to seduce a woman with improvised choreography that emphasizes intricate rhythmic footwork. In racializing the genre, Disney's introduction of the jitterbug mirrored the work of Mexican composers like Carlos Chávez and

[45] For instance, Miguel Covarrubias drew *Harlem Jitterbug* in 1935. Mexican Americans also danced the jitterbug in southern California dance halls; see Douglas Henry Daniels, "Los Angeles Zoot: Race 'Riot,' the Pachuco, and Black Music Culture," *Journal of African American History* 87 (2002): 105–6 and 112; and Anthony Macías, "Bringing Music to the People: Race, Urban Culture, and Municipal Politics in Postwar Los Angeles," *Musical Quarterly* 56, no. 3 (2004): 693–94 and 699.

[46] *The Three Caballeros*, 2-Movie Collection with *Saludos Amigos*, Walt Disney Classic Collection, DVD, 2008, 54:24–57:37.

Gerónimo Baqueiro Foster who used jazz as a vehicle to ascribe blackness to Mexican vernacular music.[47] In the middle of his improvised solo, Donald reinforces these racial associations, when he tells José to "do his thing," which not coincidentally is the Brazilian samba. This African-descended genre had become a national symbol, as *Saludos Amigos* illustrates when it features Ary Barroso's famous "Aquarela do Brasil."[48] This scene also introduces blackness for Mexican audiences, who would have likely understood the reference to a negrita and, perhaps, the more obscure allusion to blackness via the jitterbug and samba. By successfully layering Donald's jazzy improvisation onto the son jarocho and equating them both with samba, Disney forged a musical and racial compatibility among the three African-descended genres.[49]

By the mid-to-late 1940s, the son jarocho had also gained national publicity, and the association between "La bamba" and the state of Veracruz cemented in the national imaginary. In 1945, Baqueiro Foster noted that "La bamba" is "the most popular son in Veracruz."[50] Between 1946 and 1952, President Miguel Alemán Valdés, the first civilian President since the 1910 Revolution, used it as a campaign song, then a symbol of his administration. Born in the small town of Sayula in southern Veracruz, he had a well-known predilection for the son jarocho.[51] A live performance of "La bamba" greeted President Harry Truman when he arrived in Mexico on March 4, 1947. Nicolás Sosa, Baqueiro Foster's mentee, often performed the genre at presidential functions. In the state of Veracruz, local groups similarly played "La bamba" when politicians from other Mexican states or from abroad visited. "La

[47] Baqueiro Foster was still thinking about the relationship between "La bamba" and jazz in 1945; see Gerónimo Baqueiro Foster to José Barros Sierra, 31 de octubre de 1945, expediente 2732 B0154 Veracruz, Ver. Cartas y documentos en relación con los huapangos, sones del Sotavento veracruzano.

[48] *Saludos Amigos*, 32:26–36:23.

[49] References to African-descended women in the music of Veracruz were not out of the ordinary; for instance, another popular song from the region is "La morena"; see Figueroa Hernández, *Son Jarocho*, 63–64; and Kohl S., *Ecos de "La Bamba,"* 182. Walt Disney Studios did not confine these cultural parallels to this scene in Veracruz. In *Saludos Amigos*, the narrator describes the rural traditional dances of Argentina before exclaiming, "Notice how closely these steps resemble the old times square dances of North America"; see *Saludos Amigos*, 22:08–23:35.

[50] Gerónimo Baqueiro Foster to Sr. D. Martín Luis Guzmán, director de 'TIEMPO,' 2 de octubre de 1945, expediente 2732 B0154 Veracruz, Ver. Cartas y documentos en relación con los huapangos, sones del Sotavento veracruzano

[51] Bernardo Ponce, "Impresiones jarochas," *Excélsior*, 16 de junio de 1944, RP-MF 04218, expediente julio 1944, CNA-BA-FE-AGBF.

bamba" became known politically as "Alemán's hymn" and geographically as "Veracruz's hymn" and "our state's hymn." It also acquired the moniker "our jarocho hymn." As a regional neologism representing the state's history of indigenous and black racial mixture, jarocho reinforced the blackening of "La bamba" and its association with Veracruz.[52]

INTER-AMERICAN MUSICAL NETWORKS AND AFRO-CUBAN MUSIC IN VERACRUZ

During the Second World War, inter-American musical networks introduced more sophisticated ethnomusicological research methods to the postrevolutionary quest to document the nation's cultural and racial landscape. Amid the modernist vogue in the 1920s and 1930s, musicologists began to search for historical and cultural commonalities among the hemisphere's indigenous-, European-, and African-descended vernacular genres. German-born Uruguayan musicologist Francisco Curt Lange spearheaded this initiative, which he called "musical Americanism."[53] Like Chávez, he hoped the hemisphere's musical elite would preserve the ethnographic and historical peculiarities of New World music. If successful, musical Americanism would enliven vernacular cultures on the verge of disappearing and resuscitate those already lost to Western modernity. Racial assumptions undergirded the salvaging, embellishing, and modernizing of these expressions. For Curt Lange, this was a question of authenticity. Indigenous music, which he thought was less distorted by urban cultures and the mass media than black genres were, needed to anchor this newfound cultural identity.[54]

Building on Curt Lange, Mexican-born US citizen and musicologist Charles Seeger institutionalized these hemispheric networks. In 1941, he established the Music Division of the Pan American Union to counteract cultural propaganda from Nazi Germany. The Music Division sought to

[52] Kohl S., *Ecos de "La Bamba,"* 51–59; Ricardo Pérez Montfort, "Acercamientos al son mexicano: El son de mariachi, el son jarocho y el son huasteco," in *Avatares del nacionalismo cultural: Cinco ensayos* (Mexico City: Centro de Investigaciones y Estudios Superiores en Antropología Social, 2000), 137–40; and Ryan M. Alexander, *Sons of the Mexican Revolution: Miguel Alemán and His Generation* (Albuquerque: University of New Mexico Press, 2016), 15–16 and 125.

[53] F. Curt Lange, "La situación de la música en la América Latina," *El Nacional*, abril 1939, RP-MF 319074 and 29536, expediente enero-noviembre 1939, CNA-BA-FE-AGBF.

[54] Francisco Curt Lange, *Americanismo musical: La sección de investigaciones musicales. Su creación, propósitos y finalidades* (Montevideo: Instituto de Estudios Superiores, 1934), 5–6 and 11–14.

foment "international understanding, friendship and peace" by disseminating musical knowledge across national boundaries. [55] Its infrastructure gave him the tools to discuss vernacular music and the broader questions of cultural exchange ubiquitous in interwar anthropological circles. Looking simultaneously in local, national, and hemispheric arenas, he sought "to fit the many little fragments of information together into one mosaic in which an evaluation of the resultant acculturation can be made."[56] The formation of American musical genres was a product of "the historical processes of acculturation among at least three great musics – European, African and American."[57]

Seeger's rhetoric of cultural contact, exchange, and inclusion unintentionally broadened Chávez's nationalist and Curt Lange's hemispherically American agendas. According to Seeger in 1946, Mexico's cultural geography spanned from the most isolated rural communities with "slight evidence, if any at all, of acculturation with European or African traditions" to the quintessentially cosmopolitan Mexico City, where there were "productions of fine-art music in a practically 'pure' contemporary European and cosmopolitan tradition."[58] Insofar as he recognized the potential for African cultural retentions in Mexican music, Seeger sat at the precipice between hiding and recognizing Mexico's African musical heritage. In isolation, the Music Division did not intend to introduce African cultural retentions to Mexican ethnomusicology. However, the Africanization of Veracruz's music was not an undesired consequence of the musical dialogues that were in search of the racial roots of all the hemisphere's musical genres.

[55] Charles Seeger, "Brief History of the Music Division of the Pan American Union" (June 9, 1947, File Copy February 5, 1951), 2, JX 1980.53.M75.B63, OAS-CML. Pablo Palomino provides a broader musical and institutional history of Seeger's Music Division in "Nationalist, Hemispheric, and Global: 'Latin American Music' and the Music Division of the Pan American Union, 1939–1947," *Nouveaux mondes, mondes nouveaux – Novo Mundo, Mundos Novos – New World, New Worlds* (11 de juin 2015), https://doi.org/10.4000/nuevomundo.68062.

[56] Charles Seeger, foreword to *Notes on the History of Music Exchange Between the Americas before 1940*, by Eugenio Pereira Salas (Washington, DC: Music Division Pan American Union, January 1943), i, Pan American Union Music Series, vol. 1, nos. 1–13, JX 1980.58.M931 no. 1–13, OAS-CML.

[57] Charles Seeger, "Foreword to Original Edition," in *El estado presente de la música en México/The Present State of Music in Mexico*, by Otto Mayer-Serra, reprint of 3rd ed. (Washington, DC: Pan American Union, 1960), xii, JX 1980.58.M931 no. 15 1960, OAS-CML.

[58] Ibid., xii.

One of the Music Division's goals was to publish the musical history of each American nation.[59] In 1946, Otto Mayer-Serra published *The Present State of Music in Mexico* in English and Spanish as the second installment of the series. Exiled from Spain in 1939, Mayer-Serra quickly took to Chávez's musical vision and became one of its principal representatives. He too stressed the multiple cultural interactions among national, indigenous, and African-descended cultures. His analysis of the huapango epitomizes the interwar period's hemispheric reformulation of Mexican mestizaje. Echoing the musicological work done before Chávez took stewardship of the musical scene, he stated that Mexico's Spanish heritage "survives in its purest form in the huapango of the Gulf coast." The genre, he continued, is "heightened by occasional syncopation, a contribution of the Negroes."[60]

Mayer-Serra's pamphlet summarizes his 1941 book *Panorama de la música mexicana*. A synthetic account of Chávez's postrevolutionary musical aesthetic, it was the product of ten months of ethnographic research in 1940. Baqueiro Foster loomed over this project, since he "not only suggested the theme ... but also constantly and tirelessly watched over the making of this book." Mayer-Serra drew directly from a draft of Baqueiro Foster's article "El Huapango," just as Herbert Weinstock had for the program notes to the MoMA's concert series. While *Panorama de la música mexicana* follows a chronological narrative, Mayer-Serra characterized it as a sociological inquiry into national culture and modern musicological methodologies.[61] Cultural interaction and mestizaje undergirded his analysis. The decade's cautious rejection of assimilation gave him the theoretical and methodological frameworks to add African and Afro-Caribbean cultures to Mexico's musical geography. The colonial

[59] Charles Seeger, "Music and Society: Some New-World Evidence of Their Relationship," in *Studies in Musicology, 1935–1975* (Berkeley: University of California Press, 1977), 182–94; and Ann M. Pescatello, *Charles Seeger: A Life in American Music* (Pittsburgh: University of Pittsburgh Press, 1992), 178.

[60] The Spanish version refers to "Negroes" as "negros africanos"; see Otto Mayer-Serra, *El estado presente de la música en México/The Present State of Music in Mexico*, reprint of 3rd ed. (Washington, DC: Pan American Union, 1960), 5 and 28, JX 1980.58.M931 no. 14 1960, OAS-CML.

[61] Otto Mayer-Serra, *Panorama de la música mexicana: Desde la independencia hasta la actualidad* (Mexico City: El Colegio de México, 1941), 9, 10, 11, and 112. On Mayer-Serra's synthesis of Chávez's musical agenda, see Otto Mayer-Serra to Carlos Chávez, 30 de junio de 1940, expediente 33 (Otto Mayer Serra), vol. 1, caja 8, sección correspondencia, AGN-FCC; Saavedra, "Of Selves and Others," 9n9; and Alejandro L. Madrid, *Sounds of the Modern Nation: Music, Culture, and Ideas in Post-Revolutionary Mexico* (Philadelphia, PA: Temple University Press, 2009), 47.

crucible, particularly the encounters between Spanish and indigenous communities, was not the only point of departure for the nation's musical heritage: African-descended music, especially those genres honed in Cuba, could be Mexican even if Mexico did not have a visible black population. In other words, he divorced biological race from his racialization of cultural and regional identities. Constant "continental influences" and "inter-American migrations" made it impossible to connect any musical element to any particular racial group or any region of the world.[62]

Mayer-Serra cast African-descended songs as more malleable than indigenous melodies, harmonies, and rhythms, because they had withstood the trials and tribulations of slavery and had produced multiple musical genres, including jazz, danzón, and samba. "Black music – in the United States of America, in Cuba and Brazil – has kept its racial essence alive (although profoundly modified by foreign influences)," he noted. It retained its quintessential features amid the materialism of industrialism, the exploitation of capitalism, and even the absence of African-descended populations. Conversely, he argued that indigenous music was unable to withstand Western economic and cultural forces; it was destined disappear everywhere but the most remote rural communities. In this context, Mayer-Serra drew on Saldívar's and Baqueiro Foster's research as he bridged Mexican and Afro-Cuban musical genres. "The ancient dances like the *bamba* in Mexico," he explained as he implicitly explored the plasticity of racial formation, could be "called *mulattoes* in Cuba."[63] Geography and culture, not biological race, anchored his analysis: "Africa – via Cuba – has left its stamp on the *huapango*, which has been exported from Vera Cruz to all parts of the world."[64]

In 1947, Mayer-Serra solidified this inter-American perspective in his two-volume encyclopedia *Música y músicos de Latinoamérica*. He read, referred to, and cited prominent scholars throughout the Western Hemisphere while he detailed the African, indigenous, and hybrid musics that defined the region. Perhaps as a response to the US-centric initiatives of Seeger's Music Division, he declared, "it is urgent for all of Latin America to know the distinct aspects of its traditional civilization, its roots and strengths to give it inertia for the

[62] Mayer-Serra, *Panorama de la música mexicana*, 131; and Otto Mayer-Serra, "Music Made in Mexico," January 1942, 29, expediente 33 (Otto Mayer Serra), vol. 1, caja 8, sección correspondencia, FCC-AGN.

[63] Mayer-Serra, *Panorama de la música mexicana*, 97, 119, 131, and 162.

[64] Mayer-Serra, "Music Made in Mexico," 29.

future."[65] Yet, reminiscent of Seeger's inter-American sensibility, he understood the formation of national musics through the fusion of African, indigenous, and European aesthetics, a process that created "an authentic language ... a profoundly American, democratic sensibility" that jazz – and, by implication, black music – represented best.[66]

Many of Mayer-Serra's entries stressed the survival of specific African cultural practices in the Americas. While he was aware of and valued African-descended music in Mexico, he also knew that it was more important in other Latin American nations, such as Brazil and Cuba. To make these claims, he cited Melville Herskovits's publications about Dahomey and Haiti as well as the Spanish translation of Arthur Ramos's *As culturas negras no Novo Mundo* (1937).[67] Cited more than forty-five times, the works of "the great folklorist and anthropologist Fernando Ortiz" were a frequent point of departure. In particular, Ortiz's *Glosario de afronegrismos* (1924), a somewhat criminological and somewhat reverential analysis of Afro-Cuban culture served as a benchmark for Mayer-Serra's encyclopedic celebration of African cultural traditions. Practically quoting from this Afro-Cubanist dictionary, Mayer-Serra defined *El Cumbé* as "a dance of African origin" that "has given us Afro-Cubanisms as common as *cumbancha* (orgy, to go on the town partying, diversion), cumbanchar, cumbanchear." He continued with a linguistic analysis of the term that also drew on his Cuban counterpart's research. "This root *kumb*," he wrote, "has diffused in Western Africa and is observed among the Congolese where *kumba* signifies making noise, yelling, roaring." As derivative as Mayer-Serra's work was, it took the existence of African cultural retentions as an empirical fact ready to be applied to Mexican music for the first time. In describing "La bamba," he cited Ortiz and alluded to Baqueiro Foster's ethnomusicological research. His analysis therefore wed some of the most prominent scholarship about African-descended cultures in the Americas to Mexican ethnomusicology. While Baqueiro Foster had etymologically rooted the

[65] Otto Mayer-Serra, untitled introduction to *Música y músicos de Latinoamérica*, vol. A-J (Mexico City: Editorial Atlante, 1947).

[66] Mayer-Serra, *Música y músicos de Latinoamérica*, vol. A-J, 133, 279, and 307; and Otto Mayer-Serra, *Música y músicos de Latinoamérica*, vol. K-Z (Mexico City: Editorial Atlante, 1947), 566–67 and 1109.

[67] Regarding Mayer-Serra's references to Arthur Ramos, see *Música y músicos de Latinoamérica*, vol. A–J, 173 and 225; for Melville Herskovits's analysis of Haiti and Dahomey, see 465 and 496 of the same volume.

huapango in Nahuatl, Mayer-Serra followed in Ortiz's footsteps and associated the genre with Africa: *bamba* needed to be defined in relation to *mbamba*, the Congolese word for game, as well as *bumbua*, which among the MPongwe of Gabon meant improvisation. To tie these terms back to the music of Veracruz and the Huasteca, he noted that "La bamba" has recently become a popular version of the huapango.[68]

VERACRUZ ENTERS AFRO-DIASPORIC DANCE

Others joined Otto Mayer-Serra and Fernando Ortiz in perceiving the cultural and musicological flows that linked Veracruz to the Afro-Caribbean. In May 1947, African American dancer, choreographer, and ethnographer Katherine Dunham visited Mexico for the first time. Her timing was fortuitous, since she was in the midst of plotting the Caribbean as a cultural area defined by its African-descended music and dance. She arrived in Mexico City in search of new ideas, ready to set replace dance programs, like *Tropical Revue*, with new ones that took inspiration from mainland Spanish America and Brazil. Little did she know but, by the end of the summer, she would buy the rights to Baqueiro Foster's arrangement of "La bamba" and turn it into one of her signature pieces.

For Mexico's cultural elite, Dunham's performances would have been another in what, in retrospect, can be seen as series of African American cultural tours through the capital city. In May 1943, contralto Marian Anderson performed at the Palace of Fine Arts. In awe of her expansive repertoire – spanning Italian operas, modern compositions, and "the incomparable 'Negro Spirituals' that ... take on sublime accents of heart-breaking emotion" – the Mexican press fêted her artistry and elegance. With her racial heritage overlaid with class, she acquired the nickname the "black Cinderella" in reference to her humble upbringing.[69] The next year, patrons of the arts could hear William Grant Still's antilynching cantata *And They Lynched Him on a Tree* performed by the OSM. As Dunham prepared for her trip in 1947, Negro Spirituals graced the airwaves of Mexico's most prominent radio stations, and the Palace of Fine

[68] Ibid., 91, 254, and 265. Also see Fernando Ortiz, *Glosario de afronegrismos* (Havana: Imprenta "El Siglo XX": 1924), 41 and 153. Regarding the ambivalences in Ortiz's thought in the 1920s and 1930s, see Robin Moore, "Representations of Afrocuban Expressive Culture in the Writings of Fernando Ortiz," *Latin American Music Review* 15, no. 1 (1994): 32–54.

[69] "Brillante debut de Marian Anderson," 19 de mayo, RP-MF00889 and 31379; and "Marian Anderson está ya en México," expediente mayo 1943, CNA-BA-FE-AGBF.

Arts again hosted African American singers, this time a choir from Sam Houston College. Its director Gilbert Allen was amazed with the degree to which Mexicans appreciated jazz as an expression of political resistance. Commenting about the warm reception they received, particularly by President Miguel Alemán, he exclaimed, "We feel that the Mexican public was motivated by the same aspirations, sentiments, and strength to arrive at the same goals as those of the black race."[70] In July 1948, African American dancer and ethnographer Pearl Primus went to Mexico City for four weeks with a pianist, drummer, singer, and six additional dancers.[71] And, in 1952, New Negro dancer-turned-French national Josephine Baker opened and performed in her eponymous Mexico City night club.[72]

African American music and dance captivated Mexicans since it reinforced the nation's antiracist mantras. Mexican cultural producers and critics claimed to appreciate art for its intrinsic beauty, not its racial roots. The black aesthetic was, as Eduardo Pallares wrote, "revenge in art." He continued by writing that it "demonstrates to the world that color does not impede being sublime and perfect."[73] This perspective mirrored the exhortations of African Americans, like Marian Anderson, who believed the United States' segregationist policies judged them on their race rather than their artistry.[74] After Alemán appointed Carlos Chávez the Director of the INBA in 1947, Chávez helped promote this variation of Mexico's claim to racial harmony. A firm believer in the celebration of art for its intrinsic value, he became a point of contact for African Americans looking to perform in Mexico's most famous cultural institutions.[75]

In January 1946, Dunham was invited to Mexico City, a request that only began to materialize that summer. Mexico was to be a jumping off point for a tour of Central and South America.[76] She was already aware of

[70] Adame, "Varía el ritmo de la música de los negros," 3 de mayo, RP-MF 18331, expediente mayo 1947, CNA-BA-FE-AGBF. Regarding the dissemination of Negro Spirituals in Mexico, see "Programa del Instituto Salvador Díaz Mirón," 8 de junio de 1947, expediente 0040 B0080, INBA/CENIDIM-ABF.

[71] "Pearl Primus Group in Mexico Theatre," *Baltimore Afro-American*, July 3, 1948.

[72] "Jo Baker Opens New Nitery in Mexico City," *Jet*, April 10, 1952, 56.

[73] See Eduardo Pallares, "El arte de Marian Anderson," 23 de mayo de 1943, RP-MF, 00903 31392 as well as other articles in expediente mayo 1943, CNA-BA-FE-AGBF.

[74] Allan Keiler, *Marian Anderson: A Singer's Journey* (Urbana: University of Illinois Press, 2000), 166.

[75] "No hay discriminación en asuntos de música," *Excélsior*, 9 de marzo, RP-MF 28201, expediente marzo 1949, CNA-BA-FE-AGBF; and Blume[nthal] to Katherine Dunham, October 3, 1947, folder 10/7, box 10, SIUC-SCRC-KDP.

[76] On visiting Mexico, see Fernando González M. to Srita. Catherine Dunham, 29 de enero de 1946, folder 7/4, box 7, SIUC-SCRC-KDP; and Tim [Durant?] to Katherine, August 7,

the African presence in other parts of Latin America and especially in the Caribbean. On March 9, 1932, she wrote to Melville Herskovits as a New Negro intellectual who had not yet undertaken any ethnographic research in the Americas. Her interest in dance was established but her desire to resuscitate Afro-diasporic cultures was still inchoate. She was interested in "a comparative study of primitive dancing," particularly of "the American Indians and such primitive groups of American Negroes."[77] Three years later, and with letters of introduction written by Herskovits, she traveled to Jamaica, Martinique, and Trinidad to begin the research that would establish her among the most prominent figures in the ethnographic study of dance. Visiting Haiti in 1936, she embarked on a project that would become "Dances of Haiti," her master's thesis in Anthropology at the University of Chicago. Beginning in the fall of 1943, *Tropical Revue* brought this ethnographic initiative to life with musical and visual representations of the everyday life of African-descended peoples from Martinique, Haiti, Cuba, and the United States, among other locales.

Dunham arrived in Mexico City in the summer of 1947. With the assistance of Chávez and Salvador Novo, she was scheduled to perform at the city's premier venues, including the Great Theater Esperanza Isis and the Palace of Fine Arts, where she danced for President Miguel Alemán, who praised her and her troupe, just like he celebrated other African American performers.[78] Because Mexicans enjoyed Dunham's performances, she signed a contract with Ciro's nightclub to extend her stay two months.[79] The version of *Tropical Revue* she assembled for her audiences paid homage to Mexico with Harl MacDonald's "Mexican Scene," a rumba from his 1934 Symphony no. 2.[80] And, at the Palace of Fine Arts, she debuted *Rhumba Trio*, a short piece that Julie Robinson

1946, folder 8/8, box 8, SIUC-SCRC-KDP. Regarding her trip to South America, see Katherine Dunham to Organizacao "ARTS" Limitada, May 27, 1946, folder 8/5, box 8, SIUC-SCRC-KDP; and Katherine Dunham to Miss Uldarica Manas, May 6, 1947, folder 10/2, box 10, SIUC-SCRC-KDP.

77 Katherine Dunham to Melville J. Herskovits, March 9, 1932, folder 12 (Dunham, Katherine, 1932–1942), box 7, MJHP-NULA.

78 Peter Waddington, "Katherine Dunham Raises Primitive Dance Art to New Heights of Sophistication," in *Kaiso! Writings by and about Katherine Dunham*, ed. Vèvè A. Clark and Sara E. Johnson (Madison: University of Wisconsin Press, 2005), 303.

79 Eartha Kitt, *Thursday's Child* (New York: Duell, Sloan, and Pearce, 1956), 102.

80 Gran Teatro Esperanza Iris, 10–17 de mayo, folder 12, box 85, SIUC-SCRC-KDP. Also see "Hola! La Katarina," *Our World*, August 1947, 40, folder 16, box 102, SIUC-SCRC-KDP.

Belafonte, a principal dancer with the Dunham Company, described as better for nightclubs than for more formal theatrical settings.[81]

Whether Dunham realized it or not, her rumbas helped Mexico enter the Afro-Caribbean world. In the late 1920s, this musical genre became a popular dance across the Atlantic. It crossed national boundaries as black laborers traveled in search of work and as modernist elites pursued new forms of musical inspiration.[82] In the United States, it became a metonym for all Afro-Cuban musical genres, a generic symbol of Latin American music, and a window into the African ancestry of African American culture.[83] In 1946, Cuban ethnomusicologist and novelist Alejo Carpentier went as far as to claim that rumbas "proliferated in Cuba, Argentina, Chile, Mexico, Brazil, Colombia, and wherever black slaves existed in the Americas." In discussing "La bamba" in 1945, *Time* called the song "the latest dance to heat up Mexico City's cool nights." Yet the magazine also confused the song's geographic and racial origins by stating that it was a "love ritual of Spanish-Indian origin" in addition to "a Mexican version of the Cuban rumba."[84]

It should not be surprising that Mexicans responded favorably to Dunham's performances. Reviewers referenced the same racial tropes bandied about when Anderson and other African Americans sang, danced, and played musical instruments.[85] Many affectionately called Dunham "La Katarina," and her face graced the cover of *Tiempo* before she arrived. *México al Día* featured her in its June 1, 1947, issue.

[81] Vèvè A. Clark, "An Anthropological Band of Beings: An Interview with Julie Robinson Belafonte," in *Kaiso! Writings by and about Katherine Dunham*, ed. Vèvè A. Clark and Sara E. Johnson (Madison: University of Wisconsin Press, 2005), 377.

[82] Robin D. Moore, *Nationalizing Blackness:* Afrocubanismo *and Artistic Revolution in Havana, 1920–1940* (Pittsburgh, PA: University of Pittsburgh Press, 1997), 166–90.

[83] Ibid., 180; and Geoffrey Jacques, "CuBop! Afro-Cuban Music and Mid-Twentieth-Century American Culture," in *Between Race and Empire: African-Americans and Cuban before the Cuban Revolution*, ed. Lisa Brock and Digna Castañeda Fuertes (Philadelphia: Temple University Press, 1998), 257.

[84] Alejo Carpentier, *La música en Cuba* (Havana, Cuba, 1961), 38; translation from Alejo Carpentier, *Music in Cuba*, ed. Timothy Brennan, trans. Alan West-Durán (Minneapolis: University of Minnesota Press, 2001), 97. Also see "La Bamba," *Time*, October 8, 1945. These ideas reinforce what Robin D. Moore calls "the commercial 'rumba craze'"; see *Nationalizing Blackness*, 11. *Time* was not alone in conflating rumba and "La bamba." As Robert McKee Irwin explains, the 1949 film *La mujer del puerto* similarly blended these genres; see "Memín Pinguín, Rumba, and Racism: Afro-Mexicans in Classic Comics and Film," in *Hemispheric American Studies*, ed. Caroline F. Levander and Robert S. Levine (New Brunswick, NJ: Rutgers University Press, 2008), 258.

[85] African American dancer Eartha Kitt, who traveled with Dunham to Mexico, echoed these sentiments in *Thursday's Child*, 85.

Introducing her to Mexican audiences, the magazine cast her as an "anthropologist and ballerina" capable of transforming Afro-Caribbean movements into quintessential expressions of modern dance. In no uncertain terms, it called her "one of the foremost intelligent and notable women to have visited our country."[86] According to journalist Jaime Luna, Dunham's *Bal Nègre*, which was slated as the replacement for *Tropical Revue*, merited particular attention. It represented the music and dance, especially jazz, that racism in the United States had perverted. Her troupe, a "black ballet" as he described it, presented "a still misunderstood Race's unknown method of esoteric choreography." His effusive albeit exoticized praise continued. He described *Bal Nègre* as "something of which we had no idea"; more importantly, it "artistically vindicates the colored race through its most genuine expressions: Love, Sorrow, Hope, Faith, Humor, all with a tragic background." A drawing of a female black dancer, likely Dunham, accompanied Luna's article. Drawn by caricaturist Ángel Zamarripa Landi under the pseudonym Fa-Cha, this image, Luna opined, "has accurately captured the thing ... the postures and behaviors of 'Bal-Nègre' in action."[87] (See Figure 5.3.)

Dunham captivated Mexican artists, just as she took to them. The *New York Times* noted that Mexico's artistic glitterati – Diego Rivera, José Clemente Orozco, Miguel Covarrubias, and Carlos Mérida – attended her performances, socialized with her, and sketched her for a book on Mexico that was never published.[88] On May 20, 1947, Fa-Cha sent her illustrations that he hoped she would use in the future. They were, what he called, "a gift like a modest tribute to the great art that you practice." The package included a caricature of Dunham, who he addressed as "The great ballerina."[89] Covarrubias, a close friend of hers from his time in Manhattan in the 1920s and 1930s, brought his students to her troupe's dance rehearsals to draw them in action. One of his caricatures eventually graced her English and Italian program guides in 1955.[90] Documented in Mexican newspapers and magazines,

86 *Tiempo*, 25 de abril de 1947, folder 15, box 102, SIUC-SCRC-KDP; and "Ritmos primitivos: Katherine Dunham, Artista y mujer de estudio," *México al Día*, 1 de junio de 1947, folder 15, box 86, SIUC-SCRC-KDP.

87 Jaime Luna, "Bal Nègre," folder 15, box 102, SIUC-SCRC-KDP.

88 *New York Times*, May 19, 1947, folder 15, box 102, SIUC-SCRC-KDP.

89 Fa-Cha to Sra. Duham, 20 de mayo de 1947, folder 10/2, box 10, SIUC-SCRC-KDP. For the image, see folder 41/4, box 41, SIUC-SCRC-KDP.

90 Folder 17761, MHS-LRC-KDP; for program guides, see folder 3, box 86, SIUC-SCRC-KDP.

FIGURE 5.3 Ángel Zamarripa Landi, drawings of Katherine Dunham Company. KDP-SCRC-SIUC.

Dunham and Covarrubias attended the same social galas as well as more intimate meals at the homes of Mexico's cultural elite. In the spirit of their mutual admiration, she also sent him a personalized signed photo of herself with the inscription: To Miguel, who must always have a special invitation."[91]

Spearheaded by Carlos Chávez, Miguel Covarrubias, and Ana Mérida, modern dance was ascendant in the late 1940s, and Dunham was one of its main attractions. The INBA established the Mexican Academy of Dance in 1947, three years before Chávez asked Covarrubias to direct a Department of Dance that would push the boundaries of choreography beyond the high cultures of European ballet and Mexico's folkloric traditions.[92] Thinking about the history of modern dance in Mexico, Covarrubias exalted Dunham's tour. "The only contribution in 1948 to dance," he remarked, "was the arrival of Katherine Dunham and her extraordinary company, who presented two long, enormously successful seasons of modern black dance with U.S., Antillean, and Brazilian themes." Her African-descended choreography was not a threat to

[91] Katherine Dunham photograph, 5/11, 133, expediente 221, UDLAP-SACE-AMC.
[92] Williams, *Covarrubias*, 179–80.

Mexican dance but, Covarrubias hoped, an inspiration for all. Thanks to her ethnographic methods, her troupe brought "an emotivity never before seen in Mexico."[93]

In addition to her well-received performances, Dunham told Mexican audiences about her research into African-descended music and dance. A panel was organized to discuss her master's thesis about Haiti, which Mexico City's *Acta Anthropologica* was about to publish in English and Spanish. With Covarrubias translating at the Palace of Fine Arts in May, she talked about her time at the University of Chicago, her research in the Caribbean, and her modernist interpretations of African and African-descended dance. An article in the Mexico City-based newspaper *El Universal* covered the event and depicted Dunham as a "loyal interpreter" not only of African American music but also of "black art." It is unclear if Dunham already knew of the African-descended cultures of Veracruz when she gave the talk. In the question and answer session, an audience member asked if she would eventually incorporate Mexican song and dance into her oeuvre. Responding like a trained ethnographer, she retorted that she needed to spend years in Mexico in order to understand the people and cultures well enough to do justice to Mexico's cultural landscape.[94]

This conversation as well as a trip to Veracruz inspired Dunham.[95] Surrounded by artists and musicians who knew of Veracruz's African heritage and its ties to the Caribbean, she eventually recognized that the coastal state had, as she stated on July 22, 1947, "a Mexican-Negro setting."[96] She did not travel to Mexico in search of new artistic inspiration; rather, this revelation was a byproduct of her own ethnographic sensibility and the cultural circles that she entered as a much ballyhooed New Negro performer. As she began to plan the trip in 1946, her project to delimit the Afro-Caribbean as a cultural area was in the midst of blossoming into a full-fledged project to document what she called "Afro-Western Hemisphere cultures."[97] By the end of her Mexican adventure,

[93] Miguel Covarrubias, "La danza [moderna]," qtd. 8, 11051–11062, expediente 219, UDLAP-SACE-AMC.

[94] "El arte negro visto por fiel interprete," *El Universal*, 9 de mayo, RP-MF 18351, expediente mayo 1947, CNA-BA-FE-AGBF.

[95] Joyce Aschenbrenner, *Katherine Dunham: Dancing a Life* (Urbana: University of Illinois Press, 2002), 139.

[96] Katherine Dunham to Mr. William Archibald, July 22, 1947, folder 10/4, box 10, SIUC-SCRC-KDP.

[97] Katherine Dunham to Mr. Henry Allen Moe, July 29, 1946, folder 8/7, box 8, SIUC-SCRC-KDP. In addition to her interactions with Chávez and Covarrubias, she knew of Otto Mayer-Serra, who was in the process of founding a cultural institute in Xalapa,

Dunham had also learned of Baqueiro Foster's *Suite Veracruzana* no. 1. In the summer of 1947, XEQ frequently broadcast his composition during its Sunday evening program "El 'Instituto Salvador Díaz Mirón' Sección Cultural del Casino del Estado de Veracruz."[98] How Dunham learned about *Suite Veracruzana* no. 1 remains unclear. Because Chávez had performed its predecessor *Huapangos* at the MoMA in 1940, she was certainly in the correct musical circles to hear someone discuss it or, perhaps, suggest that she, as an avid collector of Afro-diasporic musical expressions, integrate it into her repertoire.[99] Baqueiro Foster knew about her, even though there is no evidence that she was previously aware of his microtonal musings, ethnographic methods, or musical compositions.[100] As her troupe prepared to leave Mexico, she gained the opportunity add *Suite Veracruzana* no. 1 to her repertoire. On stationary from the Reforma Hotel, a hastily written contract dated September 25, 1947, misspelled his name but gave her the exclusive rights to perform "Bamba," "Morena," and "Balajú" in exchange for $2,000.[101]

Baqueiro Foster never explained why he sold the rights to his most famous composition. Undoubtedly, Dunham possessed the international fame to give *Suite Veracruzana* no. 1 greater visibility on the world's stage at a time when José Pablo Moncayo's *Huapango* had Chávez's programmatic ear. Dunham's aesthetic aligned better with Baqueiro Foster's than Moncayo's. Both were careful ethnographers focused on retaining the essential spirit of vernacular song and dance. Baqueiro Foster's fascination with the Afro-Caribbean world in the late 1940s dovetailed nicely with her Afro-diasporic purview. While Dunham performed in Mexico, he was reading and acquiring books to help him understand the same Caribbean musical circuits her choreography embodied.[102] The late nineteenth- and early twentieth-century cultural exchanges that brought

Veracruz; see Katherine Dunham to Mr. Melvin Parks, November 11, 1947, folder 10/8, box 10, SIUC-SCRC-KDP.

98 Expediente 0040 B0080, INBA/CENIDIM-ABF.

99 Regarding Dunham's propensity to find new musical inspirations during her travels, see Aschenbrenner, *Katherine Dunham*, 147.

100 An avid scrapbooker, Baqueiro Foster clipped newspaper articles about Dunham and other African American performers in Mexico throughout the 1940s. See many of the folders in CNA-BA-FE-AGBF.

101 Contract between Katherine Dunham and Gerónimo Baqueiro Foster, September 25, 1947, folder 10/5, box 10, SIUC-SCRC-KDP.

102 Gerónimo Baqueiro Foster, "Francisco Curt Lange y la Escuela de Minas Geraes," *Suplemento de El Nacional*, 8 de octubre de 1961, RP-MF 27427; and Gerónimo Baqueiro Foster, "Algo más sobre la música barroca de Minas Geraes," *Suplemento*

Caribbean genres like *bambuco*, *guaracha*, *bolero*, and danzón to the coastal states of Veracruz, Tabasco, and Yucatán acquired more visibility in his publications.[103] He made sure to highlight Cuba's geographic and cultural centrality. This history, he noted, "should begin first with the state of popular music on the island of Cuba."[104]

Dunham understood "La bamba" through her own ethnographic research on African-descended music and dance. She focused on its connections to the Caribbean, chiefly Cuba and Haiti. Like many musicologists who studied the huapango in the 1930s and 1940s, she used linguistics to buttress her conclusions. She contended that bamba was part of a series of African-descended musical terms – along with *chica*, *kalenda*, *bamboula*, *meringue*, *banda*, and *juba* – that survived the crucibles of slavery and colonialism in the Caribbean and across the Western Hemisphere.[105] Reflecting on this research in the first English-only publication of "The Dances of Haiti" in 1983, she gave primacy to bamba. It was a "Social or marginal socio-religious dance of Haiti, known in other islands and southern states of America." *Chica*, *congo*, and *kalenda* all were defined with the simple note "See *bamba*."[106]

In this cultural and intellectual context, Dunham utilized Baqueiro Foster's *Suite Veracruzana* no. 1 as the foundation for her ballet *Veracruzana*. Broadway composer Dorothea Freitag rearranged his composition. Orchestral instruments as well as the jazzier saxophone gave the ballet a modernist flair. After a brief vocal opening, the score commences with a danzón, continues with "Balajú" and two more danzones, and culminates with "La bamba."[107] The inclusion of several danzones points to the Caribbean cultural flows that defined Dunham's research and choreography.[108] By artfully weaving musical genres from

de El Nacional, 13 de octubre de 1961, RP-MF 27428, cuaderno 1 enero 1961 a 31 de diciembre de 1961, CNA-BA-FE-AGBF.

[103] Gerónimo Baqueiro Foster, "La Música en Cuba," *Diario del Sureste*, 8 de septiembre de 1946; and Francisco Santamaría, *Antología folklórica y musical de Tabasco*, arr. Gerónimo Baqueiro Foster (Villahermosa, Tabasco: Publicaciones del Gobierno del Estado, 1952).

[104] Gerónimo Baqueiro Foster, *La canción popular de Yucatán (1850–1950)* (Mexico City: Editorial del Magisterio, 1970), 20.

[105] Katherine Dunham, "The Dances of Haiti/Las danzas de Haití," *Acta Anthropologica* 2, no. 4 (1947): 6.

[106] Katherine Dunham, *The Dances of Haiti* (Los Angeles: Center for Afro-American Studies, University of California, Los Angeles, 1983), 67–72.

[107] Folders 1, 2, and 3, box 113, SIUC-SCRC-KDP.

[108] For a discussion of Dunham's understanding of cultural exchange in the Caribbean, see "The Dances of Haiti."

FIGURE 5.4 Herve Derrien, Lenwood Morris dancing in *Veracruzana*, 1948. MHS-LRC-KDP.

Veracruz and Cuba together in *Veracruzana*, she situated "La bamba" in an Afro-Caribbean world that connected Mexican music to Africa.

With Baqueiro Foster's music as well as scenery and costumes by Covarrubias, *Veracruzana* gained a place in Dunham's repertoire almost immediately. Planning was under way by fall 1947, and the ballet found a place on preliminary programs the following May.[109] To critical acclaim, Dunham's troupe performed *Veracruzana* in the United States and around the world. In 1950, she performed the ballet on Broadway as part of a program entitled *Rapsodie Caribe*.[110] The plot focused on three men who sought the attention of the lead woman, "The Veracruzana," the role that Dunham always took. Other performers were "'Bamba' dancers of the village" (See Figures 5.4 and 5.5). Race was a key aspect of the ballet: Dunham was "a morena." When, as was the case in Australia,

[109] Regarding the initial planning for *Veracruzana*, see folders 10/7 and 10/8, box 10, SIUC-SCRC-KDP. For preliminary performance plans, see folder 11/6, box 11, SIUC-SCRC-KDP.

[110] "This Week and After: Katherine Dunham Billed for Broadway Series," *New York Times*, April 2, 1950.

FIGURE 5.5 Katherine Dunham and Lenwood Morris dancing in *Veracruzana*, 1948. MHS-LRC-KDP.

a dancer was not of African descent, makeup was used to provide the appropriate complexion. Program notes brought the ethnographic specificity of the music of Veracruz together with the exotic language that usually peppered Dunham's revues. "The tropical state of Vera Cruz in Mexico," Dunham's Broadway Playbill explains, "is noted both for the beauty of its girls and for its native dance, "La bamba," during whose

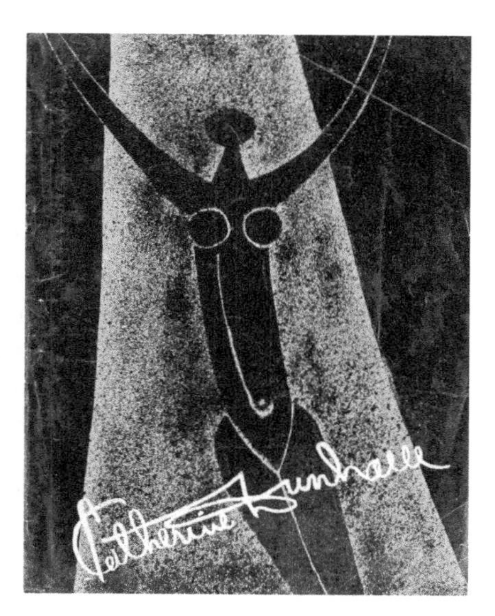

FIGURE 5.6 Rufino Tamayo, cover to Katherine Dunham Program, 1955. 2019 Tamayo Heirs/Mexico/Licensed by VAGA at Artist Rights Society (ARS), NY; and SIUC-SCRC-KDP.

course the dancers must tie a knot in a rope lying on the floor, using only their feet."[111]

In 1955, Dunham returned to Mexico with much acclaim. The First Lady María Izaguirre de Ruiz Cortines asked her perform at the Palace of Fine Arts once again.[112] She socialized with film star Dolores del Río and artist Rufino Tamayo. Taking a minimalist approach to Dunham's artistic sensibilities, Tamayo designed a cover that celebrates the black body and the clean modern lines found in her choreography (See Figure 5.6).[113] Dunham included *Veracruzana* in some of her programs, including her homecoming at Lírico Theater, which advertised her

[111] Playbill for Broadway: Katherine Dunham and Her Company [ca. 1950, May 1], folder 15, box 85, SIUC-SCRC-KDP. Regarding race in *Veracruzana*, see "La Bamba," folder 43/5, box 43, SIUC-SCRC-KDP; and "Gal from Vera Cruz!," folder Newsclippings – Dunham Press clippings, 1947–1957, vol. 2, MHS-LRC-KDP.

[112] Gabriel H. Steck, "Marlon Brando, discípulo de Katherine Dunham, será invitado a México por la famosa bailarina de color," in *Cine Mundial*, No. 817, 25 de mayo de 1955, folder "Mexico 1955 and misc. clippings," series E, box 8, MHS-LRC-KDP.

[113] For example, see "S. Hurok presents Katherine Dunham and Her Company of Dancers, Singers, Musicians," folder 3, box 86, SIUC-SCRC-KDP.

prominently on its marquee and in newspapers amid a flourish of exclamation points:

> Katherine Dunham, her ballerinas, her musicians, and her singers interpreting the ballet Veracruzana!! Judged by some! Applauded by others! And cheered by all of Mexico! Last Days! We are saying bye to Mexico![114]

Others emphasized the centrality of the exotic black body, imported from the United States but found in Veracruz. An advertisement for the National Auditorium displayed Dunham's stylized legs, exposed under a short frilly dress, wearing high heels, and ready to perform the headlining mambo. Just below, it stated that her troupe would also perform *Veracruzana*, which featured "La bamba" and Veracruz's famously beautiful women.[115]

Eight years after discovering Baqueiro Foster's composition, Dunham still took inspiration from the music of Veracruz. Placing herself at the center of this ethnomusicological project, she failed to mention his groundbreaking role in placing "La bamba" in the Afro-Caribbean world.[116] In a television interview on June 15, she discussed her interests in the Caribbean and South America. Finally, the interviewer asked, "And what about Mexico?" Her response was notably different from the one she proffered at the Palace of Fine Arts in May 1947, when she dismissed the idea of including Mexican music in her revues. This time she stated, "very strong influence to me in Mexico has been my visit to the state of Veracruz. There I fell in love with the tropical climate and the BAMBA. Perhaps Frances would sing some of the BAMBA for us."[117]

CONCLUSION

By 1955, Dunham had become a spokesperson for the African roots of "La bamba" in Mexico and across the globe. "La bamba" was not only part of Dunham's Afro-diasporic dance troupe – it was also at the center of Mexico's newfound awareness of its African heritage. The geographic

[114] Teatro Lírico Newspaper Clipping, folder "Mexico 1955 and misc. clippings," series E, box 8, MHS-LRC-KDP.

[115] "Definitivamente, Último Sábado. Katherine Dunham . . .," *Excélsior*, folder "Mexico 1955 and misc. clippings," series E, box 8, MHS-LRC-KDP.

[116] The notes for a performance at the National Auditorium only explained that the music was "arranged by Freitag"; see "New Programme For Auditorio Nacional – Saturday 25th June, 1955," folder 18/8, box 18, SIUC-SCRC-KDP.

[117] "Notes for Television Program at 291 Amsterdam, Mexico – 15th June, 1955," folder 18/7, box 18, SIUC-SCRC-KDP.

and racial connotations of this popular song had changed dramatically as a result of the pluralist ethnographic endeavors that composers, musicologists, and ethnographers initiated after the 1910 Revolution. Culturally, this indigenous and Spanish song first acquired black melodies, harmonies, and rhythms that were native to the Americas and then, in the 1940s and 1950s, musical associations with the Caribbean. As incidental and incremental as it was, the Africanization of "La bamba" was as much a spatial process as a racial one: "La bamba" traveled southward from the indigenous Huasteca to Veracruz, the state most associated with the African slave trade and therefore with the Afro-Atlantic world. Dunham did not arrive in Mexico with the intention of choreographing *Veracruzana* just as Baqueiro Foster did not arrange *Huapangos* with the goal of integrating Mexico into the song and dance of the African Diaspora. But, armed with the theoretical and methodological rigor of modern ethnomusicology, they could not ignore the African roots of "La bamba" or Veracruz's place in the Black Atlantic.

6

Caribbean Blackness

Probably in 1952, Gerónimo Baqueiro Foster argued that the "black influences in La Bamba" were "completely external and without importance."[1] The ethnomusicologist and composer who had trumpeted Veracruz's African-descended melodies, harmonies, and rhythms in the 1930s and 1940s suddenly doubted his conclusions. By the 1950s, the ethnographic mapping of Mexico's African-descended soundscapes was in decline. Radio, films, and historical accounts pushed back against the pluralist impulses of integration that had affixed African-descended musical genres to the national landscape since the Second World War. However, in the port city of Veracruz, residents continued to embrace African-descended musical genres as a window into their history and daily lives. Afro-Cuban music had tied the city's festive culture to the Atlantic world since the colonial period. *Fandangos*, rumbas, and especially counterpunctual danzones typified the genres locals performed and consumed during the Mexican Revolution and in the decades immediately after it. Disenchanted with the pace of postrevolutionary progress, the city felt estranged from a state-sponsored national culture more concerned with joining the so-called First World than with protecting the local cultural expressions, like "La bamba," that invigorated the nation's biggest and most historically significant port city.

Francisco Rivera's poetry represents the city's critique of postrevolutionary culture and politics. While the rural communities, middle-class students, workers, and lettered elites who invigorated Mexico's New Left mobilized in city streets and across the countryside to demand indigenous

[1] Gerónimo Baqueiro Foster qtd. in Kohl S., *Ecos de "La Bamba,"* 172.

rights, electoral democracy, and fair labor practices, the political critiques Rivera levied were first and foremost cultural expressions predicated on the need to reintroduce the Afro-Cuban sounds that Cold War theories of socio-economic development had dulled. Although he took inspiration from Fidel Castro, Ernesto "Che" Guevara, and the Cuban Revolution of 1959, he primarily referenced Afro-Cubanist intellectuals, like Nicolás Guillén, Alejo Carpentier, and Fernando Ortiz.[2] His verse articulates a collective cultural-cum-racial memory rooted in the history of the city's public spaces – its main square, streets, parks, and piers – rather than the political, economic, or social grievances of a particular racial community.

Rivera was a contemporary of the historians, composers, and ethnographers who, with state support, integrated African-descended cultural expressions into the national landscape in the 1940s and 1950s. Like them, he read and culled from ethnographic publications about other American nations to lend credence to his construction of blackness. He Africanized the city's history and culture, thereby allowing its inhabitants to be part of the Afro-Atlantic even if they, like him, did not consider themselves to be of African descent. He argued that the national elite needed to resuscitate Veracruz's Afro-Caribbean musical heritage by recognizing and celebrating the city's festive improvisation and polyvocality: the two pillars of the political participation that epitomized the democratic yearnings of the 1910 Revolution. Without the danzón's resurgence, the everyday forms of nation-state formation that were supposed to liberate the Mexican people would continue to oppress them and reinforce single-party rule.

RIVERA'S HISTORICAL AND CULTURAL CONTEXT

Rivera was born on February 25, 1908, in the historic district of the city of Veracruz, only a few blocks from its docks. Growing up in a modest family that needed him to sell gum and postcards, he never would have predicted that he would become a poet or that his poetry, which was published and republished for more than four decades, would eventually adorn the walls

[2] There has been a lot of research into these protest movements; for example, see Jaime M. Pensado, *Rebel Mexico: Student Unrest and Authoritarian Political Culture during the Long Sixties* (Stanford, CA: Stanford University Press, 2013); and Gladys I. McCormick, *The Logic of Compromise in Mexico: How the Countryside Was Key to the Emergence of Authoritarianism* (Chapel Hill: University of North Carolina Press, 2016).

of the city's municipal archives, where his granddaughter, Rosario Ochoa, celebrates and preserves his legacy. No one would have guessed that he would become the official chronicler of the city, with a street named after him in 1981 and an annual award bestowed in his honor.[3] He came of age not only during the 1910 Revolution but also at a moment of transition for the residents of the port city. The Porfirian government had just finished a three-decades-long project to renovate the port and provide the city with better sanitation, clean water, electricity, and other modern amenities. From 1900 to 1930, the population of the state of Veracruz increased, nearly doubling from 134,469 people to 261,223. Of the state's major cities, the population of port city grew the most. There were 29,164 residents in 1900, 48,633 in 1910, and 67,801 in 1930.[4]

In the nineteenth century, and especially during Cuba's wars of independence, Cuban exiles arrived at the port, and many chose to stay in the city and its environs as tobacco laborers, lawyers, teachers, tailors, and pharmacists.[5] As Cuban nationalists participated in the city's cultural and intellectual life, they carried Cuban politics and culture with them. Drawing on the New York City-based movement to fight for Cuban independence from Spain, they founded local branches of the Cuban Revolutionary Party in the historic district and published the newsletter *Guillermón* throughout the 1890s.[6] In 1885 José Miguel Macías – a veteran of Cuba's Ten Years War (1868–78), the President of Club Máximo Gómez, and a friend of the Governor of Veracruz Teodoro Dehesa – published a Cuban dictionary that, he hoped, would prove the linguistic similarities between Mexican and Cuban Spanish and, more broadly, establish a fellowship among Spanish-speakers on the mainland and in the Caribbean.[7]

[3] For a brief biography of Rivera, see Horacio Guadarrama Olivera, "Francisco Rivera *Paco Píldora*: Genio y figura," in *Personajes populares de Veracruz*, coord. Félix Báez-Jorge (Xalapa: Secretaría de Educación-Gobierno del Estado de Veracruz, 2010), 257–89.

[4] Andrew Grant Wood, *Revolution in the Street: Women, Workers, and Urban Protest in Veracruz, 1870–1927* (Wilmington, DE: Scholarly Resources, 2001), 3–6.

[5] Foja 109–18, vol. 350, caja 248; and foja 26–56, vol. 367, caja 261, AMV-AH. On Cuban immigration, see Yolanda Juárez Hernández, *Persistencias culturales afrocaribeñas en Veracruz: Su proceso de conformación desde la colonia hasta fines del siglo XIX* (Veracruz: Gobierno del Estado Veracruz, 2006), 191–232; and María del Socorro Herrera Barreda, "Un caso de xenofilia mexicana: La inmigración cubana entre 1868 y 1898," in *Xenofobia y xenofilia en la historia de México: Siglos XIX y XX*, coord. Delia Salazar Anaya (Mexico City: SEGOB, 2006), 181.

[6] *Guillermón*, 1897 and 1898, microfiche, 9, IIHSUV-BLCO; and Juárez Hernández, *Persistencias culturales afrocaribeñas en Veracruz*, 222.

[7] José Miguel Macías, *Diccionario cubano: Etimológico, critico, razonado y comprensivo* (Veracruz: C. Towbridge, 1885), x–xi. Also see *Guillermón*, 1897 and 1898, microfiche, 2,

Music solidified the cultural bonds between Veracruz and Cuba. In the second half of the nineteenth century, Cuban dancers and musicians, like Los Bufos Habaneros, introduced Mexicans to danzón, an offshoot of the European *contradanza* where couples danced cheek-to-cheek while swiveling their hips to the music's African-descended syncopated rhythms. By the early 1880s, this dance had gained popularity in the city of Veracruz, the state of Yucatán, and Mexico City. With the emergence of the recording industry and the radio in the 1920s and 1930s, danzón as well as other Cuban musical genres, like rumba, gained a national following.[8] Many of these Cuban musicians were of African descent, and they would have been quite visible to someone of Rivera's generation.[9]

By the 1930s, the romantic *boleros* sung by Agustín Lara and Veracruz-native Antonia del Carmen Peregrino Álvarez, or Toña la Negra as she was affectionately called, came to symbolize the nation's fascination with Afro-Caribbean musical genres.[10] Birthed from danzón, bolero was less raucous, slower, and more poetic. Associated more with the middle class in Cuba than danzón, it came to represent the modern cosmopolitan sounds of 1920s and 1930s Mexico. Also including foxtrots, bambucos, tangos, and rumbas, Lara's oeuvre gave listeners an escape from the typical sounds of Mexican music. After his first visit to Cuba in June 1932 and a second nine months later, he composed "Oración Caribe" and "Veracruz" that, as part of his *Suite Tropical*, affixed the state of Veracruz to Caribbean soundscapes.[11] His fusion of Western and African-descended musical genres, according to Mexican musicologist Daniel Castañeda in 1940, was not uniquely Mexican, but rather was something akin to the modernist aesthetics of composers across the Western Hemisphere who incorporated Afro-Cuban sounds, jazz, and

IIHSUV-BLCO; Leonardo Pasquel, prologue to *Discurso a Veracruz en su tercer centenario*, by José Miguel Macías (Mexico City: Editorial Citlaltepen, 1967), xiv; and Dalia Antonia Muller, *Cuban Émigrés and Independence in the Nineteenth-Century Gulf World* (Chapel Hill: University of North Carolina Press, 2017), 50.

[8] Jesús Flores y Escalante, *Salón México: Historia documental y gráfica del danzón en México* (Mexico City: Asociación Mexicana de Estudios Fonográficos, 1993); and Simón Jara Gámez, Aurelio Rodríguez Yeyo, and Antonio Zedillo Castillo, *De Cuba con amor . . . el danzón en México* (Mexico City: Consejo Nacional para la Cultura y las Artes, 1994).

[9] José Mancisidor, *Se llamaba Catalina* (Xalapa: Universidad Veracruzana, 1958), 10.

[10] Carlos Monsiváis, *Mexican Postcards*, ed. and trans. John Kraniauskas (New York: Verso, 2000), 179–86; and Guadalupe Loaeza and Pável Granados, *Mi novia, la tristeza* (Mexico City: Océano, 2008).

[11] Andrew Grant Wood, *Agustín Lara: A Cultural Biography* (Oxford: Oxford University Press, 2014), 14 and 76–83.

the indigenous melodies of Mexico and Peru into art music. Lara's music was therefore characteristic of any "of the music in America that has a valuable racial footprint."[12]

The son of a Spanish father and a female huapango performer from the rural town of Paso de Ovejas, Veracruz, Rivera came of age listening to the vernacular music of his home state, popular Cuban genres, and the Mexicanized versions sung by Lara. Cuba permeated all aspects of the city's daily life, something that Rivera was quick to realize. He attended a primary school named after Macías, read poems by Nicolás Guillén, and studied major events in Cuban history. As Rivera proclaimed in 1983, he learned "to love and respect Cuba" in his formative years.[13] In the late 1920s and 1930s, he worked as a waiter and a pharmacist in the states of Oaxaca and Veracruz. In 1939, he returned to the port to work at a pharmacy. Although he had always been interested in poetry and had penned a few verses in the 1930s, he did not dare become a poet until his father won the lottery. With financial stability, Rivera quit his job, traveled around the state, and began to write for local newspapers. His comic depictions of literary figures and local cultural practices were a hit. When, in the mid-1950s, he began to write for *El Dictamen*, the state's main newspaper, his local and regional celebrity increased.[14] Because of his job as a pharmacist, he even acquired the nickname *Paco Píldora*, or Paco Pill, a moniker that lovingly symbolized his jocular representations of the city of Veracruz.[15] With the publication of his 1957 epic history *Veracruz en la historia y la cumbancha*, he became known as a "humorist, folkloric poet" as well as a "jarocho poet."[16]

As the voice of the city of Veracruz, Rivera unknowingly became one of a series of local intellectuals along Mexico's Gulf Coast who preserved turn-of-the-century Afro-Caribbean musical genres at a time when newer ones, like the mambos performed by Dámaso Pérez Prado and sung by

[12] Daniel Castañeda, *Balance de Agustín Lara* (Mexico City: Ediciones Libres, 1941), 161–66.

[13] "Entrevista a Paco Píldora," in *Plano oblicuo* 1, no. 1 (Primavera 1983), expediente Reportajes periodísticos con diversos personalidades de la cultura y la política, caja Diversos reportes a Francisco Rivera Ávila, AMV-FFRA; and "Mis escuelas primarias mis condiscípulos de entonces," expediente Revolviendo Papeles, caja Cartel exposición temporal, AMV-FFRA.

[14] Guadarrama Olivera, "Francisco Rivera *Paco Píldora*," 271–75.

[15] "Entrevista a Paco Píldora."

[16] "La Semana Social," expediente Nota del libro *Veracruz en la Historia y la Cumbancha*, AMV-FFRA; and expediente Notas sobre el libro *Veracruz en la Historia y la Cumbancha*, México, D.F. 1957, caja Cartel exposición temporal, AMV-FFRA.

Beny Moré, supplanted Lara's boleros and danzones.[17] Gerónimo Baqueiro Foster encountered similar cultural elites in Yucatán. Although the state's boleros had their roots "'in mother Spain," as one of his informants told him, they had been refracted "through the marvelous prism of Cuban folklore."[18] A Yucatecan musician explained that these more recent cultural flows from Spain as well as Cuba, Colombia, and other American countries expanded the boundaries of Mexican music "through the laws of mestizaje." When faced with the statement that there were no Cuban or Colombian influences in Yucatecan popular music, many of Baqueiro Foster's interviewees "stopped him short of saying it, with the intention of showing that in earlier times these influences were strong and had produced a hybrid music of vernacular elements and bambucos, boleros, claves, criollos that have now passed into history." These musically inclined Yucatecans passionately argued that Atlantic and inter-American cultural exchanges needed to be told to younger generations so that they "do not waste away."[19]

RACE, RADIO, AND THE CARIBBEAN

Like the musicians Baqueiro Foster interviewed, Rivera felt estranged from the postwar cultural formations that sanitized the regional expressions these local intellectuals studied and performed. In the 1950s, many cultural producers, often those who had cut their teeth on the pluralist theories of the 1920s and 1930s, echoed his concerns. Radio, theater, film, and television wielded too much power. Their ability to commercialize vernacular traditions and introduce foreign cultures destroyed the nation's cultural mosaic.[20] As world-renowned artists including Diego Rivera, David Alfaro Siqueiros, and Frida Kahlo announced in 1954, the problem was that the government's cultural institutions no longer wanted to incorporate the voice of the people into national culture. For intellectuals like Rivera and José Mancisidor, the port city's heroic, seafaring, and African-descended traditions appeared to be lost.[21] In contrast, the

[17] Regarding the mambo's popularity in the 1940s and 1950s, see Vaughan, *Portrait of a Young Painter*, 56–57.

[18] Baqueiro Foster, *La canción popular de Yucatán*, 172. [19] Ibid., 85, 91–92, and 194.

[20] Profesor J. Jesús Flores Martínez, "Punto IV del Temario," expediente 2581 B0261b, INBA/CENIDIM-ABF. Also see Carlos Chavez, *Toward a New Music: Music and Electricity*, trans. Herbert Weinstock (New York: Da Capo Press, 1975).

[21] Diego Rivera et al., "Por un teatro para el pueblo: Declaración de principios," in vol. 7 of *Obras completas de José Mancisidor* (Xalapa: Gobierno del Estado de Veracruz 1982),

generation of intellectuals and statesmen born in the 1910s, 1920s, and 1930s announced a new cosmopolitan worldview that, with the assistance of the state, vowed to modernize Mexican culture and society. In the language of the Cold War, socio-economic modernization would let the country join the developed world.[22]

The postrevolutionary celebration of black cultural expressions – and, with it, Latin America's claim to be racially inclusive – was at stake domestically and across the African Diaspora.[23] In Mexico, ethnographic accounts, radio, and film nationalized the African-descended melodies, harmonies, and rhythms of the huapango and the son jarocho. By the 1950s, Baqueiro Foster even began to question the ethnomusicological value of African-descended music in Veracruz. "Some observers of the popular music of the Sotavento of Veracruz, for no reason worthy of consideration," he penned, distancing himself from his previous research, "believed to see black influences in La Bamba and, certainly, they are there; but they are completely external and without importance, and they come from the old habaneras that have left their rhythms in many songs."[24] He also reappraised the significance of Cuban music along the entire coast. Although there were varying degrees of Cuban musical influences in the states bordering the Gulf of Mexico and the Caribbean Sea, Veracruz remained unique in its welcoming embrace of Cuban and Venezuelan music. Because of the state's historical ties to the Caribbean, its inhabitants had embraced and transformed the Cuban *zapateado*, for example, more than the residents of the adjacent state of Tabasco, where the Spanish musical heritage was stronger.[25]

415–18. For a reference to the African-descended peoples of the city, see José Mancisidor, *Frontera junto al mar* (Mexico City: Fondo de Cultura Económica, 1953), 15. Ricardo Pérez Montfort provides a cultural history of Mexican regionalism and its relationship to national culture in *Estampas de nacionalismo popular mexicano: Ensayos sobre cultura popular y nacionalismo* (Mexico City: CIESAS, 1994).

[22] Deborah Cohn, "The Mexican Intelligentsia, 1950–1968: Cosmopolitanism, National Identity, and the State," *Mexican Studies/Estudios Mexicanos* 21, no. 1 (2005): 141–82.

[23] A flashpoint in the condemnation of Latin American claims of racial harmony took place when, in 1950, the Esplanda Hotel in São Paulo, Brazil, refused to give a room to Katherine Dunham. Regarding this incident and its legal ramifications, see Jerry Dávila, "Challenging Racism in Brazil: Legal Suits in the Context of the 1951 Anti-Discrimination Law," *Varia História* 33, no. 61 (2017): 163–85.

[24] Gerónimo Baqueiro Foster qtd. in Kohl S., *Ecos de "La Bamba,"* 172.

[25] Gerónimo Baqueiro Foster, "Bosquejo panorámico de la música mexicana (síntesis de una plática en el casino veracruzano)," *Diario del Sureste*, 28 de diciembre de 1947, RP-MF 17830, cuaderno no. 4, G. Baqueiro Foster Artículos – 1 de enero de 1941 a enero

Most notably, the Afro-Cuban danzón lost its Cuban heritage when it entered mainstream Mexican society. The rhythm of "the Cuban *danzón* has not really stuck, even with its half century of popularity," Baqueiro Foster asserted in 1956. In Veracruz, "they play it well and pretend to make good danzones, but nobody could say that these songs are truly veracruzano." Because of the Mexicanization of vernacular and popular music on the radio, he lamented that, "it is a difficult thing to discuss, the fact that the great popular composers of Veracruz have been trained in a metropolitan environment that necessarily bleaches and distances them from their sources."[26] In other words, the danzón's distinctly Afro-Cuban elements had been sanitized to meet the expectations of Mexican radio listeners.[27]

For example, in the late 1940s, at the peak of the "La bamba" craze, Baqueiro Foster's *Suite Veracruzana* no. 1 was performed with some regularity, but without reference to its African-descended roots. In 1947, XEQ regularly broadcast it on "El 'Instituto Salvador Díaz Mirón' Sección Cultural del Casino del Estado de Veracruz," a weekly program about the state's history and culture. Radio announcers extolled a romanticized Spanish past. At times, the program paid homage to the region's Cuban influences, particularly the "primitive Habanera Dance" that landed on the state's beaches in the late eighteenth century.[28] To Baqueiro Foster's displeasure, announcers frequently highlighted "La bamba" to such a degree that it often became the de-facto name for his composition, a simplification that not only reduced the complexity of *Suite Veracruzana* no. 1 but also ignored state's musical diversity.[29] Many of its vernacular songs, such as "El pájaro cú," were depicted as "romantic" and with "a traditional

1950, CNA-BA-FE-AGBF. On Veracruz's musical ties to Venezuela, see expediente 0249-B0622, INBA/CENIDIM-ABF.

[26] Gerónimo Baqueiro Foster, "El Estado de Veracruz, su Música y sus Músicos," *Suplemento de El Nacional*, 1 de abril de 1956, RP-MF 25129, cuaderno abril 1956 a abril 1957, CNA-BA-FE-AGBF. Emphasis in original.

[27] Ricardo Pérez Montfort, "El jarocho y sus fandangos vistos por viajeros y cronistas extranjeros de los siglos XIX y XX," in *Veracruz y sus viajeros*, by Bernardo García Díaz and Ricardo Pérez Montfort (Mexico City: BANBRAS, Gobierno del Estado de Veracruz, 2001), 157 and 180–83; and Randall Ch. Kohl S., *Escritos de un náufrago habitual: Ensayos sobre el son jarocho y otros temas etnomusicológicos* (Xalapa: Universidad Veracruzana, 2010), 23–32.

[28] "Programa del Instituto Salvador Díaz Mirón," 20 de julio de 1947, p. 1, expediente 0040 B0080, INBA/CENIDIM-ABF.

[29] Gerónimo Baqueiro Foster to Ricardo Silva, 5 de noviembre de 1949, expediente 3252 B, INBA/CENIDIM-ABF.

melody."[30] Baqueiro Foster's composition was praised for its "pure" melodic representations.[31] Similarly, radio announcers anointed him as "the most versed musicologist in the musical folklore of Veracruz."[32] Obscuring any mention of the racial and cultural origins of these vernacular traditions, one asserted that Baqueiro Foster had been successful in "conserving their essence, their traditional force."[33] On April 20, 1947, an announcer declared that "La bamba" etymologically and musically originated in Andalusia, Spain.[34] There was no mention of African or Afro-Cuban cultures, even when "La morena" was broadcast on April 6, 1947.[35]

Film also isolated Veracruz's music from Afro-Cuba. The 1948 film *Los tres huastecos* highlights a cultural geography that is distinctly Mexican, devoid of references to the Caribbean or to Africa. It begins with a map of Mexico that encircles the Huasteca. As the film zooms in on the region, the narrator states,

> La Huasteca is one of Mexico's most beautiful and picturesque regions. Just where three states meet there are three villages, which we shall call according to their state. Tamaulipeco is in the state of Tamaulipas. Potosino is in the state of San Luis Potosí and Veracruzano lives in the state of Veracruz.[36]

Los tres huastecos traces the intersecting lives of three identical triplets played by Pedro Infante: a priest from San Luis Potosí, a hustler raised in Tamaulipas, and a military captain from Veracruz. In the middle of the film, all three brothers come together for a celebration. This scene features a harpist performing music from Veracruz. To signal the beginning of a new song, one woman yells "Bamba!" when the music for "La bamba"

[30] 16 de marzo de 1947, "La Sección Cultural del Casino del Estado de Veracruz, presente en X.E.Q. . . . ," 2–3, expediente 0040 B0080, INBA/CENIDIM-ABF.

[31] 23 de marzo de 1947, "La Sección Cultural del Casino del Estado de Veracruz, presente en X.E.Q. . . . ," 3, expediente 0040 B0080, INBA/CENIDIM-ABF.

[32] "Programa del Instituto Salvador Díaz Mirón," 28 de septiembre de 1947, 2, expediente 0040 B0080, INBA/CENIDIM-ABF.

[33] 30 de marzo de 1947, "La Sección Cultural del Casino del Estado de Veracruz, presente en X.E.Q. . . . ," 3, expediente 0040 B0080, INBA/CENIDIM-ABF.

[34] 20 de abril de 1947, "El 'Instituto Salvador Díaz Mirón' Sección Cultural del Casino del Estado de Veracruz, presente en X.E.Q. . . . ," 2, expediente 0040 B0080, INBA/CENIDIM-ABF.

[35] 6 de abril de 1947, "La Sección Cultural del Casino del Estado de Veracruz, presente en X.E.Q. . . . ," expediente 0040 B0080, INBA/CENIDIM-ABF.

[36] *Los tres huastecos*, remasterizada en audio y video, El Cine de Oro Mexicano, Cinematográfica Rodríguez y Películas Rodríguez, DVD, no date, 1:29–1:56; translation provided in subtitles.

begins and later announces "Huapango!" when a huapango is performed. However, during the performance of "La bamba," the chorus references the son jarocho rather than the huapango. Similarities between the two genres – such as the use of a wood platform and the visibility of the harp – supply a regional flair, but these commonalities blend the two musical genres into a single quintessentially Mexican form bereft of any African cultural practices, ready to be enjoyed by locals, and palatable for national audiences.[37]

When African-descended cultures were visible on the big screen, they were exotic and often foreign. In the 1948 feature film *Angelitos negros* directed by Joselito Rodríguez, Infante performs in blackface for a markedly light-skinned audience. Accompanied by black dancers, he sings about "the ritual dance that black people use ... in the mangrove." This Yoruba ritual has "sexy" and "peculiar" rhythms that leave everyone who dances to them feeling "the strange influence of a ritual song."[38] An exoticized ethnographic gaze was even more prominent in Gilberto Martínez Solares's 1954 film *Mulata*. It makes frequent references to Afro-Cuban religiosity, including a *bembé* ceremony depicted through the sexualized bodies of Afro-Cuban women who rip off their clothing and, in a frenzied state, roll around topless on the beach. Perhaps for this reason, the film begins by warning the audience of the potentially lewd content:

> For the first time, a movie presents scenes of an authentic "bembé." Its incredible audacity is not immoral. Those who execute its rhythms are making a religious offering, and, far from this world, offer everything they possess, their bodies and souls, to the so-called magic of the ancient African deities. Consequently any suggestion of impurity reflect our too civilized eyes, not the pure euphoria of their frenzy.[39]

[37] *Los tres huastecos*, 48:45–54:00; also see Alegre González, "Música, migración y cine," 221–44. For another analysis of the sanitizing of African-descended music in Mexican film, see Irwin, "Memín Pinguín, Rumba, and Racism," 258.

[38] Joselito Rodríguez, *Angelitos negros*, Cinematográfica Rodríguez, 19:10–22:26. Translation in subtitles. However, I changed the word sing to song.

[39] Pedro Armendáriz, *Mulata*, Tekila Films, 2003, 1:26–1:55; and Irwin, "Memín Pinguín, Rumba, and Racism," 260–61. Dancer Yolanda Yvonne Montes Farrington, whose stage name was Tongolele, exploited these same exotic conceits. In the 1950s, she mixed African, Tahitian, Hawaiian, and Caribbean musical motifs to captivate Mexican audiences; see Vaughan, *Portrait of a Young Painter*, 84–85.

RIVERA'S LIBRARY AND AFRO-CUBANIST VOCABULARY

Rivera's verse, particularly his *Veracruz en la historia y la cumbancha*, responds to the national stereotypes that erased the city's ties to Afro-Cuba or that reduced Afro-Cuban culture to criminality and unchaste sensuality. First published in 1957, the epic poem begins with Hernán Cortés's arrival in 1519 and continues with the Atlantic economy based on slavery, tobacco, and sugar; black and indigenous resistance to the colonial regime; the wars of independence; and nineteenth-century nation-state formation. It culminates with the Revolution of 1910 and the cultural and political projects that developed in its wake. Writing for a popular audience, he hoped that the epic poem would "be used as a (free) textbook and reference guide."[40] His jocular poetry, as Victor d'Arfiere explained upon its publication, was "essential not only for the diverse topics he chose but also for the genuinely local vocabulary he employed."[41] Presumably to make it more palatable for popular audiences, Rivera followed a simple five-line stanza structure, used end rhyme, and occasionally truncated words or playfully added extra syllables to mimic popular speech patterns or to increase the fluidity of a line or a stanza.

Jarocho identity holds the epic poem together and helped make it a "decisive regional success."[42] Although Rivera was neither the first scholar nor the last to use the term jarocho to explore local culture, he innovatively grafted an Afro-Cuban vernacular onto this regional stereotype. Previously, jarocho connoted various class, geographic, and racial meanings. Dictionaries often described it as a rural field hand or rancher who lived in the areas surrounding the city.[43] Defining the colloquialism in 1885, José Miguel Macías added that, in the port city and in Cuba, jarochos could also be "individuals

[40] Paco [Francisco] Rivera, *Veracruz en la historia y en la cumbancha con una selección de poemas jarochos* (Mexico City: Impresiones Corona-Castillo, 1957), np.

[41] Victor d'Arfiere, "El sensacional libro del poeta Paco Rivera Ávila," expediente Presentación del libro *Veracruz en la historia y en la cumbancha – El Dictamen*, Veracruz, Ver., 11 de octubre de 1957, caja Danzón dedicado a Paco Píldora, AMV-FFRA.

[42] Litos, "Con toda mi estimación y aprecio para mi buen amigo Paco 'Píldora,'" 13 de diciembre de 1957, expediente Revolviendo Papeles, caja Cartel exposición temporal, AMV-FFRA.

[43] Félix Ramos y Duarte, *Diccionario de mejicanismos* (Mexico City: Imprenta de Eduardo Dublan, 1895), 320; and Francisco J. Santamaría, *Diccionario general de americanismos*, vol. 2 (Mexico City: Editorial Pedro Robredo, 1942), 141.

originating from the African race."[44] In 1924, Nicolás León claimed that the word had been harshly defined in some parts of Mexico as "a person with abrupt manners, rotten, and some rudeness." But, he noted that it could also designate people of indigenous and African descent from the state of Veracruz. In simple terms, León characterized jarochos as individuals who were half-black and half-indigenous.[45] In a culturally astute analysis of the economic exploitation of Veracruz's indigenous population, economist Moisés T. de la Peña characterized jarocho culture as a harmonious blend of indigenous, Spanish, and African biological stocks. People from Northern Africa, he claimed in 1947, had integrated into regional life to the degree that "it is no longer possible to separate them from the future of the State." Although he stressed colonial Veracruz's enslaved black population, he failed to discuss the presence of African or Afro-Cuban cultural practices in postrevolutionary society.[46] As was often the case in national histories dating back to the nineteenth century, any references to Africa in the history of Veracruz were confined to slavery, the actions of Gaspar Yanga, and the African-descended communities who resided in the state.[47]

In constructing a jarocho identity, Rivera built upon the racialized definitions that linked the term with an African ancestry. Even though Macías emphasized indigenous and Spanish languages more than African ones, the linguistic commonalities between Cuban and port life that he outlined were the closest to Rivera's formulation.[48] To highlight the port's urban features, Rivera dismissed the rural traits that were occasionally affiliated with the term. In a strategic move to ascribe Afro-Cuban culture to local identity, he used an Afro-Cubanist vocabulary in *Veracruz en la historia y la cumbancha*. However, the lack of explicit references to or citations of Cuban nationalists like Nicolás Guillén, Alejo Carpentier, and Fernando Ortiz obscure his appropriation of an Afro-Cuban dialect.[49]

[44] Macías, *Diccionario cubano*, 724. For other accounts of jarocho identity in the nineteenth century, see Ballesteros Páez, "La visión de viajeros europeos de la primera mitad del XIX de los afromexicanos," 200.

[45] León, *Las castas del México colonial*, 24 and figure 24.

[46] Moisés T. de la Peña, *Veracruz económico*, vol. 1 (Mexico City: Gobierno del Estado de Veracruz, 1946), 233.

[47] Ibid., 233; *Veracruz (Apuntes históricos)* (Mexico City: Secretaría de Educación Pública, 1947), 34; and Felipe Montemayor, *La población de Veracruz: Historia de lenguas. Culturas actuales. Rasgos físicos de la población* (Gobierno de Veracruz, 1950–1956), 14.

[48] Macías, *Diccionario cubano*, x.

[49] José Luis Melgarejo Vivanco made similar claims about the history and historiography of the city and state of Veracruz in 1960; see *Breve historia de Veracruz* (Xalapa: Universidad Veracruzana, 1960), esp. 266–68.

The title *Veracruz en la historia y la cumbancha* alludes to these linguistic connections. The word *cumbancha* was important to Rivera, since the epic's original title was the much shorter *Conquista y la cumbancha*.[50] In Cuba, cumbancha is a party that is often accompanied by live rumba music.[51] From a criminological perspective, Ortiz defined it in his *Glosario de afronegrismos* as an "orgy, partying, revelry, messy fun and noisy." It was "a term of African lineage, a derivation from the cumbé, [an] ancient black dance."[52] However, cumbancha was not in common parlance in Mexico; it had only entered musicological discussions that cited Ortiz's glossary.[53] In popular culture, Agustín Lara and Toña la Negra sang "La Cumbancha" (1934), a song that asked if the rhythmic sounds of harpsichords, bongos, and maracas made people forget troubling moments from their past.[54] While their lyrics associate cumbancha with laughter, they also strengthen the implicit connection between local festivities and African-descended cultures by mentioning African percussive instruments.

Rivera's personal library also points to his interest in Afro-Cubanist thought. His collection includes Nicolás Guillén's classic poetry collection *Sóngoro cosongo* (1931) and Alejo Carpentier's canonical *La música en Cuba* (1946).[55] Although it is not possible to know when Rivera acquired these texts, the fact that he owned first editions indicates that he was most likely concerned with Afro-Cubanism before he published *Veracruz en la historia y la cumbancha* in 1957. Throughout the 1960s and 1970s, he acquired more books by and about Guillén, Carpentier, and Ortiz.[56]

[50] Litos, "Con toda mi estimación y aprecio para mi buen amigo Paco 'Píldora.'"

[51] Hughes, *Autobiography*, 44. [52] Ortiz, *Glosario de afronegrismos*, 153.

[53] For discussion of cumbancha, see Mayer-Serra, *Música y músicos de Latinoamérica*, vol. A–J, 254.

[54] Hugo Argüelles provides lyrics to "La Cumbancha" in *Teatro vario*, vol. 4 (Mexico City: Fondo de Cultura Económica, 1998), 271. Also see Loaeza and Granados, *Mi novia, la tristeza*, 288.

[55] Nicolás Guillén, *Sóngoro consongo* (Havana, Cuba, 1931), 811–13A, AMV-FFRA; and Alejo Carpentier, *La música en Cuba* (Mexico City: Fondo de Cultura Económica, 1946), 780–4, AMV-FFRA.

[56] Nicolás Guillén, *Antología mayor/El son entero y otros poemas* (Havana, Cuba: Ediciones Unión, 1964), 811–11, AMV-FFRA; Alejo Carpentier, *Concierto barroco* (Mexico City: Siglo Veintiuno Editores, 1979), 813–7, AMV-FFRA; Fernando Ortiz, *La africanía de la música folklórica de Cuba* (Havana, Cuba: Editorial Universitaria, 1965), 780–11, AMV-FFRA; Ángel Augier, *Nicolás Guillén* (Havana, Cuba: Unidad Productora, 1971), 811–2, AMV-FFRA; and Ángel Augier, *La revolución cubana en la poesía de Nicolás Guillén* (Havana, Cuba: Editorial Letra Cubanas, 1979), 811–1, AMV-FFRA.

Although he did not own it, Ortiz's voluminous *Glosario de afronegrismos* (1924) most likely provided him with much of the vocabulary, such as cumbancha, that he deployed in his epic history of the port city.

Afro-Cuban society fascinated Rivera. As he reflected in 1983, his poem "Cundingo" "utilized Cuban terms like 'ocambo'" to mimic how "they talk in the ñáñigo dialect to the old blacks in Cuba."[57] Two years later, in his reoccurring column for the local newspaper *Notiver*, he linked Afro-Cubanist scholarship to the city of Veracruz's musical scene. Citing Carpentier's *La música en Cuba*, Rivera wrote that the Argentine tangos performed in the port possessed an African heritage and consequently were not just a derivation of European musical genres. Like the rumbas and *yambús* that also traveled from Africa, via Spain, to Cuba, Argentina, Mexico, Brazil, and other nations in the Western Hemisphere, these tangos were a product of "the coming and going of the black rhythms and dances in America and Spain and vice-versa." Drawing on Ortiz, Rivera noted that ñáñigo music originated in West Africa and could be found throughout the Americas. Although it was typically depicted as Afro-Cuban, this genre did not inhere in "a race, a people, or a country." It was present in any community with individuals who participated in the secret society. As he cited Carpentier and Ortiz, Rivera grafted their analyses of African-descended music onto his own cultural observations. Collectively, these ideas supported his belief that Afro-Cuban culture could flourish anywhere, even where blackness was not socially and demographically visible. More importantly, he hoped others, after reading his poetry, would reclaim the city's African roots. In 1985, he told his readers that he owned a small collection of books about African music and the African-descended peoples of the Americas. "If they interest you," he concluded, "you can borrow them."[58] This social consciousness and desire to disseminate knowledge about African and Afro-Cuban music reinforced his belief that *Veracruz en la historia y la cumbancha* should be available to all people who want to read it.

[57] See Francisco Rivera, "Cundingo," in *Veracruz en la historia y en la cumbancha: Poemas jarochos*, 2nd ed. (Veracruz: Juan Carlos Lara Prado, 1994), 114–16, esp. line 62; and "Entrevista a Paco Píldora."

[58] Paco Píldora, "Revolviendo Papeles: Fernando Ortiz. La Africanía de la música folklórica de Cuba," expediente Revolviendo Papeles, caja Cartel exposición temporal, AMV-FFRA.

JAROCHO IDENTITY IN VERACRUZ EN LA HISTORIA Y LA CUMBANCHA

Rivera wove myriad sounds – waves hitting the beach, musical rhythms, and the cacophony of political debate – throughout *Veracruz en la historia y la cumbancha*. These associations were not new, for the sea had been a constant motif among the state's poets and songwriters, including Lara, who saw the Atlantic Ocean, with all its shimmering colors, noises, and peoples, as a muse.[59] For Rivera, the Atlantic's currents carried Spanish settlers and enslaved Africans to Veracruz's shores. Although indigenous peoples inhabited Mexico before Cortés arrived in 1519, he depicted the majestic beaches and waters of the port as seemingly virgin land:

> Blue sky and white beaches
> white feathers of the birds;
> and silent and serious
> – like the sturdy watchtowers –
> two emerald islets
>
> Cielo azul y blancas playas
> albo plumón de las aves;
> y taciturnas y graves
> – como recias atalayas –
> dos islotes de esmeralda.[60]

While the land was silent, the Caribbean brought the sounds of crashing waves and conch shells to everyone's ears. In other words, for Veracruz to be jarocho, it had to be tied to the Atlantic and the multilingual, multiracial peoples who rode its ocean currents.[61]

Like other historians of Veracruz, Rivera frequently mentioned the constant arrival and departure of merchant ships during the colonial period. Economic exchange as well as the exploitation and, at times, enslavement of indigenous communities caused them to mix racially and

[59] Adalberto A. Esteva, "Ante el mar de Veracruz: A Pablo Macedo," in vol. 1 of *Veracruz: Dos siglos de poesía (XIX y XX)*, ed. Esther Hernández Palacios y Ángel José Fernández (Mexico City: Consejo Nacional para la Cultura y las Artes, 1991), 374; and Wood, *Agustín Lara*, 102–3.

[60] Rivera, *Veracruz en la historia y la cumbancha con una selección de poemas jarochos* (1957), 9 lines 1–5.

[61] Ibid., 9 lines 8–10. The multiracial, seafaring, and raucous traditions that Rivera equated with the port city resembles how Peter Linebaugh and Marcus Rediker describe subaltern communities in the Atlantic world in *The Many-Headed Hydra: Sailors, Slaves, Commoners, and the Hidden History of the Revolutionary Atlantic* (Boston: Beacon Press, 2000).

culturally with the Spanish population. The Atlantic economy also helped develop the city's infrastructure:

> It grows, grows like lavender
> the Vera Cruz, dressed up,
> the Cove, the royal pier,
> – the danzones from Havana –
> The parish church, the hospital.
>
> Crece, crece como espliego
> la Vera Cruz, se engalana,
> la Caleta, el muelle real,
> – los danzones de la Habana –
> La parroquia, el hospital.[62]

In discussing city's expansion in the early to mid-sixteenth century, he noted the building of hospitals and churches, two key features of Spanish civilization and Western modernity, as well as the arrival of danzón. His reference to the Cuban dance was strategic and anachronistic, considering that, by the 1950s, ethnomusicologists commonly thought that African-descended musicians, particularly Miguel Faílde, performed danzón for the first time in the late 1870s.[63] By situating the origins of the genre in the early colonial period, he established it as a foundational aspect of the city's history and culture.

With the forced importation of enslaved Africans, Rivera explained that a caste population composed of creoles, mestizos, and mulattoes took hold of the city.[64] In other words, African slavery was critical for the development of the colonial economy and the racially mixed population that would eventually become the Mexican citizenry:

> They arrive from the Windward Islands
> the blacks and the good tobacco,
> Buitrón opens its stores
> – selling fermented drinks and stews
> and growing the population –
>
> Nos llegan de Barlovento
> los negros y el buen tabaco,
> abre sus ventas Buitrón

[62] Rivera, *Veracruz en la historia y la cumbancha con una selección de poemas jarochos* (1957), 10 lines 36–40.

[63] Carpentier, *La música en Cuba*, 135–36. However, Hettie Malcomson explains that the first danzones were composed as early as 1813; see "The 'Routes' and 'Roots' of *danzón*: A Critique of the History of a Genre," *Popular Music* 30, no. 2 (2011): 267.

[64] Rivera, *Veracruz en la historia y la cumbancha con una selección de poemas jarochos* (1957), 10 lines 61–63.

– vende tepache y ajiaco
y crece la población – .[65]

As he clarified in 1973, the deplorable conditions at Buitrón founded, "by a miraculous coincidence," the culturally and racially hybrid origins of jarocho identity.[66]

The same transatlantic commercial routes that introduced enslaved Africans also brought pirates to sack the city. Rebutting the idea that blackness was equivalent to criminality, Rivera used Afro-Cuban music to depict the defense of the port against seafaring marauders. In romantic terms, he proclaimed,

The convicts are trained
armed with the rebambaramba,
they go up the watchtower
La Bamba sounds in the air
the musketry shines.

Se entrenan los presidarios
se arma la rebambaramba,
sube a la torre el vigía
suena en los aires La Bamba
brilla la fusilería.[67]

This musical reference to "La bamba" was also historically inaccurate. As version of the huapango, "La bamba" emerged from the Spanish fandango around 1790, not in the sixteenth and seventeenth centuries. By placing this initial reference to the song more than a century earlier than the ethnomusicological studies he read, he ahistorically rendered this quintessentially jarocho song a pillar of the city's history.[68]

There was another purpose for mentioning "La bamba." Since the mid-1800s, the residents of city and state of Veracruz prided themselves on their courageous defense of the port and the entire nation during foreign invasions, an idea that President Miguel Alemán reasserted when, in 1948,

[65] Ibid., 10 lines 11–15.

[66] "Raíz del jarocho," 16 de octubre de 1973, expediente Raíz del jarocho, caja M-V, AMV-FFRA.

[67] Rivera, *Veracruz en la historia y la cumbancha con una selección de poemas jarochos* (1957), 11 lines 56–60. Rivera's depiction of the city's heroic defense, however, glossed over Spanish fears of racial violence that encouraged the colonial state to regulate who had access to weapons; see García de León, *Tierra adentro*, 566–72.

[68] Pérez Montfort, "El jarocho y sus fandangos vistos por viajeros y cronistas extranjeros de los siglos XIX y XX," 157. The association between pirates and "La bamba" however is widespread; see Arce *México's Nobodies*, 150.

he called the port city "Four Times Heroic." In this stanza, Rivera used the alliteration between *bamba* and *bomba*, or bomb, to associate blackness with the valiant defense of the city. In another history of "La bamba," he utilized a comic strip to visualize this playful word-game. In it, the song "La bamba" etymologically and stylistically emerges from the sounds made by "La bomba" after cannons are fired to ward off attacking pirates.[69]

Rebambaramba also alludes to Afro-Cuban culture. Rivera associated this word with popular noises that often upset elites.[70] Similarly for Ortiz, it was a "scandal, disorder, confusion."[71] In this sense, bamba and rebambaramba resonate with the popular festivities that frame his entire history in verse. However, rebambaramba also refers to the classical composition *La Rebambaramba* that Cuban Amadeo Roldán debuted in 1928. Based on a libretto by Carpentier, the opera illustrates everyday life in Havana in 1830, including the popular religions of the Congolese and Yoruban slaves who lived there.[72] In *Música en Cuba*, Carpentier noted that Roldán's composition, which had been performed in Mexico, expertly fuses African motifs and modernist musical accoutrements.[73] By tying Congolese and Yoruban religiosity to the subaltern defense of the port, Rivera characterized Afro-Cuban cultures as integral – not dangerous – to Veracruz's history.

While Rivera located the origins of the city's jarocho identity in the colonial period, he specifically referenced it for the first time on the eve of the wars of independence, when a national spirit was kindling.[74] In short,

[69] Paco Rivera Ávila "¡¡Así se escribió la historia!!" expediente La bamba: *El Dictamen*, caja M-Z, AMV-FFRA. On the comic book genre role in fashioning alternative cultural narratives in postrevolutionary Mexico, see Anne Rubenstein, *Bad Language, Naked Ladies, and Other Threats to the Nation: A Political History of Comic Books in Mexico* (Durham, NC: Duke University Press, 1998).

[70] Paco Píldora, "Condes y condesas varones y marqueses de la rancia aristocracia veracruzana," expediente Revolviendo Papeles, caja Cartel exposición temporal, AMV-FFRA.

[71] Ortiz, *Glosario de afronegrismos*, 405.

[72] Alejo Carpentier, "The Rebambaramba," trans. Jill A. Netchinsky, *Latin American Literary Review* 15, no. 30 (1987): 68–70.

[73] Carpentier, *La música en Cuba*, 175–76.

[74] Rivera, *Veracruz en la historia y la cumbancha con una selección de poemas jarochos* (1957), 13 line 50. José Emilio Pacheco echoes this chronology when he explains that the term jarocho has two potential origins, either during the city's defense against the British in 1764 or as an epithet associating the city with its African-descended population that went out of favor in the eighteenth century and then reemerged during and after independence as a point of local pride; see "De Clavijero a Carranza," in *Crónica del Puerto de Veracruz*, by Fernando Benítez and José Emilio Pacheco (Mexico: Gobierno del Estado de Veracruz, 1986), 158–59.

these two identities – one regional and the other Mexican – could not be separated. They both drew on subaltern caste resistance, such as the actions of enslaved Africans like Gaspar Yanga and Mayan rebels like Jacinto Canek.[75] After all, the postcolonial soundscape included musical genres with origins in the state's history of African slavery, as he explained in relation to two classic huapangos, "El pájaro cú" and "El balajú":

> The jarocho enters at last
> and spreads through the population
> singing el pájaro Cú,
> and even the Galicians
> happily sing el balajú.
>
> Entra el jarocho por fin
> y en la población se riega
> cantando el pájaro Cú,
> y hasta la gente gallega
> canta alegre el balajú.[76]

Although Mexican identity crystallized with independence, the city's jarocho culture had not yet blossomed into its fullest self. Afro-Cuban music, like rumba, helped it solidify at mid-century. This genre represented the liberal struggles for national sovereignty that took place during Mexican independence, Mexico's victory over Austrian Archduke Maximilian in 1867, and Cuba's wars of independence from Spain, which began in 1868.[77] The city's identity continued to mature when Porfirio Díaz introduced modern amenities, like railroads and electricity. In eugenic terms, Rivera argued that the city's population finally had come of age, becoming fully jarocho at the end of the century:

> The strong and healthy population
> one hundred percent jarocha
>
> La población fuerte y sana
> jarocha ciento por ciento.[78]

[75] Rivera, *Veracruz en la historia y la cumbancha con una selección de poemas jarochos* (1957), 13, lines 26–30 and 68.

[76] Ibid., 14 lines 46–50.

[77] Ibid., 14 lines 1–35 and 18 lines 66–70. As historian Dalia Antonia Muller explains, Mexicans, especially in Veracruz, and Cubans frequently made ideological comparisons between Cuba's wars of independence and Mexico's struggles to gain and maintain independence before Porfirio Díaz came to power in 1876; see *Cuban Émigrés and Independence in the Nineteenth-Century Gulf World*, esp. 132–67.

[78] Rivera, *Veracruz en la historia y la cumbancha con una selección de poemas jarochos* (1957), 20 lines 46–48.

Having foreshadowed this idea numerous times, Rivera finally placed danzón in its correct historical context:

Veracruz vibrates in danzones,
the emigration arrives
of the happy Cubans,
they are teachers and craftsmen
in arts and the danzón.

Veracruz vibra en danzones,
pues llega la emigración
de los alegres cubanos,
son maestros y artesanos
en las letras y el danzón.[79]

Although a racially diverse set of white and blue collar Cubans arrived in the port during the island's wars with Spain and the United States, Rivera subsumed their diverse phenotypes, ideologies, skills, and cultural practices to their ability to perform danzón. Because of them, the musical genre became a "ritual [rito]" for all of the city's inhabitants, regardless of racial or national origin. In essence, danzón embodied the city's modernity, cultural identity, and racial inclusivity on the eve of the 1910 Revolution.[80]

AFRO-CUBAN MUSIC AND POSTREVOLUTIONARY DEMOCRACY

Rivera depicted a peaceful picture of the city at the turn of the century to construct an idealized jarocho identity that transcended class lines and embraced its indigenous, Afro-Cuban, and Spanish heritages. He asserted:

No scandals or conundrums
there is peace and tranquility,
with agility the jarocho
waters the entire city
his happiness and liveliness.

No hay escándalos ni brete
hay paz y tranquilidad,
el jarocho con soltura

[79] Ibid., 21 lines 1–5.

[80] Ibid., 21 line 13. Danzón, however, was fraught with racial connotations that Rivera eschewed. Prior to the 1890s, lighter-skinned Cubans associated the genre with poorer Afro-Cubans; see Muller, *Cuban Émigrés and Independence in the Nineteenth-Century Gulf World*, esp. 57–59.

riega en toda la ciudad
su alegría y su sabrosura.[81]

To paint such a benevolent scene, he downplayed the social tensions that undergirded city life throughout the nineteenth century.[82] He also mitigated the racist refrains about the inferiority of African-descended cultures and black criminality that dominated prerevolutionary conceptions of Mexican blackness and world history.

Of course, Rivera's idyllic representations of the Porfirian period, when read in relation to the revolutionary violence that followed, were also a sarcastic appraisal of Díaz's dictatorship. Turning to the first decade of the twentieth century, he was more critical of national politics. Bereft of any glimmers of social peace, his verse juxtaposes the port's heroic tenacity with Díaz's antidemocratic politics. The port city embraced Madero's call for political reform.[83] Social protest emerged when the city's ebullient atmosphere changed from raucous to revolutionary:

There are already workers protests,
unease, although apparent,
everything is in turmoil
and the people talk now
about no reelection.

Hay ya protestas obreras,
malestar, aunque aparente,
todo está en ebullición
y ya platica la gente
sobre la no reelección.[84]

Similar to his portrayal of the Porfiriato, Rivera did not merely glorify or condemn the Revolution of 1910. While praising Madero's electoral goals, he noted that many revolutionary leaders desired money and power more than they sought to democratize Mexican politics.[85] When self-serving politicians succumbed to avarice and treason, popular discontent spread, and new leaders – such as Emiliano Zapata, Francisco "Pancho" Villa, and Venustiano Carranza – marshaled popular support and initiated agrarian reforms. Divisions between indigenous communities and the lettered elite

[81] Rivera, *Veracruz en la historia y la cumbancha con una selección de poemas jarochos* (1957), 22 lines 26–30.
[82] Wood, *Revolution in the Street*, 1–20.
[83] Rivera, *Veracruz en la historia y la cumbancha con una selección de poemas jarochos* (1957), 23 lines 46–60.
[84] Ibid., 23 lines 61–65. [85] Ibid., 24 lines 31–35.

exacerbated these social and political fissures. Yet, for Rivera, the cultural, linguistic, and spatial articulations of blackness symbolized the broadest contours of postrevolutionary politics.[86]

Accordingly, Rivera traced the ebb and flow of revolutionary optimism through the port city's musical culture. When Madero's uprising introduced the expectation of democratic elections, "The Port continues to party [El Puerto sigue rumbero]," just as it had done in the nineteenth century when foreign powers invaded.[87] After the initial revolutionary euphoria subsided, and as violence continued,

> the parties of high society
> were postponed several months
>
> las fiestas de sociedad
> muchos meses se aplazaron.[88]

With the US invasion of the port in 1914, "The hot rumba sounds [Suena la rumba caliente]." Again, these rumbas represented the people's valiant defense of the city.[89] Shortly thereafter he depicted the city as

> Danzón fun and docile
> in a cumbanchero atmosphere
>
> Danzón sabrosón y manso
> en ambiente cumbanchero.[90]

His use of the term *cumbanchero*, a derivation of cumbancha, was not accidental. Danzones did not just enliven weekend bacchanalias. They were also a fundamental part of the political agitation and the proliferation of multiple voices that inhered in electoral democracy.

Rivera was not alone in associating danzón with democracy and popular protest. In the late nineteenth and early twentieth centuries, Mexicans discontent with Díaz's dictatorship embraced the liberal proclamations of Cuba's wars of independence while they advocated for political reform if not outright revolution.[91] Cuban musician and folklorist Odilio Urfé, who spent some time working on Mexican films in the 1950s, made a similar argument. "Today the danzón is justly proclaimed to be the *national dance* of Cuba," he explained, "since it often has served as a vehicle to reveal the emotions, pleasures and complaints of our

[86] Ibid., 24 line 46 to 25 line 40. [87] Ibid., 24 line 36. [88] Ibid., 25 lines 14–15.
[89] Ibid., 25 lines 64–66. [90] Ibid., 27 lines 66–67.
[91] Muller, *Cuban Émigrés and Independence in the Nineteenth-Century Gulf World*, 222–30.

people."[92] Noting danzón's ability to bring popular opinions into the public sphere, Rivera introduced it to local politics. Amid worker discontent,

> The people get caught up in the burundanga
> and in the heat of the danzón
>
> Se prende en la burundanga
> y en caliente danzoneo.[93]

The word *burundanga* gave Rivera the opportunity to make a poetic leap from the musical spontaneity and polyvocality of Afro-Cuban music to the cacophony of political rallies and popular suffrage. Meaning scandal, agitation, and jubilation, it brought a more austere political connotation to the city's free-spirited atmosphere.[94]

This revolutionary electoral impulse gathered momentum by 1917. Accordingly, and in one of the epic poem's most important stanzas, Rivera wrote:

> Speech, Rally, Danzón,
> there are already liberal parties,
> getting into the ring Domingo Ramos
> for personal merits,
> we begin democracy.
>
> Discursos, Mitin, Danzón,
> ya hay partidos liberales,
> sube al ring Domingo Ramos
> por méritos personales,
> la democracia empezamos.[95]

In recounting this history of political participation, he referred to Domingo Ramos, the city's democratically elected mayor who, in 1917, tried to pave local streets and improve living conditions for the working poor.[96] For Rivera, this historical moment signified the peak of Mexico's revolutionary potential. Local elections were taking place, and there was hope that national ones would emerge with the ratification of the

[92] Odilio Urfé, "Historia del danzón," expediente 0056 B0127, INBA/CENIDIM-ABF.
[93] Rivera, *Veracruz en la historia y la cumbancha con una selección de poemas jarochos* (1957), 29 lines 1–2.
[94] For a discussion of burundanga, see Ortiz, *Glosario de afronegrismos*, 76–77.
[95] Rivera, *Veracruz en la historia y la cumbancha con una selección de poemas jarochos* (1957), 29 lines 16–20.
[96] Wood, *Revolution in the Street*, 30.

Constitution of 1917.[97] Most importantly, this stanza explicitly links the rabble-rousing energy of speeches and the ruckus of political assemblies with danzón. Just like the weekend festivities that typified the city's everyday life, political rallies saw "the people shout themselves hoarse [el pueblo se desgañita]."[98] The multiple voices inhering in these musical and political gatherings united them, rendering this historical moment the apex of city's cumbanchera merriment.[99] Repeated throughout the rest of the epic poem, the line "Speech, Rally, Danzón" signifies this fusion of local Afro-Cuban culture and postrevolutionary democracy.

The political optimism that Rivera associated with 1917 vanished in the 1920s and 1930s. He lamented:

> The Revolution forgets
> its beginnings, its loyalty
>
> La Revolución olvida
> sus principios, su lealtad.[100]

The federal government had not made the necessary improvements, such as the rebuilding of the piers, needed to help the city's residents maintain their musical connections to the Caribbean. Elections became mere lotteries, games played among political power brokers. After Plutarco Elías Calles ascended to the presidency in 1924, oppression marked the beginning of the end of the democratic politics unleashed in 1917.[101]

For Rivera, the 1910 Revolution's democratic proclivities came to a close in 1938, when President Lázaro Cárdenas expropriated the oil industry. In discussing the period from 1917 to 1938, Rivera contrasted national political stagnation with the port city's cultural jubilance. In 1924, Carnival returned to Veracruz, reestablishing another convivial, African-descended celebration he treasured and attended annually.[102]

[97] Rivera, *Veracruz en la historia y la cumbancha con una selección de poemas jarochos* (1957), 29 lines 41–45.

[98] Ibid., 31 line 18.

[99] Paco Rivera, "El 3 de mayo: A Domingo Ramos, afectuosamente," in *Veracruz en la historia y la cumbancha con una selección de poemas jarochos* (1957), 68 lines 1–13 and 69 lines 32–34.

[100] Rivera, *Veracruz en la historia y la cumbancha con una selección de poemas jarochos* (1957), 31 lines 76–77.

[101] Ibid., 31 line 36 to 42 line 35.

[102] Rivera frequently wrote about his love of Carnival; see *Sobredosis de humor de Paco Píldora* (Veracruz: Instituto Veracruzano de Cultura, 1996), 19–48. Regarding the politics surrounding blackness and Carnival in Veracruz, see Sagrario Cruz Carretero, *El Carnaval en Yanga: Notas y comentarios sobre una fiesta de la negritud* (Mexico City:

Rumbas and danzones continued to sound. To demonstrate that revolutionary ideas still permeated local politics, he wrote that residents still deployed the slogan "Speech, Rally, Danzón" when they commented on the presidential election in 1928.[103] The nationalization of the oil industry ended any hope of revolutionary progress either locally or nationally. While many on the left celebrated Cárdenas's decree, Rivera bemoaned its economic ramifications:

> and the Port deserted,
> of the ships, there were no sign
>
> y el Puerto deshabitado,
> de los barcos ni señal.[104]

Cultural and economic ties to Cuba and the rest of the Caribbean, he explained, would continue a little longer, but they were in decline without petroleum constantly being loaded onto ships at the piers.

Criticizing postrevolutionary progress, Rivera recast the dominant historical narrative. The ruling party, the PRI, claimed that the state apparatus would unite the nation and overcome the political and social fissures left by Spanish colonialism and nineteenth-century liberalism. Conversely, he linked the PRI to the Spanish colonial enterprise. At the very beginning of the chapter on the colonial period, he proclaimed:

> The P.R.I. was erected. Lottery!
> Vote for Portocarrero!
> Photos of Jack, democracy,
> even postmen registering to vote
> and there begins our misfortune.
>
> With shrewdness, with audacity,
> the town council is founded,
> born the city of boards
> – already murmuring and speaking
> the story begins to form –

Consejo Nacional para la Cultura y las Artes, 1990); Pérez Montfort, "El jarocho y sus fandangos vistos por viajeros y cronistas extranjeros de los siglos XIX y XX," 179–83; and Horacio Guadarrama Olivera, "Los carnavales del puerto de Veracruz," in *La Habana/Veracruz, Veracruz/La Habana: Las dos orillas*, coord. Bernardo García Díaz and Sergio Guerra Vilaboy (Mexico City: Universidad Veracruzana, 2002), 482.

[103] Rivera, *Veracruz en la historia y la cumbancha con una selección de poemas jarochos* (1957), 37 line 50.

[104] Ibid., 42 lines 29–30.

Se instala el P.R.I. ¡Lotería!
¡Vote por Portocarrero!
Fotos de Jack, democracia,
se empadrona hasta el cartero
y empieza nuestra desgracia.

Con astucia, con audacia,
se funda el Ayuntamiento,
nace la ciudad de tablas
– ya se murmura y se habla
se empieza a formar el cuento – .[105]

The postrevolutionary state was nothing more than the heir to Cortés's search for wealth and power. To highlight this point, Rivera invented the campaign slogan "Vote for Portocarrero!" that referenced Alonso Hernández Portocarrero, a captain who the Spanish undemocratically named mayor of the city of Veracruz after they defeated the Aztecs.[106] The motto represented the farcical notions that the indigenous peoples had the choice to vote for Portocarrero and that Mexicans could decide whether or not to vote for the PRI.

The lack of open presidential elections and political rallies throughout the nation mirrored the cultural changes in city of Veracruz after the Cárdenas presidency. New less revolutionary musical genres, such as mambo and rural *ranchero* music, supplanted the city's cumbanchera heritage.[107] The cultural expressions that shaped Rivera's childhood and the Mexican Revolution's democratic rhetoric were not only becoming less popular but also "sickly-sweet [melosa]."[108] Even Agustín Lara, his longtime friend, unofficially went into retirement in 1953.[109] Rivera lamented this cultural erasure:

[105] Ibid., 10 lines 1–10.

[106] Fernando Benítez, "De Cortés a Humboldt," in *Crónica del Puerto de Veracruz*, by Fernando Benítez and José Emilio Pacheco (Mexico: Gobierno del Estado de Veracruz, 1986), 37.

[107] For a discussion of mambo, see Malcomson, "The 'Routes' and 'Roots' of *danzón*," 268. Regarding the popularity of ranchero music after 1940, see Marco Velázquez and Mary Kay Vaughan, "*Mestizaje* and Musical Nationalism in Mexico," in *The Eagle and the Virgin: Nation and Cultural Revolution in Mexico, 1920–1940*, ed. Mary Kay Vaughan and Stephen E. Lewis (Durham, NC: Duke University Press, 2006), 110–13.

[108] Rivera, *Veracruz en la historia y la cumbancha con una selección de poemas jarochos* (1957), 44 line 72.

[109] Loaeza and Granados, *Mi novia, la tristeza*, 329, 377, and 390; and Wood, *Agustín Lara*, 129 and 180–82.

Tradition has gone away,
the "taro" has finished
the "skullcap" and the "chestnut",
everything today is burundanga
nobody "cuts the cane" any longer.

Se va lo tradicional,
ya se acabó la "malanga"
el "casquete" y la "castaña",
ahora todo es burundanga
ya nadie "tumba la caña."[110]

The inability to remember the city's African past and its Atlantic connections – embodied in the images of cutting cane and eating tubers like taro – pointed to the sanitized cultural expressions disseminated on the radio. Rivera mourned that

There is silence and solitude
in the parks and on the streets

Hay silencio y soledad
en los parques y paseos.[111]

"Speech, Rally, Danzón" no longer bounced off the port city's streets or resonated with the cultural politics of the postrevolutionary state.

In spite of a few glimmers of democratic promise in local politics, the national scene was even less promising. Nonetheless, Rivera concluded the 1957 epic with the hope that the city's residents would unite and rebel once again:

So the time comes
to change the authorities
and there is an uproar in the spirit
among the jarocho people
for the new city council.

Así se llega el momento
de cambiar autoridad
y hay bulla en el elemento
de la jarocha entidad
por el nuevo ayuntamiento.[112]

[110] Rivera, *Veracruz en la historia y la cumbancha con una selección de poemas jarochos* (1957), 44 lines 16–20.
[111] Ibid., 46 lines 51–52. [112] Ibid., 56 lines 66–70.

TO THE SECOND EDITION OF VERACRUZ EN LA HISTORIA Y LA CUMBANCHA

Rivera's optimism at the end of *Veracruz en la historia y la cumbancha* manifested itself one year later. In 1958, he helped his friend Salvador Kuri Jatar run for municipal president of the city of Veracruz.[113] Under the sardonic banner of the Immaculate Reformist Party, or *Partido Reformista Inmaculado*, they redeployed the PRI acronym that had heretofore signified the state's postrevolutionary achievements. While the ruling party's name, the Partido Revolucionario Institucional, highlighted the institutionalization of the Mexican Revolution's democratic aims, Rivera and Kuri Jatar's variation stressed the purity of their party and the corruption of the PRI, with its tradition of having each President select his successor. Echoing the refrain "Speech, Rally, Danzón" from Rivera's epic history, they used danzones to spread the party platform and gain local support. For one meeting, they even hired a female dancer to parade around the city to the genre's rhythms.[114] After the campaign failed, Rivera turned away from politics and became the director of the city's public library in 1959.[115]

Nostalgia replaced the optimism of *Veracruz en la historia y la cumbancha*. Rivera's 1959 poem "Añoranzas" painted a somber picture of the city's future:

> Play a jarocho danzón
> that brings to my memory
> those glorious times
> of the danzonero Veracruz.
>
> Toca un danzón jarocho
> que me traiga a la memoria
> aquéllos tiempos de gloria
> del Veracruz danzonero.[116]

As labor unions aligned with the authoritarian state, Rivera's hopefulness continued to wane in the 1960s and early 1970s. Seeing the negative impact of inflation and lower wages on the city's workers, he claimed

113 Guadarrama Olivera, "Francisco Rivera *Paco Píldora*," 280–81.
114 "El segundo mitin de Sakuja," expediente Revolviendo Papeles, caja Cartel exposición temporal, AMV-FFRA.
115 Guadarrama Olivera, "Francisco Rivera *Paco Píldora*," 274.
116 "Añoranzas" in "Entrevista a Paco Píldora," lines 9–12, expediente Reportajes periodísticos con diversas personalidades de la cultura y la política, caja Diversos Reportajes a Francisco Rivera Ávila, AMV-FFRA.

that the state's interest in developing industries merely exploited the people and caused foodstuffs to become too expensive.[117] To return to their glorious past, he and some friends founded *El Chakiste*, a weekly local newspaper that he directed in 1974, after they changed its name to *El Chaquiste Versador*. The newspaper was subtitled "Juguetón y Bullanguero" in reference to the city's playful, fun-loving, and noisy denizens.[118] By the 1970s, the picturesque and satirical narrative that he wrote in 1957 had transformed into an even more biting condemnation of the PRI. The lack of popular suffrage begat sadness and a lack of confidence in the government. With each election

> We already have a candidate
> appointed by the P.R.I.
>
> Ya tenemos candidato
> designado por el P.R.I.[119]

Popular quiescence replaced the bellicose atmosphere of the revolutionary period:

> The people are no longer scared
> because they are getting used to it,
> the bad will come to pass
> between fasting and lamenting,
> declarations and tales
> and we keep waiting.
>
> La gente ya ni se escama
> porque se va acostumbrando,
> los males se van pasando
> entre ayunos y lamentos,
> declaraciones y cuentos
> y seguimos esperando.[120]

A prominent voice in the city's public sphere, Rivera updated *Veracruz en la historia y la cumbancha*. Although it is not clear when he made these

[117] See various poems in expediente "El Chaquiste Versador," Caja Así se escribió la historia, AMV-FFRA.

[118] Expediente "El Chaquiste Versador," caja Así se escribió la historia, AMV-FFRA; and Guadarrama Olivera, "Francisco Rivera *Paco Píldora*," 279.

[119] Paco Píldora, "¿Como ira la cosa?," 10 de junio de 1974, *El Chakiste*, expediente "El Chaquiste Versador," caja Así se escribió la historia, AMV-FFRA.

[120] Paco Píldora, "Catorce sobres y una estampilla," lines 5–10, 12 de septiembre de 1973, *El Chakiste*, expediente "El Chaquiste Versador," caja Así se escribió la historia, AMV-FFRA.

additions, it is likely that he made them in the early 1970s. The second edition's indignant tone mirrors the pessimism of his poems in *El Chakiste* and *El Chaquiste Versador*. Also, because it concludes in the wake of the 1968 Olympics and most likely in the days leading up to Agustín Lara's death on November 7, 1970, its chronology aligns with the historical moment in which he wrote his some of his most inflammatory attacks on the PRI.[121] The second edition, with the ever so slightly different title, *Veracruz en la historia y en la cumbancha*, continues to describe the port city as rowdy, loud, and festive. However, the democratic danzonera culture that he associated with the city in 1957 is absent in the verses he tacked on at the end of the epic. Politics – or what he called "The National Lottery" – no longer united the city and rarely provided the economic development or infrastructure that locals needed. Class divisions reigned.[122] The 1968 Olympics in Mexico City epitomized the state's desire to construct a modern veneer that hid popular discontent. Tourism, he contended, segregated the beautiful, modernized, and wealthy segments of the city from working-class communities. And, the beaches used by foreigners and national elites hid the voices of the proletarian workers.[123]

Amid these social fissures, the line "There are demonstrations, ruckus and revelry [Hay mitin, bulla y jolgorio]" replaced the slogan "Speech, Rally, Danzón" that Rivera had equated with democracy in 1957.[124] The dangerous but necessary riotousness of resistance replaced the danzón's democratic aspirations. Of course he wanted to return to a culture that

[121] As historian Andrew Grant Wood explains, Rivera was acutely aware of Lara's declining health. Rivera traveled to see his dying friend in Mexico City before publishing several articles memorializing the singer; see *Agustín Lara*, 201–4. Considering that, in 1953, Rivera wrote a poem addressed to Lara that centers him in the city's musical culture, a pillar of Rivera's conception of jarocho life, it would not be surprising that Lara's death represented a logical end point for the second edition of *Veracruz en la historia y en la cumbancha*; see Francisco Rivera Ávila, "Salutación: Afectuosamente al flaco Agustín Lara," 30 de diciembre de 1953, expediente Varias décimas, caja Fotos – Dirección general de correos, AMV-FFRA.

[122] Francisco Rivera, *Veracruz en la historia y en la cumbancha: Poemas jarochos*, 2nd ed. (Veracruz: Juan Carlos Lara Prado, 1994), 79 line 26. Also see Paco Píldora, "Inflación," 15 de noviembre de 1973, expediente El Chaquiste Versador, caja Primeras décimas, AMV-FFRA.

[123] Rivera, *Veracruz en la historia y en la cumbancha*, 2nd ed., 82 lines 19–20 and 88 lines 6–20. For an overview of the state's goals for the Olympics and how they reflected Mexican modernity, see Eric Zolov, "Showcasing the 'Land of Tomorrow': Mexico and the 1968 Olympics," *The Americas* 61, no. 2 (2004): 159–88.

[124] Rivera, *Veracruz en la historia y en la cumbancha*, 2nd ed., 79 line 48.

was both Mexican and Afro-Cuban, one that was "mulatto from infancy [mulata de pañalón]."[125] Concluding the second edition of *Veracruz en la historia y en la cumbancha*, Rivera wrote that danzón was a hollowed shell of its previous self. It was

> without conceited "strength," without mulatto,
> without the rhythm that pulls the waist,
> the old danzón wanders rootless,
> outside of time, like a suit of armor
> that extols the glory of the past.
>
> sin "ñeques" parejeros, sin mulata,
> sin el compás que arrastra a la cintura,
> vaga el viejo danzón desarraigado,
> fuera de tiempo, como una armadura
> que pregona la gloria del pasado.[126]

The city's residents had forgotten the Afro-Cuban aspects of their heritage. This was not a local problem but a national one. According to Rivera, the young countercultural generation of political dissidents who emerged on the national scene in the 1960s were unaware of the plight facing most of Mexico's popular classes. Favoring rebellion for the sake of rebellion, they were made "of meringue and coconut candy [de merengue y alfajor]."[127] They did not dance danzones or rumbas or follow in Lara's footsteps. They could not carry forth the adage "Speech, Rally, Danzón." The rock-and-roll tunes these student protesters enjoyed, he concluded, were not real music and certainly were not what Mexico needed if the country was to fulfill the democratic aims of the 1910 Revolution.[128]

[125] Francisco Rivera, "Mulata Veracruz," in *Veracruz en la historia y en la cumbancha: Poemas jarochos*, 2nd ed., 117 line 3. In 1985, to celebrate the Cuban Revolution of 1959, he clarified this relationship between the city of Veracruz and Cuba, exclaiming "AND THE JAROCHO WAS CUBAN [Y EL JAROCHO FUE CUBANO]"; see Paco Píldora, "Glosas sencillas con motive del aniversario de la Revolución Cubana," verano de 1985, expediente Glosas a un cubano, caja Primeras decimas, AMV-FFRA.

[126] Francisco Rivera, "El arremanga (Apología del danzón)," in *Veracruz en la historia y en la cumbancha: Poemas jarochos*, 2nd ed., 126 lines 15–19.

[127] Rivera, *Veracruz en la historia y en la cumbancha*, 2nd ed., 80 line 22.

[128] Ibid., 85 lines 21–50. In the wake of Agustín Lara's death, Rivera remarked that he alone continued the sonorous verses that Lara made famous. Others only made bad renditions of them and therefore were incapable of representing the port city's true spirit; see "Soneto para Agustín Lara," noviembre de 1973, caja Décimas del 21 de abril: Trípticos danzón y La bamba, AMV-FFRA. For an analysis of how rock music influenced Mexico City's urban middle-class youth, see Eric Zolov, *Refried Elvis: The Rise of the Mexican Counterculture* (Berkeley: University of California Press, 1999).

CONCLUSION

While Rivera's political objections to the PRI resonated with indigenous, working-class, and middle-class disenchantment, he employed an alternative cultural and racial language to articulate them. Assuming that the discussions of African-descended cultural practices in the ethnographic works of Ortiz and Carpentier were accurate, he applied an Afro-Cubanist lexicon to characterize danzón and rumba as quintessentially jarocho. The cacophony inherent to these African-descended musical genres best represented the city's heroic history just like they signified the democratic possibilities of the 1910 Revolution. Rivera's cultural history mirrored the pluralist ideals of nation-state formation that by the Second World War had introduced African cultural retentions to the national mosaic. It also pointed to the cultural limitations of PRI politics. The national embrace of mestizaje was insufficient, since jarocho identity was mulatto, the mixture of Mexican and Afro-Cuban cultures, histories, and identities. Local intellectuals had to guard these vernacular expressions against the homogenizing tendencies of the national culture industries that defined mestizaje as the fusion of the indigenous and the Spanish. Otherwise, as Rivera understood it, the Mexican Revolution was doomed to fail.

7

The Black Body in Mexico

In 1948, Pedro Infante starred as José Carlos Ruiz in *Angelitos negros*. The feature film tells the story of Ruíz, an internationally known singer, and his eventual wife Ana Luisa de la Fuente (played by Emilia Guiú), a light-skinned blonde woman who, unbeknownst to her, is a half-black. The plot thickens when they have a baby girl, Belén, who Ana Luisa rejects because of her darker complexion. As the film reaches its climax, and Ana Luisa learns that her dying black nanny Mamá Mercé (played by Rita Montaner) is her mother, she realizes the dangers of racial discrimination and asks for forgiveness. Framed by Venezuela's Andrés Eloy Blanco's poem "Píntame angelitos negros," which asks why there are no black angels in heaven, the film provides a window into postrevolutionary narratives about the racialized body, black visibility, and racial intolerance. Infante's use of blackface, for instance, pushes back on the egalitarian mantras of the 1910 Revolution at the same time that Ana Luisa's climactic epiphany suggests that those antiracist claims still shaped racial formations in 1948.[1]

Angelitos negros, however, does more than address the prejudicial underpinnings of Mexican society. It tackles postrevolutionary Mexico's ambivalent relationship to the black body. With the nation's African heritage outlined by 1946, ethnographers and cultural producers began

[1] Regarding the place of blackness in postrevolutionary society, see Hernández Cuevas, *African Mexicans and the Discourse on Modern Nation*, 69–85; and Arce, *México's Nobodies*, 205–12. For the historical context surrounding *Angelitos negros*, see Theresa Delgadillo, "Singing 'Angelitos Negros': African Diaspora Meets *Mestizaje* in the Americas," *American Quarterly* 58, no. 2 (2006): 407–30.

to identify African-descended communities in the contemporary ethnographic landscape and, as a result, integrated them into political debates about mestizaje, socio-economic development, and social justice. To render blackness socially visible, a Mexicanized variation of the black body, usually the racially and culturally mixed mulatto, took hold in the national imaginary. Mexicans across the nation could see African-descended peoples – or their artistic representation – in films, art, and ethnographies.

The visibility of black bodies redefined the relationship between Mexico and the African Diaspora just as it blurred the distinction between racial visibility and invisibility. An extension of the cultural brand of race trumpeted during the Second World War, the visual and ethnographic recognition of African-descended communities in certain locales expanded the social parameters of postrevolutionary mestizaje, even while it continued the postcolonial project to explore national unity through black disappearance. Blackness symbolized the successful integration of local communities into the nation-state, even if the realities encountered daily in communities in the states of Veracruz, Oaxaca, and Guerrero were less egalitarian than the national narrative proclaimed.

From abroad, African Americans were also aware of the newfound recognition of African-descended peoples in contemporary Mexico. No longer merely a place to escape Jim Crow's gaze, Mexico became another archeological, historical, and ethnographic site for the study of Afro-diasporic peoples and cultures. Concerned with the silencing of African cultural ingenuity and historical agency globally, Black Nationalists articulated a more critical vision of racial integration and a more corporeal definition of black identity than Mexican social scientists, artists, and policy makers did. The shared political sensibilities about cultural race forged during the Second World War, when Mexico briefly sat at the center for Afro-diasporic research in the Western Hemisphere, crumbled without the specter of fascism hovering over Europe and Asia. In sum, the black body came to signify two different, albeit intersecting, political projects about biology and culture, visibility and invisibility, and diaspora and nation by the 1970s.

GONZALO AGUIRRE BELTRÁN AND THE ETHNOGRAPHIC PRESENT

The year 1946 signified a new epoch in the histories of Mexico and Afro-Mexico. Miguel Alemán's election as President signaled a generational shift: the civilians who came of age during and after the Mexican Revolution had replaced revolutionary combatants as the spokesmen of national progress.[2] The former Governor of the state of Veracruz was well aware of the inter-American ethnographic projects that framed the wartime recognition of Mexico's African past and that envisioned democracy through cultural definitions of indigeneity, blackness, and mestizaje. Aguirre Beltrán likely met if not befriended Alemán before or at the First Inter-American Demographic Congress in 1943. When Alemán ascended to the presidency in 1946, Aguirre Beltrán quickly affiliated his research agenda with his political ally. That year he dedicated *La población negra de México* to three people: Alemán, Melville Herskovits, and his wife Frances.

With Mexico's African heritage documented in the annals of history, scholars and policy makers needed to link it to the ethnographic present. Aguirre Beltrán led the charge to establish the theoretical and methodological parameters necessary to trace the cultural and social legacies of colonial slavery. After completing *La población negra de México*, his intellectual trajectory and lasting influence within Afro-American ethnographic networks was not obvious, particularly because of his ties to Alemán. Herskovits feared that his protégé would no longer have sufficient time to devote to the study of African-descended peoples and cultures in Mexico or in another part of the Americas.[3] By January 1947, Aguirre Beltrán was already under consideration for various government positions, including General Director of Population and General Director of Indigenous Affairs, an office he briefly held.[4] However, as a result of what Aguirre Beltrán called the "astonishing" shift to the right in Mexican politics in the 1940s, he and other left-leaning intellectuals like ethnographers Julio de la Fuente and Miguel Covarrubias faced "the dilemma of accommodating themselves to the new situation or renounce" their government positions. Aguirre Beltrán chose to distance himself from public service and returned to anthropological research on both indigenous and African-descended peoples and cultures.[5]

[2] Alexander, *Sons of the Mexican Revolution*.

[3] Melville J. Herskovits to Gonzalo Aguirre Beltrán, September 23, 1946, folder 17 (Beltrán, Gonzalo Aguirre, 1946–1948), box 37, NULA-MJHP. These fears were aggravated by Aguirre Beltrán's inability, even with Herskovits's support in 1945, to acquire a permanent academic position; see Lewis, *Chocolate and Corn Flour*, 124–25.

[4] Gonzalo Aguirre Beltrán to Melville J. Herskovits, 2 de enero de 1947, folder 17 (Beltrán, Gonzalo Aguirre, 1946–1948), box 37, NULA-MJHP.

[5] Gonzalo Aguirre Beltrán to Melville J. Herskovits, 26 de marzo de 1948, folder 17 (Beltrán, Gonzalo Aguirre, 1946–1948), box 37, NULA-MJHP. Also see Covarrubias, *Mexico South*, xxvi; and Dawson, *Indian and Nation in Revolutionary Mexico*, 135.

Aguirre Beltrán needed to determine what aspect of African-descended identity he wanted to study next: would it be another archival project like *La población negra de México*? Or, something more ethnographic and directly attuned to the exigencies of postrevolutionary nation building? Would it focus on cultural behaviors? Socially visible communities? Or, both? Concerned with the global development of African American anthropology, Herskovits wanted him to expand his research agenda to other unexplored nations, such as Honduras, Colombia, or Venezuela. Nevertheless, Aguirre Beltrán's dedication to Mexico never wavered; nationalism guided his career more than Herskovits's diasporic agenda and comparative methods.[6] To build on the colonial data he uncovered for *La población negra de México*, Aguirre Beltrán hoped "to begin a series of field work on the mulatto population of the nation."[7] Even before visiting Herskovits at Northwestern, Aguirre Beltrán knew that an ethnographic study of contemporary African-descended communities would be needed to complement his historical inquiries into colonial slavery. In 1942, Manuel Gamio had suggested that he study the Costa Chica of Guerrero to connect his historical research into African slaves to postrevolutionary society.[8] In the *Journal of Negro History* in 1946, Aguirre Beltrán echoed this sentiment. "It is easy to prove in colonial archives the role they played in the integration of the patterns of culture of the colony," he explained, "and the persistence of their influx will surely be recognized when ethnographic investigations motivated by the Negro groups which still live in Mexico are under-taken."[9]

In 1948, Aguirre Beltrán sought funds from the INAH and the Wenner-Gren Foundation for a ten-month study of the isolated rural town of Cuajinicuilapa (or Cuijla), Guerrero (See Map 7.1). As part of the post-revolutionary impulse to document all the peoples and cultures of the nation, the Demographic Department of the Ministry of the Interior provided additional support. This new project sat awkwardly between Mexico's historical emphasis on black cultural visibility and the diasporic methodologies that embraced black social visibility. On January 28, 1949,

[6] Melville J. Herskovits to Richard Evans, April 9, 1945, folder 26 (Rockefeller Foundation, 1944–1946), box 35, NULA-MJHP.

[7] Gonzalo Aguirre Beltrán to Melville J. Herskovits, 26 de marzo de 1948, folder 17 (Beltrán, Gonzalo Aguirre, 1946–1948), box 37, NULA-MJHP.

[8] Gonzalo Aguirre Beltrán, "Gonzalo Aguirre Beltrán," in *Vidas en la antropología mexicana*, ed. and comp. María José Con Uribe and Magalí Daltabuit Godás (Mexico City: Instituto Nacional de Antropología e Historia, 2004), 18–19.

[9] Aguirre Beltrán, "Tribal Origins of Slaves in Mexico: Historical Background," 281.

MAP 7.1 Map of the Costa Chica of Guerrero and Oaxaca.

after a month of field research, he explained to Herskovits that Cuijla was "a community with a high percentage of blacks." Perhaps to translate Mexican racial formations into a language more familiar to Herskovits, he continued "there only existed four 'mestiza' families, which according to the cultural patterns of the United States would surely also be classified as black." The chasm between US constructions of blackness defined by the one-drop rule and Mexican ones built on racial and cultural mixture gave credence to the uniqueness of his research. Of course, these comparisons also risked imposing foreign racial conceptions onto postrevolutionary society. Despite the visibility of black bodies, "the majority of the cultural patterns of this community are indigenous," he observed, "even though some elements could frankly be described as black and, for others, it is not known if they are black or indigenous."[10]

[10] Gonzalo Aguirre Beltrán to Melville J. Herskovits, 28 de enero de 1949, folder 8 (Beltrán, Gonzalo Aguirre, 1948–1949), box 43, NULA-MJHP.

In a typically Mexican fashion, Aguirre Beltrán noted that racialized cultural behaviors were not inextricably bound to a particular community or ancestral line. Some indigenous peoples adopted African cultural practices just as Cuijla's African-descended residents adopted certain indigenous customs. Consequently, he continued to reference the community's racial and cultural hybridity. In September 1949, just one month before he completed the first draft of his manuscript about Cuijla, he presented the theoretical and historical underpinnings of his research at the twenty-ninth International Congress of Americanists in New York City. Pushing back on Herskovits's steadfast quest to discover Africanisms, he stated that Mexico's African-descended population was no longer "'pure' black, neither biologically nor culturally."[11] His October 1949 manuscript reaffirmed the ubiquity of the cultural and racial exchanges between the descendants of enslaved Africans in Cuijla and the more European and indigenous communities who lived nearby. Structurally, the region had to be characterized in relation to its more economically developed center, the mestizo town of Ometepec, which "serves as an intermediary for the commercial transactions, exchange of products, and the cultural mixture, exchange, and reinterpretation" among the area's indigenous, indomestizo, afromestizo, and euromestizo communities.[12] Herskovits called this new project "the first real word of any Afroamerican ethnography in Mexico."[13] Aguirre Beltrán claimed that scholarly research about Mexican communities "suffer, by default, from a gap of incalculable proportions that had to be filled with the study of the remnants of our great colonial black population." As such, he selectively embraced the often-criticized practice that Herskovits made famous: the search for the most palpable African cultural survivals he could encounter. Such ethnographic myopia encouraged simplistic conclusions, like the assumption that all "elements, features, complexes and cultural configurations – not yet identified or not held by the indigenous or the Spanish – were of black origin."[14]

11 Gonzalo Aguirre Beltrán, "La etnohistoria y el estudio del negro en México," in *Acculturation in the Americas: Proceedings and Selected Papers of the XXIXth International Congress of Americanists*, ed. Sol Tax (Chicago, IL: University of Chicago Press, 1951), 164.

12 Gonzalo Aguirre Beltrán, "Estudio antropológico de la población negra de Cuajinicuilapa de la Costa Chica de Guerrero," 1 de octubre de 1949 (1572.-1), p. 130, tomo CCXXIII, INAH-AT-CNA.

13 Melville J. Herskovits to Gonzalo Aguirre Beltrán, February 2, 1949, folder 8 (Beltrán, Gonzalo Aguirre, 1948–1949), box 43, NULA-MJHP.

14 Aguirre Beltrán, "Estudio antropológico de la población negra de Cuajinicuilapa de la Costa Chica de Guerrero," 1–2.

Aguirre Beltrán couched the romantic quest to find Africanisms in geographical terms. Migrations directly from Africa to Mexico left the purest African cultural retentions. The footprints of subsequent inter-American cultural and demographic passages were hybrid less authentic African expressions. This historical schema laid the foundation for how he affixed race to region and how he searched for African cultural retentions in contemporary Mexico. The Gulf and Caribbean coasts had an "easily accessible" African-descended presence that possessed strong historical ties to the Atlantic world. These cosmopolitan communities "had suffered frequent and continual contacts with individuals with Western culture" and were not suitable for a study of African cultural expressions. Conversely, African-descended peoples on the Pacific Coast – the offspring of the Bantu-speaking peoples of Angola, Mozambique, and Congo, as he understood them – were ideal case studies, since they "have remained in total isolation," with their cultural behaviors and physical types comparatively unblemished by cultural and biological exchanges.[15]

Incorrectly believing that the African-descended peoples of Cuijla were descendants of runaway slave communities, Aguirre Beltrán assumed that they lacked the cultural exchanges that typified black cultural practices in other parts of the country. To explain what he perceived as their cultural conservatism and comparative racial purity, he constantly referred to what he called their violent ethos, a cultural behavior born in Africa but emboldened in Mexico. As maroon communities, the town's first African settlers had to ward off Spaniards attempting to reenslave them. This survival strategy, he claimed, defined their cultural behaviors, most notably their marriage practices. While Western societies followed the practice of marriage "by asking," when the groom asks the parents of his suitor for her hand in marriage, most of the African-descended people of Cuijla practiced marriage "by robbery," the kidnapping of the bride by the groom.[16] To corroborate these conclusions, Aguirre Beltrán looked to the colonial archives he had mined for *La población negra de México*. One of his most useful sources was the 1609 inquisitional testimony of Brother Alonso de Benavides, who made similar claims about marriage customs in

[15] Ibid., 1, 138, and 140–41.

[16] Gonzalo Aguirre Beltrán to Melville J. Herskovits, 28 de enero de 1949, folder 8 (Beltrán, Gonzalo Aguirre, 1948–1949), box 43, NULA-MJHP; and Lewis, *Chocolate and Corn Flour*, 56 and 127–30. As Antonio García de León explains, maroon communities had to integrate themselves into colonial governance to ensure their survival; thus, even their existence as a free-black community required a certain amount of integration; see *Tierra adentro*, 753–54.

the runaway community led by Gaspar Yanga in Veracruz. "The distinction between 'marriage of the mountain' and 'marriage of the city,'" Aguirre Beltrán wrote, "remains in the black town of Cuajinicuilapa, Gro. – nicknamed Cuijla – despite the 340 years that passed. Now, like then, the marriage patterns of blacks, which are seen as an abominable practice, continue being a motive of profound worry for the Christian evangelizers."[17] By comparing colonial records with his observations, he assumed that these marriage practices had identical African roots and discounted the possibility that they could be indigenous or hybrid. Neither ethnographic upstreaming (the application of contemporary ethnographic evidence to the past) nor downstreaming (the use of historical sources to understand the present), this conclusion could not be proven empirically. Rather, it points to the methodological maneuvers required to explain the presence of an African-descended community in a nation that everyone assumed lacked black social visibility.

Nine years later, *Cuijla* appeared in bookstores. The social significance of black identity in Mexico in 1958 was fundamentally different than it had been when Aguirre Beltrán completed his manuscript in 1949. New information about regional, cultural, social, and economic dynamics – the sociological and historical underpinnings of mestizaje – nuanced his Herskovits-ian search for Africanisms. The catalyst for this change occurred in 1948, when President Alemán founded the INI under the directorship of Alfonso Caso. The INI brought new theories of applied anthropology and socio-economic development to Mexican indigenist policies. During its heyday in the 1950s, INI officials like Aguirre Beltrán established innovative policy programs, such as training locals to be cultural promoters and establishing bilingual hand puppet troupes, to educate and modernize isolated indigenous peoples and thus to break them free from regional mestizo domination. Conceiving of indigenous integration in interethnic terms, the INI established Coordinating Centers across the country to study relations between mestizo cities and the indigenous hinterlands. State funding also allowed the INI to solidify postrevolutionary Mexico's place at the vanguard of indigenism in the Western Hemisphere.[18]

Accordingly, the Coordinating Centers provided Aguirre Beltrán with access to ethnographic information about the mestizo elites who exploited

[17] Aguirre Beltrán, "Estudio antropológico de la población negra de Cuajinicuilapa de la Costa Chica de Guerrero," 114–15.

[18] Lewis, *Rethinking Mexican Indigenismo*, 30–154.

nearby indigenous communities. These regional dynamics, he quickly realized, resembled the socio-economic structures he had already explored among the African-descended people in Cuijla and the mestizos in Ometepec. Nonetheless, the INI armed him with new data, which he used to adjust the paradigms of culture change he learned from Melville Herskovits. Determined not only by historical context and power dynamics but also by regional racial demographics, cultural encounters varied and so did mestizaje. For instance, in the Basin of Tepalcatepec of Michoacán in 1949 and 1950, he noticed the clearly demarcated distinctions between indigenous communities who spoke native languages and nonindigenous Spanish-speaking individuals. The cultural vocabulary of the euro-, indo-, and afromestizo he honed in *La población negra de México* returned, adapted to the region's historical and cultural peculiarities. He contended that "one can consider the population of the basin in three strata: the mestizo, of a predominately Western culture; the Indian, of predominately native culture; and the mestindio, where Western and indigenous cultures are at equilibrium." There were no longer any African-descended cultures, since they had undergone regional processes of "dilution, assimilation, and extinction."[19]

The relative strength or weakness of the socio-economic bonds between locals and the Mexican state figured prominently in determining whether mestizaje was a benevolent process guided by national integration or an exploitative one buttressed by regional seclusion and mestizo domination. In regions where African slavery had not invigorated the colonial economy, blackness disappeared. Conversely, in Cuijla, where there was a critical mass of African-descended peoples, it survived even while the region's peoples and cultures mixed. In 1957, Aguirre Beltrán calculated that there were approximately 120,000 afromestizos but no individuals with pure African lineages in Mexico.[20] The search for pure Africanisms that he selectively championed in 1949 now aligned even less with the exigencies of nation-state formation or with the local realities he observed.

[19] In part to explain such awkward classificatory divisions among the Basin's residents, Aguirre Beltrán admitted that the lack of racial classification in government documents hindered ethnographic research; see Gonzalo Aguirre Beltrán, *Problemas de la población indígena de la Cuenca del Tepalcatepec*, vol. 3 of *Memorias del Instituto Nacional Indigenista* (Mexico City: Ediciones del Instituto Nacional Indigenista, 1952), 9, 12–13, and 87.

[20] Gonzalo Aguirre Beltrán, *El proceso de la aculturación* (Mexico City: Universidad Autónoma de México, 1957), 128.

By 1958, Aguirre Beltrán applied this new formulation of cultural and racial interaction to his research in Cuijla. In *Cuijla*, he argued that scholars and policy makers needed to analyze social relations beyond the schematic continuum from cultural homogeneity to heterogeneity and from purely isolated to fully integrated. Applying colonial-era and prerevolutionary stereotypes about black violence and maroonage, he assumed black isolation did not operate in absolute terms even though its legacy, what he still called "a violent and aggressive *ethos*," persisted. Aguirre Beltrán used a combination of ethnographic research and historical intuition to determine who was afromestizo and who was not. He employed a cautious language that straddled the line between the cultural mosaic he saw in Cuijla and the Afro-Americanist methodologies rooted in the socially visible communities of other nations in the Western Hemisphere. "No one could deny or affirm," he penned neither recognizing nor hiding the presence of racially unmixed black bodies, "that at one time the population of Cuijla was completely black." As close as he would ever come to establishing a racial type for Cuijla's inhabitants, he concluded, "It is undeniable also that, in this hybridization, the black element prevailed and that, consequently, the mixed-race Cuileño is currently predominantly black, that is to say, an afro-mestizo."[21]

To reveal the histories of African-descended communities required that Aguirre Beltrán account for mestizaje's local and regional variations. In Cuijla and the nearby afromestizo towns of Maldonado and San Nicolás, the preponderance of African-descended individuals, 90 percent of all locals, rendered mestizaje the blackening of indigenous and European peoples. Black social visibility had pernicious social affects in a region dominated by Ometepec's mestizo elite. Having ascended the social ladder on the back of the discriminatory refrains of the Spanish caste system, urban mestizos rejected postrevolutionary cultural pluralism and instead maintained their regional status by keeping hamlets like Cuijla isolated from the state capital of Chilpancingo as well as Mexico City. Aguirre Beltrán concluded that afromestizos, unaware of the egalitarian ideologies of the postrevolutionary state, continued to embrace colonial-era caste terms as a survival strategy to combat elite exploitation and to maintain a sense of community.[22]

[21] Gonzalo Aguirre Beltrán, *Cuijla: Esbozo etnográfico de un pueblo negro* (Mexico City: Fondo de Cultura Económica, 1958), 12, 65, and 225n87. For a discussion of the tropes of black violence that buttressed Aguirre Beltrán's research, see Lewis, *Chocolate and Corn Flour*; and Milstead, "Afro-Mexicans and the Making of Modern Mexico."

[22] Aguirre Beltrán, *Cuijla*, 69–76.

REGIONALISM AND NATIONAL INTEGRATION

Conceived of regionally, African-descended social and demographic realities sat in contrast to the national thrust of indigenous integration, which was now spurred on by the INI's developmentalist initiatives. Nonetheless, Mexican intellectuals and artists described both blackness and indigeneity through the concept of interethnic relations: the dominance and exploitation of mestizos over the indigenous and African-descended peoples in nearby satellite communities. The postrevolutionary state needed to rectify the structural and historical inequalities that indigenous and African-descended communities shared. Social scientists and policy makers, including Alfonso Caso and Gonzalo Aguirre Beltrán, the INI's initial directors, did not speak of black or indigenous problems but rather of ones that were shaped by the interactions among the Mexican people and between them and the land they inhabited. The reduction of these complex regional interethnic dynamics to a singular racial issue, they feared, would codify discrimination and reduce Mexican concepts of racial harmony to US racial formations.[23]

Across the nation, professionally trained and amateur ethnographers placed black social visibility in conversation with the indigenous communities whose visibility had never been in doubt. In 1947, anthropologist Julio de la Fuente singled out the sociological peculiarity of Mexico's African-descended communities. He claimed that they were the only Mexicans whose racial identity could be determined biologically. No one else, he believed, had maintained a history of geographic isolation and racial endogamy.[24] The following year, at the Second Inter-American Indigenist Conference in Cuzco, Peru, the Demographic Department explained in quantitatively and spatially vague terms that mulattoes

[23] For example, see Alfonso Caso to Presidente Miguel Alemán, 24 de diciembre de 1948, 545.3/172, AGN-FMAV; and Gonzalo Aguirre Beltrán, "Declaración de México en materia indigenista," in Gonzalo Aguirre Beltrán, *La labor indigenista del gobierno de la Revolución*, FD 09/0012, CDI-CDJR. Antonio Salas Ortega provided a legal foundation for these beliefs in "La naturaleza jurídica del I.N.I.," in *Los centros coordinadores indigenistas* (Mexico City: Instituto Nacional Indigenista, 1962), 15–24. For an alternative perspective that explores the intersection between Mexican and US concepts of integration, see Ruben Flores, *Backroads Pragmatists: Mexico's Melting Pot and Civil Rights in the United States* (Philadelphia: University of Pennsylvania Press, 2014).

[24] Julio de la Fuente, *Relaciones interétnicas* (Mexico City: Instituto Nacional Indigenista, 1965), 68–70. The idea that there was a distinct and scientifically verifiable black race was present among some Mexican social scientists, even while they argued that these biological types were not relevant to Mexican society. For example, see Juan Comas, *Las razas humanas* (Mexico City: Secretaría de Educación Pública, 1946).

were "particularly abundant" along the Gulf and Pacific coasts and in a few unnamed locales in central Mexico. Because the state rarely recognized a black demographic presence, the Department struggled to define black social visibility in relation to mestizaje. "It is possible," the Department concluded, "that there is not currently a single pure Indian, unmixed white person, or truly black person." Yet, even if these African-descended peoples could be identified by their physical traits, they were culturally indistinguishable from mestizos and thus could not be cataloged "as a special group."[25]

This shift in Mexican racial formation was most evident in Veracruz, where the state's Geographic Commission tasked the INAH's Johanna Faulhaber with documenting all of the state's communities. With Veracruz's official history written and its African heritage acknowledged, the existence of African-descended peoples was no longer up for debate.[26] Anthropologist Jorge A. Vivó stated that anthropological research required an analysis of the mulatto locales with a "black-African influence."[27] Tamiahua, Gutiérrez Zamora, Las Higueras, Almolonga, Manuel González, Úrsulo Galván, Yanga, Mata Clara, and Veracruz were all communities identified as having large African-descended populations.[28] As such, Faulhaber devoted hundreds of pages to physiological and demographic data – median age, height, core body temperature, hair color and texture, nose length and width, skin color, and cephalic index, among other categories – that described indigenous, white, mestizo, and mulatto communities.[29]

[25] Departamento Demográfico, "Proyecto de ponencia sobre política demográfica," *Segundo Congreso Indigenista Interamericano* (Cuzco, 1948), 211 and 214, FD AI/0004, CDI-CDJR. Not everyone at the conference agreed with the belief that there were no African-descended cultural behaviors in contemporary Mexico. Wigberto Jiménez Moreno explained that enslaves Africans had left "an indelible footprint" that needed to be recognized alongside the nation's indigenous and Iberian cultures; see "Preservación y fomento de la cultura regional," *Segundo Congreso Indigenista Interamericano* (Cuzco: 1948), 326, FD AI/0004, CDI-CDJR.

[26] For the state's comprehensive history of Veracruz, see Manuel B. Trens and José Luis Melgarejo Vivanco, *Historia de Veracruz*, 6 vols. (Jalapa-Enríquez: Talleres Gráficos del Estado de Veracruz, 1947–1950).

[27] Jorge A. Vivó, introduction to vol. 1 of *Antropología física de Veracruz*, by Johanna Faulhaber (Gobierno de Veracruz, 1950–56), xii.

[28] José Luis Melgarejo Vivanco, "Carta etnográfica de Veracruz," in vol. 2 of *Antropología física de Veracruz*, by Johanna Faulhaber (Gobierno de Veracruz, 1950–56), np.

[29] Johanna Faulhaber, *Antropología física de Veracruz*, 2 vols. (Gobierno de Veracruz, 1950–56). As Alexandra Minna Stern explains, Mexican social scientists were not trying to copy nineteenth-century racial norms venerating Western civilization. They used statistical averages of physical, mental, and psychological data in tandem with demographic and

In broader terms, social scientists applied indigenist theories of regional integration to visible African-descended communities. It is not surprising that Aguirre Beltrán took the lead, in part by theorizing this initiative. Cuijla had been his first point of entry into questions of interethnic relations and the theory of regional mestizo exploitation that he called "a region of refuge" in 1967.[30] According to the INI, the introduction of new infrastructure, like roads and electricity, in addition to modern technologies – such as DDT, tractors, and sewing machines – would undermine these regional structures and provide secluded rural communities with direct access to the state.[31] Most notably, the federal government was in the process of integrating villages like Cuijla as part of a larger project to transform Acapulco, Guerrero, into an internationally renown resort haven. Aided by the interstate highway that connected Acapulco to Mexico City in 1927, a vast infrastructure of roads and hotels, along with the co-requisite amenities needed to sustain this tourist economy, was under construction.[32] The completion of a Pacific-coastal highway between Acapulco and Puerto Angel, Oaxaca, was supposed to unite the Costa Chica.[33] Yet, as the 1940s came to a close, the region had not fully felt the effects of socio-economic development and national integration. Reflecting on why he chose to study Cuijla, Aguirre Beltrán explained that, because of the region's relative isolation, Cuijla was one of the few places where he felt safe enough to complete his ethnography.[34]

While the INI hoped to conserve the positive aspects of these indigenous and African-descended communities' cultural expressions, national integration was fraught with risks. Anthropologist Julio de la Fuente

anthropological methods to classify peoples through typologies, for instance, based on the ratio of chest to limb size. However, these methodologies were still saddled with many of the same problematic racial assumptions found in previous generations of social scientific research; see "From Mestizophilia to Biotypology," 187–210.

[30] Gonzalo Aguirre Beltrán, *Regiones de refugio* (Mexico City: Instituto Indigenista Interamericano, 1967).

[31] For example, see Julian H. Steward, "Acculturation and the Indian Problem," *América Indígena* 3, no. 4 (1943): 326–28; and Manuel Gamio, "The Director of the National Indian Institute of Mexico," *América Indígena* 9, no. 1 (1949): 6.

[32] Andrew Jonathan Sackett, "The Making of Acapulco: People, Land, and the State in the Development of the Mexican Riviera, 1927–1973" (PhD diss., Yale University, 2009); and Tomás Bustamante Álvarez, "La reconstrucción," in vol. 4 of *Historia general de Guerrero* (Mexico City: Instituto Nacional de Antropología e Historia, 1998), 289–92.

[33] Gral. Baltazar R. Leyva M. to Pres. Ávila Camacho, 23 de noviembre de 1945, 515.1/5, AGN-FMAC.

[34] Aguirre Beltrán, "Estudio antropológico de la población negra de Cuajinicuilapa de la Costa Chica de Guerrero," 1–2.

framed the terms of this debate in 1947. Concerned with the potential dangers of poorly conceived indigenist policies, he wrote, "If the term Indian is rejected for its connotations of inferiority and government agencies address the Indian as a campesino more than as an Indian, and if, finally, the qualities and characteristics are associated with local people and places – communities, regions and cities – Indianness and the Indian disappear."[35] In his 1949 manuscript about Cuijla, Aguirre Beltrán took a more fatalistic approach. Cuijla "would undoubtedly disappear through mestizaje." The specter of disappearance reared its head as a scientifically predestined fact. According to the state, economic modernization was beneficial, and Aguirre Beltrán was no critic of it. The inevitable loss of racial and cultural diversity – in this case, African-descended social, demographic, and possibly cultural visibility – was the darker side of this newest template for Mexican modernity. An ethnography of Cuijla, he concluded, could slow if not prevent the erasure of blackness in the region.[36]

Researching Pinotepa Nacional, Oaxaca, Gutierre Tibón, an Italian immigrant and professor at the National Autonomous University of Mexico, arrived at a similar spatial understanding of blackness to Aguirre Beltrán's. A small village about ninety miles southeast of Cuijla, Pinotepa Nacional also sat along the proposed highway route that would connect the Costa Chica to Mexico City. Inspired by Aguirre Beltrán's research, Tibón traced the isolated community's roots back to pre-Columbian indigenous communities and the subsequent arrival of Spanish settlers and African slaves. In slightly more poetic terms than his contemporary, he acknowledged the presence of black phenotypes: "Skin of all shades, from the white of the Goths of Asturias to the blackest of the blacks of the black continent, passed through by the copper colors that are the most beautiful that the human skin can have." In part because of Aguirre Beltrán's emphasis on African cultural retentions, Tibón arrived in Pinotepa Nacional expecting to encounter exotic African cultural behaviors that locals openly expressed and that he could easily

[35] De la Fuente, *Relaciones interétnicas*, 73. This chapter, "Definición, pase y desaparición del indio en México," had already been published in the January 1947 issue of *América Indígena*.

[36] Aguirre Beltrán, "Estudio antropológico de la población negra de Cuajinicuilapa de la Costa Chica de Guerrero," 1–4 and 141. Historian Karin Rosemblatt explores these debates about culture contact in relation to indigenous integration in Mexico and the United States; see *The Science and Politics of Race in Mexico and the United States*, 169–75.

observe. "I believed," he recalled, "that in all of the black population centers certain African rites were conserved: ceremonial dances in step with tam-tams, with frenzied crescendos and people falling into a cataleptic state; or acts of black magic in which roosters' throats are slashed." Locals, however, did not advertise their African heritage "out of caution." It only appeared in public during festivals, when drunkenness cast social inhibitions and racial stigmas aside. Tibón did not doubt the presence of African-descended cultures, but he pushed back against the degree to which Aguirre Beltrán highlighted their purity. "To speak of a 'Mexican Congo' is a cheap literary resource," he noted without any explicit reference to his predecessor.[37]

Tibón attributed the African-descended cultural visibility he witnessed to the community's seclusion. "Africa, Africa. Their pure African race," he commented, "has been maintained here thanks to the isolation in which they live." Access to these communities from major urban hubs, like Mexico City and Oaxaca City, was difficult. If there was no plane available to drop a visitor off at the nearby beach, then it was an eight-day trek by horse from the state capital through the forests and mountains to Pinotepa Nacional. Highway 200, which Aguirre Beltrán thought would destroy local cultures, was still under construction in 1961, despite the fact that locals "say there is not a more important center along the entire coast between Acapulco and the Isthmus."[38] The images accompanying Tibón's ethnography *Pinotepa Nacional: Mixtecos, negros y triques* reaffirm his spatial conclusions. To depict the indigenous and African-descended residents of Oaxaca's Pacific Coast, illustrator Alberto Beltrán drew a map of the coastal area where the states of Oaxaca and Guerrero meet. He placed the image of a black man, shirtless and carrying a sword, facing Pinotepa Nacional. Reminiscent of the masculine images of Mexican insurgents from the 1930s and of the violent ethos that Aguirre Beltrán described, this

[37] Guiterre Tibón, *Pinotepa Nacional: Mixtecos, negros y triques* (Mexico City: Universidad Autónoma de México, 1961), 12, 40–41, and 49; also see Lewis, *Chocolate and Corn Four*, 134–36. Tibón was not alone in recognizing the presence of African-descended peoples in Oaxaca. Reynaldo Salvatierra, the director of Coordinating Center along the coast of Oaxaca, explained that there were "Mixtecs, mestizos, and blacks" in the region; see "El centro coordinador de la Mixteca de la costa," in *Los centros coordinadores indigenistas* (Mexico City: Instituto Nacional Indigenista, 1962), 103.

[38] Tibón, *Pinotepa Nacional*, 11–12 and 40. Aguirre Beltrán similarly noted the difficulty of finding air travel into the Costa Chica; see "Estudio antropológico de la población negra de Cuajinicuilapa de la Costa Chica de Guerrero," 1. Also see Lewis, *Chocolate and Corn Flour*, 17.

African-descended everyman appears strong and armed. None of the people representing the Costa Chica, regardless of race or gender, look to Mexico City or Oaxaca City, neither of which are pictured (See Map 7.2).

This was not Beltrán's first time depicting the region's African-descended communities as insulated from postrevolutionary nation-state formation. Coming of age during the radicalism of the 1930s, he was familiar with Mexico's ethnographic tradition and historical glorification of the poor, both urban and rural, African-descended and indigenous. In the 1950s, he observed indigenous regional isolation and exploitation at the INI's Coordinating Center in Chiapas; he illustrated several of Aguirre Beltrán's monographs, including *Cuijla*; and he provided images for other Mexicans and foreigners fascinated by indigeneity and mestizaje. The INI's rhetoric of indigenous integration, particularly its attempts to bring all of the nation's secluded populations into the national electoral arena and hopefully the arms of the PRI, caught his eye (See Map 7.3).[39] For Aguirre Beltrán's 1953 *Formas de gobierno indígena*, an ethnography written with this Mexico City-centric political project in mind, Beltrán contributed images of indigenous peoples and cultures. To illustrate Aguirre Beltrán's blueprint for indigenous integration and postrevolutionary democracy, he drew the Tarascan Indians of Michoacán with political banners, like the PRI's, in the background (See Figure 7.4). Conversely, Beltrán's illustrations for *Cuijla*, like those from *Pinotepa Nacional*, emphasize regional isolation. In *Cuijla*, he drew the African-descended inhabitants of Cuijla facing the Pacific Ocean to illustrate either their separation from the postrevolutionary state or their rejection of it (See Map 7.5).

With black bodies visible in specific locales, ethnographers such as Aguirre Beltrán and Tibón needed to describe their informants' physical characteristics in relation to others in the region. Tibón poetically acknowledged the presence of a color continuum in Pinotepa Nacional and in nearby communities, such as Collantes, where European features, like thinner lips and straight hair, were visible. African-descended peoples who possessed these physical traits could possibly pass for another racial group and therefore overcome the

[39] Sergio Gómez Montero, "El arte indígena es contemporáneo: Vive y se transforma a su propio ritmo. (Alberto Beltrán recuerda cuando se ilustraba la acción educativa 'quitando la venda de la ignorancia a los indios')," in *INI: 30 años después. Revisión crítica* (Mexico City: Instituto Nacional Indigenista, 1978), 189–94; Elena Poniatowska, "Alberto Beltrán," in *Alberto Beltrán, 1923–2002: Cronista e ilustrador de México* (Mexico City: Universidad Nacional Autónoma de México, 2003), 11–12; and Lewis, *Rethinking Mexican Indigenismo*, 177.

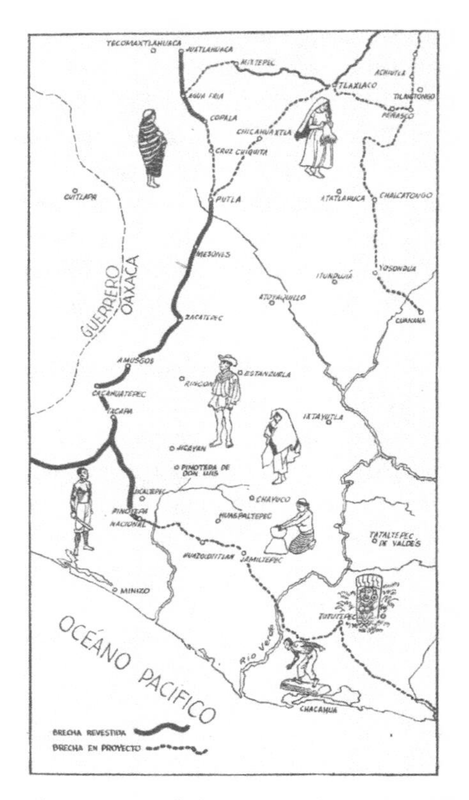

MAP 7.2 Alberto Beltrán, map of the Costa Chica, 1961. In Tibón, *Pinotepa Nacional*. 2019 Artist Rights Society (ARS), New York/SOMAAP, Mexico City.

stigmas attributed to their heritage.[40] Aguirre Beltrán went further, detailing a deleterious social hierarchy built on a combination of culture, race, and caste. Euromestizos sat at the top of the region's social ladder, followed by racially mixed *blanquitos* who had some black physiological and cultural characteristics. Afromestizos and the few people considered to be black were at the bottom. Locals as well as ethnographers could identify them by their wavy hair, flat and wide noses, protruding lips, large mouths, and skin color, which varied from coffee-colored to black. To help readers visualize Cuijla's residents, he included photographs of the local racial types, including a "blanquita woman," a "black woman," and a "black boy."[41]

[40] Tibón, *Pinotepa Nacional*, 12 and 39.
[41] Aguirre Beltrán, *Cuijla*, 71–73; photographs follow pages 48, 96, and 112.

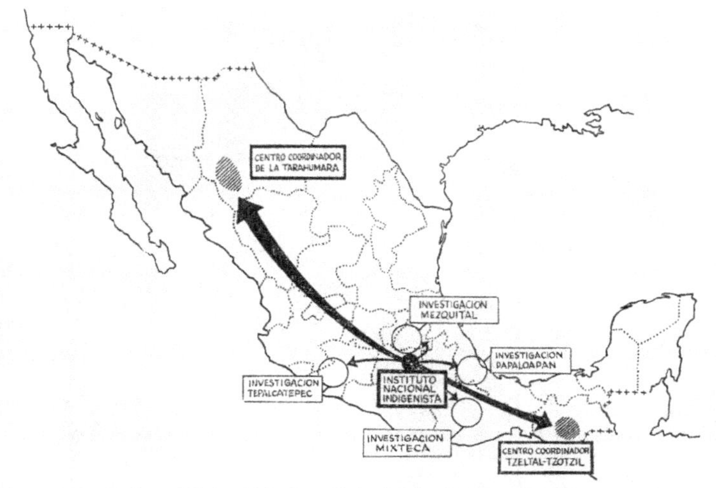

MAP 7.3 Map of INI activities, 1953. Subtitle: "Map that shows the activities of the National Indigenist Institute with headquarters in Mexico City, and the Coordinating Centers in the states of Chiapas and Chihuahua, as well as the four regions in which there were already research underway." From Instituto Nacional Indigenista (1953, julio). Los Centros Coordinadores. *Acción Indigenista: Boletín Mensual del Instituto Nacional Indigenista* 1, 2. Cortesía del Instituto Nacional de los Pueblos Indígenas.

BLACK VISIBILITY

When scholars and cultural producers interested in African-descended peoples in Mexico conceived of blackness nationally, that is beyond the Costa Chica and the state of Veracruz, the ethnographic and visual cues surrounding the black body were less visible. The national lens emphasized the successful, benevolent incorporation of enslaved Africans into Mexican history and society, just as it had for more than a century. In short, mestizaje's centripetal forces reigned. Secluded hamlets with black social visibility, like Cuijla, were the historical, ethnographic, and even biological anomalies. As such, African-descended peoples became the model for indigenous integration, and Mexican racial formations, the model for global programs to forge racial harmony.[42]

[42] For this global perspective, particularly as part of the United Nations' postwar human rights initiatives, see Gonzalo Aguirre Beltrán to Melville J. Herskovits, August 6, 1952, folder 267 (Northwestern University – Beltrán, Gonzalo Aguirre (Visit, Anthropology), 1944–1952), box 19, series 216.S, record group 1.1, RAC-RFR.

FIGURE 7.4 Alberto Beltrán, image of indigenous political participation, 1953. From Aguirre Beltrán, *Formas de gobierno indígena.* 2019 Artist Rights Society (ARS), New York/SOMAAP, Mexico City.

MAP 7.5 Alberto Beltrán, map of people in the Costa Chica, 1957. From Aguirre Beltrán, *Cuijla.* Source: 2019 Artist Rights Society (ARS), New York/SOMAAP, Mexico City.

Miguel Covarrubias's sketch of *El Negrito* is emblematic of this national perspective (See Figure 7.6). Drawn for Vicente T. Mendoza's ethnomusicological research on the colonial *Danza de los negritos* in the late 1940s or early 1950s, El Negrito is one of the few images, if not the only one, he drew of an African-descended Mexican. To indicate the degree to which African-descended peoples assimilated into colonial society, he drew three individuals: El Negrito, an indigenous chicken farmer, and a Spanish majordomo. This black man, whose legal status is unclear, carries two woven baskets and is dressed, like the Spaniard, in a blue coat, breeches, and stockings. In contrast, the chicken farmer, who has not assimilated, dons sandals, a sombrero, and a poncho in a complementary orange. As such, culture, not skin color or heritage, best reflects an individual's degree of integration into colonial and Mexican society.[43] Covarrubias's art echoes Mendoza's analysis of black musical hybridity. According to Mendoza, this colonial dance, made famous by the painted masks that dancers wear depicting African, Spanish, and indigenous peoples, spread from the free black town of San Lorenzo de Cerralvo, Veracruz, to the states of Puebla, Tlaxcala, Hidalgo, Oaxaca, Guerrero, and Michoacán. While there were regional variations, it always combined Spanish culture and an African spirit of resistance. It mimicked liturgical music, paid homage to Mexican patron saints, and used violins, guitars, and harps.[44]

Academics in Mexico and the United States reaffirmed the assumption that African-descended people eagerly threw off slavery's racial stigmas and integrated into Mexican society. Across the Americas, social scientists invoked the language of postwar development to discuss the formation of socially mobile class societies that rejected caste divisions. Amid the Cold War's developmentalist paradigms, caste often operated as a euphemism for the scientifically unsound, socially dangerous concept of biological race.[45] In

[43] 3/10,950, expediente 216, UDLAP-SACE-AMC. Following his typical fusion of ethnography and art, Covarrubias also clipped images of people dancing the Danza de los negritos; see 5/10763, expediente 210, UDLAP-SACE-AMC.

[44] Vicente T. Mendoza, "La danza durante la colonia en México," 1/108912–108913, expediente 215, UDLAP-SACE-AMC. For an analysis of the Danza de los negritos, see Anita González, *Afro-Mexico: Dancing between Myth and Reality* (Austin: University of Texas Press, 2010).

[45] Karin Alejandra Rosemblatt, "Other Americas: Transnationalism, Scholarship, and the Culture of Poverty in Mexico and the United States," *Hispanic American Historical Review* 89, no. 4 (2009): 603–41. Regarding the mutual constructions of caste and class, see Cope, *The Limits of Racial Domination*; and Laura A. Lewis, *Hall of Mirrors: Power, Witchcraft, and Caste in Colonial Mexico* (Durham, NC: Duke University Press, 2003), 4 and 185–86n6.

FIGURE 7.6 Miguel Covarrubias, “Danza Colonial Mexicana: Historia III.” María Elena Covarrubias/Archivo Miguel Covarrubias. Sala de Archivo y Colecciones Especiales. Dirección de Bibliotecas, Universidad de las Américas Puebla.

the late 1960s, Mexican historian Moisés González Navarro stated that the abolition of slavery incorporated African-descended peoples into a class system and therefore functioned as a window into Mexican socio-economic integration.[46] In 1965, Magnus Mörner, a Swedish historian of colonial Latin America, brought scholars from across the Western Hemisphere, including Aguirre Beltrán and González Navarro, together to discuss the transition from caste to class. His sociological approach mirrored those found in Mexico, where black integration and indigenous isolation was the point of departure. He pled for new research into the "survival or destruction of representative 'indigenous' communities" on the one hand and "the economic and social effects of abolition and the absorption of the emancipated Negroes into society" on the other.[47]

Aguirre Beltrán was at the forefront of Mexico's narrative of national integration. He too imagined that African-descended peoples were more willing to assimilate into colonial and postindependence society than indigenous communities were. By the end of the 1960s, this nation-wide history of African integration undergirded his sociological conception of indigenous development. Interethnic relations between afromestizos and mestizos were "as egalitarian as possible between persons of different classes." Accordingly, he assumed that the INI did not need to be preoccupied with African-descended communities, because the caste dynamics that indigenists were obliged to resolve only remained in areas near Cuijla. "Ethnographic studies of the Negro in Mexico and, in particular, of interethnic relations between the national populations and the Negroes and between the Negro and Indian populations," he wrote, "will provides [*sic*] us with a knowledge of those integrative mechanisms which encourage unity and those seigneurial mechanisms which oppose it."[48] In other words, if the state effectively encouraged indigenous communities to follow the processes of cultural

[46] Moisés González Navarro, "*Mestizaje* in Mexico during the National Period," in *Race and Class in Latin America*, ed. Magnus Mörner (New York: Columbia University Press, 1970), 149.

[47] Magnus Mörner, "Historical Research on Race Relations in Latin America during the National Period," in *Race and Class in Latin America*, ed. Magnus Mörner (New York: Columbia University Press, 1970), 230.

[48] Gonzalo Aguirre Beltrán, "The Integration of the Negro into the National Society of Mexico," in *Race and Class in Latin America*, ed. Magnus Mörner (New York: Columbia University Press, 1970), 12 and 14. He reaffirmed these ideas in *Medicina y magia: El proceso de aculturación en la estructura colonial*, vol. 8 of *Obra antropológica* (Mexico City: Fondo de Cultura Económica, 1992); and *La población negra de México*, 2nd ed. (1972).

encounter and exchange that afromestizos had already navigated, then there would be, "for the first time, an element of social justice in indigenist politics." All Mexicans would enjoy a democratic class system built upon the liberal notions of "the equality of all people without limitations according to sex, race, or creed."[49]

At the national level, African-descended social invisibility paved the way for the black body to be visible in cultural expressions, like art, music, and film, where the national populace could consume it allegorically and in contrast to the seemingly ubiquitous racial violence in the United States. During the Golden Age of Mexican cinema (1940–60), movie theaters operated as an alternative form of education. In front of the big screen, people of all classes could learn about Mexican society, the United States, and the world at large in a less pretentious way than they could by reading schoolbooks.[50] Postwar films made black corporeality visible either with blackface or by introducing actors from other parts of the Black Atlantic. The black body was ready for audiences to observe in *Angelitos negros* (1948), *La negra Angustias* (1949), *Negro es mi color* (1951), and *Mulata* (1954).[51] To address these cinematic propensities in 1995, screenwriter and director Matilde Landeta recalled her experiences with black social visibility, which she first observed abroad during a chance encounter as a twelve year old visiting the United States. She thought that blackness was invisible in Mexico; consequently it was impossible for her to cast African-descended Mexicans in her films, even when the plot warranted it. "Although I knew that there were black people because I had cried when I read *Uncle Tom's Cabin*, I had never physically seen one in person. Mexico had not had a black population," she stated, "and we still do not have one."[52]

[49] Gonzalo Aguirre Beltrán, "Un postulado de política indigenista," *América Indígena* 27, no. 3 (1967): 559–65; and Aguirre Beltrán, *Regiones de refugio*, 154–59, 166, and 210.

[50] Historian Mary Kay Vaughan discusses the role of film as an educative device in *Portrait of a Young Painter*. For a discussion of movie theaters' roles in socializing society before the Golden Age, see Serna, *Making Cinelandia*.

[51] See Irwin, "Memín Pinguín, Rumba, and Racism," 256–61; and Selfa A. Chew, "Representation of Black Womanhood in Mexico," *Studies in Latin American Popular Culture* 36 (2018): 108–27. As Eli Bartra argues, audiences likely recognized the use of blackface in the film *La negra Angustias*. This racial inauthenticity, what she calls "a masquerade," lent credence to the supposition that blackness was socially invisible in contemporary Mexico; see "How Black Is *La Negra Angustias*?," *Third Text* 26, no. 3 (2012): 281.

[52] Isabel Arredondo, "'Tenía bríos, aún vieja, los sigo teniendo': Entrevista a Matilde Landeta," *Mexican Studies/Estudios Mexicanos* 18, no. 1 (2002): 200.

These cultural inquiries into what was the black body and who possessed one were fundamentally interethnic examinations of Mexico claims of racial tolerance. Embodying these racial tropes, mixed-race women, whether they were African-descended or not, were mothers to the next generation of mestizo citizens. The film *Angelitos negros* best captures the relationship between the female black body and mestizaje. Once José Carlos learns that his wife, Ana Luisa, is half-black, he wonders if and when he should tell her about her ancestry. The family's priest as well as Ana Luisa's mother and former nanny, Mamá Mercé, act as his moral guideposts. They tell him to keep the secret and shoulder the blame for harboring the black blood that stained their daughter Belén. Unity – the creation of a happy household emblematic of the PRI's own version of a harmonious national family – is the goal. Of course, prejudice destroys this fantasy. Mamá Mercé, for instance, points to the divisions racial hatred sows when she talks to a distraught Ana Luisa: "What did black people do so you hate us? Think how much your girl will suffer in a few years. She'll suffer as much hardship as I had. My God. If she were white and blonde, just like you."[53] Mirroring other postrevolutionary constructions of blackness, racial prejudice caused social instability and discord – black visibility was not the problem.

The history of overt racial discrimination that African Americans encountered in the United States reinforced Mexico's solution to racial injustice. In a review of *Angelitos negros* for the NAACP's the *Crisis* in 1950, Gena Cerminara celebrated the film's nuanced portrayal of interpersonal racism. "Perhaps the whole psychological problem in breaking down attitudes of race prejudice," she explained as she distilled the film's message and applied it to US racial formations, "is the problem of making white people understand that the Negro Problem is not a remote mass sociological phenomenon, but rather a very close and a very personal thing, in which they themselves are often unconscious participants, and which deeply affects people very much like themselves who feel and love and suffer and aspire like themselves." Fearing *Angelitos negros* was too sentimental for audiences north of the border, she hoped that a more suitable equivalent would soon make its way to US theaters.[54]

[53] Rodríguez, *Angelitos negros*, 1:20:45–1:21:06. Cultural scholars have called the representation of blackness through women like Ana Luisa a mulatta archetype, see Cedric J. Robinson and Luz Maria Cabral, "The Mulatta on Film: From Hollywood to the Mexican Revolution," *Race and Class* 45, no. 2 (2003): 1–20; and Arce, *México's Nobodies*, 147–224.

[54] Gina Cerminara, "Little Black Angels," *Crisis*, April 1950, 267.

When African Americans crossed the border to escape from Jim Crow's watchful eye, they frequently noticed the new social and cultural capital that Mexico's interethnic conception of integration offered them. Border crossing transformed how they conceptualized black visibility and invisibility and thus their sense of humanity. With anticommunism setting the acceptable boundaries for cultural expression in the United States during the Cold War, those African Americans artists whose leftist sensibilities sat at the margins of society doubly felt the need to move abroad. Others used their newfound expendable income to live in Mexico City or to visit Acapulco.[55] As Langston Hughes described in 1965, African Americans visiting or migrating to Mexico encountered "a complete change of racial climate."[56] In 1982, African American feminist poet and activist Audre Lorde fondly recalled her extended visit in 1954. Living in a nation defined by its indigeneity proved to be particularly empowering: "For me, walking hurriedly back to my own little house in this land of color and dark people who said *negro* and meant something beautiful, who noticed me as I moved among them – this decision felt like a promise of some kind that I half-believed in, in spite of myself, a possible validation." As she explained, "I had never felt visible before, nor even known I lacked it."[57]

Lorde was not alone. Virgil Richardson, a Tuskegee airman during the Second World War, referenced the skin color of the people he saw in Acapulco. Women had "caramel complexion" or were of "chocolate color." Their "beautiful dark bodies" captivated him and helped him have "a sense of homecoming in a foreign land." Entranced by Mexican culture and racial formations, he moved to Mexico City, where he too felt a newfound sense of visibility:

In the early 1950s, the black author Ralph Ellison published his highly acclaimed masterpiece *Invisible Man*, about a nameless black character searching for his place in America. While a lot of what Ellison wrote concerning the experience of blacks in America was true, I cannot say that I felt the same in Mexico. Here, I was

[55] Rebecca Schreiber, *Cold War Exiles in Mexico: U.S. Dissidents and the Culture of Critical Resistance* (Minneapolis: University of Minnesota Press, 2008); and Vinson, *Flight*, 168. By late 1960s and early 1970s, American Airlines often teamed up with African American magazines, like *Crisis* and *Ebony*, to advertise vacations to Acapulco; for example, see *Crisis*, August–September 1969, 294; and "Americans Summer Deals to Mexico and the Caribbean," *Ebony*, June 1975, 113.

[56] Langston Hughes, "Remembrances," June 25, 1965, 34, folder A1, box 1, reel 1, NYPL-SCRBC-LM-LHC.

[57] Audre Lorde, *Zami: A New Spelling of My Name* (Freedom, CA: Crossing Press, 1982), 156 and 173.

always visible. People always looked at me with admiration, envy, affection, and friendship. I was and became "*un negro*."[58]

The racial visibility that Lorde and Richardson celebrated was most evident among the artists who continued the racial conversations forged in the 1920s and 1930s by New Negro, Afro-Cubanist, and Mexican cultural producers. Founded by former LEAR members Leopoldo Méndez, Pablo O'Higgins, and Luis Arenal in 1937, the TGP frequently took inspiration from photographs its Mexican audiences would have likely recognized. This methodology provided Alberto Beltrán with the tools to take Aguirre Beltrán's photographs of Cuijla's residents and turn them into gripping illustrations that accompanied every chapter (See Figure 7.7).[59] In essence, the TGP's members were amateur ethnographers – and their linocuts were romantic visual ethnographies of the oppressed.[60] As Beltrán explained in 1957, for the Workshop's twentieth anniversary, "what is indispensable is having a clear sense of popular struggles; thus the artist who thinks alone, who dialogues only with himself and not with the people, who is not an interpreter but someone who exerts his meta-feelings, is not able to identify with the people."[61]

When African American artists, such as Margaret Taylor Gross Burroughs, Elizabeth Catlett, and her first husband Charles White, reached Mexico City, they looked to the TGP for institutional support and inspiration.[62] A sculptor, Catlett arrived with a Julius Rosenwald Fund Fellowship for a project entitled *The Negro Woman* in 1946. As part of the 1949 exhibit *T.G.P. México*, she introduced the black body to the Workshop's aesthetic. With her instruction, members produced linocuts of famous African Americans for series like *Against Discrimination in the*

[58] Virgil Richardson qtd. in Vinson, *Flight*, 87–90. His words have been transcribed, reordered, and edited by Ben Vinson III.

[59] "Estatutos del Taller de Gráfica Popular, aprobados en la Asamblea General del 17 de marzo de 1938," Francisco Reyes Palma Archive, Mexico City, Record ID: 826866, ICAA-MFAH; and Fabiola Martha Villegas Torres, *Alberto Beltrán y el libro ilustrado* (Mexico City: Consejo Nacional para la Cultura y las Artes, 2007), 41–42.

[60] Ceferino Palencia, "La gran labor del Taller de Gráfica Popular," *México en la cultura: Suplemento cultural de Novedades*, 15 de enero de 1950, Record ID: 781749, ICAA-MFAH.

[61] Raquel Tibol, "Mesa redonda en el Taller de Gráfica Popular," *Artes de México*, no. 18 (1957): 10.

[62] Schreiber, *Cold War Exiles in Mexico*, 27–58; and Lizzetta LeFalle-Collins, "African-American Modernists and the Mexican Muralist School," in *In the Spirit of Resistance: African-American Modernists and the Mexican Muralist School*, ed. Lizzetta LeFalle-Collins and Shifra M. Goldman (New York: American Federation of Arts, 1996), 27–67.

FIGURE 7.7 Photograph of Alberto Beltrán, 1977. CID "Alberto Beltrán." Copyright 1977, Durango.

United States.[63] Four linoleum prints representing the African American radical tradition – Catlett's *Harriet Tubman*, Leopoldo Méndez's *Paul Robeson*, Alberto Beltrán's *Nat Turner*, and Ángel Bracho's more historically ambiguous *Héroe negro* – were reproduced in 1957 for *Artes de México.*[64] The TGP's populist message and collective techniques inspired African Americans who, as White explained, saw its methods as "a milestone" for their own aesthetic and political development. "I saw artists," he continued, "working to create an art about and for the people. That had the strongest influence on my whole approach." Taking inspiration from him as well, the TGP printed the lithograph "Un miembro del T.G.P. víctima del racismo" in response to a "racist assault" on White on April 14, 1947, in Greenwich Village (See Figure 7.8).[65] TGP artists also brought these cultural

[63] Melanie Anne Herzog, *Elizabeth Catlett: An American Artist in Mexico* (Seattle: University of Washington Press, 2000), 47, 80, and 100–107; and Schreiber, *Cold War Exiles in Mexico*, 44.

[64] Tibol, "Mesa redonda en el Taller de Gráfica Popular."

[65] John Murphy and Ashley James, "Chronology," in *Charles White: A Retrospective*, ed. Sarah Kelly Oehler and Esther Adler (Chicago, IL: Art Institute of Chicago, 2018), 197.

FIGURE 7.8 Anonymous, "Un miembro del T.G.P. víctima del racismo." #2001-004-0011 from Taller de Gráfica Popular Pictorial Collection (PICT 2001-025), Center for Southwest Research, University of New Mexico Libraries.

conversations to the postwar international arena, where questions of decolonization dominated headlines and where condemnations of US racism were an issue of Cold War propaganda. For example, in 1960, Francisco Mora, Catlett's second husband, took several of the prints from *Against Discrimination in the United States* to the Third International Educators Conference in Guinea.[66]

In 1960, the TGP also recognized Mexico's African heritage when it published *450 años de lucha: Homenaje al pueblo mexicano*. With contributions from Alberto Beltrán, Elizabeth Catlett, and Francisco Mora, among others, the book reiterates the pantheon of heroes – such as Gaspar Yanga, Father Hidalgo, José María Morelos, and Vicente Guerrero – that Marxists had carved into the national narrative in the 1930s. After the TGP depicted pre-Columbian societies, the Spanish Conquest, and the inhuman enslavement of indigenous communities, Adolfo Quinteros provided the fourth linocut *Rebeliones de negros*. Accompanied by runaway slaves wielding swords, Yanga, with his shackles broken, holds a knife. Glorifying slave insurrection, the caption describes him as "a brave black man" before ending with an integrationist statement that still renders

[66] Schreiber, *Cold War Exiles in Mexico*, 49–50 and 56–57.

blackness visible: "The blacks brought from Africa are also part of the history of Mexico."[67]

In the 1960s and 1970s, US scholars were less attuned to Mexico's interethnic constructions of blackness than they had been in previous decades. Melville Herskovits provided the most loyal summary of Gonzalo Aguirre Beltrán's research in Cuijla when, in the late 1950s or early 1960s, he included Guerrero in his charting of African cultural retentions in the Americas. Emphasizing the state's comparatively limited presence of African-descended cultures, he explained that there was little to no trace of African economic, artistic, or linguistic patterns. In contrast, some social organizations and institutions as well as aspects of the region's magic and folklore were "quite African."[68] African Americans also reveled in the recovery of Mexico's African past. In June 1969 *Jet* magazine mentioned in passing that African-descended peoples shaped Mexican culture and helped lead the nation into the 1910 Revolution. As such, Mexico offered African Americans interested in traveling to Mexico City or Acapulco a worthwhile opportunity "to see how high their black brothers are regarded in the custom-rich society."[69] Finally, in the February 1969 issue of *Negro Digest*, historian Gwendolyn Midlo Hall correctly made the point, likely reflecting on her time studying in Mexico in 1963, that Africans not only supplanted indigenous labor but also outnumbered Spaniards throughout the colonial period.[70]

[67] Taller de Gráfica Popular, *450 años de lucha: Homenaje al pueblo mexicano*, 1st ed. (1960). For a discussion of how the TGP previously recounted Mexican history, see Mary Theresa Avila, "Chronicles of Revolution and Nation: El Taller de Gráfica Popular's 'Estampas de la Revolución Mexicana' (1947)" (PhD diss., University of New Mexico, 2013).

[68] See Melville J. Herskovits, "Problem, Method, and Theory in Afroamerican Studies," in *The New World Negro: Selected Papers in Afroamerican Studies*, ed. Frances S. Herskovits (Bloomington: Indiana University Press, 1966), 53. As part of a posthumously published anthology, this chapter is supposedly a reprint of an article of the same name published in *Afroamérica* in 1945. The 1945 article, however, did not include Guerrero, Mexico. The bibliography at the end of the reproduced chapter does not include a citation explaining where Herskovits acquired this ethnographic data, but he likely added it after he corresponded with Aguirre Beltrán about the latter's research in Cuijla in 1949.

[69] "Journalists See Black Achievements in Mexico," *Jet*, June 12, 1969, 46.

[70] Gwendolyn Midlo Hall, "Africans in the Americas," *Negro Digest*, February 1969, 41. As Jonathan Fenderson explains, *Negro Digest*, which renamed itself *Black World* in May 1970, was one of the most widely read African American magazines in the 1960s and 1970s; see *Building the Black Arts Movement: Hoyt Fuller and the Cultural Politics of the 1960s* (Urbana: University of Illinois Press, 2019), 4–5.

Nonetheless, a methodological and political chasm about the significance of black demographic visibility was emerging between Mexican ethnographers and Afro-diasporic intellectuals. Gonzalo Aguirre Beltrán's research fed both sides. His 1945 article "Races in 17th Century Mexico" points to this divergence. In *Phylon*, an academic journal founded by W. E. B. Du Bois and Irene Diggs to give an African American perspective on the social sciences, he reduced his research on the African roots of Mexican mestizaje to an analysis of the black body, its diverse phenotypes and ancestries, and the myriad racial vocabularies associated with them.[71] Employing the one-drop rule to recalibrate Aguirre Beltrán's demographic data, *Ebony* magazine concluded that Mexico had a black population approaching 12 million in 1948, a number well in excess of Aguirre Beltrán's claim that Mexico was home to 120,000 afromestizos.[72] In contrast to the integrationist interethnic sentiments found in Mexican social scientific research in the 1940s and 1950s, Diggs described the former maroon community San Lorenzo de los Negros (or Yanga) as a "black republic" that "represented attempts to destroy the *castas*."[73]

Jim Tuck, a writer living in the Costa Chica, touted the existence of an enclave of 20,000 pure-blooded Africans in the region surrounding Cuijla. His August 1965 article for *Negro Digest* "The Afro-Mexicans: Black 'Republic' in Modern Mexico" claims that the Costa Chica was home to "a 'lost' – or to put it more accurately – completely overlooked civilization, a culture so atypical, so alien, and so different from anything Americans associate with Mexico that it seems like an importation from another continent and another world." A map accompanying the text marks four sites: Mexico City; Acapulco; Ometepec, the mestizo town that Aguirre Beltrán described as the main hub for the residents of Cuijla; and Pinotepa Nacional, Tibón's ethnographic locale. "Africa in

[71] Gonzalo Aguirre Beltrán, "Races in 17th Century Mexico," *Phylon* 6, no. 3 (1945): 212–18.

[72] Vinson, *Flight*, 165–66. For a more nuanced African American discussion of blackness in Mexico, which likely references Aguirre Beltrán's trip to Fisk University during the 1944–45 academic year, see Antoinette H. Demond, "On 'Passing,'" *Crisis*, December 1956, 591–92. Other scholars have been more loyal to Aguirre Beltrán's demographic conclusions. Using his research almost exclusively to discuss African-descended peoples in Mexico, French sociologist Roger Bastide claimed in 1967 that Mexico was home to 80,000 people of pure African heritage and 40,000 mulattoes; see *Les Amériques noires*, 22 and 78–81.

[73] Irene Diggs, "Color in Colonial Spanish America," *Journal of Negro History* 38, no. 4 (1953): 404.

miniature!" he proudly called it with his US-centric conception of black racial solidarity. Aguirre Beltrán's and Tibón's analyses of racial and cultural mixture are absent. So too are many of the integrationist refrains trumpeted in postrevolutionary ethnographic theory. More a sensationalized tourist advertisement geared toward brining African Americans to the Costa Chica than a scholarly text, "The Afro-Mexicans" concludes with the following pitch:

> If any remain unconvinced, I make the following suggestion. On their next trip to Acapulco, let them invest $16 – the round trip per passenger price of a small charter plane – and visit either Cuajinicuilapa, Guerrero, or Santo Domingo, Oaxaca, both communities serviced by airfields. *Then* let them say that Mexico has no lost civilization.[74]

CODA: THE OLMEC HEADS AND AFRO-DIASPORIC POLITICS

In "The Afro-Mexicans," Tuck argued that the African-descended communities of the Costa Chica were the descendants of enslaved peoples brought from Africa during the colonial period. Such an assertion would not have ruffled Mexicans concerned with the importation of US racial formations. "Its members are not," he penned, "as might be supposed, descendants of Aztecs or Mayans, undiscovered by the *conquistadores* and living as they did in Montezuma's day."[75] This passing comment also would not have elicited ire from Mexican archeologists, ethnographers, or historians – and, if anything, Mexicans likely would have chuckled at the need to make such an obvious claim. Rather, it was a conscious rebuttal of an alternative conception of black corporeality that was gaining currency within Black Nationalist circles: the idea that Africans inhabited the Americas before 1492.

In the United States in the 1960s and 1970s, a second generation of postwar African American activists and scholars navigated what they perceived as the social, cultural, and ideological failures of liberal integration, whether it was the United States' so-called melting pot or Latin America's claim to racial harmony. As part of broader demands for self-determination, economic self-sufficiency, and social justice at home and abroad, some advocated for an Afrocentric history of the peoples and cultures of the diaspora. Reading scholars like Melville Herskovits,

[74] Jim Tuck, "The Afro-Mexicans: Black 'Republic' in Modern Mexico," *Negro Digest*, August 1965, 14–17, and 19.
[75] Ibid., 15.

Carter G. Woodson, and W. E. B. Du Bois, they ensconced themselves in the same intellectual genealogies and cultural debates about African cultural retentions in the Western Hemisphere as had the pioneers of African ethnography in Mexico: Gonzalo Aguirre Beltrán and Miguel Covarrubias.[76]

The rejection of all things Eurocentric and the allure of all things African led some Black Nationalists down the slippery slope toward a racial essentialism that rejected Mexico's cultural brand of race. Acting as amateur archeologists, they defined the Olmec's large basalt heads through the black body, a project that most archeologists in Mexico and the United States deemed invalid.[77] As artifacts of pre-Columbian African settlements in the Americas, these heads were proof of what Harold G. Lawrence called "Negro Colonies" in the June–July 1962 issue of the *Crisis*.[78] As described in Chapter 1, the colossal head uncovered by José María Melgar y Serrano in the 1860s was at the root of this disagreement over the pre-Columbian black body in Mexico. The head's Old World roots refuted the long-held assumption that Africans had not contributed to world history. In the minds of nineteenth-century Mexicans uncritically conflating race and culture, the sculpture's protruding lips, flat nose, and large nostrils indicated that it had been carved by Africans rather than indigenous peoples before 1492. Residing somewhere between archeological novelty and mystery, the head continued to enliven debate after the 1910 Revolution. The most enduring proclamation of this pre-Columbian blackness came from Harvard philologist and Slavic Studies professor Leo Wiener. Between 1920 and 1922, he published the three-volume *Africa and the Discovery of America*, which

[76] Martha Biondi, *The Black Revolution on Campus* (Berkeley: University of California Press, 2012), 17 and 23; and Ibram X. Kendi, "Reigning Assimilationists and Defiant Black Power: The Struggle to Define and Regulate Racist Ideas," in *New Perspectives on the Black Intellectual Tradition*, ed. Keisha N. Blain, Christopher Cameron, and Ashley D. Farmer (Evanston, IL: Northwestern University Press, 2018), 157–74.

[77] There is an extensive literature on the international dimensions of Black Nationalism and Black Power in the 1960s and 1970s; for example, see Robin D. G. Kelley, *Freedom Dreams: The Black Radical Imagination* (Boston, MA: Beacon Press, 2002); Brenda Gayle Plummer, *In Search of Power: African Americans in the Era of Decolonization, 1956–1974* (New York: Cambridge University Press, 2013); Sean L. Malloy, *Out of Oakland: Black Panther Party Internationalism during the Cold War* (Ithaca, NY: Cornell University Press, 2017); and Christopher M. Tinson, *Radical Intellect:* Liberator *Magazine and Black Activism in the 1960s* (Chapel Hill: University of North Carolina Press, 2017).

[78] Harold G. Lawrence, "African Explorers of the New World," *Crisis*, June–July 1962, 328.

used linguistic analysis and Spanish colonial accounts to trace the West African – Berber, Wolof, Soninke, Malinke, and Bambara – origins of indigenous words. Discussing Melgar's colossal head, he hoped "only to do homage to the man who long ago had suspected the African influence in Mexican civilization."[79]

Most Mexicans and their US colleagues remained perplexed by the head but grew weary of its supposed African origin. In the 1920s, the belief that it proved the African discovery of the hemisphere had quieted. Wiener's controversial statements went unmentioned in Mexico, even while questions about pre-Columbian migratory patterns continued. In 1922, Miguel Othón de Mendizábal placed the Olmecs, the people associated with the head, squarely within the history of pre-Columbian indigenous communities and their migration from Asia to the Americas. Unsure of the origins of the earliest civilizations in the hemisphere, he asked, "Could there perhaps be another community more ancient?"[80] In 1925, Tulane University archeologist Frans Blom traveled with Oliver La Farge to the states of Veracruz and Tabasco, where they discovered La Venta, an archeological site with another head and countless other artifacts. Although born in Denmark and affiliated with Tulane's Department of Middle American Research, Blom had already worked with Mexico's Bureau of Anthropology in 1922 and was therefore well connected in Mexican intellectual circles. Versed in the debates about the colossal head, Blom and La Farge recognized Melgar's contribution to pre-Columbian history and noted that some archeologists claimed that the Mayans "came from Egypt, or even are descendants of African races." Like Mendizábal, they did not embrace that line of thought, even though they shared the belief that these archeological sites pointed researchers toward the first breaths of Mayan civilization if not of all the indigenous peoples of the Americas.[81]

79 Leo Wiener, *Africa and the Discovery of America*, vol. 1 (Philadelphia, PA: Innes, 1920), ix; and Leo Wiener, *Africa and the Discovery of America*, vol. 3 (Philadelphia, PA: Innes, 1922), esp. 322.

80 Miguel O. de Mendizábal, *Las artes aborígenes mexicanas* (Mexico City: Imprenta del Museo Nacional de Arqueología, Historia y Etnografía, 1922), 11, C14–4, C14 Historia Antigua #21, UDLAP-SACE-FMQ.

81 Oliver La Farge and Frans Blom, *Tribes and Temples: A Record of the Expedition to Middle America Conducted by the Tulane University of Louisiana in 1925*, vol. 1 (New Orleans, LA: Tulane University, 1926), 17, 94–95, and 150, qtd. 94. For their discussion of Melgar, see Oliver La Farge and Frans Blom, *Tribes and Temples: A Record of the Expedition to Middle America Conducted by the Tulane University of Louisiana in 1925*, vol. 2 (New Orleans, LA: Tulane University, 1927), 506 and 531.

By the late 1930s, Mexican and US archeologists exhuming these curiosities were on the verge of concluding that the Olmecs were indigenous. But to translate Olmec aesthetics into terms that their readers could visualize, they often used stereotyped references to black bodies to describe Olmec art. In 1939, under the auspices of the National Geographic Society and the Smithsonian Institute, Matthew Stirling made his way to Veracruz to examine the colossal head Meglar uncovered. Completely covered in dirt, archeologists and antique dealers had long ignored it. Stirling asked, "What would be revealed by the complete excavation of the head? Was it attached to a body? If so, what would be its position – crouching, seated, or standing?" Like his predecessors, he realized that these artifacts could shed light on the first civilizations in the Americas, even when he rejected the assumption that the heads were African and instead concluded they were probably Mayan or Huastecan. To describe the heads and to accompany the black and white photos his readers saw in *National Geographic*, he wrote that their "features are bold and amazingly negroid in character."[82]

Mexicans also grappled with historical and cultural significance of these Olmec artifacts. Taking the helm, Alfonso Caso and Miguel Covarrubias claimed that this civilization not only predated the Maya but, as the first indigenous civilization in human history, was the foundation for all of indigenous America.[83] Covarrubias joined Stirling on some digs and began to collect pre-Columbian relics. He became an expert on ancient indigenous art and a professor on the subject at the National School of Anthropology and History. Moreover, Covarrubias and Caso helped coordinate Mexico's *Twenty Centuries of Mexican Art*, a massive display of Mexico's pre-Columbian, colonial, and modern art, at the MoMA. Referring to the recent archeological discoveries in Veracruz, the exhibition catalog states, "Until recently, it would have not been possible to understand the whole course of Mexican art, from the Olmec figurines to the creations of [José Clemente] Orozco."[84]

[82] Matthew W. Stirling, "Discovering the New World's Oldest Dated Work of Man: Maya Monument Inscribed 291 B.C. is Unearthed Near a Huge Stone Head by a Geographic-Smithsonian Expedition in Mexico," *National Geographic*, August 1939, 192 and 209.

[83] Miguel Covarrubias was uncomfortable with the term Olmec. He often chose to put it in scare quotes for two reasons: it was a term invented by Spanish conquistadores; and this civilization's cultural influence was better represented by the term "La Venta," his preferred descriptor; see "Tlatilco: Archaic Mexican Art and Culture," *Dyn* 4–5 (1943): 40–46; and Miguel Covarrubias, "La Venta: Colossal Heads and Jaguar Gods," *Dyn* 6 (1944): 27.

[84] Antonio Castro Leal, introduction to *Twenty Centuries of Mexican Art* (New York: Museum of Modern Art, 1940), 14.

In 1942, an impressive array of Mexican and US scholars came together at a roundtable in Chiapas to reach a conclusion about Olmec history and culture. The relationship between Mayan and Olmec societies, especially which was the mother civilization of all of Mesoamerica, was at the heart of the proceedings. The African origins of the Olmecs received no attention. Only Jorge R. Acosta related black corporeality to Olmec aesthetics. Artifacts from Monte Albán, he explained, "present features invariably negroid ... that are also like the Olmecs of Veracruz."[85] No article, including Covarrubias's first published statement on the subject, associated the wide flat noses and thick lips with the black body.[86] Presumably to affix the Olmecs to indigenous civilizations and the history of Asian migration to the Americas during the Ice Age, many participants mentioned the sculptures' "Mongoloid eyes." To decouple aesthetics and human physiology and therefore to reject any declaration of the African origins of Mesoamerica, Juan Comas opined, "The anthropomorphic representations of 'Olmec' art should not be taken as an expression of the physical type of the Olmecs."[87]

Pre-Columbian civilizations and their twentieth-century footprints guided Covarrubias until his premature death in 1957. These inquiries initially led to *Mexico South*, the first book to integrate African-descended cultures into the postrevolutionary ethnographic landscape (See Chapter 4). Recognition of Afro-Cuban music in Veracruz as well as the legacies of the slave trade in the state accompanies a much longer discussion of Olmec culture and society. Upon reaching the archeological sites exhumed by Blom, La Farge, and Stirling, Covarrubias introduced his readers to the debates about this grand civilization. He inveighed against its supposed African origins and the nineteenth-century theories of human migration that buttressed such fallacious conclusions. New scientific methods, like radiocarbon dating, and the discovery of new artifacts and archeological sites reinvigorated Olmec history, even while Mexican archeology was acquiring its disciplinary and institutional footing. Covarrubias self-servingly noted that, for the

[85] Jorge R. Acosta, "Rasgos olmecas en Monte Albán," in *Mayas y olmecas: Segunda reunión de mesa redonda sobre problemas antropológicas de México y Centro América* (Tuxtla Gutiérrez, Chiapas: 1942), 56.

[86] Miguel Covarrubias, "Origen y desarrollo del estilo artístico 'olmeca,'" in *Mayas y olmecas*, 46. Also see Villela, "Miguel Covarrubias and Twenty Centuries of Pre-Columbian Latin American Art, from the Olmec to the Inka," 52.

[87] Juan Comas, "El problema de la existencia de un tipo racial olmeca," in *Mayas y olmecas*, 69.

first time since Melgar discovered the first colossal head, "real progress has been made in the knowledge of how they came into being." These excavations brought scientific integrity to the previously unchecked "dilettante speculation as to where these arts originated: Egypt, China, the legendary Atlantis, and the absurd 'continent of Mu' have all taken turns as sources of high civilization in America."[88]

In *Mexico South*, Covarrubias wrote that the heads were "seven feet high, powerfully carved in the likeness of a flat-nosed, thick-lipped, rather Negroid man's head, wearing a headdress reminiscent of a football-player's helmet."[89] His posthumously published *Indian Art of Mexico and Central America* (1957) continues to describe the Olmec heads as having "Negroid features." Other smaller Olmec statuettes were "Mongoloid and Negroid at the same time." But, he cautioned "It is, of course, dangerous to attempt to identify a people by physical characteristics shown in their art; there is no such a thing as a uniform ethnic type, and it is well known that peoples seldom portray their characteristic type."[90] There was a logic to these references to black corporeality. Texts written in English for US readers, like *Mexico South* and *Indian Art of Mexico and Central America*, tend to describe the heads' features as black to translate their visual cues into words familiar to his north-of-the-border audiences. When writing for Mexicans less familiar with the black body, he minimized these allusions and instead described the sculptures with references to their Mongoloid eyes and jaguar lips.[91]

Covarrubias's texts were anything but veritable transcriptions of the pre-Columbian past. Since the 1920s, he had played with the relationships among culture, race, and the human body. Although the black body was the visual touchstone of his New Negro art, he followed the modernist desire to delve into the inner spirit of a particular person or community. Alfred A. Knopf, Inc., noted that his caricatures had been "tentative

[88] Covarrubias, *Mexico South*, 120. Regarding the political and methodological debates surrounding Mexican archeology following the Second World War, see Paul Gillingham, *Cuauhtémoc's Bones: Forging National Identity in Modern Mexico* (Albuquerque: University of New Mexico Press, 2011).

[89] Covarrubias, *Mexico South*, 84. Also see Miguel Covarrubias, *The Eagle, the Jaguar, and the Serpent: Indian Art of the Americas. North America: Alaska, Canada, the United States* (New York: Alfred A. Knopf, 1954), 65–71.

[90] Miguel Covarrubias, *Indian Art of Mexico and Central America* (New York: Alfred A. Knopf, 1957), 50, 58, and 65.

[91] Miguel Covarrubias, "Tipología de la industria de piedra tallada y pulida de la cuenca del Rio Mezcala," 14256–14259, expediente 284; and various documents in expediente 327, UDLAP-SACE-AMC.

experiments with racial characteristics." But, by 1927, they had transformed into "something new – neither the absurdity of the comic strip, nor the weak sentimentality of 'idealistic' painting, nor even a meaningless realism."[92] In a review of *Negro Drawings*, Walter Pach of the *New York Herald Tribune* depicted the caricatures as character studies tied to culture not race. The "primitive passion, religiosity and heroism" ubiquitous in Mexico City made it "natural for Covarrubias to succeed in portraying the men and women who evolved the cake-walk – and the spirituals."[93] His famous caricature, "A Prediction for Carl, from Covarrubias," best illustrates the aesthetic and spiritual nature of Covarrubias's art: Van Vechten, a prominent white patron of the New Negro Movement, appears as an African American (See Figure 7.9). Now interested in the Olmecs, Covarrubias often drew himself, as one of these large basalt heads, not because he was Olmec or looked like the heads, but because he was fascinated by them (See Figure 7.10).

With Alfonso Caso, Covarrubias helped usher a historiographic shift in Mexican archeology. Of course, he was aware of and cited the nineteenth-century excavations done by Melgar. More frequently, he looked to Blom, La Farge, and Stirling for empirical data regarding the indigenous roots of Olmec society. Building on Caso's and Covarrubias's research, US archeologist Michael Coe called these African theses "wild speculations." Covarrubias set the parameters for Coe's analysis of pre-Columbian artifacts. "No other person," Coe wrote in 1968, "could rival him in his intuition about the Mesoamerican past and in his feeling for objects and styles."[94] This revisionist stance, like Mexican postrevolutionary nationalism in general, wholeheartedly rejected Melgar's findings and Wiener's Afrocentricity. In 1975, Beatriz de la Fuente, one of Mexico's leading scholars of pre-Columbian art, synthesized the revisions that had taken place since the 1930s. "Certainly, the Colossal Heads," she unequivocally stated, "do not represent

[92] "Negro Drawings by Miguel Covarrubias," 1/6429, expediente 125, UDLAP-SACE-AMC.

[93] Walter Pach, "An Artist Looks on Harlem," *New York Herald Tribune*, November 6, 1927, 2/6576, expediente 128, UDLAP-SACE-AMC.

[94] Michael D. Coe, *America's First Civilization: Discovering the Olmec* (New York: American Heritage, 1968), 39 and 47. Also see, Jesús Romero Flores, *Historia de la cultura mexicana* (Mexico City: Editorial B. Costa-AMIC, 1963), 20–21; and Elizabeth P. Benson, ed., *Dumbarton Oaks Conference on the Olmec* (Washington, DC, 1968). This historiographic revision made its way into Mexican print culture; see "La cultura de la Venta," *Histórica Gráfico de México – Novedades* (1952), 14310, expediente 289, UDLAP-SACE-AMC.

FIGURE 7.9 Miguel Covarrubias, "A Prediction to Carl, from Covarrubias." María Elena Covarrubias/Archivo Miguel Covarrubias. Sala de Archivo y Colecciones Especiales. Dirección de Bibliotecas, Universidad de las Américas Puebla.

individuals of the black or Ethiopic race."[95] Even Aguirre Beltrán, the Mexican intellectual with the strongest desire to find pure Africanisms, rejected the African origins of pre-Columbian Mexico. In discussing West African influences on sixteenth-century Mexican society, he took Wiener to task: "It is not possible to accept, like Wiener expects, the Mandinka influence in pre-Columbian Nahuatl language, since the existence of contact between Africa and the Americas has not been demonstrated prior to its discovery."[96]

[95] Beatriz de la Fuente, *Las cabezas colosales olmecas* (Mexico City: Fondo de Cultura Económica, 1975), 59.
[96] Aguirre Beltrán, *La población negra de México* (1946), 104.

FIGURE 7.10 Miguel Covarrubias, self-portrait as an Olmec head. María Elena Covarrubias/Archivo Miguel Covarrubias. Sala de Archivo y Colecciones Especiales. Dirección de Bibliotecas, Universidad de las Américas Puebla.

However, not everyone was willing to accept Covarrubias's assertion about the Olmecs or his place at the center of Mexican archeology. *National Geographic* depicted him as an artist fascinated with the recently exhumed monuments; not trained in archeology, he seemed to be more a dilettante than a researcher.[97] Some reviewers of *Mexico South* in the United States questioned Covarrubias's steadfast declarations that the Olmecs, as Mesoamerica's mother civilization, predated the Mayans.[98] Long fascinated with indigenous cultures, Texas expatriate and Cuernavaca resident Eudora Garrett was riveted by the Olmecs. In spite of having translated ethnographic and historical texts about Mexico into English, she seemed to be unaware of Covarrubias's and Caso's new interpretations. As her lover Audre Lorde recounted in 1982, "She told me about the Olmec stone heads of African people that were being found in Tabasco, and the ancient contacts between Mexico and Africa and Asia that were just now coming to light." Her interest piqued, Lorde hoped to

[97] Marion Stirling, "Jungle Housekeeping for a Geographic Expedition," *National Geographic*, September 1941, 323.

[98] For reviews of *Mexico South*, see "The Book Shelf," 3/28681; and Rodney Gallup's review in the November 1948 issue of *Man*, 3/28686, expediente 544, UDLAP-SACE-AMC.

return to Mexico to see the pre-Columbian ruins of Chichén Itzá and the Olmec heads.[99]

The disjuncture between Mexican and US histories of the colossal heads was most clearly found in Black Nationalist circles, where Melgar's outdated conclusions and Wiener's Afrocentrism informed decades-long political projects to redeem Africa's image in world history and to establish sovereign black nation-states.[100] Emblematic of these potent albeit discredited racial typologies, the Olmec heads signaled the global reach of Africa's civilizational prowess. On March 10, 1960, Henry Willcox wrote to W. E. B. Du Bois about his trip to Xalapa, Veracruz. Willcox had visited a museum that displayed six-to-eight of these "beautifully carved" heads. His enthusiasm was palpable, in part because African American history and culture had not yet been established in museums in the United States. "There is as yet no authoritative theory about them," Willcox exclaimed, "but they are supposed to date between 1000 BC and 200 AD – definitely not Maya." He noted that the heads' "features are unmistakably negroid, utterly unlike any American Indians we know of." Clearly not everyone in Mexico had adopted the newest archeological findings that trumpeted the civilization's indigenous origins. By chance, Willcox had stumbled into the museum's director, who stated they were of African descent. After hearing this, Willcox and his wife "immediately thought we must have your opinion on them."[101] Responding quickly on March 14, Du Bois mentioned Wiener's *Africans and the Discovery of America*, which "pointed out innumerable proofs of African influence in America."[102] Du Bois's reference to Wiener's discredited monograph is telling. His Afro-diasporic politics trumped any interest in Mexican archeology. Covarrubias's theories about human

[99] Lorde, *Zami*, 164, 170, and 176; and Richard Zelade, *Austin in the Jazz Age* (Charleston, SC: History Press, 2015), 145–47.

[100] As historian Keisha N. Blain explains in regard to African American emigration to Liberia, Black Nationalist political and cultural projects could align with the separatist dictums of White Nationalism; see *Set the World on Fire: Black Nationalist Women and the Global Struggle for Freedom* (Philadelphia: University of Pennsylvania Press, 2018), 104–32. As such, the citing and quoting outmoded racial assumptions, like Meglar's and Wiener's, was a sometimes a pillar of Black Nationalism.

[101] Henry Willcox to W. E. B. Du Bois, March 10, 1960, UMAL-SCUA-WDP. For another example of Mexicans in the late 1950s and 1960s considering the African origins of the Olmec heads, see Tibón, *Pinotepa Nacional*, 78. Historian Andrea A. Burns provides a history of the black museum movement that began in the 1960s in *From Storefront to Monument: Tracing the Public History of the Black Museum Movement* (Amherst: University of Massachusetts Press, 2013).

[102] W. E. B. Du Bois to Henry Willcox, March 14, 1960, UMAL-SCUA-WDP.

migration and the origins of the heads not only went unmentioned but, considering Willcox's lament about the lack of a true theory about them, also outside his scholarly and political interests.

Willcox saw these heads during a moment of transition in Mexican archeology, when the Mexican state was retelling the nation's pre-Columbian history. Because they caught everyone's attention, the PRI displayed them as a centerpiece of the nation's history and culture in European cities such as Paris, Rome, and Moscow and at World's Fairs in New York City and San Antonio in 1964 and 1968.[103] It was investing huge amounts of money, intellectual effort, and institutional support in Mexico City and Xalapa to build state-of-the-art anthropology museums that celebrated the Olmecs as the foundation for Mexican civilization. The artifacts Willcox saw in Xalapa, for instance, would have been by November of that year at the forefront of the nation's indigenous-centric origin story, a narrative crafted at the Museum of Anthropology in Xalapa, Veracruz, under the auspices of Gonzalo Aguirre Beltrán, Rector of the University of Veracruz, and built on the back of Covarrubias's archeological and historical synthesis.[104]

Some Black Nationalists were slightly more attuned to the debates surrounding the Olmecs than Willcox and Du Bois were. By the late 1960s, they established an alternative intellectual genealogy that asserted the civilization's African origins. Trailblazers like Melgar and Wiener made appearances, but this historiographic tradition was decidedly African American in origin and in politics. They cited Carter G. Woodson for his pioneering discussions of African civilizations in world history. Regarding the Olmecs, a subject outside of his geographic specialties, Woodson took Wiener's conclusions at face value. "According to Leo Wiener, of Harvard University," he penned, "the Africans were the first to discover America."[105] Others read, cited, and distributed the many

[103] Luis M. Castañeda, *Spectacular Mexico: Design, Propaganda, and the 1968 Olympics* (Minneapolis: University of New Mexico Press, 2014), 31–51.

[104] Néstor Garcia Canclini, *Hybrid Cultures: Strategies for Entering and Leaving Modernity*, trans. Christopher L. Chiappari and Silvia L. López (Minneapolis: University of Minnesota Press, 1995), 116–30; and Álvaro Brizuela Absalón, "Museo de Antropología de la Universidad Veracruzana," in vol. 7 of *La antropología en México: Panorama histórico*, coord. Carlos García Mora (Mexico City: Instituto Nacional de Antropología e Historia, 1988), 437–43. Gonzalo Aguirre Beltrán saw the university as a fundamental pillar for the making and celebration of local and regional cultures; see "El Instituto de Antropología y el florecimiento cultural de Veracruz," in *La universidad latinoamericana y otros ensayos* (Xalapa: Universidad Veracruzana, 1961), 173–76.

[105] Woodson, *The Negro in Our History*, 58–59.

pamphlets and books written by Joel Augustus Rogers, who often used phenotypes to prove, for example, Diego Rivera's "Negro strain" and the African origins of the Olmec heads.[106] To introduce Rogers's *World's Great Men of Color* in 1972, John Henrik Clarke synthesized this intellectual history. "There has been a revolution in research and scholarship," he proclaimed, "relating to this still developing area of our hemisphere." The reclamation of Wiener's, Woodson's, and Rogers's investigations to prove "the presence of African peoples in pre-Columbian South and Central America, and in the United States" was at the forefront of this historiographic revision. In political terms, these historians had freed African history from the racist assumptions of Western thought, and their conclusions underscored "the current cry for Black History and Black Power."[107]

Postrevolutionary Mexican archeology was largely absent from this intellectual genealogy. Clarke for instance failed to mention Covarrubias – and his only direct reference to Mexican archeology was Alexander von Wuthenau's English-language *The Art of Terracotta Pottery in Pre-Columbian Central and South America*. German by birth, von Wuthenau was a researcher at Mexico City's University of the Americas who acknowledged Covarrubias's importance to pre-Columbian art. Yet, he too rejected the indigenous narrative espoused by Mexican archeologists and their US colleagues. He used the bodily features of pre-Columbian art to determine the races of their sculptors. Not all were of African origin, since some artifacts resembled Mongol, Chinese, Japanese, and Semitic peoples. Based in rhetorical assumptions that diminished the aesthetic creativity of all human communities, he stated:

> Because the individual and racial characteristics of the human face are something that no one would be able to invent by accident, it seems to me that if ever anything were created by God, it was surely the racial differentiations of mankind. It is in contradiction, moreover, to the most elementary logic and to all artistic experience that an Indian could depict in a masterly way the head of a Negro or of a white

[106] Rogers, *Sex and Race*, vol. 2, 9, and 76; and J. A. Rogers, *100 Amazing Facts about the Negro with Complete Proof: A Short Cut to the World History of the Negro* (Bay Street, St. Johns ANU: Brawtley Press, 1995). On Rogers's political and intellectual significance, for instance, among Black Panthers in Baltimore, Maryland, see Ta-Nehisi Coates, *The Beautiful Struggle: A Memoir* (New York: Spiegel and Grau, 2009), 13, 90, and 136.

[107] John Henrik Clarke, introduction to vol. 2 of *World's Great Men of Color*, by J. A. Rogers, ed. John Henrik Clarke (New York: Collier Books, 1972), xi–xv and xviii.

person without missing a single racial characteristic, unless he had actually seen such a person.[108]

Unlike Caso, Covarrubias, and Coe, von Wuthenau couched his research in diasporic terms. He presented photographs and terracotta "of pre-Columbian Negroid representations" at the First World Festival of Negro Art in Dakar in April 1966.[109] Focused on African decolonization and interracial harmony, the Festival sought to give African-descended peoples the opportunity "to return periodically to the sources of their art."[110] His conclusions sat awkwardly between the global dimensions of Black Nationalism and the cultural constructions of race in Mexico. Most notably, he thought Covarrubias's art was a veritable representation of the Olmecs' racial roots, an idea that was antithetical to Covarrubias's modernist aesthetic. Through a corporeal reading of pre-Columbian terracotta, what von Wuthenau called faciology, he asserted that Africans discovered the Americas and, in rhetoric more typical of postrevolutionary Mexico's veneration of racial unity, that "*all the races of mankind*" inhabited the Americas before Columbus's 1492 voyage.[111]

Writing for *Black World* in July 1973, Floyd W. Hayes III was mystified by the fact that "Africanists fail to recognize Leo Wiener ... or J. A. Rogers." He too went out of his way to analyze Olmec art phenotypically. Quoting Matthew Stirling, he italicized the archeologist's statement that heads were "flat-nosed and sensually thick-lipped." Hayes also paraphrased the more recent work done by Michael Coe, even while he maintained the biological assumptions that underpinned the diasporic appropriation of Olmec aesthetics. Responding rhetorically to the Mexican narrative that Coe extended, he asked:

108 Alexander von Wuthenau, *The Art of Terracotta Pottery in Pre-Columbian Central and South America* (New York: Crown, 1969), esp. 40–52.

109 Ibid., 178.

110 "The First World Festival of Negro Arts," *Negro Digest*, August 1965, 63–64.

111 Von Wuthenau, *The Art of Terracotta Pottery in Pre-Columbian Central and South America*, 11, 52, and 85. Regarding his misreading of Miguel Covarrubias, see Román Piña Chan and Luis Covarrubias, *El pueblo del jaguar (Los olmecas arqueológicos)*, drawings by Miguel Covarrubias (Mexico City: Museo Nacional de Antropología, 1964). By the mid-1960s, the artistic reimagination of the pre-Columbian past had the financial and institutional support of the Mexican state, which sponsored artists to work with archeologists, like Piña Chan, as they painted images for the National Anthropology Museum in Mexico City. As such, von Wurthenau's incorrect assumptions about Covarrubias's Olmec aesthetics were part of a broader exploration of the relationship between modern art and archeology. For a discussion of the murals created for the National Anthropology Museum, see Vaughan, *Portrait of a Young Painter*, 173–83.

If Africans were not present in the Americas before Columbus, why the typically African physiognomy of the monuments? It is in contradiction to the most elementary logic and to all artistic experience to suggest that these ancient Olmec artists could have depicted, with such detail, African facial features they had never seen.[112]

Guyanese-born Ivan Van Sertima expanded von Wurthenau assertions and became the face of this intellectual project with the publication of his 1976 book *They Came Before Columbus.*[113] After stumbling into Leo Wiener's research, Van Sertima became "fascinated by the subject." This history "if proven," he acknowledged, "could have far-reaching consequences for both American and African history." In a slight variation, possibly to reflect newer archeological findings, he explained that the Olmecs were not Africans but were aesthetically inspired by African corporeality – their lips, noses, skin color, and bone structure – and by African cultural attributes, such as the cotton caps of Gambian warriors. Taking Aguirre Beltrán's research out of context, Van Sertima cited his discussion of the African tradition of carrying heavy items on top of the head to prove the presence of pre-Columbian Africans in Mexico.[114]

CONCLUSION

By the 1960s and 1970s, the flat noses and large lips of Olmec plastic arts pointed toward two diverging but overlapping conceptions of the African Diaspora: one rooted more in black corporeality and the other based in regional cultural expressions. Two intellectual genealogies of social and demographic visibility, one Afro-diasporic and the other Mexican, had

[112] Floyd W. Hayes III, "The African Presence in America Before Columbus," *Black World*, July 1973, 8n10 and 13.

[113] Among the many scholars who have drawn on Van Sertima's research, see Kelley, "But a Local Phase of a World Problem," 1061–62; Jameelah S. Muhammad, "Mexico," in *No Longer Invisible: Afro-Latin Americans Today*, ed. Minority Rights Group (London: Minority Rights Group, 1995), 178n1; Pero Gaglo Dagbovie, *What Is African American History?* (Malden, MA: Polity Press, 2015), 30; and Ramsey, *Afro-Mexican Constructions of Diaspora, Gender, Identity and Nation*, 2. Van Sertima's ideas also have a following in Mexico; see Mario Moya Palencia, *Madre África: Presencia del África negra en el México y Veracruz antiguos*, 2nd ed. (Mexico City: Miguel Ángel Porrúa, 2006), esp. 155–218. For an overview of these debates and their fallacies, see Bernard Ortiz de Montellano et al., "They Were *NOT* Here before Columbus: Afrocentric Hyperdiffusionism in the 1990s," *Ethnohistory* 44, no. 2 (1997): 199–234.

[114] Ivan Van Sertima, *They Came Before Columbus* (New York: Random House, 1976), xiii, 25–26, 33, 98, and 106n21.

emerged from the political synchronicity buttressed by interwar era anti-fascism and inter-Americanism. Although Mexico's cultural version of race had its origins long before the Second World War, the need to reconcile the nation's African heritage with its contemporary ethnographic landscape was a new, often nettlesome project set against the backdrop of Mexican racial formations and Cold War socio-economic paradigms.

The ability to trace cultural expressions back to Africa unleashed a host of political and methodological conundrums about Mexico's place in the African Diaspora. While some artists, undoubtedly influenced by Elizabeth Catlett, basked in the history of African American activism and the plight of colonized Africans globally, models detailing interethnic integration predominated within Mexican cultural and policy circles. Postrevolutionary artists and ethnographers inverted the Afrocentric desire to give primacy to the black body in world history and instead queried: where had African-descended peoples failed to integrate into a national society defined by class mobility and mestizaje? In other words, they wondered why there were a few visibly African-descended communities along the Costa Chica and in Veracruz when the well-worn national narrative assumed black social and demographic invisibility. Black visibility sat at the confluence of cultural and social constructions of race and therefore elucidated the disparate historical pasts, social presents, and political potentialities of African-descended identities by the 1970s. These two visions of what and who was African-descended were products of the mutual constructions of biology and culture, race and space, indigeneity and blackness, and nation and diaspora in Mexico and the United States.

Conclusion

Images from Mexico City in October 1968 instantly evoke controversy in Afro-diasporic and Mexican histories. On the evening of October 16, African American sprinters Tommie Smith and John Carlos took to the Olympic podium to receive their respective gold and bronze medals in the 200-meter dash. During the national anthem, they stood shoeless to protest income inequality in the United States; Smith raised his right arm, and Carlos, his left, with their respective fists covered in black gloves. This last and most famous action, Smith recalled in his 2007 autobiography, "is described as a Black Power salute; it was not ... It was more than civil rights; that's why it was called human rights ... What we as black athletes took on for the whole world was a very basic platform that should have drawn support from everybody everywhere." Made possible by the gold medal around his neck, his visibility as a black athlete was secondary to his position "as a representative of oppressed people all over America, as a spokesman for the ambitious goal of the Olympic Project for Human Rights."[1] Almost immediately the US Olympic Committee rescinded Smith's and Carlos's athletic credentials and forced them to leave the Olympic Village. Many in the United States were infuriated by the duo's overt politics, which not only carried US racial concerns to the world's stage but also tarnished the spirit of human

[1] Tommie Smith, *Silent Gesture: The Autobiography of Tommie Smith*, with David Steele (Philadelphia, PA: Temple University Press, 2007), 1 and 22. Regarding the symbolism of their clothing, see John Carlos, *The John Carlos Story: The Sports Moment That Changed the World*, with Dave Zinn (Chicago, IL: Haymarket Books, 2013), 110 and 120.

solidarity that the games were supposed to foster and that spectators were supposed to enjoy.[2]

Mexican officials quickly sent word that Smith and Carlos could remain in the country if they procured the proper tourist visas. Booker Griffin of the *Los Angeles Sentinel*, an African American newspaper, spoke favorably of Mexico's chivalrous embrace of the track stars. "The brown brothers on the other side of the border," he penned six days after the medal ceremony, "roll out the red carpet for American blacks." Resembling the exhortations of the vast majority of African Americans who commented on Mexican racial formations, he continued, "Black is truly beautiful to the Mexico City natives."[3] In the United States, the often-reproduced photograph of Smith and Carlos has come to symbolize the generational shift from the mainstream Civil Rights Movement to the Black Power critique of liberal integration. It also verified, as Griffin's commentary shows, the endurance of Mexico's claim to racial tolerance. But, amid the Civil Rights Movement, even this rhetorical vestige of nineteenth-century Mexican liberalism had taken on new a veneer: Mexico transformed into a place where African Americans were not only culturally accepted or socially visible but also where "Black is Beautiful."

Just two weeks earlier, on October 2, the Mexican military injured and killed at least 100 Mexican students, much to the chagrin of African American activists like John Carlos.[4] After months of demonstrations and skirmishes with the police, middle-class students inspired by the New Left descended on Tlatelolco Plaza demanding that President Gustavo Díaz Ordaz disband the police's special riot forces, release political prisoners, and end the army's occupation of the National Autonomous University of Mexico. With people on all continents watching Mexico on the eve of the Olympics, the protesters snatched the nation's global platform away from the PRI and its carefully crafted image of Mexico as the first Third World country to host the games.

[2] On the response to Smith's and Carlos's actions on the medal stand, see Amy Bass, *Not the Triumph but the Struggle: The 1968 Olympics and the Making of the Black Athlete* (Minneapolis: University of Minnesota Press, 2002), 233–348.

[3] Booker Griffin qtd. in Bass, *Not the Triumph but the Struggle*, 268–69.

[4] Carlos, *The John Carlos Story*, 106–8. The Black Panthers also hoped to connect with the student protesters; see Malloy, *Out of Oakland*, 114 and 272n22. For example, the March 9, 1969, issue of *Black Panther* discussed the struggle in Mexico. Its cover featured Hugo Brehme's famous photo of Emiliano Zapata from Cuernavaca, Morelos, in May 1911. The article "Children of Zapata," trans. Jackie Stiles Quayle, provides transcripts of interviews with three student protestors; see 10–11.

Photographs and firsthand accounts of the massacre quickly symbolized the unsavory underbelly of Mexican modernity under the PRI. To pull the country back together and to reign in the students who had come of age in the 1960s, Luis Echeverría Álvarez, who had been Minister of the Interior during the fateful events of October 1968, embarked on a new populist program reminiscent of Lázaro Cárdenas's a generation earlier. As President from 1970 to 1976, he aligned himself with Third Worldism, redistributed land, expanded the INI, and brought some of the student protesters into the state apparatus, giving them the tools to shape the next generation of postrevolutionary nation-state formation.[5]

Neither of these vignettes directly tells us anything new about Mexico's relationship to the African Diaspora. If anything, they reaffirm the rhetorical propensity of foreigners to affix racial egalitarianism to Mexico. They also confirm the stagnancy of the postrevolutionary reforms forged through the simultaneous refashioning of indigeneity, blackness, and mestizaje. The absence of a stronger correlation is more indicative of the diverging postwar trajectories between Mexico's cultural and spatial constructions of race and the social and demographic constructions more common in the United States.[6] Mexican racial formations – which, as I have argued, gained international renown during the Second World War as the antidote to fascism, racism, and segregation – appeared insufficient once a new generation of Mexican and Afro-diasporic intellectuals radicalized in the 1960s and 1970s. Black cultural visibility – and its twin, social invisibility – were suddenly nothing more than a relic of the assimilationist doctrines that needed to be toppled if the 1910 Revolution's goals were finally to be achieved.

[5] For an analysis of these two waves of Mexican populism, see Amelia M. Kiddle and María L. O. Muñoz, ed., *Populism in Twentieth Century Mexico: The Presidencies of Lázaro Cárdenas and Luis Echeverría* (Tucson: University of Arizona Press, 2010).

[6] As Eric Zolov observes, scholars have remembered these two moments in Mexico in October 1968 as distinct histories, not as intertwined narratives about the global sixties; see "Showcasing the 'Land of Tomorrow,'" 159–60 and 186–88. Lance Wyman's art points to a potential unexplored link between them. As the architect of Mexico's Olympic imagery, he designed the famous Mexico '68 logo and the signage for the Mexico City metro, among other examples. However, in response to the assassination of Martin Luther King Jr., he also designed a Mexican stamp with King's portrait in his typical op-art style; see Elena Gonzales, "Who Are We Now? Roots, Resistance, and Recognition," in *The African Presence in México: From Yanga to the Present*, coord. Claudia Herrera (Chicago, IL: Mexican Fine Arts Center Museum, 2006), 182.

THE POLITICS OF BLACKNESS AFTER 1968

These 1960s generational conflicts exacerbated the growing rift between US and Mexican conceptions of the African Diaspora that had been building since the late 1940s, when blackness started to gain social and demographic visibility south of the Rio Grande and the Civil Rights Movement entered mainstream politics north of it. By the late 1960s and 1970s, once integration had given way to the anti-assimilationist mantras of Black Power, the black body flowered as a physical site on which the African American experience could be authenticated, owned, and performed. Wearing dashikis, afros, and bubas, learning Swahili, and taking an African name were ways for African Americans to use the body to visualize and celebrate their African heritage.[7] Accordingly, the failures of federal and state governments to enact the nation's founding credos, which Thomas Jefferson famously penned in 1776, framed African American history.

In Mexico, intellectuals and activists questioned the nation's cultural and regional constructions of blackness for the first time since independence. According to the generation of anthropologists who cut their teeth under the tutelage of Gonzalo Aguirre Beltrán and the INI, postrevolutionary narratives about unity and progress merely offered a shiny new veneer to state programs dedicated to indigenous disappearance, capitalist encroachment, and national homogeneity. In sum, democracy under the PRI was no more than political chicanery.[8] Rejecting the state's top-down approach to nation-state formation, these newly minted indigenists yearned for a nation-state forged from the bottom-up, beginning with grassroots indigenous campaigns and bilingual education. Integration and democracy were no longer assumed to be two sides of the same coin. In the 1960s, they dialogically read ethnographic theories written by postrevolutionary intellectuals, like Aguirre Beltrán, through Karl Marx's and Andre Gunder Frank's analyses of the political economy at the same time that they saw the INI's budget cut and the PRI shift its focus toward

[7] Jonathan Scott Holloway, *Jim Crow Wisdom: Memory and Identity in Black America since 1940* (Chapel Hill: University of North Carolina Press, 2013), 67–101; and Russell Rickford, *We Are an African People: Independent Education, Black Power, and the Radical Imagination* (New York: Oxford University Press, 2016), 100–130.

[8] On this new generation of anthropologists' relationship with Aguirre Beltrán, see Andrés Fábregas Puig, "Gonzalo Aguirre Beltrán y los análisis antropológicos de la política en México," in *Gonzalo Aguirre Beltrán: Memorial crítico. Diálogos con la obra de Gonzalo Aguirre Beltrán en el centenario de su natalicio*, coord. Félix Báez-Jorge (Mexico City: Editora de Gobierno del Estado de Veracruz, 2008), 38–48.

urban development, which in their minds came at the expense of the 1910 Revolution's popular aims.

With internal colonialism, decolonization, ethnocentrism, and paternalism – touchstones of the global 1960s – at the tip of their pens, this cohort of up-and-coming anthropologists, historians, sociologists, and political scientists ushered in a new variation of Marxist thought that pushed their predecessors' visions of blackness, Mexicanness, and democracy aside. They rejected the paternalist treatises proclaimed by light-skinned Mexican indigenists, like Aguirre Beltrán, at the same time that Black Power activists and scholars looked to reclaim the study of African-descended peoples and cultures from academics, like Melville Herskovits, who were not of African descent. Polemics written by Albert Memmi, Georges Balandier, and Frantz Fanon not only struck a chord with Mexico's newest indigenists but also brought an alternative politics of race to the forefront. Most acutely, Fanonian ideas of decolonization honed in Algeria provided a new model of political and cultural domination that fundamentally rejected the integrationist aims that the postrevolutionary Mexican state made famous. Relegated to the abstractions of revolutionary theories and epistemologies born abroad, blackness lived primarily in the footnotes of Mexico's young dissidents, not in their empirical observations.[9]

According to Francisco Rivera, the popular chronicler of the city of Veracruz, the countercultural movement replaced the polyvocal democratic ruckus of political debate with the cacophony of rock-and-roll. Youthful protesters were made "of meringue and coconut candy," the satiating opiates of a generation not yet versed in the nuances of Mexican

[9] For instance, see Pablo González Casanova, *La democracia en México* (Mexico City: Ediciones Era, 2006); and Arturo Warman et al., *De eso que llaman antropología mexicana* (Mexico City: Editorial Nuestro Tiempo, 1970). Recent historical research has detailed these generational debates and their importance for INI policies in the 1960s and 1970s; see María L. O. Muñoz, *Stand Up and Fight: Participatory Indigenismo, Populism, and Mobilization in Mexico, 1970–1984* (Tucson: University of Arizona Press, 2016); A. S. Dillingham, "Indigenismo Occupied: Indigenous Youth and Mexico's Democratic Opening (1968–1975)," *The Americas* 72, no. 4 (2015): 549–82; and Lewis, *Rethinking Mexican Indigenismo*, 175–204 and 227–44. Jaime M. Pensado and Enrique C. Ochoa's edited collection *México beyond 1968: Revolutionaries, Radicals, and Repression during the Global Sixties and Subversive Seventies* (Tucson: University of Arizona Press, 2018) explores the decade's new theories of democracy and Mexicanness. Regarding the relationship between Mexican nation-state formation and French colonial policies in Algeria, see Todd Shepard, "Algeria, France, Mexico, UNESCO: A Transnational History of Anti-racism and Decolonization, 1932–1962," *Journal of Global History* 6, no. 2 (2011): 273–97.

cultural history or postrevolutionary nationalism. Without Rivera's poetic verve, Aguirre Beltrán also criticized the anthropologists he helped to train for what he saw as their ingenuous denunciations of INI policies. In particular, he took umbrage with the 1970 anthology *De eso que llaman antropología mexicana* written by five anthropologists, nicknamed "*los magníficos*," who would steer the course of the discipline and of indigenist policy in the last quarter of the century. According to Aguirre Beltrán, the theory of internal colonialism they trumpeted was irrelevant to a Mexican society predicated on social mobility and class relations. While structures of socio-cultural domination were applicable in other parts of the world, notably in the Soviet Union and apartheid South Africa, they were, he argued, only present in Mexican regions where mestizo elites still exploited local indigenous and African-descended communities.[10]

In retrospect, Aguirre Beltrán's regions of refuge paradigm, his interethnic model of regional dominance, points to the different politics of blackness at stake in these generational diatribes. For him, this theory was rooted empirically in Cuijla, Guerrero, and theoretically in his engagement with the Afro-Atlantic dialogues he learned from Melville Herskovits and Fernando Ortiz.[11] His critics concealed these intellectual genealogies by tying his model of regional exploitation, like postrevolutionary nation-state formation in general, exclusively to indigeneity. There was a certain irony to this generational silencing of blackness in Mexico, since these iconoclastic indigenists articulated these critiques at the very moment when blackness was entering into the nation's social and demographic fabric for the first time since independence. Arguing that scholars needed to bring other racial and cultural communities into the conversation, Arturo Warman, one of the magníficos, bemoaned what he perceived as a false equivalency between nation-state formation and indigenism. His compatriot Mercedes Olivera de Vázquez went further,

[10] Gonzalo Aguirre Beltrán, "De eso que llaman antropología mexicana," in *Obra polémica*, vol. 11 of *Obra antropológica* (Mexico City: Fondo de Cultural Económica, 1992), 110–14. These debates in Mexican social science made their way back to African American print culture. For instance, the December 25, 1969, issue of *Jet* cited an article about racial discrimination by Raúl Béjar Navarro to declare that Mexicans discriminated against African-descended peoples just like they discriminated against indigenous, mestizo, and Chinese populations; see "Cites Bias against, Indians, Black in Mexico," *Jet*, December 25, 1969, 44; and Raúl Béjar Navarro, "Prejuicio y discriminación racial en México," *Revista Mexicana de Sociología* 31, no. 2 (1969): 417–33.

[11] Regarding Aguirre Beltrán's broader theoretical approach to culture change and interethnic relations, see *El proceso de la aculturación*.

explaining that they have introduced "new comparative elements, above all about what has been researched in Africa, Asia, and South America."[12]

Citing his own work as well as others from the 1950s and 1960s, Aguirre Beltrán criticized this hasty repudiation of exactly what these younger anthropologists wanted: a broader ethnographic engagement with world history.[13] With few exceptions, an empirical, theoretical, and political rift grew between Aguirre Beltrán's work on the nation's indigenous and African-descended communities. His inclinations – and those of countless other Mexican intellectuals, cultural producers, and policy makers since the 1930s – to use the cultural legacies of African slavery to contextualize, catalyze, and craft indigenous integration and class-based social justice disappeared.[14] The marginalization of his research was already a sore spot for Aguirre Beltrán, and it undoubtedly continued to rankle him when his students took stewardship of the indigenous institutions, like the INI, that he helped build. With the publication of a second slightly revised edition of his seminal *La población negra de México* in 1972, he complained about the minimal influence of the first.[15] In 1994, his lamentations remained. "Africanist studies in Mexico," he exclaimed, "enjoy poor acceptance."[16]

In the United States, Black Power laid the foundation for new studies of African slavery in colonial Mexico and across the Western Hemisphere. Student activists wanting to decolonize university curricula advocated for ethnic studies programs like Black Studies. Similarly, professional historians promoted new historical methodologies that explored the social

[12] Mercedes Olivera de Vázquez, "Algunos problemas de la investigación antropológica actual," in Warman et al., *De eso que llaman antropología mexicana*, 114; and Arturo Warman, "Todos santos y todos difuntos: Crítica histórica de la antropología mexicana," in Warman et al., *De eso que llaman antropología mexicana*, 40–41.

[13] Aguirre Beltrán, "De eso que llaman antropología mexicana," 102 and 105–6.

[14] Mexican social scientists divided Aguirre Beltrán's research projects on indigeneity and blackness into two separate topics of inquiry; see the essays in Instituto Indigenista Interamericano, *Homenaje a Gonzalo Aguirre Beltrán*, 3 vols. (Mexico City: Instituto Indigenista Interamericano, 1973–74). One notable exception is Félix Báez-Jorge, "Aculturación e integración intercultural: Un momento histórico del indigenismo mexicano," in *INI: 30 años después. Revisión crítica* (Mexico City: México Indígena, Diciembre de 1978), 290–99.

[15] Aguirre Beltrán, *La población negra de México*, 2nd ed. (1972), 11.

[16] Gonzalo Aguirre Beltrán, *El negro esclavo en Nueva España: La formación colonial, la medicina popular y otros ensayos*, vol. 16 of *Obra antropológica* (Mexico City: Universidad Veracruzana, 1994), 13. Rolando Pérez Fernández drew directly on Aguirre Beltrán's research to make a similar argument in *La música afromestiza mexicana*, 3.

histories of African Americans "from below."[17] Much like the comparative study of African cultural retentions that had unified Afro-Atlantic conversations in the 1930s and 1940s, research on the demographics of the slave trade now provided a common point of departure for scholars to compare slave systems in the Americas.[18] Latin America was not immune to this historiographic revision or to the political ferment buttressing it. References to Martin Luther King Jr., Malcolm X, and the Black Panthers bolstered nationalist projects to recover the history of African-descended peoples across the hemisphere.[19]

Jamaican-born historian Colin A. Palmer embraced the task of bringing Mexico into this new generation of Afro-diasporic politics. In 1968, as a graduate student at the University of Wisconsin, he began to research African slavery in sixteenth- and seventeenth-century Mexico. Demands for "courses dealing with the black experience" resonated with him, even while he pushed back against the presentism of the more radical cultural and intellectual conversations that, I argue, imposed US constructions of the black body onto Mexican demographics and declared the African origins of pre-Columbian civilizations. The African American experience in the United States could not act as a springboard for a wholescale revision of world history. According to Palmer, it needed to be historicized and put in conversation with "the history of other peoples of African descent in the New World, particularly in Latin America." Mexico caught his attention, not only for its early dependence on the Atlantic slave trade

[17] Fabio Rojas, *From Black Power to Black Studies: How a Radical Social Movement Became an Academic Discipline* (Baltimore: Johns Hopkins University Press, 2007); and Biondi, *The Black Revolution on Campus*. For a discussion of the mainstreaming of African American history and its embrace of social history, see Dagbovie, *What Is African American History?*, 6–52.

[18] Philip D. Curtain, "The African Diaspora," *Historical Reflections* 6, no. 1 (1979): 1–2. In Mexico, for example, see Fernando Winfield Capitaine, "Población rural en Córdoba, 1788," *La Palabra y el Hombre*, no. 30 (1979): 64–72. As a PhD student interested in the history of African-descended peoples in nineteenth-century Argentina, George Reid Andrews began his dissertation research in 1975 hoping to use "municipal censuses to document the disappearance of that population over the course of the 1800s"; see "Epilogue: Whiteness and Its Discontents," in *Rethinking Race in Modern Argentina*, ed. Paulina L. Alberto and Eduardo Elena (New York: Cambridge University Press, 2016), 318.

[19] Karin Alejandra Rosemblatt, "Modernization, Dependency, and the Global in Mexican Critiques of Anthropology," *Journal of Global History* 9, no. 1 (2014): 112–17; and Alfonso Cassiani Herrera, "La diáspora africana y afrodescendiente en Latinoamérica: Las redes de organizaciones como puntos de encuentros," in *Identidades políticas en tiempos de afrodescendencia: Auto-identificación, ancestralidad, visibilidad y derechos*, ed. Silvia Valero and Alejandro Campos García (Buenos Aires: Corregidor, 2015), 132.

but also because of the nation's comparative obliviousness to its African heritage. As he stated at the outset of his pioneering book *Slaves of the White God* (1976), one unnamed Mexican graduate student remarked to him that he "certainly made a mistake in coming to Mexico to study African slavery, since Africans had never been enslaved in his country!"[20]

In the 1980s, a historiography of African slavery in Mexico, replete with its own political implications, was coalescing. Aguirre Beltrán's research loomed over all of these inquiries but more recent works by US historians like Patrick Carroll and Colin Palmer also provided footing. Adriana Naveda Chávez-Hita, for instance, began to research the sugar plantations surrounding Córdoba, Veracruz, in 1975, before she studied with Carroll in the United States. She was surprised to see the region's "well-stocked documentation about black slavery." The nation's propensity to hide its African heritage still cast a shadow over academia and civil society decades after Aguirre Beltrán established himself as the father of this interdisciplinary field.[21] Despite the increasing ethnographic recognition of African-descended communities in the 1950s and 1960s, archival examinations of the nation's African-descended peoples in the nineteenth and twentieth centuries lacked the ample record books the colonial bureaucracy left for researchers concerned with colonial slavery.

FINDING AFRO-MEXICO, 1989–2015

Building on these historical works as well as the firsthand observations of earlier decades, the state established a bevy of regional and national institutions in the late 1980s and 1990s. The era witnessed wholescale attempts to unify the diverse disciplinary pursuits, cultural representations, and political initiatives that had marked previous articulations of Mexico's relationship to the African Diaspora.[22] Scholarly interests in the ethnographic study of African-descended communities, first by Mexicans

[20] Palmer, *Slaves of the White God*, vii.

[21] Naveda, *Esclavos negros en las haciendas azucareras de Córdoba, Veracruz*, 7; and Patrick J. Carroll, prologue to *Esclavos negros en las haciendas azucareras de Córdoba, Veracruz*, by Adriana Naveda Chávez-Hita (Xalapa: Universidad Veracruzana, 1987), 11.

[22] For an overview of some of these projects, see María Elisa Velázquez, "Afrodescendientes en museos de México: Silencio y olvido," *Gaceta de Museos*, no. 58 (2014): 27–31. As Mara Loveman explains, the gradual recognition of Mexico's African-descended population is just one example of a broader moment when Latin American nations sought to craft more inclusive, multicultural nations in the last decades of the twentieth century and the beginning of the twenty-first; see *National Colors*, 312–18.

in the 1980s and then by anthropologists in the United States in the 1990s, reemerged. Blackness and its relationship to mestizaje seemed particularly poignant once Mexico declared itself a multicultural nation in 1992.[23] Three years earlier, Guillermo Bonfil Batalla, the Director of Mexico's Popular Cultural Administration of the National Board for Culture and the Arts, gave credence to the idea that the nation's African-descended peoples and cultures were "Our Third Root." For the first time in Mexican history, there was a national organization dedicated to the nation's African heritage. The state no longer relegated the study and celebration of African-descended peoples and cultures to the furthest margins of institutions like the Bureau of Anthropology, INBA, and INI. One of the iconoclastic contributors to *De eso que llaman antropología mexicana*, Bonfil Batalla preserved many of his generation's critiques of postrevolutionary indigenism, including the proclivity to reduce Aguirre Beltrán's ethnographic contributions to an indigenous-centric version of his regions of refuge paradigm. Bonfil Batalla grounded Mexican identity in the pre-Columbian past, not the colonial-era racial and cultural mixtures that incorporated the descendants of enslaved Africans into the nation. To the chagrin of Aguirre Beltrán, he almost completely dismissed the nation's African heritage. He condensed this history to a few passing comments about the slave trade, black violence against indigenous communities, and the Spanish caste system. From this perspective, Bonfil Batalla's historical narrative mirrors prerevolutionary histories more than the postrevolutionary revisions driven by black cultural and spatial visibility. In 1987, he quipped that blackness "has been little studied," with its cultural footprint defined regionally "according to the size of the Black population, its relative magnitude in the local demography, and the particular conditions of the relationship with the rest of local society."[24]

Popular and academic pressure encouraged Bonfil Batalla to expand the social and cultural visibility of blackness. As the first action of Our Third Root, he convened eighteen researchers under Aguirre Beltrán's

[23] Vinson, "La historia del estudio de los negros en México," 67; and Gloria Lara, "Una corriente etnopolítica en la Costa Chica, México (1980–2000)," in *Política e identidad: Afrodescendientes en México y América Central*, coord. Odile Hoffmann (Mexico City: Instituto Nacional de Antropología e Historia, 2010), 307–34.

[24] Guillermo Bonfil Batalla, *México Profundo: Reclaiming a Civilization*, trans. Philip A. Dennis (Austin: University of Texas Press, 1996), 43; and Gonzalo Aguirre Beltrán, "Del materialismo dialéctico al culturalismo utópico: Guillermo Bonfil y su obra antropológica," *La Palabra y el Hombre*, no. 92 (1994): 25.

stewardship at the first Meeting of Afro-Mexicanists in 1989. The conference provided a scaffolding for the INAH to establish annual conferences on the topic beginning in 1997. While there had been sporadic seminars about Mexico's African heritage in the 1940s, Bonfil Batalla integrated these diverse disciplinary pursuits into a coherent interdisciplinary field. Previously, scholars had generally confined the subject to disciplinary-specific classes about comparative ethnography, like those envisioned by Nicolás León in 1906 or those Bonfil Batalla developed in 1974.[25] Bonfil Batalla also helped publish new ethnographic and historical works about African slavery. This scholarly pursuit contributed to a broader multicultural initiative to understand the contributions of disparate immigrant communities – African, Japanese, Arab, North American, and Spanish – to national culture. For academics and activists like Luz María Martínez Montiel, who were interested more specifically in colonial slavery and its legacies, Our Third Root provided the institutional support to celebrate the hidden regional histories and cultures of the African Diaspora in Mexico.[26]

Two geographies of blackness, with two competing notions of diasporic authenticity, hardened under the auspices of Our Third Root.[27] Following Aguirre Beltrán's archival footsteps, historians have tended to begin their inquiries in the port cities of the Gulf and Caribbean coasts, whereas ethnographers have prioritized the Costa Chica, where he observed what he considered to be the purest Africanisms. In the 1990s and 2000s, Trinidad's Father Glyn Jemmott Nelson helped develop a racial consciousness among Oaxaca's and Guerrero's African-

[25] Regarding the development of courses on Afro-Mexico by the 1990s, see Chege Githiora, *Afro-Mexicans: Discourse of Race and Identity in the African Diaspora* (Trenton, NJ: Africa World Press, 2008), 217; Luz María Martínez Montiel, *Afroamérica I: La ruta del esclavo* (Mexico City: Universidad Nacional Autónoma de México, 2006), 9; and María Elisa Velázquez and Ethel Correa, "Seminario: Estudios sobre poblaciones y culturas con herencia africana en México," *Diario de Campo*, no. 21 (2000): 19.

[26] Guillermo Bonfil Batalla, comp., *Simbiosis de culturas: Los inmigrantes y su cultura en México* (Mexico City: Fondo de Cultura Económica, 1993); and Luz María Martínez Montiel, coord., *Presencia africana en México* (Mexico City: Consejo Nacional para la Cultura y las Artes, 1997).

[27] The racial authenticities associated with the state of Veracruz and the Costa Chica, however, eschew other regions with histories of African slavery; for example, see Sierra Silva, *Urban Slavery in Colonial Mexico*, 5–6. Genomic research in Mexico has shown that African slaves left autosomal markers throughout much of Mexico, not just in these two coastal regions; see Peter Wade, "Conclusion: Race, Multiculturalism, and Genomics in Latin America," in *Mestizo Genomics: Race Mixture, Nation, and Science in Latin America*, ed. Peter Wade et al. (Durham, NC: Duke University Press, 2014), 217.

descended communities. As the parish priest of St. John of the Cross in Pinotepa Nacional, he organized the first annual Meeting of Black Communities in March 1997 and was instrumental in founding Black Mexico, a grassroots organization that advocated for the racial recognition of African-descended Mexicans on regional and national censuses.[28] These interests intersected when Our Third Root contributed funds to Cuijla's Museum of Afromestizo Cultures, which opened its doors to the public in 1996. Yet, the raising of a diasporic consciousness, as anthropologist Laura Lewis demonstrates, has been fraught with tensions among the community's older residents not comfortable with the homogenizing politics of the Museum, its local organizers, and the academics who revived Aguirre Beltrán's quest to find and preserve unblemished African cultural retentions among the Costa Chica's secluded towns.[29]

In contrast to the linear narrative of cultural transmission and diasporic authenticity articulated along the coasts of Guerrero and Oaxaca, people in the city and state of Veracruz have embraced a cosmopolitan geography more akin to Paul Gilroy's Black Atlantic.[30] Of course, the recognition of the constant cultural exchanges between Mexico and the Caribbean were not new in the 1980s and 1990s. Immediately after the 1910 Revolution, composers and musicologists feared the introduction of African-descended musical genres. By the late 1940s, and in the wake of the International Institute of Afro-American Studies, these cultural flows gave Miguel Covarrubias sufficient qualitative impressions to wed blackness in Veracruz to the Caribbean and provided Katherine Dunham with the ethnographic evidence to affix "La bamba" to the Afro-Cuban danzón. Francisco Rivera's verse has become the benchmark for the city of Veracruz's ties to the Atlantic world. After his death in 1994, the second edition of *Veracruz en la historia y en la cumbancha* was published with a new prologue praising him for helping "to create a poetry with the

[28] For example, see Jean-Philibert Mobwa Mobwa N'Djoli, "The Need to Recognize Afro-Mexicans as an Ethnic Group," in *Black Mexico: Race and Society from Colonial to Modern Times*, ed. Ben Vinson III and Matthew Restall (Albuquerque: University of New Mexico Press, 2009), 228–29. The states of Oaxaca and Guerrero gave their African-descended residents statewide recognition in 2013 and 2014, respectively; see Ramsay, *Afro-Mexican Constructions of Diaspora, Gender, Identity and Nation*, 162.

[29] Lewis, *Chocolate and Corn Flour*, esp. 94, 151, and 177–78.

[30] For example, see Luz María Martínez Montiel, "Mexico's Third Root," in *Africa's Legacy in Mexico/El legado de África en México*, by Tony Gleaton (Washington, DC: Smithsonian Institution, 1993), 24–30. Also see Paul Gilroy, *The Black Atlantic: Modernity and Double Consciousness* (Cambridge, MA: Harvard University Press, 1993).

features of the land, a sense of feeling that is without social circles, a language at times full of local idioms."[31]

In 1987, Governor Fernando Gutiérrez Barrios founded the Veracruz Cultural Institute to disseminate historical and cultural information, chiefly through museums, festivals, classes, books, and magazines. The next year, for Rivera's eightieth birthday, the Institute compiled and republished many of his poems in *Estampillas jarochas*. This anthology was part of a larger series celebrating the state's prominent intellectual and cultural icons, a series that also published a Festschrift to honor Aguirre Beltrán that same year.[32] The 1990s saw these multicultural calls flourish under the banner "Veracruz is also Caribbean," a cultural geography that, often invoking Rivera's poetry, helped resuscitate Afro-Caribbean musical genres, like danzón, along Mexico's Gulf Coast.[33]

COMPARISON AND THE POLITICS OF DIASPORA

Despite the institutional, intellectual, and cultural capital that policy makers, intellectuals, and cultural producers affixed to blackness by the beginning of the twenty-first century, its history is still told in relation to what is presumed to be missing, not what is expressed. In 2005, Mexican and US citizens found themselves at odds over a series of stamps featuring Memín Pinguín, a popular comic book figure conceived by Yolanda Vargas Dulché in 1943. For many Mexicans, Memín was (and still is) a jocular representation of popular culture and a window

[31] Lic. Francisco Ramírez Govea, prologue to the 2nd ed. of *Veracruz en la historia y en la cumbancha: Poemas jarochos*, by Francisco Rivera (Veracruz: Juan Carlos Lara Prado, 1994), np.

[32] Francisco Rivera Ávila, *Estampillas jarochas* (Veracruz: Instituto Veracruzano de Cultura, 1988); and Instituto Veracruzano de Cultura, *Jornadas de homenaje a Gonzalo Aguirre Beltrán* (Veracruz: Instituto Veracruzano de Cultura, 1988). Veracruz continued to celebrate these two figures after their respective deaths in 1994 and 1996; see Rivera, *Sobredosis de humor de Paco Píldora*; and *Gonzalo Aguirre Beltrán: Homenaje nacional* (Xalapa: Universidad Veracruzana, 1996).

[33] Instituto Veracruzano de Cultura, *2o. foro Veracruz también es Caribe: Veracruz 10–12 de octubre 1990* (Veracruz: Instituto Veracruzano de Cultura, 1992); and Instituto Veracruzano de Cultura, *Festival internacional afrocaribeño: Programa general y cartelera de junio* (Veracruz: Instituto Veracruzano de Cultura, 1996). Also see Pérez Fernández, *La música afromestiza*, 4 and 230–32; Hettie Malcomson "La configuración racial del danzón: los imaginarios raciales del puerto de Veracruz," in *Mestizaje, diferencia y nación: Lo "negro" en América Central y el Caribe*, coord. Elisabeth Cunin (Mexico City: Instituto Nacional de Antropología e Historia, 2010), 267–98; and Arce, *México's Nobodies*, 251–52.

into the country's penchant to elide biological race and reject racism. Vargas Dulché's childhood in Guerrero and her interactions with Afro-Cubans inspired her to create the comic to celebrate Mexican racial formations. However, the United States, including the administration of President George W. Bush, condemned the stamps. Memín's big ears and lips harkened back to the stereotyped pickaninny figures Jim Crow had long surveilled. As Emanuel Cleaver, a democratic congressman from Missouri explained, these stamps were a "kind of cultural terrorism," whose true meaning could be determined without even reading the comic books.[34] Mexico's cultural brand of blackness was hidden, lost amid, as some in the United States claimed, its apparent insufficiency or, as Mexicans decried, the imposition of a foreign brand of diasporic authenticity.[35]

Activists and scholars have typically identified the lack of self-identifying or externally classified African-descended peoples as the main problem. "In Mexico," Aguirre Beltrán's last student and the co-curator of the 2006 art exhibit *The African Presence in México* Sagrario Cruz-Carretero wrote, "the black population does not currently have a recognized separate legal and judicial status."[36] Included in the traveling exhibition, Alfred J. Quiroz's *La Raza Kósmica* (2005) takes this reevaluation of postindependence racial egalitarianism further, condemning what was left of Mexico's once ballyhooed racial imaginary. A professor of art at the University of Arizona, Quiroz linguistically and visually fused José Vasconcelos's cosmic vision of Mexican mestizaje, one of the post-revolutionary state's foundational fictions and the most widely accepted

[34] Darryl Fears, "White House Denounces Art on Mexican Stamps," *Washington Post*, July 1, 2005, www.washingtonpost.com/wp-dyn/content/article/2005/06/30/AR2005063002112.html; Hugh Dellios, "In Mexico, 'They Just Don't See Us,'" *Chicago Tribune*, July 10, 2005, www.chicagotribune.com/news/ct-xpm-2005-07-10-0507100296-story.html; and 109 Cong. Rec. H5630–H5633 (daily ed. July 11, 2005) (statements of Rep. Cleaver and Rep. Payne, "Introduction of Resolution Condemning Mexico's Issuance of Offensive Stamps"). On the historical context for this controversy and the terms with which it was articulated, see Irwin, "Memín Pinguín, Rumba, and Racism," 249–65; and Ramsay, *Afro-Mexican Constructions of Diaspora, Gender, Identity and Nation*, 29.

[35] Staking an important middle ground, María Elisa Vázquez explained that the Memín controversy pointed to the difficulty African Americans had understanding racial scripts that differed from theirs. Yet, she also exclaimed that these polemics gave Mexicans the opportunity to better come to grips with their nation's own forms of racism; see María Elisa Vázquez, "Detrás de Memín Pinguín," *Diario de Campo*, no. 79 (2005): 66–68.

[36] Sagrario Cruz-Carretero, "The African Presence in México/La presencia africana en México," in Herrera, *The African Presence in México: From Yanga to the Present*, 32.

symbol of blackness in postrevolutionary nationalism, with the Ku Klux Klan and the symbolic violence Quiroz claimed inhered in Memín Pinguín.[37] No longer a model of national unity and indigenous integration, blackness represented the most ethnocentric pillar of national identity: the destruction of nonwhite peoples and cultures.

The propensity to understand blackness in Mexico from a comparative perspective is not new, just as the politics of racial and national comparison are not.[38] For the vast majority who have come of age since the 1960s, the Civil Rights Movement, Black Power, and decolonization set the stage to invert the comparisons that heralded Mexico – and Latin America – as a paragon of racial tolerance and that cast the United States as a symbol of racial discrimination. Indicative of this political and historiographic shift, sociologist Pierre Van Den Berghe wrote the following while citing the first edition of Aguirre Beltrán's *La población negra de México* in 1976:

> In fact, the United States, with its rigid racial caste society is highly socially pluralistic.
>
> Mexico exhibits no social pluralism at all on that dimension; there is no socially recognized group of Afro-Mexicans, and most Mexicans do not even know that a substantial number of their fellow citizens are of partly African descent (Aguirre Beltrán).[39]

In the past fifty years, African American political activism has blossomed as a point of departure for the study of Mexico's African heritage. Among scholars concerned with the African Diaspora in Latin America, it has become fashionable to ask what political scientist Michael Hanchard inquired for Brazil in 1994: "Why has there been no social movement generated by Afro-Brazilians in the postwar period that corresponds to social movements in the United States, sub-Saharan Africa, and the Caribbean?"[40]

[37] Cesáreo Moreno, "An Historical Survey: Afro-Mexican Depictions and Identity in the Visual Arts/Una visión histórica: Representaciones afro-mexicanas e identidad en las artes visuales," in Herrera, *The African Presence in México: From Yanga to the Present*, 88–91.

[38] Micol Seigel, "Beyond Compare: Historical Method after the Transnational Turn," *Radical History Review* 91 (2005): 62–90.

[39] Pierre L. Van Den Berghe, "The African Diaspora in Mexico, Brazil, and the United States," *Social Forces* 54, no. 3 (1976): 532.

[40] Michael George Hanchard, *Orpheus and Power: The* Movimento Negro *of Rio de Janeiro and São Paulo, Brazil, 1945–1988* (Princeton, NJ: Princeton University Press, 2004), 6.

Caution is necessary, even when queries like Hanchard's effectively deconstruct the relationship between assimilation and pluralism, social control and popular resistance, inclusion and exclusion, nation and diaspora. As anthropologist David Scott warns us, our research questions not only provide us with a problem to resolve – in this case, the marginalized place of African-descended peoples in Mexican history and society – but also the political futures to be desired: demographic visibility and social recognition. In other words, they sit dialogically at the intersection of history and historiography.[41] The questions we ask, like those probed by the intellectuals, cultural producers, and policy makers analyzed in *Finding Afro-Mexico*, frame the histories we tell and determine whether black disappearance was tragic; whether mestizaje and national integration were romantic, benevolent, and pluralist; whether academic and popular constructions of blackness in Mexico were, and still are, a fragment of their diasporic potentialities.[42]

Generations of pre- and postrevolutionary liberals, Marxists, antifascists, Cold War developmentalists, New Left radicals, and turn-of-the-century multiculturalists each constructed blackness while they decided how to situate Mexican and African civilizations in world history. Based on their ideological fears and fantasies, they arrived at their own disciplinary and spatial conclusions about whether African-descended peoples and cultures could be Mexican and how, if at all, they could contribute to the making of a more just society. In other words, there was no coherent state-sponsored policy to erase – or to integrate – blackness, in all its

[41] David Scott, *Conscripts of Modernity: The Tragedy of Colonial Enlightenment* (Durham, NC: Duke University Press, 2004). Literary scholar Charles Henry Rowell's research about the African-descended populations of Veracruz for the Afro-diasporic journal *Callaloo* illustrates the intimate political connections between research questions and the historical narratives they produce. Thinking about black social visibility, he and his research team were surprised by what appeared to be the lack of African-descended people in the communities surrounding the maroon community-turned-free black town of Yanga. In 2008, he queried, "But, each time we visit Yanga, one question declares itself incessantly: Why is it that no one we have met in Yanga has ever been able to tell us what happened to the descendants of the black people who founded the town?" "Without an answer to that question," he continued, bemoaning the insufficient responses he encountered, "we are led to read contemporary Yanga, then, as a symbol of Mexico's failure to remember, to recover, and to reclaim vital narratives that constitute its national history and that inform its contemporary life and culture"; see "'El primer libertador de las Américas'/The First Liberator of the Americas: The Editor's Notes," *Callaloo* 31, no. 1 (2008): 3–4.

[42] Hayden White discusses tragedy and other narrative tropes in historical writing in "The Historical Text as Literary Artifact," in *Tropics of Discourse: Essays in Cultural Criticism* (Baltimore, MD: Johns Hopkins University Press, 1985), esp. 83 and 87.

vicissitudes, during the two centuries when African-descended peoples were socially and demographically excluded from most local, regional, and national expressions of race and nation.

In the twenty-first century, the paradigm of invisibility has supplanted the trope of black disappearance that was always, it seemed, on the verge of becoming a reality. When Mexican nationalists and foreigners began to investigate African-descended cultural behaviors in the 1940s and 1950s, they erected their observations on recent historical research documenting Mexico's history of colonial slavery; they traced the processes of racial disappearance and integration that, in their minds, were already under way. Following the path cleared by anthropologist Manuel Gamio, Gonzalo Aguirre Beltrán and Miguel Covarrubias argued that ethnography could guide the state toward a more democratic society. Since the multicultural declarations of Our Third Root, ethnographers and grassroots organizers have invoked the trope of black disappearance differently, as something ethnocentric social scientists and an assimilationist state desired rather than a fait accompli destined by the innate laws of racial evolution, cultural contact, or socio-economic modernization.

It is not surprising that local demands to recognize African-descended Mexicans have their roots in one of the main critiques levied in the 1960s and 1970s: that mestizaje was a colonialist project to whiten the national populace and thereby render African-descended Mexicans invisible.[43] The slogan "Black is Beautiful" has come to symbolize an Afro-diasporic politics built on racial visibility and its foil, invisibility, a motif that, like disappearance a century earlier, is rarely divided into its social, demographic, cultural, and spatial pillars. Accordingly, beginning in July 1970, the magazine *Black World* conveyed the centrality of the racialized body in the making of diasporic authenticities in its monthly section "Reports from the Black World."[44] Using the black head as a metonym for the African Diaspora, it only left Mexico, Canada, and Europe out of its plotting of the Black Atlantic (See Figure 8.1). In 1976, Leslie B. Rout Jr.'s classic *The African Experience in Spanish America* classified Mexico – along with

[43] Githiora, *Afro-Mexicans*, 204 and 207–8; Andrew Juan Rosa, "El Que No Tiene Dingo, Tiene Mandingo: The Inadequacy of the 'Mestizo' as a Theoretical Construct in the Field of Latin American Studies – The Problem and Solution," *Journal of Black Studies* 27, no. 2 (1996): 278–91. Gene Andrew Jarrett similarly discusses the politics surrounding the African American literary canon after the Black Power Movement in *Representing the Race: A New Political History of African American Literature* (New York: New York University Press, 2011), 12–15.

[44] "Reports from the Black World," *Black World*, July 1970, 32.

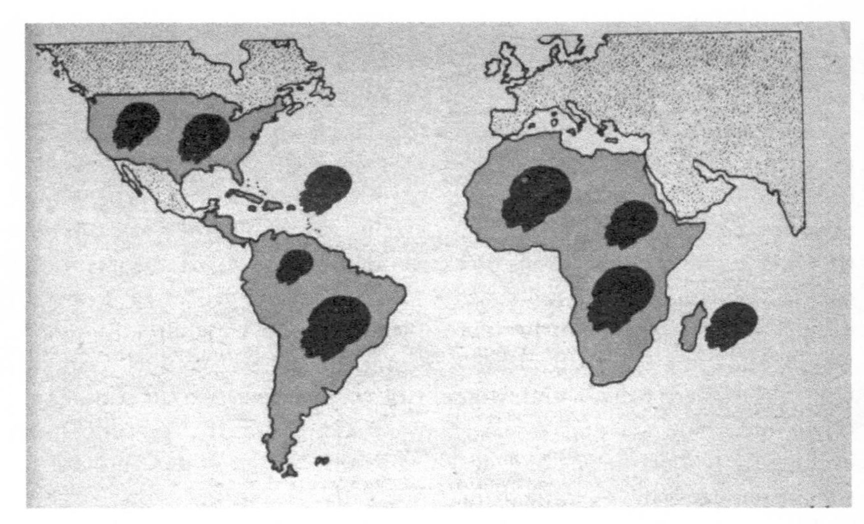

FIGURE 8.1 "Reports from the Black World." *Black World* (October 1975): 79.

Bolivia, Chile, and Argentina – in demographic terms whereby "The Negroid population has disappeared, or become almost totally amalgamated (1% or less)." The lack of racial questions in the national census led him to ask "How many Afro-Mexicans are there now?" and to respond lamentingly that "The answer could only be a conjecture based on a shred of evidence."[45] Finally, reading Latin American literature through the themes and racial vocabularies of US history in 1976, literary scholar Richard L. Jackson went as far as to claim that mestizaje, which he defined as "ethnic lynching," begat a "crisis of black identity."[46]

This line of inquiry indicated that advocates of Mexican mestizaje could no longer take refuge in the claims of racial tolerance and cultural syncretism popularized on both sides of the border. Questions of visibility and invisibility have gained traction as a way to bridge social justice initiatives driven by multiculturalism and academic pursuits looking to retell regional, national, and global histories.[47] Drawing directly on

[45] Leslie B. Rout Jr., *The African Experience in Spanish America* (Princeton, NJ: Markus Wiener, 2003), 211 and 280.

[46] Richard L. Jackson, *The Black Image in Latin American Literature* (Albuquerque: University of New Mexico Press, 1976), 1–2.

[47] For a discussion of invisibility in Afro-Latin America, see George Reid Andrews, *Afro-Latin America: Black Lives, 1600–2000* (Cambridge, MA: Harvard University Press, 2016). On the question of social justice and racial visibility, see Juliet Hooker, *Race and*

Jackson's conclusions in 2004, literary critic Marco Polo Hernández Cuevas applauded the "apartheid system that forced African Americans in the United States to look into themselves in search of identity, as there was no hope of entering the mainstream." Conversely, people of African descent in Mexico suffered a racial holocaust. In identifying themselves as Mexican and succumbing to the national narrative of racial and cultural mixture, they have "yet to discover a truer picture of themselves."[48] Similarly, Henry Louis Gates Jr. subtitled the section of his monograph and accompanying four-part documentary *Black in Latin America* about Mexico and Peru "The Black Grandma in the Closet." Blackness in Mexico appeared to be almost a nihilistic prophesy, built around a concerted desire "to hide one's blackness in a mixed-race culture."[49] Cloaked in invisibility, blackness seemed to exist in a truer form unbeknown to most Mexicans but ready to be discovered by the scholars who know where to look, who to study, and what to ask.

Definitions of blackness in Mexico have been and continue to be contextualized by the same motifs that enliven the histories of nations more often associated with the African Diaspora in the Western Hemisphere: slavery and abolition, civil rights and national integration, liberalism and racism, visibility and invisibility.[50] Mexican historians, social scientists, and policy makers, however, did not always couple them in the ways that their counterparts in the United States had. Most notably, they did not take the twinned concepts of integration and race-based civil rights, which Black Power deconstructed in the United States,

the Politics of Solidarity (Oxford: Oxford University Press, 2009), 5–6. More empirical studies can be found in Minority Rights Group, ed., *No Longer Invisible: Afro-Latin Americans Today* (London: Minority Rights Group, 1995); and Dixon and Burdick, *Comparative Perspectives on Afro-Latin America*.

48 Hernández Cuevas, *African Mexicans and the Discourse on Modern Nation*, 24–25.

49 Henry Louis Gates Jr., *Black in Latin America* (New York: New York University Press, 2011), 59 and 67. B. Christine Arce calls the simultaneous invisibility of blackness in Mexican nationalism and its culturally exoticized popular consumption "the paradox of invisibility," a paradigm that leaves African-descended Mexicans "in the closet"; see *México's Nobodies*, 1 and 145.

50 There is a growing literature about the relationship between racism and liberalism. Saidiya V. Hartman brilliantly unpacks the liberal narrative of slavery to freedom in *Scenes of Subjection: Terror, Slavery, and Self-making in Nineteenth-Century America* (New York: Oxford University Press, 1997). Jonathan Fenderson considers these ideas specifically in relation to the Black Art Movement; see *Building the Black Arts Movement*. For more synthetic accounts, see Robin Blackburn, *The American Crucible: Slavery, Emancipation and Human Rights* (London: Verso, 2011); and Domenico Losurdo, *Liberalism: A Counter-history*, trans. Gregory Elliott (London: Verso, 2011).

as obvious bedfellows. In the name of national integration, the nineteenth-century Mexicans who took Enlightenment ideas of natural rights at face value naively believed the abolition of slavery and caste signified equality. They failed to consider the underlying structures of racism and the socio-economic inequalities that persisted after Father Hidalgo, José María Morelos, and Vicente Guerrero each abolished slavery. More than their Mexican brethren, US policy makers and activists have expanded the tenets of liberalism in a piecemeal fashion, from abolition, through Reconstruction and the Civil Rights Movement, to protests broadcast on live television and launched on social media under the hashtag Black Lives Matter.[51] Accordingly, the politics of blackness diverged in the early nineteenth century when Mexico abolished slavery and the United States allowed slavery to expand westward. Although these histories briefly reunited in the interwar period with the New Negro Movement, modernism, and the specter of global fascism, postwar social movements exploded this cultural and political unity. A new diasporic politics rooted in decolonization, social visibility, and the primacy of the black body birthed the assumption that Mexico left the African Diaspora.

By 2015, Afro-diasporic politics appeared to be coalescing again as a result of eerily similar cultural and political circumstances: the politics of racial activism in a supposedly raceless moment. In the United States, the 2008 election of Barack Obama, the son of a white woman from Kansas and a Kenyan man with no ancestral ties to slavery or the Middle Passage, ushered in hopes for new race relations. Not only throwing the politics of African American cultural authenticity into the fray, his sudden rise to national prominence also unleashed optimism that, for many on the left, the African American quest for equality had triumphed or that, for some on the right, racial protest was no longer expedient.[52] Upon hearing that Mexico had an African-descended President, Vicente Guerrero, almost 120 years before the United States, Henry Louis Gates Jr. exclaimed in 2011, "So you had your Barack Obama in 1829!"[53] In making this comparison, Gates made a more important political and historiographic

[51] Keeanga-Yamahtta Taylor, *From #BlackLivesMatter to Black Liberation* (Chicago, IL: Haymarket Books, 2016).

[52] The academic and popular literature on post-racialism and the historical, political, and sociological importance of Barack Obama's election is rapidly growing. For instance, see Ta-Nehisi Coates, *Between the World and Me* (New York: Spiegel and Grau, 2015); and Kimberlé Williams Crenshaw et al., eds., *Seeing Race Again: Countering Colorblindness across the Disciplines* (Oakland: University of California Press, 2019).

[53] Gates, *Black in Latin America*, 77.

point: the main themes in African American history are present in modern Mexican history.

Mexico came to this synchronous moment from the other extreme, as a nation theoretically post-racial for nearly 200 years. African-descended individuals, like Sergio Peñaloza Pérez and Father Glyn Jemmott Nelson, had only recently gained national and international attention for their advocacy of black social visibility, an activist agenda that itself was unimaginable only a few decades earlier.[54] As a result of their efforts, the federal government recognized African-descended peoples as a demographic category on the INEGI's intercensal survey in 2015. Reframing longstanding questions about black disappearance the following year, Mexico's National Commission for Human Rights asserted that the INEGI had rectified "the statistic invisibility of the African-descended population."[55] Working with UNESCO, the INAH has named Cuijla, the city of Veracruz, and Yanga "places of memory" to preserve the history of African slavery and to recognize the nation's African-descended heritage.[56] Most notably, on December 1, 2018, during Andrés Manuel López Obrador's presidential inauguration, blackness was present for the entire country to see. From the Costa Chica of Oaxaca, African-descended activist Elena Ruiz Salinas joined indigenous elders in performing a purification ritual to anoint him the leader of the nation's indigenous and Afro-Mexican communities.[57] A visible part of contemporary society, blackness was no longer confined to regional idiosyncrasy or the abstractions of historical metaphor and cultural symbolism.

[54] Mónica G. Moreno Figueroa and Emiko Saldívar Tanaka, "'We Are Not Racists, We Are Mexicans': Privilege, Nationalism and Post-Race Ideology in Mexico," *Critical Sociology* 42, no. 4–5 (2016): 515–33. For an overview of the rhetorical strategies surrounding Afro-Mexican political activism since 1990s, see Vinson, *Before Mestizaje*, 203–6.

[55] Comisión Nacional de Derechos Humanos, *Estudio especial de la CNDH sobre la situación de la población afrodescendiente de México a través de la encuesta intercensal 2015*, Octubre de 2016, 85, http://informe.cndh.org.mx/menu.aspx?id=15010.

[56] María Elisa Velázquez and José Luis Martínez Maldonado, *Cuajinicuilapa, Guerrero: Sitio de memoria de la esclavitud y de las poblaciones afrodescendientes* (Mexico City: Instituto Nacional de Antropología e Historia, 2016); and Citlalli Domínguez et al., *El puerto de Veracruz y Yanga: Sitios de memoria de la esclavitud y las poblaciones africanas y afrodescendientes* (Mexico City: Instituto Nacional de Antropología e Historia, 2017).

[57] Alberto López, "Comunidad negra abandona Oaxaca por pobreza," 6 de junio de 2005, *El Universal*, https://archivo.eluniversal.com.mx/estados/57582.html; and Mario Méndez, "Afromexicanos entregan bastón de mando a AMLO," *El Imparcial de la Costa*, 4 de diciembre de 2018, http://imparcialoaxaca.mx/costa/251599/afromexicanos-entregan-baston-de-mando-a-amlo/.

When US citizens asked in the immediate wake of the 2008 presidential election whether racial identification had become irrelevant, Mexicans wondered whether the centuries spent eschewing racial categories bred structural injustice and cultural violence. The inequalities born from slavery and the making of liberal societies buttressed polemics in both countries, just as they had in the nineteenth century when Mexicans contrasted their adherence to abolition with the expansion of slavery in the United States. Fundamentally ensnared in the everyday realities of nation-state formation, these questions demonstrated that intellectual and cultural debates about African-descended identities as well as broader investigations into narratives about race and nation were not unique to either country.[58] Mexico never left the African Diaspora – it merely took an alternative historical course toward the social recognition of its African-descended citizens.

[58] Most notably, beginning in 2012, artists and intellectuals affiliated with the Zapatista Army of National Liberation in the state of Chiapas have worked with former Black Panthers, like Emory Douglas, to fuse the politics and aesthetics of indigenous and Afro-diasporic liberation under the banner of global humanism, antiracism, and the rejection of neoliberalism; see Marc James Léger and David Tomas, eds., *Zapantera Negra: An Artistic Encounter between Black Panthers and Zapatistas* (Brooklyn, NY: Common Notions, 2017).

Bibliography

ARCHIVES

Mexico

Archivo General de la Nación (AGN), Mexico City
Fichera Abelardo Rodríguez (FAR)
Fichera Lázaro Cárdenas del Río (FLCR)
Fichera Manuel Ávila Camacho (FMAC)
Fichera Miguel Alemán Valdez (FMAV)
Fondo Carlos Chávez #239 (FCC)

Archivo General del Estado de Veracruz (AGEV), Xalapa, Veracruz

Archivo Municipal de Veracruz (AMV), Veracruz, Veracruz
Archivo Histórico (AH)
Fondo Francisco Rivera Ávila (FFRA)

Centro Nacional de las Artes, Biblioteca de las Artes, Fondos Especiales, Archivo Gerónimo Baqueiro Foster (CNA-BA-FE-AGBF), Mexico City
Cuadernos
Expedientes

Comisión Nacional para el Desarrollo de los Pueblos Indígenas, Centro de Documentación "Juan Rulfo" (CDI-CDJ), Mexico City

Instituto de Investigaciones Históricos-Sociales de la Universidad Veracruzana, Biblioteca Luis Chávez Orozco (IIHSUV-BLCO), Xalapa, Veracruz

Instituto Indigenista Interamericano, Archivo Histórico, México en el Archivo Histórico, 1940–1959 (III-AH-MAH), Mexico City

Instituto Nacional de Antropología e Historia, Archivo Técnico, Coordinación Nacional de Arqueología (INAH-AT-CNA), Mexico City

Instituto Nacional de Bellas Artes/Centro Nacional de Investigación, Documentación e Información Musical "Carlos Chávez," Archivo Baqueiro Foster (INBA/CENIDIM-ABF), Mexico City

Universidad Autónoma de México, Instituto de Investigaciones Antropológicas, Fondo Alfonso Caso (UNAM-IIA-FAC), Mexico City

Universidad de las Américas, Puebla, Sala de Archivos y Colecciones Especiales (UDLAP-SACE), Cholula, Puebla
  Archivo Miguel Covarrubias (AMC)
  Folletería Miguel Quintana (FMQ)

United States

Georgetown University Library, Booth Family Center for Special Collections, Papers of Katherine Biddle (GUL-BFCSC-PKB), Washington, DC

Missouri History Society, Library and Research Center, Katherine Dunham Papers (MHS-LRC-KDP), St. Louis, Missouri

New York Public Library, Schomburg Center for Research in Black Culture (NYPL-SCRBC), New York City, New York
  Library Microfilm (LM)
    Langston Hughes Collection (LHC)
  Manuscripts and Archives (MA)
    Melville & Frances Herskovits Papers (MFHP)

Northwestern University Library Archives, Melville J. Herskovits Papers (NULA-MJHP), Evanston, Illinois

Organization of American States, Columbus Memorial Library (OAS-CML), Washington, DC

Rockefeller Archive Center, Rockefeller Foundation Records (RAC-RFR), Sleepy Hollow, New York

Smithsonian Institute, National Anthropology Archives (SI-NAA), Suitland, Maryland
  Institute of Social Anthropology (ISA)
  Pan American Institute of Geography and History (PAIGH)
  Ralph Leon Beals Papers (RLBP)

Southern Illinois University, Carbondale, Special Collections Research Center, Katherine Dunham Papers, 1906–2006 (SIUC-SCRC-KDP), Carbondale, Illinois

University of Arkansas, Special Collections, William Grant Still and Verna Arvey Papers (Manuscripts Collection MC1125) (UAL-SC-WGSVAP), Fayetteville, Arkansas

Online

Museum of Fine Arts, Houston, Documents of 20th-Century Latin American and Latino Art, Digital Archive (ICAA-MFAH), Houston, Texas, http://icaadocs.mfah.org

Museum of Modern Art, Press Release Archives (MoMA-PRA), New York City, New York, www.moma.org/research-and-learning/archives/

University of Massachusetts Amherst Libraries, Special Collections and University Archives, W. E. B. Du Bois Papers (MS 312) (UMAL-SCUA-WDP), Amherst, Massachusetts, https://credo.library.umass.edu/view/collection/mums312

Yale University, Beinecke Rare Book and Manuscripts Library, James Weldon Johnson Collection in the Yale Collection of American Literature, Langston Hughes Papers, 1862–1980, JWJ MSS 26 (YU-BRBML-JWJCYCAL-LHP), New Haven, Connecticut, https://beinecke.library.yale.edu/collections/highlights/langston-hughes-papers-1862–1980

PRIMARY SOURCES

Films

Angelitos negros
Mulata
Redes (The Wave)
Saludos Amigos
The Three Caballeros
Los tres huastecos

Bulletins, Magazines, and Newspapers

América Indígena
Atlantic Monthly
Baltimore Afro-American
Black Panther
Boletín Bibliográfico de Antropología Americana

Boletín de la Sociedad Mexicana de Geografía y Estadística
Bulletin of the Museum of Modern Art
Chicago Tribune
Colorlines
The Crisis
Diario del Sureste
Ebony
Ethnos
Frente a Frente
Huffington Post
El Imparcial de la Costa
Internal Bulletin: Socialist Workers Party
Jet
La Jornada
Mexican Folk-ways
National Geographic
Negro Digest/Black World
Negro World
New International
New York Times
Opportunity
Partisan Review
Phylon
Pittsburgh Courier
Population Index
Science
Survey Graphic
Time
El Universal
El Universal Ilustrado
Washington Post

Books, Essays, and Chapters

Acosta, Jorge R. "Rasgos olmecas en Monte Albán." In *Mayas y olmecas*, 55–56.

Agea, Francisco. *21 años de la Orquesta Sinfónica de México, 1928–1948*. Mexico City: Nuevo Mundo, 1948.

Aguirre Beltrán, Gonzalo. *Cuijla: Esbozo etnográfico de un pueblo negro*. Mexico City: Fondo de Cultura Económica, 1958.

"De eso que llaman antropología mexicana." In *Obra polémica*. Vol. 11 of *Obra antropológica*, 101–20. Mexico City: Fondo de Cultural Económica, 1992.

"La etnohistoria y el estudio del negro en México." In *Acculturation in the Americas: Proceedings and Selected Papers of the XXIXth International Congress of Americanists*, edited by Sol Tax, 161–66. Chicago, IL: University of Chicago Press, 1951.

"Gonzalo Aguirre Beltrán." In *Vidas en la antropología mexicana*, edited and compiled by María José Con Uribe and Magalí Daltabuit Godás, 15–27. Mexico City: Instituto Nacional de Antropología e Historia, 2004.

"El Instituto de Antropología y el florecimiento cultural de Veracruz." In *La universidad latinoamericana y otros ensayos*, 173–76. Xalapa: Universidad Veracruzana, 1961.

"The Integration of the Negro into the National Society of Mexico." In *Race and Class in Latin America*, edited by Magnus Mörner, 11–27. New York: Columbia University Press, 1970.

"Del materialismo dialéctico al culturalismo utópico: Guillermo Bonfil y su obra antropológica." *La Palabra y el Hombre*, no. 92 (1994): 5–29.

Medicina y magia: El proceso de aculturación en la estructura colonial. Vol. 8 of Obra antropológica. Mexico City: Fondo de Cultura Económica, 1992.

El negro esclavo en Nueva España: La formación colonial, la medicina popular y otros ensayos. Vol. 16 of Obra antropológica. Mexico City: Universidad Veracruzana, 1994.

La población negra de México, 1519–1810: Estudio etnohistórico. Mexico City: Ediciones Fuente Cultural, 1946.

La población negra de México, 1519–1810: Estudio etnohistórico. 2nd ed., corrected and expanded. Mexico City: Fondo de Cultura Económica, 1972.

Problemas de la población indígena de la Cuenca del Tepalcatepec. Vol. 3 of Memorias del Instituto Nacional Indigenista. Mexico City: Ediciones del Instituto Nacional Indigenista, 1952.

El proceso de la aculturación. Mexico City: Universidad Autónoma de México, 1957.

Regiones de refugio. Mexico City: Instituto Indigenista Interamericano, 1967.

El señorío de Cuauhtochco: Luchas agrarias en México durante el Virreinato. Vol. 1 of Obra antropológica. Mexico City: Fondo de Cultura Económica, 1991.

"The Slave Trade in Mexico." *Hispanic American Historical Review* 24, no. 3 (1944): 412–31.

"Tribal Origins of Slaves in Mexico: Historical Background." *Journal of Negro History* 31, no. 3 (1946): 269–89.

"Tribal Origins of Slaves in Mexico: San Thome." *Journal of Negro History* 31, no. 3 (1946): 317–52.

"Tribal Origins of Slaves in Mexico: The Rivers of Guinea." *Journal of Negro History* 31, no. 3 (1946): 290–316.

Alamán, Lucas. *Historia de México*. Vols. 2 and 5. Mexico City: Victoriano Agüeros, 1884–85.

"The History of Mexico (1849–1852) (selection)." In *Nineteenth-Century Nation Building and the Latin American Intellectual Tradition: A Reader*, edited and translated by Janet Burke and Ted Humphrey, 175–98. Indianapolis, IN: Hackett, 2007.

Alemán, Miguel. "Discurso del licenciado Miguel Alemán, Secretario de Gobernación, al inaugurarse el Congreso." In *Corresponde a las Américas: La forjación del mundo que ya llega*, 7–11. Mexico City: Secretaría de Gobernación, 1943.

Arredondo, Isabel. "'Tenía bríos, aún vieja, los sigo teniendo': Entrevista a Matilde Landeta." *Mexican Studies/Estudios Mexicanos* 18, no. 1 (2002): 189–204.

Arvey, Verna. *In One Lifetime*. Fayetteville: University of Arkansas Press, 1984.

Báez-Jorge, Félix. "Aculturación e integración intercultural: Un momento histórico del indigenismo mexicano." In *INI: 30 años después. Revisión crítica*, 290–99. Mexico City: México Indígena, 1978.

Baqueiro Foster, Gerónimo. *La canción popular de Yucatán (1850–1950)*. Mexico City: Editorial del Magisterio, 1970.

"El Huapango." *Revista Musical Mexicano*, no. 8 (1942): 174–83.

Barton, Ralph. Preface to *Negro Drawings*, by Miguel Covarrubias. New York: Alfred A. Knopf, 1927.

Basauri, Carlos. *Breves notas etnográficas sobre la población negra del distrito de Jamiltepec, Oax*. Mexico City: Primer Congreso Demográfico Interamericano, 1943.

La población indígena de México. 3 vols. Mexico City: Secretaría de Educación Pública, 1940.

La población negroide mexicana. Mexico City: Secretaría de Gobernación/Primero Congreso Demográfico Interamericano, 1943.

Bastide, Roger. *Les Amériques noires: Les civilisations africaines dans le nouveau monde*. Paris: Payot, 1967.

Bastien, Auguste Rémy. "Las características del negro americano." *Afroamérica* 2, no. 3 (1946): 38–41.

Beals, Carleton. *Mexican Maze*. Philadelphia, PA: J. B. Lippincott, 1931.

Beals, Ralph L. Review of *Mexico South* by Miguel Covarrubias. *Pacific Historical Review* 16, no. 1 (1947): 83–84.

Béjar Navarro, Raúl. "Prejuicio y discriminación racial en México." *Revista Mexicana de Sociología* 31, no.2 (1969): 417–33.

Benítez, José R. *Morelos, su casta y su casa en Valladolid (Morelia)*. Guadalajara, Mexico, 1947.

Benson, Elizabeth P., ed. *Dumbarton Oaks Conference on the Olmec*. Washington, DC, 1968.

Boas, Franz. *The Mind of Primitive Man*. New York: Macmillan, 1911.

Bonfil Batalla, Guillermo. *México Profundo: Reclaiming A Civilization*. Translated by Philip A. Dennis. Austin: University of Texas Press, 1996.

comp. *Simbiosis de culturas: Los inmigrantes y su cultura en México*. Mexico City: Fondo de Cultura Económica, 1993.

Bonilla, José María. *La evolución del pueblo mexicano*. Mexico City: Herrero Hermanos Sucesores, 1922.

Bustos Cerecedo, Miguel. "Carta a Nueva York." In vol. 2 of *Veracruz: Dos siglos de poesía (XIX y XX)*, edited by Esther Hernández Palacio and Ángel José Fernández, 77–82. Mexico City: Consejo Nacional para la Cultura y las Artes, 1991.

Campos, Rubén M. *El folklore musical de las ciudades: Investigación acerca de la música mexicana para bailar y cantar*. Mexico City: Publicaciones de la Secretaría de Educación Pública, 1930.

El folklore y la música mexicana: Investigación acerca de la cultura musical en México (1525–1925). Mexico City: Secretaría de Educación Pública, 1928.

Carlos, John. *The John Carlos Story: The Sports Moment That Changed the World*. With Dave Zinn. Chicago, IL: Haymarket Books, 2013.

Carpentier, Alejo. *Music in Cuba*. Edited by Timothy Brennan. Translated by Alan West-Durán. Minneapolis: University of Minnesota Press, 2001.

La música en Cuba. Havana, Cuba, 1961.

"The Rebambaramba." Translated by Jill A. Netchinsky. *Latin American Literary Review* 15, no. 30 (1987): 69–77.

Carreño, Alberto María. *México y los Estados Unidos de América: Apuntaciones para la historia* [...]. Prologue by Francisco Sosa. Mexico City: Imprenta Victoria, 1922.

El peligro negro. Mexico City: Sociedad Mexicana de Geografía y Estadística, 1910.

Castañeda, Daniel. *Balance de Agustín Lara*. Mexico City: Ediciones Libres, 1941.

Castro Leal, Antonio. Introduction to *Twenty Centuries of Mexican Art*, 14–17. New York: Museum of Modern Art, 1940.

Chavero, Alfredo. *Historia antigua y de la conquista*. Vol. 1 of Riva Palacio, *México a través de los siglos*.

Chávez, Carlos. Introduction to *Mexican Music: Notes by Herbert Weinstock for Concerts Arranged by Carlos Chávez*, translated by Herbert Weinstock, 5–11. New York: Museum of Modern Art, 1940.

Toward a New Music: Music and Electricity. Translated by Herbert Weinstock. New York: Da Capo Press, 1975.

"Chávez, Mexican Composer, Sees Promise in Swing." *Washington Star*, February 2, 1940. In *Carlos Chávez: North American Press, 1936–1950*, 50. Mexico City: Ediciones Mexicanas de Música, 1951.

Chávez Orozco, Luis. *Historia de México (1808–1836)*. Mexico City: Instituto Nacional de Estudios Históricos de la Revolución Mexicana, 1985.

Las instituciones democráticas de los indígenas mexicanos en la época colonial. Mexico City: Ediciones del III, 1943.

Clark, Vèvè A. "An Anthropological Band of Beings: An Interview with Julie Robinson Belafonte." In *Kaiso! Writings by and about Katherine Dunham*, edited by Vèvè A. Clark and Sara E. Johnson, 365–81. Madison: University of Wisconsin Press, 2005.

Clarke, John Henrik. Introduction to vol. 2 of *World's Great Men of Color*, by J. A. Rogers, edited by John Henrik Clarke, xi–xxiv. New York: Collier Books, 1972.

Coates, Ta-Nehisi. *The Beautiful Struggle: A Memoir*. New York: Spiegel and Grau, 2009.

Between the World and Me. New York: Spiegel and Grau, 2015.

Coe, Michael D. *America's First Civilization: Discovering the Olmec*. New York: American Heritage, 1968.
Comas, Juan. "El problema de la existencia de un tipo racial olmeca." In *Mayas y olmecas*, 69–70.
Las razas humanas. Mexico City: Secretaría de Educación Pública, 1946.
Comisión Nacional de Derechos Humanos. *Estudio especial de la CNDH sobre la situación de la población afrodescendiente de México a través de la encuesta intercensal 2015*. Octubre de 2016. http://informe.cndh.org.mx/menu.aspx?id=15010.
Consejo Nacional de Población. *La situación demográfica de México, 2013*. Mexico City: Consejo Nacional de Población, 2013. www.gob.mx/cms/uploads/attachment/file/112476/La_Situacion_Demografica_de_Mexico_2013.pdf.
Copland, Aaron. *Our New Music*. New York: McGraw-Hill, 1941.
Covarrubias, Miguel. "Blues Singer." In *The New Negro: Voices of the Harlem Renaissance*, edited by Alain Locke, 227. New York: Touchstone, 1992.
"Los djukas: 'Bush Negroes' de la Guayana Holandesa." *Afroamérica* 2, no.3 (1946): 121–22.
The Eagle, the Jaguar, and the Serpent: Indian Art of the Americas. North America: Alaska, Canada, the United States. New York: Alfred A. Knopf, 1954.
Indian Art of Mexico and Central America. New York: Alfred A Knopf, 1957.
Mexico South: the Isthmus of Tehuantepec. New York: Alfred A. Knopf, 1946.
"Origen y desarrollo del estilo artístico 'olmeca.'" In *Mayas y olmecas*, 46–49.
"Tlatilco: Archaic Mexican Art and Culture." *Dyn* 4–5 (1943): 40–46.
Untitled Lithograph. In *Uncle Tom's Cabin; or, Life among the Lowly*, by Harriet Beecher Stowe, after page 236. New York: The Heritage Press, 1938.
"La Venta: Colossal Heads and Jaguar Gods." *Dyn* 6 (1944): 24–33.
Crew, Spencer R., Lonnie G. Bunch, and Clement A. Price, eds. *Memories of the Enslaved: Voices from the Slave Narratives*. Santa Barbara, CA: ABC-CLIO, 2015.
Crowninshield, Frank. Introduction to *Negro Drawings*, by Miguel Covarrubias, np. New York: Alfred A. Knopf, 1927.
Cruz-Carretero, Sagrario. "The African Presence in México/La presencia africana en México." In Herrera, *The African Presence in México: From Yanga to the Present*, 14–59.
Curt Lange, Francisco. *Americanismo musical: La sección de investigaciones musicales. Su creación, propósitos y finalidades*. Montevideo: Instituto de Estudios Superiores, 1934.
Curtain, Philip D. "The African Diaspora." *Historical Reflections* 6, no.1 (1979): 1–17.
de la Fuente, Beatriz. *Las cabezas colosales olmecas*. Mexico City: Fondo de Cultura Económica, 1975.
de la Fuente, Julio. *Relaciones interétnicas*. Mexico City: Instituto Nacional Indigenista, 1965.

de la Peña, Moisés T. *Veracruz económico*. Vol. 1. Mexico City: Gobierno del Estado de Veracruz, 1946.

Diggs, Irene. "Color in Colonial Spanish America." *Journal of Negro History* 38, no.4 (1953): 403–27.

Dirección General de Estadística. "6°Censo general de población, 6 de marzo de 1940." nd. www.beta.inegi.org.mx/programas/ccpv/1940/default.html.

Domínguez, Citlalli, Alfredo Delgado, María Elisa Velázquez, and José Luis Martínez. *El puerto de Veracruz y Yanga: Sitios de memoria de la esclavitud y las poblaciones africanas y afrodescendientes*. Mexico City: Instituto Nacional de Antropología e Historia, 2017.

Du Bois, W. E. B., and Guy B. Johnson. *Encyclopedia of the Negro: Preparatory Volume with Reference Lists and Reports*. New York: The Phelps-Stokes Fund, 1945.

Du Bois, W. E. Burghardt. *The Gift of Black Folk: The Negroes in the Making of America*. Boston, MA: Stratford, 1924.

Duby, Gertrude. *¿Hay Razas Inferiores?* Mexico City: Secretaría de Educación Pública, 1946.

Dunham, Katherine. *The Dances of Haiti*. Los Angeles, CA: Center for Afro-American Studies, University of California, Los Angeles, 1983.

"The Dances of Haiti/Las danzas de Haití." *Acta Anthropologica* 2, no. 4 (1947): 5–60.

"Dynamic Chávez Arrives as Symphony Conductor." Pittsburgh Post-Gazette, November 8, 1937. In Carlos Chávez: North American Press, *1936–1950*, 31. Mexico City: Ediciones Mexicanas de Música, 1951.

Eisenstein, Sergei. *Eisenstein on Disney*. Edited by Jay Leyda. Translated by Alan Upchurch. Calcutta: Seagull Books, 1986.

Esteva, Adalberto A. "Ante el mar de Veracruz: A Pablo Macedo." In vol. 1 of *Veracruz: Dos siglos de poesía (XIX y XX)*, edited by Esther Hernández Palacios and Ángel José Fernández, 374. Mexico City: Consejo Nacional para la Cultura y las Artes, 1991.

Faulhaber, Johanna. *Antropología física de Veracruz*. 2 vols. Gobierno de Veracruz, 1950–56.

Gamio, Manuel. *Forjando patria (pro nacionalismo)*. Mexico City: Librería de Porrúa Hermanos, 1916.

Hacia un México nuevo: Problemas sociales. Mexico City, 1935.

"The Indian Basis of Mexican Civilization." In *Aspects of Mexican Civilization*, by José Vasconcelos and Manuel Gamio, 103–86. Chicago, IL: University of Chicago Press, 1926.

Introduction, Synthesis and Conclusions of the Work the Population of the Valley of Teotihuacan. Mexico City: Talleres Gráficos de la Nación, 1922.

García Cubas, Antonio. *Atlas geográfico, estadístico e histórico de la República Mexicana*. Mexico City: Imprenta de José Mariano Fernández de Lara, 1858.

Cuadro geográfico, estadístico, descriptivo é histórico de los Estados Unidos Mexicanos. Mexico City: Oficina Tip. de la Secretaría de Fomento, 1884.

Gómez Montero, Sergio. "El arte indígena es contemporáneo: Vive y se transforma a su propio ritmo. (Alberto Beltrán recuerda cuando se ilustraba la acción educativa 'quitando la venda de la ignorancia a los indios')." In *INI: 30 años después. Revisión crítica*, 189–94. Mexico City: Instituto Nacional Indigenista, 1978.

González Casanova, Pablo. *La democracia en México*. Mexico City: Ediciones Era, 2006.

González Navarro, Moisés. "*Mestizaje* in Mexico during the National Period." In *Race and Class in Latin America*, edited by Magnus Mörner, 145–69. New York: Columbia University Press, 1970.

Gonzalo Aguirre Beltrán: Homenaje nacional. Xalapa: Universidad Veracruzana, 1996.

Guillén, Nicolás. "Conversación con Langston Hughes." In vol. 1 of *Prosa de prisa, 1929–1972*, compiled by Ángel Augier, 16–19. Havana: Editorial Arte y Literatura, 1975.

Hanke, Lewis. "The Incorporation of Indians and Negroes into Latin American Life." *Journal of Negro Education* 10, no. 3 (1941): 504–9.

Herrera, Claudia, coord. *The African Presence in México: From Yanga to the Present*. Chicago, IL: Mexican Fine Arts Center Museum, 2006.

Herrera Moreno, Enrique. *El cantón de Córdoba: Apuntes de geografía, estadística, historia, etc.* Cordoba: Tip. "La Prensa" de R. Valdecilla, 1892.

Herrera y Ogazón, Alba. *El arte musical en México*. Mexico City: Departamento Editorial de la Dirección General de las Bellas Artes, 1917.

Herskovits, Melville J. "The Cattle Complex in East Africa." *American Anthropologist* 28, no. 1–4 (1926).

The Myth of the Negro Past. New York: Harper, 1941.

"The Negro in the New World: The Statement of a Problem." *American Anthropologist* 32, no. 1 (1930): 145–55.

"Problem, Method and Theory in Afroamerican Studies." *Afroamérica* 1, no. 1–2 (1945): 5–24.

"Problem, Method, and Theory in Afroamerican Studies." In *The New World Negro: Selected Papers in Afroamerican Studies*, edited by Frances S. Herskovits, 43–61. Bloomington: Indiana University Press, 1966.

Hughes, Langston. "Autobiography: I Wonder as I Wander." In vol. 14 of *The Collected Works of Langston Hughes*, edited by Joseph McLaren. Columbia: University of Missouri Press, 2003.

The Big Sea. New York: Hill and Wang, 1993.

"Negroes in Spain." In *Volunteer for Liberty* 1, no. 14 (1937). Reprinted in *African Americans in the Spanish Civil War: "This Ain't Ethiopia, but It'll Do,"* edited by Danny Duncan Collum, 103–5. New York: G. K. Hall, 1992.

Instituto Indigenista Interamericano. *Homenaje a Gonzalo Aguirre Beltrán*. 3 vols. Mexico City: Instituto Indigenista Interamericano, 1973–74.

Instituto Nacional de Estadística y Geografía. "Resultados definitivos de la encuesta intercensal 2015." December 8, 2015. www.inegi.org.mx/contenidos/programas/intercensal/2015/doc/especiales2015_12_3.pdf.

Instituto Nacional de Migración. "Ley de Migración de 1926." In *Compilación histórica de la legislación migratoria en México, 1821–2002*, 3rd ed., corrected and expanded, 121–45. Mexico City: Secretaría de Gobernación, 2002.

"Ley de Migración de 1930." In *Compilación histórica de la legislación migratoria en México, 1821–2002*, 3rd ed., corrected and expanded, 147–77. Mexico City: Secretaría de Gobernación, 2002.

"Ley General de Población de 1936." In *Compilación histórica de la legislación migratoria en México, 1821–2002*, 3rd ed., corrected and expanded, 179–212. Mexico City: Secretaría de Gobernación, 2002.

Instituto Veracruzano de Cultura. *20. foro Veracruz también es Caribe: Veracruz 10–12 de octubre 1990*. Veracruz: Instituto Veracruzano de Cultura, 1992.

Festival internacional afrocaribeño: Programa general y cartelera de junio. Veracruz: Instituto Veracruzano de Cultura, 1996.

Jornadas de homenaje a Gonzalo Aguirre Beltrán. Veracruz: Instituto Veracruzano de Cultura, 1988.

"Introduction of Resolution Condemning Mexico's Issuance of Offensive Stamps." 109 Cong. Rec. H5630–H5633 (daily ed. July 11, 2005) (statements of Rep. Cleaver and Rep. Payne).

Kitt, Eartha. *Thursday's Child*. New York: Duell, Sloan, and Pearce, 1956.

La Farge, Oliver, and Frans Blom. *Tribes and Temples: A Record of the Expedition to Middle America Conducted by the Tulane University of Louisiana in 1925*. 2 vols. New Orleans, LA: Tulane University, 1926–27.

Léger, Marc James, and David Tomas, eds. *Zapantera Negra: An Artistic Encounter Between Black Panthers and Zapatistas*. Brooklyn, NY: Common Notions, 2017.

León, Nicolás. *Las castas del México colonial o Nueva España: Noticias etno-antropológicas*. Mexico City: Talleres Gráficos del Museo Nacional de Arqueología y Etnografía, 1924.

Compendio de la historia general de México: Desde los tiempos prehistóricos hasta el año de 1900. Mexico City: Herrero Hermanos, 1902.

Logan, Rayford W. "The Crisis of Democracy in the Western Hemisphere." *Journal of Negro Education* 10, no. 3 (1941): 344–52.

Lorde, Audre. *Zami: A New Spelling of My Name*. Freedom, CA: The Crossing Press, 1982.

Loyo, Gilberto. *La política demográfica de México*. Mexico City: Secretaría de Prensa y Propaganda, 1935.

Luna Arroyo, Antonio. *Ana Mérida en la historia de la danza mexicana moderna*. Mexico City: México Técnica Gráf, 1959.

Macías, José Miguel. *Diccionario cubano: Etimológico, critico, razonado y comprensivo*. Veracruz: C. Towbridge, 1885.

Magner, James A. Review of *Mexico South: The Isthmus of Tehuantepec* by Miguel Covarrubias. *The Americas* 3, no. 4 (1947): 561–62.

Mancisidor, José. "30 minutos con Picasso." In *Imágenes de mi tiempo*, in vol. 5 of *Obras completas de José Mancisidor*, 739–44. Xalapa: Gobierno del Estado de Veracruz, 1980.

La asonada: Novela mexicana. 1st ed. Jalapa, Veracruz: Editorial Integrales, 1931.

Ciento veinte días. Editorial México Nuevo, 1937.

Frontera junto al mar. Mexico City: Fondo de Cultura Económica, 1953.

"Índice de la decoración mural de la Escuela Normal Veracruzana." In vol. 5 of *Obras completas de José Mancisidor*, 141–61. Xalapa: Gobierno del Estado de Veracruz, 1980.

"Lenin (Conferencia)." In vol. 5 of *Obras completas de José Mancisidor*, 507–47. Xalapa: Gobierno del Estado de Veracruz, 1980.

"Lenin en el corazón del pueblo." In *Imágenes de mi tiempo*, vol. 5 of *Obras completas de José Mancisidor*, 651–60. Xalapa: Gobierno del Estado de Veracruz, 1980.

Nueva York revolucionario. Xalapa: Editorial "Integrales," 1935.

"La risa de Langston Hughes." In *Imágenes de mi tiempo*, vol. 5 of *Obras Completas de José Mancisidor*, 645–49. Xalapa: Gobierno del Estado de Veracruz, 1980.

Se llamaba Catalina. Xalapa: Universidad Veracruzana, 1958.

"Stalin: El hombre de acero." In vol. 5 of *Obras completas de José Mancisidor*, 549–89. Xalapa: Gobierno del Estado de Veracruz, 1980.

Yanga. In vol. 7 of *Obras Completas de José Mancisidor*, 129–76. Xalapa: Gobierno del Estado de Veracruz, 1982.

Martínez Montiel, Luz María. "Mexico's Third Root." In *Africa's Legacy in Mexico/El legado de África en México*, by Tony Gleaton, 24–30. Washington, DC: Smithsonian Institution, 1993.

Mayas y olmecas: Segunda reunión de mesa redonda sobre problemas antropológicas de México y Centro América. Tuxtla Gutiérrez, Chiapas, 1942.

Mayer-Serra, Otto. *Música y músicos de Latinoamérica*. 2 vols. Mexico City: Editorial Atlante, 1947.

Panorama de la música mexicana: Desde la independencia hasta la actualidad. Mexico City: El Colegio de México, 1941.

Melgarejo Vivanco, José Luis. "Carta etnográfica de Veracruz." In vol. 2 of *Antropología física de Veracruz*, by Johanna Faulhaber, np. Gobierno de Veracruz, 1950–56.

Breve historia de Veracruz. Xalapa: Universidad Veracruzana, 1960.

Mobwa Mobwa N'Djoli, Jean-Philibert. "The Need to Recognize Afro-Mexicans as an Ethnic Group." In *Black Mexico: Race and Society from Colonial to Modern Times*, edited by Ben Vinson III and Matthew Restall, 224–31. Albuquerque: University of New Mexico Press, 2009.

Molina Enríquez, Andrés. *Esbozo de la historia de los primeros diez años de la revolución agraria de México (de 1910 a 1920)*. 5 vols. Mexico City: Talleres Gráficos del Museo Nacional de Arqueología, Historia y Etnografía, 1932–36.

Los grandes problemas nacionales. Mexico City: A. Carranza e Hijos, 1909.

Montemayor, Felipe. *La población de Veracruz: Historia de lenguas. Culturas actuales. Rasgos físicos de la población*. Gobierno de Veracruz, 1950–56.

Monzón, Luis G. *Detalles de la educación socialista implantables en México*. Mexico City: Talleres Gráficas de la Nación, 1936.

Mora, José María Luis. *Méjico y sus revoluciones*. Vols. 1 and 4. Paris: Librería de Rosa, 1836.

Morelos, José María. "Sentiments of the Nation, or Points Outlined by Morelos for the Constitution." In *The Mexico Reader: History, Culture, Politics*, edited by Gilbert M. Joseph and Timothy J. Henderson, 189–91. Durham, NC: Duke University Press, 2002.

Moreno, Cesáreo. "An Historical Survey: Afro-Mexican Depictions and Identity in the Visual Arts/Una visión histórica: Representaciones afro-mexicanas e identidad en las artes visuales." In Herrera, *The African Presence in México: From Yanga to the Present*, 60–95.

Moreno Fraginals, Manuel. Review of *La población negra de México, 1510–1810: Estudio etnohistórico* by Gonzalo Aguirre Beltrán. *Hispanic American Historical Review* 27, no. 1 (1947): 117–19.

Mörner, Magnus. "Historical Research on Race Relations in Latin America during the National Period." In *Race and Class in Latin America*, edited by Magnus Mörner, 199–230. New York: Columbia University Press, 1970.

Myrdal, Gunnar. *An American Dilemma: The Negro Problem and Modern Democracy*. New York: Harper, 1944.

Nelson, Glyn Jemmott. Foreword to Paulette A. Ramsay, *Afro-Mexican Constructions of Diaspora, Gender, Identity and Nation*, by Paulette A. Ramsay, xi–xiv. Kingston, Jamaica: University of the West Indies Press, 2016.

Neve, Brian. "A Past Master of His Craft: An Interview with Fred Zinnemann." In *Fred Zinnemann: Interviews*, edited by Gabriel Miller, 145–56. Jackson: University Press of Mississippi, 2005.

Noriega, Eduardo. *Geografía de la República Mexicana*. Mexico City: Librería de la Viuda de Ch. Bouret, 1898.

Olavarría y Ferrari, D. Enrique. *México independiente*. Vol. 4 of Riva Palacio, *México a través de los siglos*.

Olivera de Vázquez, Mercedes. "Algunos problemas de la investigación antropológica actual." In Warman et al., *De eso que llaman antropología mexicana*, 94–118.

Orozco, José Clemente. *An Autobiography*. Translated by Robert C. Stephenson. Austin: University of Texas Press, 2014.

Orozco y Berra, Manuel. *Historia antigua y de la conquista de México*. 2 vols. Mexico City: Tipografía de Gonzalo A. Esteva, 1880.

Ortiz, Fernando. *Glosario de afronegrismos*. Havana: Imprenta "El Siglo XX": 1924.

Pasquel, Leonardo. Prologue to *Discurso a Veracruz en su tercer centenario*, by José Miguel Macías, xi–xix. Mexico City: Editorial Citlaltepen, 1967.

Peñafiel, Antonio. *Estadística general de la República Mexicana*. Mexico City: Ministerio de Fomento, 1890.

Pimentel, D. Francisco. *Cuadro descriptivo y comparativo de las lenguas indígenas de México*. 2 vols. Mexico City: Imprenta de Andrade y Escalante, 1862–65.

Piña Chan, Román, and Luis Covarrubias. *El pueblo del jaguar (Los olmecas arqueológicos)*. Drawings by Miguel Covarrubias. Mexico City: Museo Nacional de Antropología, 1964.

Ponce, Manuel M. "Cultura: Escritos y composiciones musicales." *Cultura* 4, no. 1–6: 1–48.

"El folk-lore musical mexicano: Lo que se ha hecho. Lo que puede hacerse." *Revista musical de México* 1, no. 5 (1919): 5–9.

Primer Congreso Demográfico Interamericano. *Acta final del Primer Congreso Demográfico Interamericano: Celebrado en México, D.F. del 12 al 21 de octubre de 1943*. Mexico City, 1943.

Ramírez Govea, Lic. Francisco. Prologue to the 2nd ed. of *Veracruz en la historia y en la cumbancha: Poemas jarochos*, by Francisco Rivera, np. Veracruz, Mexico: Juan Carlos Lara Prado, 1994.

Ramos Pedrueza, Rafael. *José María Morelos y Pavón: Precursor del socialismo en México*. Mexico City: Dirección General de Acción Educativa Recreativa, 1930.

La lucha de las clases a través de la historia de México. Mexico City: Ediciones Revista LUX, 1934.

Rusia soviet y México revolucionario: Vicente Guerrero, precursor del socialismo. Mexico City: Secretaría de Educación Pública, 1922.

Sugerencias revolucionarias para la enseñanza de la historia. Mexico City: Universidad Nacional de México Autónomo, 1932.

Ramos y Duarte, Félix. *Diccionario de mejicanismos*. Mexico City: Imprenta de Eduardo Dublan, 1895.

Rayón, Ignacio López. "Elementos constitucionales circulados por el Sr. Rayón." In *Leyes fundamentales de México, 1808–1994*, coordinated by Felipe Tena Ramírez, 23–27. Mexico City: Editorial Porrúa, 1994.

"Report." *American Anthropologist* 51, no. 2 (1949): 345–76.

"Resolución del Primer Congreso Demográfico Interamericano sobre la población negra." *Afroamérica* 1, no. 1–2 (1945): 147–66.

Riva Palacio, Vicente. "Los treinta y tres negros." In vol. 1 of *El libro rojo, 1520–1867*, by Vicente Riva Palacio et al., 351–68. Mexico City: A. Pola, 1905.

El Virreinato. Vol. 2 of Riva Palacio, *México a través de los siglos*.

ed. *México a través de los siglos: Historia general y completa* [...]. 5 vols. Mexico City: Ballescá, 1888–89.

Rivera, Diego, et al. "Por un teatro para el pueblo: Declaración de principios." In vol. 7 of *Obras completas de José Mancisidor*, 415–18. Xalapa: Gobierno del Estado de Veracruz, 1982.

Rivera Ávila, Francisco [Paco Píldora, pseud.]. *Estampillas jarochas*. Veracruz: Instituto Veracruzano de Cultura, 1988.

Sobredosis de humor de Paco Píldora. Veracruz: Instituto Veracruzano de Cultura, 1996.

Veracruz en la historia y en la cumbancha con una selección de poemas jarochos. Mexico City: Impresiones Corona-Castillo, 1957.

Veracruz en la historia y en la cumbancha: Poemas jarochos. 2nd ed. Veracruz: Juan Carlos Lara Prado, 1994.

Rogers, Joel A. *100 Amazing Facts about the Negro with Complete Proof: A Short Cut to The World History of The Negro*. Bay Street, St. Johns ANU: Brawtley Press, 1995.

Sex and Race: A History of White, Negro, and Indian Miscegenation in the Two Americas. 2 vols. St. Petersburg, FL: Helga M. Rogers, 1970.
Romero Flores, Jesús. *Historia de la cultura mexicana*. Mexico City: Editorial B. Costa-AMIC, 1963.
Roncal, Joaquín. "The Negro Race in Mexico." *Hispanic American Historical Review* 24, no. 3 (1944): 530–40.
Rosenfeld, Paul. *By Way of Art: Criticisms of Music, Literature, Painting, Sculpture, and the Dance*. New York: Coward-McCann, 1928.
Rout, Leslie B., Jr. *The African Experience in Spanish America*. Princeton, NJ: Markus Wiener, 2003.
Salas Ortega, Antonio. "La naturaleza jurídica del I.N.I." In *Los centros coordinadores indigenistas*, 15–25. Mexico City: Instituto Nacional Indigenista, 1962.
Salazar Mallén, Rubén. *Morelos*. Ediciones de la Universidad Nacional, 1936.
Saldívar, Gabriel. *Historia de la música en México (épocas precortesiana y colonial)*. Mexico City: Secretaría de Educación Pública, 1934.
Salvatierra, Reynaldo. "El centro coordinador de la Mixteca de la costa." In *Los centros coordinadores indigenistas*, 103–9. Mexico City: Instituto Nacional Indigenista, 1962.
Santamaría, Francisco. *Antología folklórica y musical de Tabasco*. Arranged by Gerónimo Baqueiro Foster. Villahermosa, Tabasco: Publicaciones del Gobierno del Estado, 1952.
Diccionario general de americanismos. 3 vols. Mexico City: Editorial Pedro Robredo, 1942.
Sartorius, Carl. *Mexico, Landscapes and Popular Sketches*. Edited by Dr. Gaspey. London: Trübner, 1859.
Schoen, Harold. "The Free Negro in the Republic of Texas." *Southwestern Historical Quarterly* 39, no. 4 (1936): 292–308.
Seeger, Charles. "Music and Society: Some New-World Evidence of Their Relationship." In *Studies in Musicology, 1935–1975*, 182–94. Berkeley: University of California Press, 1977.
Sierra, Justo. *Evolución política del pueblo mexicano*. Mexico City: Editorial Porrúa, 1986.
Historia General. Vol. 11 of *Obras completas*. Mexico City: Universidad Nacional Autónoma de México, 1948.
The Political Evolution of the Mexican People. Translated by Charles Ramsdell. Austin: University of Texas Press, 1969.
En tierra yankee (Notas á todo vapor). Mexico City: Tipografía de la Oficina Impresora del Timbre, 1898.
Slonimsky, Nicolas. *Music of Latin America*. New York: Thomas Y. Crowell, 1945.
Smith, Tommie. *Silent Gesture: The Autobiography of Tommie Smith*. With David Steele. Philadelphia, PA: Temple University Press, 2007.
Starr, Frederick. "The Mexican Situation: Manuel Gamio's Program." *American Journal of Sociology* 24, no. 2 (1918): 128–38.
Taller de Gráfica Popular. *450 años de lucha: Homenaje al pueblo mexicano*. 1st ed. 1960.

Teja Zabre, Alfonso. *Biografía de México: Introducción y sinopsis*. Mexico City: Universidad Nacional de México Autónoma, 1931.

Breve historia de México. Mexico City: Talleres Gráficos de la Nación, 1934.

Guide to the History of Mexico: A Modern Interpretation. Translated by P. M. del Campo. Mexico City: Press of the Ministry of Foreign Affairs, 1935.

Historia de México: Una moderna interpretación. Mexico City: Secretaría de Relaciones Exteriores, 1935.

Morelos: Caudillo de la independencia mexicana. 1st ed. Madrid: España-Calpe, 1934.

Panorama histórico de la Revolución Mexicana. Mexico City: Ediciones Botas, 1939.

Teoría de la revolución. Mexico City: Ediciones Botas, 1936.

Tibol, Raquel. "Mesa redonda en el Taller de Gráfica Popular." *Artes de México*, no. 18 (1957): 3–16.

Tibón, Guiterre. *Pinotepa Nacional: Mixtecos, negros y triques*. Mexico City: Universidad Autónoma de México, 1961.

Toor, Frances. *A Treasury of Mexican Folkways*. New York: Crown, 1947.

Tornel y Mendivil, José María. *Breve reseña histórica de los acontecimientos más notables de la nación mexicana desde el año de 1821 hasta nuestros días*. Mexico City: Imprenta de Cumplido, 1852.

Trens, Manuel B., and José Luis Melgarejo Vivanco. *Historia de Veracruz*. 6 vols. Jalapa-Enríquez: Talleres Gráficos del Estado de Veracruz, 1947–50.

Van Den Berghe, Pierre L. "The African Diaspora in Mexico, Brazil, and the United States." *Social Forces* 54, no. 3 (1976): 530–45.

Van Sertima, Ivan. *They Came Before Columbus*. New York: Random House, 1976.

Vasconcelos, José. *Breve historia de México*. 1st ed. Mexico City: Acción Moderna Mercantil, 1937.

"The Latin-American Basis of Mexican Civilization." In *Aspects of Mexican Civilization*, by José Vasconcelos and Manuel Gamio, 3–102. Chicago, IL: University of Chicago Press, 1926.

A Mexican Ulysses: An Autobiography. Translated by W. Rex Crawford. Bloomington: Indiana University Press, 1963.

Qué es el comunismo: Por qué se pelea en España. Mexico City: Ediciones Botas, 1936.

La raza cósmica. Vigesimoquinta edition. Mexico City: Colección Austral, 2002.

Velázquez, María Elisa, and Ethel Correa. "Seminario: Estudios sobre poblaciones y culturas con herencia africana en México." *Diario de Campo*, no. 21 (2000): 19.

Velázquez, María Elisa, and José Luis Martínez Maldonado. *Cuajinicuilapa, Guerrero: Sitio de memoria de la esclavitud y de las poblaciones afrodescendientes*. Mexico City: Instituto Nacional de Antropología e Historia, 2016.

Veracruz (Apuntes históricos). Mexico City: Secretaría de Educación Pública, 1947.

Villaurrutia, Xavier. "La mulata de Córdoba: Escenario cinematográfico." In *Obras: Poesía/Teatro/Prosas varias/Crítica*, 2nd ed., compiled by Miguel

Capistrán, Alí Chumacero, and Luis Mario Schneider, 191–226. Mexico City: Fondo de Cultura Económica, 1966.

"La mulata de Córdoba: Ópera en un acto y tres cuadros [en colaboración con Agustín Lazo, Música de J. Pablo Moncayo]." In *Obras: Poesía/Teatro/ Prosas varias/Crítica*, 2nd. ed., compiled by Miguel Capistrán, Alí Chumacero, and Luis Mario Schneider, 227–49. Mexico City: Fondo de Cultura Económica, 1966.

Vivó, Jorge A. Introduction to vol. 1 of *Antropología física de Veracruz*, by Johanna Faulhaber, ix–xxi. Gobierno de Veracruz, 1950–56.

von Wuthenau, Alexander. *The Art of Terracotta Pottery in Pre-Columbian Central and South America*. New York: Crown, 1969.

Waddington, Peter. "Katherine Dunham Raises Primitive Dance Art to New Heights of Sophistication." In *Kaiso! Writings by and about Katherine Dunham*, edited by Vèvè A. Clark and Sara E. Johnson, 302–5. Madison: University of Wisconsin Press, 2005.

Warman, Arturo. "Todos santos y todos difuntos: Crítica histórica de la antropología mexicana." In Warman et al., *De eso que llaman antropología mexicana*, 9–38.

Warman, Arturo, et al. *De eso que llaman antropología mexicana*. Mexico City: Editorial Nuestro Tiempo, 1970.

Weinstock, Herbert. *Mexican Music: Notes by Herbert Weinstock for Concerts Arranged by Carlos Chávez*. New York: Museum of Modern Art, 1940.

Whitaker, Arthur P. "Cultural Interchange and the Teaching of History in the United States." In *Inter American Intellectual Exchange*, 121–34. Austin: Institute of Latin American Studies of the University of Texas, 1943.

Wiener, Leo. *Africa and the Discovery of America*. Vols. I and III. Philadelphia, PA: Innes, 1920–22.

Winfield Capitaine, Fernando. "Población rural en Córdoba, 1788." *La Palabra y el Hombre*, no. 30 (1979): 64–72.

Winsor, Justin, ed. *Narrative and Critical History of America*. Vol. 1. Boston: Houghton, Mifflin, 1889.

Woodson, Carter G. *The Negro in Our History*. 7th ed., further revised and enlarged. Washington, DC: Associated Publishers, 1941.

"Review of *La población negra de México, 1510–1810: Estudio etnohistórico* by Gonzalo Aguirre Beltrán." *Journal of Negro History* 31, no. 4 (1946): 491–94.

Zárate, D. Julio. *La guerra de la independencia*. Vol. 3 of Riva Palacio, *México a través de los siglos*.

de Zayas, Marius. *African Negro Art: Its Influence on Modern Art*. New York: Modern Gallery, 1916.

How, When, and Why Modern Art Came to New York. Edited by Francis M. Naumann. Cambridge, MA: MIT Press, 1996.

de Zayas, Marius, and Paul B. Haviland. *A Study of the Modern Evolution of Plastic Expression*. New York: "291," 1913.

de Zayas Enríquez, R. *La redención de una raza: Estudio sociológico*. Veracruz, Mexico: Tip. de R. de Zayas, 1887.

SECONDARY SOURCES

Ades, Dawn. *Art in Latin America: The Modern Era, 1820–1980*. New Haven, CT: Yale University Press, 1989.

Aguirre Beltrán, Gonzalo. "Manuel Gamio." In *Crítica antropológica: Hombres e ideas. Contribuciones al estudio del pensamiento social en México*, in vol. 15 of *Obra antropológica*, 269–80. Mexico City: Fondo de Cultura Económica, 1990.

Alberto, Paulina L. "El Negro Raúl: Lives and Afterlives of an Afro-Argentine Celebrity, 1886 to the Present." *Hispanic American Historical Review* 96, no. 4 (2016): 669–710.

Alberto, Paulina L., and Jesse Hoffnung-Garskof. "'Racial Democracy' and Racial Inclusion: Hemispheric Histories." In *Afro-Latin American Studies: An Introduction*, edited by Alejandro de la Fuente and George Reid Andrews, 264–316. New York: Cambridge University Press, 2018.

Alegre González, Lizette. "Música, migración y cine: *Los Tres Huastecos*. Un ejemplo de entrecruzamiento cultural." In *Música sin fronteras: Ensayos sobre migración, música e identidad*, 221–47. Mexico City: Consejo Nacional para la Cultura y las Artes, 2006.

Alexander, Ryan M. *Sons of the Mexican Revolution: Miguel Alemán and His Generation*. Albuquerque: University of New Mexico Press, 2016.

Andrews, George Reid. *Afro-Latin America, 1800–2000*. Oxford: Oxford University Press, 2004.

Afro-Latin America: Black Lives, 1600–2000. Cambridge, MA: Harvard University Press, 2016.

Blackness in the White Nation: A History of Afro-Uruguay. Chapel Hill: University of North Carolina Press, 2010.

"Epilogue: Whiteness and Its Discontents." In *Rethinking Race in Modern Argentina*, edited by Paulina L. Alberto and Eduardo Elena, 318–26. New York: Cambridge University Press, 2016.

Arce, B. Christine. *México's Nobodies: The Cultural Legacy of the Soldadera and Afro-Mexican Women*. Albany: State University of New York Press, 2017.

Archer-Straw, Petrine. *Negrophilia: Avant-Garde Paris and Black Culture in the 1920s*. New York: Thames and Hudson, 2000.

Argüelles, Hugo. *Teatro vario*. Vol. 4. Mexico City: Fondo de Cultura Económica, 1998.

Arnáiz y Freg, Arturo. "Alfonso Teja Zabre (1888–1962): El historiador." *Revista de Historia de América*, nos. 53–54 (1962): 229–31.

Aschenbrenner, Joyce. *Katherine Dunham: Dancing a Life*. Urbana: University of Illinois Press, 2002.

Avila, Mary Theresa. "Chronicles of Revolution and Nation: El Taller de Gráfica Popular's 'Estampas de la Revolución Mexicana' (1947)." PhD diss., University of New Mexico, 2013.

Azuela, Alicia. "*El Machete* and *Frente a Frente*: Art Committed to Social Justice in Mexico." *Art Journal* 52, no. 1 (1993): 82–87.

Baker, Lee D. *From Savage to Negro: Anthropology and the Construction of Race, 1896–1954*. Berkeley: University of California Press, 1998.

Ballesteros Páez, María Dolores. "La visión de viajeros europeos de la primera mitad del XIX de los afromexicanos." *Cuicuilco Revista de Ciencias Antropológicas*, no. 69 (2017): 185–206.

Bartra, Eli. "How Black Is *La Negra Angustias*?" *Third Text* 26, no. 3 (2012): 275–83.

Basave Benítez, Agustín. *México mestizo: Análisis del nacionalismo mexicano en torno a la mestizofilia de Andrés Molina Enríquez*. 2nd ed. Mexico City: Fondo de Cultura Económica, 2002.

Bass, Amy. *Not the Triumph but the Struggle: The 1968 Olympics and the Making of the Black Athlete*. Minneapolis: University of Minnesota Press, 2002.

Benítez, Fernando. "De Cortés a Humboldt." In *Crónica del Puerto de Veracruz*, by Fernando Benítez and José Emilio Pacheco, 11–138. Veracruz: Gobierno del Estado de Veracruz, 1986.

Benjamin, Thomas. *La Revolución: Mexico's Great Revolution as Memory, Myth, and History*. Austin: University of Texas Press, 2000.

Bennett, Herman. *Africans in Colonial Mexico: Absolutism, Christianity, and Afro-Creole Consciousness, 1570–1640*. Bloomington: Indiana University Press, 2003.

Colonial Blackness: A History of Afro-Mexico. Bloomington: Indiana University Press, 2009.

"The Subject in the Plot: National Boundaries and the 'History' of the Black Atlantic." *African Studies Review* 43, no. 1 (2000): 101–24.

Berlin, Ira. *The Making of African America: The Four Great Migrations*. New York: Viking, 2010.

Many Thousands Gone: The First Two Centuries of Slavery in North America. Cambridge, MA: Harvard University Press, 1998.

Berrios, Alfonso. "Vida y Obras de José Mancisidor." In vol. 1 of *Obras Completas de José Mancisidor*, 11–224. Xalapa: Gobierno del Estado de Veracruz, 1978.

Biondi, Martha. *The Black Revolution on Campus*. Berkeley: University of California Press, 2012.

Blackburn, Robin. *The American Crucible: Slavery, Emancipation and Human Rights*. London: Verso, 2011.

Blain, Keisha N. *Set the World on Fire: Black Nationalist Women and the Global Struggle for Freedom*. Philadelphia: University of Pennsylvania Press, 2018.

Blanco, José Joaquín. *Se llama Vasconcelos: Una evocación crítica*. Mexico City: Fondo de Cultura Económica, 1979.

Bourdieu, Pierre, and Loïc Wacquant. "On the Cunning of Imperialist Reason." *Theory, Culture, and Society* 16, no. 1 (1999): 41–58.

Brading, David A. "Manuel Gamio and Official Indigenismo in Mexico." *Bulletin of Latin American Research* 7, no. 1 (1988): 75–89.

Bristol, Joan C. "Afro-Mexican Saintly Devotion in a Mexico City Alley." In *Africans to Spanish America: Expanding the Diaspora*, edited by Sherwin K. Bryant, Rachel Sarah O'Toole, and Ben Vinson III, 114–35. Urbana: University of Illinois Press, 2012.

Britton, John A. *Carleton Beals: A Radical Journalist in Latin America*. Albuquerque: University of New Mexico Press, 1987.

Brizuela Absalón, Álvaro. "Museo de Antropología de la Universidad Veracruzana." In vol. 7 of *La antropología en México: Panorama histórico*, coordinated by Carlos García Mora, 437–54. Mexico City: Instituto Nacional de Antropología e Historia, 1988.

Bronfman, Alejandra. *Measures of Equality: Social Science, Citizenship, and Race in Cuba, 1902–1940*. Chapel Hill: University of North Carolina Press, 2004.

Brunk, Samuel. *The Posthumous Career of Emiliano Zapata: Myth, Memory, and Mexico's Twentieth Century*. Austin: University of Texas Press, 2008.

Buck-Morss, Susan. *Hegel, Haiti, and Universal History*. Pittsburgh, PA: University of Pittsburgh Press, 2009.

Bueno, Christina. *The Pursuit of Ruins: Archaeology, History, and the Making of Modern Mexico*. Albuquerque: University of New Mexico Press, 2016.

Burns, Andrea A. *From Storefront to Monument: Tracing the Public History of the Black Museum Movement*. Amherst: University of Massachusetts Press, 2013.

Burns, Kathryn. "Unfixing Race." In *Histories of Race and Racism: The Andes and Mesoamerica from Colonial Times to the Present*, edited by Laura Gotkowitz, 57–71. Durham, NC: Duke University Press, 2011.

Bustamante Álvarez, Tomás. "La reconstrucción." In vol. 4 of *Historia general de Guerrero*, 189–311. Mexico City: Instituto Nacional de Antropología e Historia, 1998.

Bustos Cerecedo, Miguel. "José Mancisidor: El Hombre." In vol. 1 of *Obras Completas de José Mancisidor*, by José Mancisidor, 225–306. Xalapa: Gobierno del Estado de Veracruz, 1978.

Butler, Judith. "Restaging the Universal: Hegemony and the Limits of Formalism." In *Contingency, Hegemony, Universality, Contemporary Dialogues on the Left*, by Judith Butler, Ernesto Laclau, and Slavoj Žižek, 11–43. London: Verso, 2000.

Butler, Kim D. "Defining Diaspora, Refining a Discourse." *Diaspora: A Journal of Transnational Studies* 10, no. 2 (2001): 189–219.

Caballero, Paula López, and Ariadna Acevedo-Rodrigo, eds. *Beyond Alterity: Destabilizing the Indigenous Other in Mexico*. Tucson: University of Arizona Press, 2018.

Campos, Luis Eugenio. "Caracterización étnica de los pueblos de negros de la costa chica de Oaxaca: Una visión etnográfica." In Velázquez Gutiérrez and Correa Duró, *Poblaciones y culturas de origen africano en México*, 411–25.

Campos García, Alejandro. Introduction to *Identidades políticas en tiempos de afrodescendencia: Auto-identificación, ancestralidad, visibilidad y derechos*, edited by Silvia Valero and Alejandro Campos García, 15–64. Buenos Aires: Corregidor, 2015.

Carr, Barry. *Marxism and Communism in Twentieth-Century Mexico*. Lincoln: University of Nebraska Press, 1992.

Carrera, Magali M. *Traveling from New Spain to Mexico: Mapping Practices of Nineteenth-Century Mexico*. Durham, NC: Duke University Press, 2011.

Carrera Stampa, Manuel. "Alfonso Teja Zabre (1888–1962): El Hombre." *Revista de Historia de América*, nos. 53/54 (1962): 232–34.

Carroll, Patrick J. *Blacks in Colonial Veracruz: Race, Ethnicity, and Regional Development*. 2nd ed. Austin: University of Texas Press, 2001.

"Los mexicanos negros, el mestizaje y los fundamentos olvidados de la 'Raza Cósmica': una perspectiva regional." Translated by Jeffrey N. Lamb. *Historia Mexicana* 44, no. 3 (1995): 403–38.

Prologue to *Esclavos negros en las haciendas azucareras de Córdoba, Veracruz*, by Adriana Naveda Chávez-Hita, 11–12. Xalapa: Universidad Veracruzana, 1987.

Cassiani Herrera, Alfonso. "La diáspora africana y afrodescendiente en Latinoamérica: Las redes de organizaciones como puntos de encuentros." In *Identidades políticas en tiempos de afrodescendencia: Auto-identificación, ancestralidad, visibilidad y derechos*, edited by Silvia Valero and Alejandro Campos García, 127–64. Buenos Aires: Corregidor, 2015.

Castañeda, Luis M. *Spectacular Mexico: Design, Propaganda, and the 1968 Olympics*. Minneapolis: University of Minnesota Press, 2014.

Cházaro, Laura. "From Anatomical Collection to National Museum, circa 1895: How Skulls and Female Pelvises Began to Speak the Language of Mexican National History," translated by Lucía Cirianni and Benjamín de Buen, in López Caballero and Acevedo-Rodrigo, *Beyond Alterity*, 173–98.

Chew, Selfa A. "Representation of Black Womanhood in Mexico." *Studies in Latin American Popular Culture* 36 (2018): 108–27.

Childs, Gregory. "Conspiracies, Seditions, Rebellions: Concepts and Categories in the Study of Slave Resistance." In *New Perspectives on the Black Intellectual Tradition*, edited by Keisha N. Blain, Christopher Cameron, and Ashley D. Farmer, 217–31. Evanston, IL: Northwestern University Press, 2018.

Clifford, James. "Diasporas." *Cultural Anthropology* 9, no. 3 (1994): 302–38.

Cohn, Deborah. "The Mexican Intelligentsia, 1950–1968: Cosmopolitanism, National Identity, and the State." *Mexican Studies/Estudios Mexicanos* 21, no. 1 (2005): 141–82.

Contreras Soto, Eduardo. *Silvestre Revueltas: Baile, duelo y son*. Mexico City: CONACULTA, 2000.

Cooper, Frederick, and Rogers Brubaker. "Identity." In *Colonialism in Question: Theory, Knowledge, History*, by Frederick Cooper, 59–90. Berkeley: University of California Press, 2005.

Cope, R. Douglas. *The Limits of Racial Domination: Plebeian Society in Colonial Mexico City, 1660–1720*. Madison: University of Wisconsin Press, 1994.

Cornell, Sarah E. "Citizens of Nowhere: Fugitive Slaves and Free African Americans in Mexico, 1833–1857." *Journal of American History* 100, no. 2 (2013): 351–74.

Craib, Raymond B. *Cartographic Mexico: A History of State Fixations and Fugitive Landscapes*. Durham, NC: Duke University Press, 2004.

Crenshaw, Kimberlé Williams, Luke Charles Harris, Daniel Martinez HoSang, and George Lipsitz, eds. *Seeing Race Again: Countering Colorblindness across the Disciplines*. Oakland: University of California Press, 2019.

Cruz Carretero, Sagrario. *El Carnaval en Yanga: Notas y comentarios sobre una fiesta de la negritud.* Mexico City: Consejo Nacional para la Cultura y las Artes, 1990.

Cunin, Elisabeth. "Introducción: ¿Por qué una antología?" In *Textos en diáspora: Una antología sobre afrodescendientes en América*, edited by Elisabeth Cunin, 11–29. Mexico City: Instituto Nacional de Antropología e Historia, 2008.

Dagbovie, Pero Gaglo. *What Is African American History?* Malden, MA: Polity Press, 2015.

Daniels, Douglas Henry. "Los Angeles Zoot: Race 'Riot,' the Pachuco, and Black Music Culture." *Journal of African American History* 87 (2002): 98–118.

Dávila, Jerry. "Challenging Racism in Brazil: Legal Suits in the Context of the 1951 Anti- Discrimination Law." *Varia História* 33, no. 61 (2017): 163–85.

Dawson, Alexander S. *Indian and Nation in Revolutionary Mexico.* Tucson: University of Arizona Press, 2004.

de la Peña, Guillermo. "Gonzalo Aguirre Beltrán." In vol. 9 of *La antropología en México: Panorama histórico*, coordinated by Lina Odena Güemes and Carlos García Mora, 63–95. Mexico City: Instituto Nacional de Antropología e Historia, 1988.

"Nacionales y extranjeros en la historia de la antropología mexicana." In *La historia de la antropología en México: Fuentes y transmisión*, compiled by Mechthild Rutsch, 41–81. Mexico City: Plaza y Valdés, 1996.

Delgadillo, Theresa. "Singing 'Angelitos Negros': African Diaspora Meets *Mestizaje* in the Americas." *American Quarterly* 58, no. 2 (2006): 407–30.

Delpar, Helen. *The Enormous Vogue of Things Mexican: Cultural Relations between the United States and Mexico, 1920–1935.* Tuscaloosa: University of Alabama Press, 1992.

Derbez, Alain. *El jazz en México: Datos para una historia.* Mexico City: Fondo de Cultura Económica, 2001.

Dillingham, A. S. "Indigenismo Occupied: Indigenous Youth and Mexico's Democratic Opening (1968–1975)." *The Americas* 72, no. 4 (2015): 549–82.

Dixon, Kwame, and John Burdick, eds. *Comparative Perspectives on Afro-Latin America.* Gainesville: University Press of Florida, 2012.

Earle, Rebecca. *The Return of the Native: Indians and Myth-Making in Spanish America, 1810–1930.* Durham, NC: Duke University Press, 2007.

Edwards, Brent Hayes. *The Practice of Diaspora: Literature, Translation, and the Rise of Black Internationalism.* Cambridge, MA: Harvard University Press, 2003.

"The Uses of *Diaspora*." *Social Text* 19, no. 1 (2001): 45–73.

Edwards, Erika. "Mestizaje, Córdoba's patria chica: Beyond the Myth of Black Disappearance in Argentina." *African and Black Diaspora: An International Journal* 7, no. 2 (2014): 89–104.

Ellis, Keith. "Nicolás Guillén and Langston Hughes: Convergences and Divergences." In *Between Race and Empire: African-Americans and Cubans before the Cuban Revolution*, edited by Lisa Brock and Digna Castañeda Fuertes, 129–67. Philadelphia, PA: Temple University Press, 1998.

Ellison, Ralph. *Invisible Man.* New York: Vintage International, 1995.

Fábregas Puig, Andrés. "Gonzalo Aguirre Beltrán y los análisis antropológicos de la política en México." In *Gonzalo Aguirre Beltrán: Memorial crítico. Diálogos con la obra de Gonzalo Aguirre Beltrán en el centenario de su natalicio*, coordinated by Félix Báez-Jorge, 38–48. Mexico City: Editora de Gobierno del Estado de Veracruz, 2008.

Feldman, Heidi. *Black Rhythms of Peru: Reviving African Musical Heritage in the Black Pacific*. Middletown, CT: Wesleyan University Press, 2006.

Fell, Claude. *José Vasconcelos: Los años del águila (1920–1925). Educación, cultura e iberoamericanismo en el México postrevolucionario*. Mexico City: Universidad Autónoma de México, 1989.

Fenderson, Jonathan. *Building the Black Arts Movement: Hoyt Fuller and the Cultural Politics of the 1960s*. Urbana: University of Illinois Press, 2019.

Fernández Repetto, Francisco, and Genny Negroe Sierra. *Una población perdida en la memoria: Los negros de Yucatán*. Mérida: Universidad Autónoma de Yucatán, 1995.

Figueroa Hernández, Rafael. *Son Jarocho: Guía histórico-musical*. Mexico City: CONACULTA, 2007.

Flores, Ruben. *Backroads Pragmatists: Mexico's Melting Pot and Civil Rights in the United States*. Philadelphia: University of Pennsylvania Press, 2014.

Flores y Escalante, Jesús. *Salón México: Historia documental y gráfica del danzón en México*. Mexico City: Asociación Mexicana de Estudios Fonográficos, 1993.

Florescano, Enrique. *Etnia, Estado y Nación*. Mexico City: Taurus, 2002.

National Narratives in Mexico: A History. Translated by Nancy Hancock. Norman: University of Oklahoma Press, 2006.

Gaitors, Beau Dayeon Jovan. "Traders, Vendors, and Society in Early-Independence Veracruz, 1821–1850." PhD diss., Tulane University, 2017.

Garcia Canclini, Néstor. *Hybrid Cultures: Strategies for Entering and Leaving Modernity*. Translated by Christopher L. Chiappari and Silvia L. López. Minneapolis: University of Minnesota Press, 1995.

García de León, Antonio. *Tierra adentro, mar en fuera: El puerto de Veracruz y su litoral a Sotavento, 1519–1821*. Mexico City: Fondo de Cultura Económica, 2011.

Gates, Henry Louis, Jr. *Black in Latin America*. New York: New York University Press, 2011.

"Parable of the Talents." In *The Future of the Race*, by Henry Louis Gates Jr. and Cornell West, 1–52. New York: Vintage Books, 1996.

George, Ann, and Jack Selzer. "What Happened at the First American Writers Congress? Kenneth Burke's 'Revolutionary Symbolism in America'." *Rhetoric Society Quarterly* 33, no. 2 (2003): 47–66.

Gibson, Christina Taylor. "The Music of Manuel M. Ponce, Julián Carrillo, and Carlos Chávez." PhD diss., University of Maryland, 2008.

Gillingham, Paul. *Cuauhtémoc's Bones: Forging National Identity in Modern Mexico*. Albuquerque: University of New Mexico Press, 2011.

Gillingham, Paul, and Benjamin T. Smith, eds. *Dictablanda: Politics, Work, and Culture in Mexico, 1938–1968*. Durham, NC: Duke University Press, 2014.

Gilmore, Glenda Elizabeth. *Defying Dixie: The Radical Roots of Civil Rights, 1919–1950*. New York: W. W. Norton, 2008.

Gilroy, Paul. *Against Race: Imagining Political Culture beyond the Color Line*. Cambridge, MA: Harvard University Press, 2000.

The Black Atlantic: Modernity and Double Consciousness. Cambridge, MA: Harvard University Press, 1993.

Giraudo, Laura. "Neither 'Scientific' nor 'Colonialist': The Ambiguous Course of Inter-American Indigenismo in the 1940s." Translated by Victoria J. Furio. *Latin American Perspectives* 39, no. 186 (2012): 12–32.

Githiora, Chege. *Afro-Mexicans: Discourse of Race and Identity in the African Diaspora*. Trenton, NJ: Africa World Press, 2008.

Gonzales, Elena. "Who Are We Now? Roots, Resistance, & Recognition." In Herrera, *The African Presence in México: From Yanga to the Present*, 132–97.

González, Anita. *Afro-Mexico: Dancing between Myth and Reality*. Austin: University of Texas Press, 2010.

González, Fredy. *Paisanos Chinos: Transpacific Politics among Chinese Immigrants in Mexico*. Oakland: University of California Press, 2017.

González Gamio, Ángeles. *Manuel Gamio: Una lucha sin final*. 2nd ed. Mexico City: Universidad Nacional Autónoma de México, 2003.

González Navarro, Moisés. *Los extranjeros en México y los mexicanos en el extranjero, 1821–1970*. Vol. 3. Mexico City: El Colegio de México, 1994.

Gotkowitz, Laura. "Introduction: Racisms of the Present and the Past in Latin America." In *Histories of Race and Racism: The Andes and Mesoamerica from Colonial Times to the Present*, edited by Laura Gotkowitz, 1–53. Durham, NC: Duke University Press, 2011.

ed. *Histories of Race and Racism: The Andes and Mesoamerica from Colonial Times to the Present*. Durham, NC: Duke University Press, 2011.

Graham, Jessica Lynn. *Shifting the Meaning of Democracy: Race, Politics, and Culture in the United States and Brazil*. Berkeley: University of California Press, 2019.

Guadarrama Olivera, Horacio. "Francisco Rivera *Paco Píldora*: Genio y figura." In *Personajes populares de Veracruz*, coordinated by Félix Báez-Jorge, 257–89. Xalapa: Secretaría de Educación-Gobierno del Estado de Veracruz, 2010.

"Los carnavales del puerto de Veracruz." In *La Habana/Veracruz, Veracruz/La Habana: Las dos orillas*, coordinated by Bernardo García Díaz and Sergio Guerra Vilaboy, 469–94. Mexico City: Universidad Veracruzana, 2002.

Guardino, Peter. *The Dead March: A History of the Mexican-American War*. Cambridge, MA: Harvard University Press, 2017.

"La identidad nacional y los afromexicanos en el siglo XIX." In *Practicas populares, cultura política y poder en México, siglo XIX*, edited by Brian Connaughton, 259–301. Mexico City: Casa Juan Pablos, 2008.

Gudmundson, Lowell, and Justin Wolfe. Introduction to *Blacks and Blackness in Central America: Between Race and Place*, edited by Lowell Gudmundson and Justin Wolfe, 1–23. Durham, NC: Duke University Press, 2010.

Guevara Sanginés, María. "Perspectivas metodológicas en los estudios historiográficos sobre los negros en México hacia finales del siglo XX." In Velázquez Gutiérrez and Correa Duró, *Poblaciones y culturas de origen africano en México*, 65–84.

Guridy, Frank A., and Juliet Hooker. "Currents in Afro-Latin American Political Thought." In *Afro-Latin American Studies: An Introduction*, edited by Alejandro de la Fuente and George Reid Andrews, 179–221. New York: Cambridge University Press, 2018.

Guridy, Frank Andre. *Forging Diaspora: Afro-Cubans and African Americans in a World of Empire and Jim Crow*. Chapel Hill: University of North Carolina Press, 2010.

Guzmán, Alicia Inez. "Miguel Covarrubias's World: Remaking Global Space at the 1939 Golden Gate International Exposition." In *Miguel Covarrubias: Drawing a Cosmopolitan Line*, edited by Carolyn Kastner, 19–48. Austin: University of Texas Press, 2014.

Hale, Charles A. "The War with the United States and the Crisis in Mexican Thought." *The Americas* 14, no. 2 (1957): 153–73.

Hamilton, Nora. *The Limits of State Autonomy: Post-Revolutionary Mexico*. Princeton, NJ: Princeton University Press, 1982

Hanchard, Michael. "Identity, Meaning and the African-American." *Social Text*, no. 24 (1990): 31–42.

Orpheus and Power: The Movimento Negro *of Rio de Janeiro and São Paulo, Brazil, 1945–1988*. Princeton, NJ: Princeton University Press, 2004.

Hartman, Saidiya V. *Scenes of Subjection: Terror, Slavery, and Self-Making in Nineteenth-Century America*. New York: Oxford University Press, 1997.

Hellier-Tinoco, Ruth. *Embodying Mexico: Tourism, Nationalism and Performance*. Oxford: Oxford University Press, 2011.

Hellwig, David, ed. *African-American Reflections on Brazil's Racial Paradise*. Philadelphia, PA: Temple University Press, 1992.

Hernández Cuevas, Marco Polo. *African Mexicans and the Discourse on Modern Nation*. Lanham, MD: University Press of America, 2004.

Herrera Barreda, María del Socorro. "Un caso de xenofilia mexicana: La inmigración cubana entre 1868 y 1898." In *Xenofobia y xenofilia en la historia de México: Siglos XIX y XX*, coordinated by Delia Salazar Anaya, 175–202. Mexico City: SEGOB, 2006.

Herrera Casasús, María Luisa. *Presencia y esclavitud del negro en la Huasteca*. Mexico City: Universidad Autónoma de Tamaulipas, 1989.

"Raíces africanas en la población de Tamaulipas." In Martínez Montiel, *Presencia africana en México*, 463–523.

Herzog, Melanie Anne. *Elizabeth Catlett: An American Artist in Mexico*. Seattle: University of Washington Press, 2000.

Hoffmann, Odile. "Negros y afromestizos en México: Viejas y nuevas lecturas de un mundo olvidado." Translated by Camila Pascal. *Revista Mexicana de Sociología* 68, no. 1 (2006): 103–35.

Holloway, Jonathan Scott. *Jim Crow Wisdom: Memory and Identity in Black America since 1940*. Chapel Hill: University of North Carolina Press, 2013.

Hooker, Juliet. *Race and the Politics of Solidarity*. Oxford: Oxford University Press, 2009.

Theorizing Race in the Americas: Douglass, Sarmiento, Du Bois, and Vasconcelos. New York: Oxford University Press, 2017.

Horne, Gerald. *Black and Brown: African Americans and the Mexican Revolution, 1910–1920*. New York: New York University Press, 2005.

Iber, Patrick. *Neither Peace nor Freedom: The Cultural Cold War in Latin America*. Cambridge, MA: Harvard University Press, 2015.

Irwin, Robert McKee. "Memín Pinguín, Rumba, and Racism: Afro-Mexicans in Classic Comics and Film." In *Hemispheric American Studies*, edited by Caroline F. Levander and Robert S. Levine, 249–65. New Brunswick, NJ: Rutgers University Press, 2008.

Jackson, Jeffrey H. *Making Jazz French: Music and Modern Life in Interwar Paris*. Durham, NC: Duke University Press, 2003.

Jackson, Lawrence P. *The Indignant Generation: A Narrative History of African American Writers and Critics, 1934–1960*. Princeton, NJ: Princeton University Press, 2011.

Jackson, Richard L. *The Black Image in Latin American Literature*. Albuquerque: University of New Mexico Press, 1976.

Jacoby, Karl. *The Strange Career of William Ellis: The Texas Slave Who Became a Mexican Millionaire*. New York: W. W. Norton, 2016.

Jacques, Geoffrey. "CuBop! Afro-Cuban Music and Mid-Twentieth-Century American Culture." In *Between Race and Empire: African-Americans and Cuban before the Cuban Revolution*, edited by Lisa Brock and Digna Castañeda Fuertes, 249–65. Philadelphia, PA: Temple University Press, 1998.

James, Winston. *Holding Aloft the Banner of Ethiopia: Caribbean Radicalism in Early Twentieth-Century America*. London: Verso, 1998.

Janken, Kenneth Robert. *Rayford W. Logan and the Dilemma of the African-American Intellectual*. Amherst: University of Massachusetts Press, 1993.

Jara Gámez, Simón, Aurelio Rodríguez Yeyo, and Antonio Zedillo Castillo. *De Cuba con amor . . . el danzón en México*. Mexico City: Consejo Nacional para la Cultura y las Artes, 1994.

Jarrett, Gene Andrew. *Representing the Race: A New Political History of African American Literature*. New York: New York University Press, 2011.

Johnson, Jessica Marie. "Markup Bodies: Black [Life] Studies and Slavery [Death] Studies at the Digital Crossroads." *Social Text* 36, no. 4 (2018): 57–79.

Joseph, Gilbert M., and Daniel Nugent, eds. *Everyday Forms of State Formation: Revolution and the Negotiation of Rule in Modern Mexico*. Durham, NC: Duke University Press, 1994.

Juárez Hernández, Yolanda. *Persistencias culturales afrocaribeñas en Veracruz: Su proceso de conformación desde la colonia hasta fines del siglo XIX*. Veracruz: Gobierno del Estado Veracruz, 2006.

Karp, Matthew. *This Vast Southern Empire: Slaveholders at the Helm of American Foreign Policy*. Cambridge, MA: Harvard University Press, 2016.

Keiler, Allan. *Marian Anderson: A Singer's Journey*. Urbana: University of Illinois Press, 2000.
Kelley, Robin D. G. "'But a Local Phase of a World Problem': Black History's Global Vision, 1883–1950." *Journal of American History* 86, no. 3 (1999): 1045–77.
Freedom Dreams: The Black Radical Imagination. Boston, MA: Beacon Press, 2002.
Race Rebels: Culture, Politics, and the Black Working Class. New York: The Free Press, 1996.
Kendi, Ibram X. "Reigning Assimilationists and Defiant Black Power: The Struggle to Define and Regulate Racist Ideas." In *New Perspectives on the Black Intellectual Tradition*, edited by Keisha N. Blain, Christopher Cameron, and Ashley D. Farmer, 157–74. Evanston, IL: Northwestern University Press, 2018.
Kiddle, Amelia M., and María L. O. Muñoz, eds. *Populism in Twentieth Century Mexico: The Presidencies of Lázaro Cárdenas and Luis Echeverría*. Tucson: University of Arizona Press, 2010.
Knight, Alan. "The Mexican Revolution: Bourgeois? Nationalist? Or Just a 'Great Rebellion'?" *Bulletin of Latin American Research* 4, no. 2 (1985): 1–37.
"Racism, Revolution, and *Indigenismo*: Mexico, 1910–1940." In *The Idea of Race in Latin America, 1870–1940*, edited by Richard Graham, 71–114. Austin: University of Texas Press, 1990.
Kohl S., and Ch. Randall. *Ecos de "La Bamba": Una historia etnomusicológica sobre el son jarocho de Veracruz, 1946–1959*. Veracruz: Instituto Veracruzano de Cultura, 2007.
Escritos de un náufrago habitual: Ensayos sobre el son jarocho y otros temas etnomusicológicos. Xalapa: Universidad Veracruzana, 2010.
Kolb-Neuhaus, Roberto. "Silvestre Revueltas's *Redes*: Composing for Film or Filming for Music?" *Journal of Film Music* 2, nos. 2–4 (2009): 127–44.
Kourí, Emilio. "Interpreting the Expropriation of Indian Pueblo Lands in Porfirian Mexico: The Unexamined Legacies of Andrés Molina Enríquez." *Hispanic American Historical Review* 82, no. 1 (2002): 69–118.
coord. *En busca de Andrés Molina Enríquez: Cien años de Los grandes problemas nacionales*. Mexico City: El Colegio de México, 2009.
Krippner, James. *Paul Strand in Mexico*. New York: Aperture Foundation, 2010.
LaCapra, Dominick. *Rethinking Intellectual History: Texts, Contexts, Language*. Ithaca, NY: Cornell University Press, 1983.
Laclau, Ernesto, and Chantal Mouffe. *Hegemony and Socialist Strategy: Towards a Radical Democratic Politics*. London: Verso, 1985.
Lamothe, Daphne. *Inventing the New Negro: Narrative, Culture, and Ethnography*. Philadelphia: University of Pennsylvania Press, 2008.
Lara, Gloria. "Una corriente etnopolítica en la Costa Chica, México (1980–2000)." In *Política e identidad: Afrodescendientes en México y América Central*, coordinated by Odile Hoffmann, 307–34. Mexico City: Instituto Nacional de Antropología e Historia, 2010.
Lasso, Marixa. *Myths of Harmony: Race and Republicanism during the Age of Revolution, Colombia, 1795–1831*. Pittsburgh, PA: University of Pittsburgh Press, 2007.

Lear, John. *Picturing the Proletariat: Artists and Labor in Revolutionary Mexico, 1908–1940*. Austin: University of Texas Press, 2017.

LeFalle-Collins, Lizzetta. "African-American Modernists and the Mexican Muralist School." In *In the Spirit of Resistance: African-American Modernists and the Mexican Muralist School*, edited by Lizzetta LeFalle-Collins and Shifra M. Goldman, 27–67. New York: American Federation of Arts, 1996.

Lesser, Jeff H. "Are African-Americans African or American? Brazilian Immigration Policy in the 1920s." *Review of Latin American Studies* 4, no. 1 (1991): 115–37.

Lewis, David Levering. *When Harlem Was in Vogue*. New York: Penguin Books, 1997.

Lewis, Earl. "To Turn as on a Pivot: Writing African Americans into a History of Overlapping Diasporas." *American Historical Review* 100, no. 3 (1995): 765–87.

Lewis, Laura A. "African Mexicans." In *Concise Encyclopedia of Mexico*, edited by Michael S. Werner, 1–5. Chicago: Fitzroy Dearborn, 2001.

"Blacks, Black Indians, Afromexicans: The Dynamics of Race, Nation, and Identity in a Mexican 'Moreno' Community (Guerrero)." *American Ethnologist* 27, no. 4 (2000): 898–926.

Chocolate and Corn Flour: History, Race, and Place in the Making of "Black" Mexico. Durham, NC: Duke University Press, 2012.

Hall of Mirrors: Power, Witchcraft, and Caste in Colonial Mexico. Durham, NC: Duke University Press, 2003.

Lewis, Stephen E. *Ambivalent Revolution: Forging State and Nation in Chiapas, 1910–1945*. Albuquerque: University of New Mexico Press, 2005.

Rethinking Mexican Indigenismo: The INI's Coordinating Center in Highland Chiapas and the Fate of a Utopian Project. Albuquerque: University of New Mexico Press, 2018.

Lim, Julian. *Porous Borders: Multiracial Migrations and the Law in the U.S.–Mexico Borderlands*. Chapel Hill: University of North Carolina Press, 2017.

Linebaugh, Peter, and Marcus Rediker. *The Many-Headed Hydra: Sailors, Slaves, Commoners, and the Hidden History of the Revolutionary Atlantic*. Boston, MA: Beacon Press, 2000.

Loaeza, Guadalupe, and Pável Granados. *Mi novia, la tristeza*. Mexico City: Océano, 2008.

Lomnitz, Claudio. "Bordering on Anthropology: Dialectics of a National Tradition." In *Deep Mexico, Silent Mexico: An Anthropology of Nationalism*, 228–62. Minneapolis: University of Minnesota Press, 2001.

López, Rick A. *Crafting Mexico: Intellectuals, Artisans, and the State after the Revolution*. Durham, NC: Duke University Press, 2010.

Losurdo, Domenico. *Liberalism: A Counter-history*. Translated by Gregory Elliott. London: Verso, 2011.

Loveman, Mara. "The Modern State and the Primitive Accumulation of Symbolic Power." *American Journal of Sociology* 110, no. 6 (2005): 1651–83.

National Colors: Racial Classification and the State in Latin America. Oxford: Oxford University Press, 2014.
Luis-Brown, David. *Waves of Decolonization: Discourses of Race and Hemispheric Citizenship in Cuba, Mexico, and the United States*. Durham, NC: Duke University Press, 2008.
Macías, Anthony. "Bringing Music to the People: Race, Urban Culture, and Municipal Politics in Postwar Los Angeles." *Musical Quarterly* 56, no. 3 (2004): 693–717.
Madrid, Alejandro L. *Sounds of the Modern Nation: Music, Culture, and Ideas in Post-Revolutionary Mexico*. Philadelphia, PA: Temple University Press, 2009.
Madrid, Alejandro L., and Robin D. Moore. *Danzón: Circum-Caribbean Dialogues in Music and Dance*. Oxford: Oxford University Press, 2013.
Maguire, Emily A. *Racial Experiments in Cuban Literature and Ethnography*. Gainesville: University Press of Florida, 2011.
Malcomson, Hettie. "La configuración racial del danzón: los imaginarios raciales del puerto de Veracruz." In *Mestizaje, diferencia y nación: Lo "negro" en América Central y el Caribe*, coordinated by Elisabeth Cunin, 267–98. Mexico City: Instituto Nacional de Antropología e Historia, 2010.
"The 'Routes' and 'Roots' of *danzón*: A Critique of the History of a Genre." *Popular Music* 30, no. 2 (2011): 263–78.
Malloy, Sean L. *Out of Oakland: Black Panther Party Internationalism during the Cold War*. Ithaca, NY: Cornell University Press, 2017.
Malmström, Dan. *Introduction to Twentieth Century Mexican Music*. Uppsala, Sweden: Institute of Musicology, Uppsala University, 1974.
Manela, Erez. "Imagining Woodrow Wilson in Asia: Dreams of East-West Harmony and the Revolt against Empire in 1919." *American Historical Review* 111, no. 5 (2006): 1327–51.
Manning, Patrick. *Navigating World History: Historians Create a Global Past*. New York: Palgrave Macmillan, 2003.
Martin, Cheryl English. *Rural Society in Colonial Morelos*. Albuquerque: University of New Mexico Press, 1985.
Martínez, María Elena. "The Black Blood of New Spain: Limpieza de Sangre, Racial Violence, and Gendered Power in Early Colonial Mexico." *William and Mary Quarterly* 61, no. 3 (2004): 479–520.
Martínez Maranto, Alfredo. "Dios pinto como quiere: Identidad y cultura en un pueblo afromestizo de Veracruz." In Martínez Montiel, *Presencia africana en México*, 525–73.
Martínez Montiel, Luz María. *Afroamérica I: La ruta del esclavo*. Mexico City: Universidad Nacional Autónoma de México, 2006.
coord. *Presencia africana en México*. Mexico City: Consejo Nacional para la Cultura y las Artes, 1997.
Matera, Marc. *Black London: The Imperial Metropolis and Decolonization in the Twentieth Century*. Oakland: University of California Press, 2015.
McCormick, Gladys I. *The Logic of Compromise in Mexico: How the Countryside Was Key to the Emergence of Authoritarianism*. Chapel Hill: University of North Carolina Press, 2016.

Meade, Teresa, and Gregory Alonso Pirio. "In Search of the Afro-American 'Eldorado': Attempts by North American Blacks to Enter Brazil in the 1920s." *Luso-Brazilian Review* 25, no. 1 (1988): 85–110.

Méndez Reyes, Salvador. "Hacia la abolición de la esclavitud en México: El dictamen de la comisión de esclavos de 1821." In *De la libertad y la abolición: Africanos y afrodescendientes en Iberoamérica*, coordinated by Juan Manuel de la Serna, 170–93. Mexico City: Instituto Nacional de Antropología e Historia, 2010.

Meierovich, Clara. *Vicente T. Mendoza: Artista y primer folclorólogo musical.* Mexico City: Universidad Nacional Autónoma de México, 1995.

Meriwether, James H. *Proudly We Can Be Africans: Black Americans and Africa, 1935–1961.* Chapel Hill: University of North Carolina Press, 2002.

Middlebrook, Kevin J. *The Paradox of the Revolution: Labor, the State, and Authoritarianism in Mexico.* Baltimore, MD: Johns Hopkins University Press, 1995.

Miller, Marilyn Grace. *Rise and Fall of the Cosmic Race: The Cult of* Mestizaje *in Latin America.* Austin: University of Texas Press, 2004.

Mills, Charles W. *Blackness Visible: Essays on Philosophy and Race.* Ithaca, NY: Cornell University Press, 1998.

Milstead, John Radley. "Afro-Mexicans and the Making of Modern Mexico: Citizenship, Race, and Capitalism in Jamiltepec, Oaxaca (1821–1910)." PhD diss., Michigan State University, 2019.

Minority Rights Group, ed. *No Longer Invisible: Afro-Latin Americans Today.* London: Minority Rights Group, 1995.

Miranda, Ricardo. "'*The Heartbeat of an Intense Life*': Mexican Music and Carlos Chávez's Orquesta Sinfónica de México, 1928–1948." In *Carlos Chávez and His World*, edited by Leonora Saavedra, 46–61. Princeton, NJ: Princeton University Press, 2015.

Monroe, John Warne. "Surface Tensions: Empire, Parisian Modernism, and 'Authenticity' in African Sculpture, 1917–1939." *American Historical Review* 117, no. 2 (2012): 445–75.

Monsiváis, Carlos. *Mexican Postcards.* Edited and translated by John Kraniauskas. New York: Verso, 2000.

Moore, Robin D. *Nationalizing Blackness*: Afrocubanismo *and Artistic Revolution in Havana, 1920–1940.* Pittsburgh, PA: University of Pittsburgh Press, 1997.

"Representations of Afrocuban Expressive Culture in the Writings of Fernando Ortiz." *Latin American Music Review* 15, no. 1 (1994): 32–54.

Moreno Figueroa, Mónica G., and Emiko Saldívar Tanaka. "'We Are Not Racists, We Are Mexicans': Privilege, Nationalism and Post-Race Ideology in Mexico." *Critical Sociology* 42, nos. 4–5 (2016): 515–33.

Moreno Rivas, Yolanda. *Rostros del nacionalismo en la música mexicana: Un ensayo de interpretación.* Mexico City: Fondo de Cultura Económica, 1989.

Mota Sánchez, J. Arturo. "El censo de 1890 del estado de Oaxaca." In *El rostro colectivo de la nación mexicana*, coordinated by María Guadalupe Chávez Carbajal, 127–41. Mexico City: Instituto de Investigaciones Históricas, 1997.

Muhammad, Jameelah S. "Mexico." In *No Longer Invisible: Afro-Latin Americans Today*, edited by Minority Rights Group, 163–80. London: Minority Rights Group, 1995.

Muhammad, Khalil Gibran. *The Condemnation of Blackness: Race, Crime, and the Making of Modern Urban America*. Cambridge, MA: Harvard University Press, 2010.

Muller, Dalia Antonia. *Cuban Émigrés and Independence in the Nineteenth-Century Gulf World*. Chapel Hill: University of North Carolina Press, 2017.

Muñoz, María L. O. *Stand Up and Fight: Participatory Indigenismo, Populism, and Mobilization in Mexico, 1970–1984*. Tucson: University of Arizona Press, 2016.

Murphy, John, and Ashley James. "Chronology." In *Charles White: A Retrospective*, edited by Sarah Kelly Oehler and Esther Adler, 192–209. Chicago, IL: Art Institute of Chicago, 2018.

Naveda Chávez-Hita, Adriana. *Esclavos negros en las haciendas azucareras de Córdoba, Veracruz, 1690–1830*. Xalapa: Universidad Veracruzana, 1987.

Ochoa Serrano, Álvaro. *Afrodescendientes: Sobre piel canela*. Zamora, MI: El Colegio de Michoacán, 1997.

Oja, Carol J. *Making Modern Music: New York in the 1920s*. Oxford: Oxford University Press, 2000.

Olcott, Jocelyn. *Revolutionary Women in Postrevolutionary Mexico*. Durham, NC: Duke University Press, 2005.

Ortiz, Paul. *An African American and Latinx History of the United States*. Boston, MA: Beacon Press, 2018.

Ortiz de Montellano, Bernard, et al. "They Were *NOT* Here before Columbus: Afrocentric Hyperdiffusionism in the 1990s." *Ethnohistory* 44, no. 2 (1997): 199–234.

Ortiz Monasterio, José. *México eternamente: Vicente Riva Palacio ante la escritura de la historia*. Mexico City: Fondo de Cultura Económica, 2004.

Osten, Sarah. *The Mexican Revolution's Wake: The Making of a Political System, 1920–1929*. New York: Cambridge University Press, 2018.

Pacheco, José Emilio. "De Clavijero a Carranza." In *Crónica del Puerto de Veracruz*, edited by Fernando Benítez and José Emilio Pacheco, 139–251. Veracruz: Gobierno del Estado de Veracruz, 1986.

Palencia, Mario Moya. *Madre África: Presencia del África negra en el México y Veracruz antiguos*. 2nd ed. Mexico City: Miguel Ángel Porrúa, 2006.

Palmer, Colin A. "Defining and Studying the Modern African Diaspora." *Perspectives on History*, September 1998. www.historians.org/publications-and-directories/perspectives-on-history/september-1998/defining-and-study ing-the-modern-african-diaspora.

Slaves of the White God: Blacks in Mexico, 1570–1650. Cambridge, MA: Harvard University Press, 1976.

Palomino, Pablo. "Nationalist, Hemispheric, and Global: 'Latin American Music' and the Music Division of the Pan American Union, 1939–1947." *Nouveaux mondes, mondes nouveaux – Novo Mundo, Mundos Novos – New World, New Worlds*, June 11, 2015. https://doi.org/10.4000/nuevomundo.68062.

Paredes Martínez, Carlos, and Blanca Lara Tenorio. "La población negra en los valles centrales de Puebla: Orígenes y desarrollo hasta 1681." In Martínez Montiel, *Presencia africana en México*, 19–77.

Paschel, Tianna S. *Becoming Black Political Subjects: Movements and Ethno-Racial Rights in Colombia and Brazil*. Princeton, NJ: Princeton University Press, 2016.

Pensado, Jaime M. *Rebel Mexico: Student Unrest and Authoritarian Political Culture during the Long Sixties*. Stanford, CA: Stanford University Press, 2013.

Pensado, Jaime M., and Enrique C. Ochoa, eds. *México Beyond 1968: Revolutionaries, Radicals, and Repression during the Global Sixties and Subversive Seventies*. Tucson: University of Arizona Press, 2018.

Pérez Fernández, Rolando A. *La música afromestiza mexicana*. Xalapa: Universidad Veracruzana, 1990.

Pérez Montfort, Ricardo. "Acercamientos al son mexicano: El son de mariachi, el son jarocho y el son huasteco." In *Avatares del nacionalismo cultural: Cinco ensayos*, 117–49. Mexico City: Centro de Investigaciones y Estudios Superiores en Antropología Social, 2000.

Estampas de nacionalismo popular mexicano: Ensayos sobre cultura popular y nacionalismo. Mexico City: CIESAS, 1994.

"El jarocho y sus fandangos vistos por viajeros y cronistas extranjeros de los siglos XIX y XX." In *Veracruz y sus viajeros*, by Bernardo García Díaz and Ricardo Pérez Montfort, 123–87. Mexico City: BANBRAS, Gobierno del Estado de Veracruz, 2001.

Pescatello, Ann M. *Charles Seeger: A Life in American Music*. Pittsburgh: University of Pittsburgh Press, 1992.

Piedra, José. "Pato Donald's Gender Ducking." In *Disney Discourse: Producing the Magic Kingdom*, edited by Eric Smoodin, 148–68. New York: Routledge, 1994.

Plummer, Brenda Gayle. *Black Americans and U.S. Foreign Affairs, 1935–1960*. Chapel Hill: University of North Carolina Press, 1996.

In Search of Power: African Americans in the Era of Decolonization, 1956–1974. New York: Cambridge University Press, 2013.

Poniatowska, Elena. "Alberto Beltrán." In *Alberto Beltrán, 1923–2002: Cronista e ilustrador de México*, 9–15. Mexico City: Universidad Nacional Autónoma de México, 2003.

Pool, Christopher A. *Olmec Archeology and Early Mesoamerica*. New York: Cambridge University Press, 2007.

Price, Richard, and Sally Price. *The Roots of Roots; or, How Afro-American Anthropology Got Its Start*. Chicago, IL: Prickly Paradigm Press, 2003.

Priego, Natalia. *Positivism, Science, and "The Scientists" in Porfirian Mexico: A Reappraisal*. Liverpool: Liverpool University Press, 2016.

Proctor, Frank "Trey," III. "African Diasporic Ethnicity in Mexico City to 1650." In *Africans to Spanish America: Expanding the Diaspora*, edited by Sherwin K. Bryant, Rachel Sarah O'Toole, and Ben Vinson III, 50–72. Urbana: University of Illinois Press, 2012.

Putnam, Lara. *Radical Moves: Caribbean Migrants and the Politics of Race in the Jazz Age*. Chapel Hill: University of North Carolina Press, 2013.

Ramos, Marisela Jiménez. "Black Mexico: Nineteenth-Century Discourses of Race and Nation." PhD diss., Brown University, 2009.

Rampersad, Arnold. *The Life of Langston Hughes: I, Too, Sing America*, vol. 1, *1902–1941*. Oxford: Oxford University Press, 1986.

Ramsay, Paulette A. *Afro-Mexican Constructions of Diaspora, Gender, Identity and Nation*. Kingston, Jamaica: University of the West Indies Press, 2016.

Revueltas, Eugenia. "La Liga de Escritores y Artistas Revolucionarios y Silvestre Revueltas." In *Diálogo de resplandores: Carlos Chávez y Silvestre Revueltas*, edited by Yael Bitrán and Ricardo Miranda, 173–81. Mexico City: Consejo Nacional para la Cultura y las Artes, 2002.

Reyes G., and Juan Carlos. "Negros y afromestizos en Colima, siglos XVI-XIX." In Martínez Montiel, *Presencia africana en México*, 259–335.

Rickford, Russell. *We Are an African People: Independent Education, Black Power, and the Radical Imagination*. New York: Oxford University Press, 2016.

Roberts, Dorothy. *Killing the Black Body: Race, Reproduction, and the Meaning of Liberty*. New York: Vintage Books, 1999.

Robinson, Cedric J., and Luz Maria Cabral. "The Mulatta on Film: From Hollywood to the Mexican Revolution." *Race and Class* 45, no. 2 (2003): 1–20.

Rochfort, Desmond. *Mexican Muralists: Orozco, Rivera, Siqueiros*. San Francisco, CA: Chronicle Books, 1998.

Rodríguez, Alberto. "Nacionalismo y folklore en la Escuela Nacional de Música." In *Preludio y fuga: Historias trashumantes de la Escuela Nacional de Música de la UNAM*, coordinated by María Esther Aguirre Lora, 375–418. Mexico City: Universidad Nacional Autónoma de México, 2008.

Rodríguez Díaz, María del Rosario. "Mexico's Vision of Manifest Destiny during the 1847 War." *Journal of Popular Culture* 35, no. 2 (2001): 41–50.

Rojas, Fabio. *From Black Power to Black Studies: How a Radical Social Movement Became an Academic Discipline*. Baltimore, MD: Johns Hopkins University Press, 2007.

Rosa, Andrew Juan. "El Que No Tiene Dingo, Tiene Mandingo: The Inadequacy of the 'Mestizo' as a Theoretical Construct in the Field of Latin American Studies – The Problem and Solution." *Journal of Black Studies* 27, no. 2 (1996): 278–91.

Rosemblatt, Karin Alejandra. "Modernization, Dependency, and the Global in Mexican Critiques of Anthropology." *Journal of Global History* 9, no. 1 (2014): 94–121.

"Other Americas: Transnationalism, Scholarship, and the Culture of Poverty in Mexico and the United States." *Hispanic American Historical Review* 89, no. 4 (2009): 603–41.

The Science and Politics of Race in Mexico and the United States, 1910–1950. Chapel Hill: University of North Carolina Press, 2018.

Rosenberg, Emily S., and Shanon Fitzpatrick, eds. *Body and Nation: The Global Realm of US Body Politics in the Twentieth Century*. Durham, NC: Duke University Press, 2014.

Rowell, Charles Henry. "'El primer libertador de las Américas'/The First Liberator of the Americas: The Editor's Notes." *Callaloo* 31, no. 1 (2008): 1–11.

Rowley, Hazel. *Richard Wright: The Life and Times*. Chicago: University of Chicago Press, 2001.

Rubenstein, Anne. *Bad Language, Naked Ladies, and Other Threats to the Nation: A Political History of Comic Books in Mexico*. Durham, NC: Duke University Press, 1998.

Ruiz, Luis F. "Where Have All the Marxists Gone? Marxism and the Historiography of the Mexican Revolution." *A Contra corriente* 5, no. 2 (2008): 196–219.

Runstedtler, Theresa. *Jack Johnson, Rebel Sojourner: Boxing in the Shadow of the Global Color Line*. Berkeley: University of California Press, 2012.

Rupprecht, Tobias. *Soviet Internationalism after Stalin: Interaction and Exchange between the USSR and Latin America during the Cold War*. Cambridge: Cambridge University Press, 2015.

Rutsch, Mechthild. *Entre el campo y el gabinete: Nacionales y extranjeros en la profesionalización de la antropología mexicana (1877–1920)*. Mexico City: INAH, 2007.

Saavedra, Leonora. "Carlos Chávez and the Myth of the Aztec Renaissance." In *Carlos Chávez and His World*, edited by Leonora Saavedra, 134–64. Princeton, NJ: Princeton University Press, 2015.

"Of Selves and Others: Historiography, Ideology, and the Politics of Modern Mexican Music." PhD diss., University of Pittsburgh, 2001.

"Staging the Nation: Race, Religion, and History in Mexican Opera of the 1940s." *The Opera Quarterly* 23, no. 1 (2007): 1–21.

Sackett, Andrew Jonathan. "The Making of Acapulco: People, Land, and the State in the Development of the Mexican Riviera, 1927–1973." PhD diss., Yale University, 2009.

Sacks, Marcy S. *Before Harlem: The Black Experience in New York City before World War I*. Philadelphia: University of Pennsylvania Press, 2006.

Sanders, James E. *The Vanguard of the Atlantic World: Creating Modernity, Nation, and Democracy in Nineteenth-Century Latin America*. Durham, NC: Duke University Press, 2014.

Sansone, Livio. *Blackness without Ethnicity: Constructing Race in Brazil*. New York: Palgrave Macmillan, 2003.

Schaefer, Timo H. *Liberalism as Utopia: The Rise and Fall of Legal Rule in Post-Colonial Mexico, 1820–1900*. New York: Cambridge University Press, 2017.

Schreiber, Rebecca. *Cold War Exiles in Mexico: US Dissidents and the Culture of Critical Resistance*. Minneapolis: University of Minnesota Press, 2008.

Schuler, Friedrich E. *Mexico between Hitler and Roosevelt: Mexican Foreign Relations in the Age of Lázaro Cárdenas, 1934–1940*. Albuquerque: University of New Mexico Press, 1998.

Schwartz, Stuart B. "Black Latin America: Legacies of Slavery, Race, and African Culture." *Hispanic American Historical Review* 82, no. 3 (2002): 429–33.

Scott, David. *Conscripts of Modernity: The Tragedy of Colonial Enlightenment*. Durham, NC: Duke University Press, 2004.

Seigel, Micol. "Beyond Compare: Historical Method after the Transnational Turn." *Radical History Review* 91 (2005): 62–90.

Uneven Encounters: Making Race and Nation in Brazil and the United States. Durham, NC: Duke University Press, 2009.

Serna, Laura Isabel. *Making Cinelandia: American Films and Mexican Film Culture before the Golden Age.* Durham, NC: Duke University Press, 2014.

Sheehy, Daniel Edward. "The 'Son Jarocho': The History, Style, and Repertory of a Changing Mexican Musical Tradition." PhD diss., University of California, Los Angeles, 1979.

Shepard, Todd. "Algeria, France, Mexico, UNESCO: A Transnational History of Anti-racism and Decolonization, 1932–1962." *Journal of Global History* 6, no. 2 (2011): 273–97.

Shirley, Wayne D. "William Grant Still's Choral Ballad *and They Lynched Him on a Tree.*" *American Music* 12, no. 4 (1994): 425–61.

Sierra Silva, Pablo Miguel. *Urban Slavery in Colonial Mexico: Puebla de los Ángeles, 1531–1706.* New York: Cambridge University Press, 2018.

Smith, Benjamin T. *The Roots of Conservatism in Mexico: Catholicism, Society, and Politics in the Mixteca Baja, 1750–1962.* Albuquerque: University of New Mexico Press, 2012.

Smith, Stephanie J. *The Power and Politics of Art in Postrevolutionary Mexico.* Chapel Hill: University of North Carolina Press, 2017.

Smoodin, Eric. *Animating Culture: Hollywood Cartoons from the Sound Era.* New Brunswick, NJ: Rutgers University Press, 1993.

Spellacy, Amy. "Mapping the Metaphor of the Good Neighbor: Geography, Globalism, and Pan-Americanism during the 1940s." *American Studies* 47, no. 2 (2006): 39–66.

Spenser, Daniela. *Stumbling Its Way through Mexico: The Early Years of the Communist International.* Translated by Peter Gellert. Tuscaloosa: University of Alabama Press, 2011.

Stallings, Stephanie N. "The Pan/American Modernisms of Carlos Chávez and Henry Cowell." In *Carlos Chávez and His World*, edited by Leonora Saavedra, 28–45. Princeton, NJ: Princeton University Press, 2015.

Stern, Alexandra Minna. "From Mestizophilia to Biotypology: Racialization and Science in Mexico, 1920–1960." In *Race and Nation in Modern Latin America*, edited by Nancy P. Appelbaum, Anne S. Macpherson, and Karin Alejandra Rosemblatt, 187–210. Chapel Hill: University of North Carolina Press, 2003.

Stevens, Margaret. *Red International and Black Caribbean: Communists in New York City, Mexico and the West Indies, 1919–1939.* London: Pluto Press, 2017.

Stevenson, Alva Moore, ed. "Africans in México: History, Race, and Place." Special issue, *Journal of Pan African Studies* 6, no. 1 (2013).

Stocking, George W., Jr. "The Ethnographic Sensibility of the 1920s and the Dualism of the Anthropological Tradition." In *Romantic Motives: Essays on Anthropological Sensibility*, in vol. 6 of History of Anthropology, ed. George W. Stocking Jr., 208–76. Madison: University of Wisconsin Press, 1989.

Sue, Christina A. *Land of the Cosmic Race: Race Mixture, Racism, and Blackness in Mexico*. Oxford: Oxford University Press, 2013.

"Hegemony and Silence: Confronting State-Sponsored Silences in the Field." *Journal of Contemporary Ethnography* 44, no. 1 (2015): 113–40.

Taylor, Keeanga-Yamahtta. *From #BlackLivesMatter to Black Liberation*. Chicago, IL: Haymarket Books, 2016.

Tenorio-Trillo, Mauricio. *I Speak of the City: Mexico City at the Turn of the Twentieth Century*. Chicago, IL: University of Chicago Press, 2012.

Tinson, Christopher M. *Radical Intellect:* Liberator *Magazine and Black Activism in the 1960s*. Chapel Hill: University of North Carolina Press, 2017.

Torget, Andrew J. *Seeds of Empire: Cotton, Slavery, and the Transformation of the Texas Borderlands, 1800–1850*. Chapel Hill: University of North Carolina Press, 2015.

Torres Chibrás, Armando Ramón. "José Pablo Moncayo, Mexican Composer and Conductor: A Survey of His Life with a Historical Perspective of His Time." DMA, University of Missouri–Kansas City, 2002.

Valdez Aguilar, Rafael. *Sinaloa: Negritud y Olvido*. Culiacán, Sinaloa, Mexico: Talleres Gráficos, 1993.

Van Young, Eric. "No Human Power to Impede the Impenetrable Order of Providence: The Historiography of Mexican Independence." In *Writing Mexican History*, by Eric Van Young, 127–63. Stanford, CA: Stanford University Press, 2012.

Vaughan, Mary Kay. *Cultural Politics in Revolution: Teachers, Peasants, and Schools in Mexico, 1930–1940*. Tucson: University of Arizona Press, 1997.

Portrait of a Young Painter: Pepe Zúñiga and Mexico City's Rebel Generation. Durham, NC: Duke University Press, 2015.

The State, Education, and Social Class in Mexico, 1880–1928. DeKalb: Northern Illinois University Press, 1982.

Vaughan, Mary Kay, and Theodore Cohen. "Brown, Black, and Blues: Miguel Covarrubias and Carlos Chávez in the United States and Mexico." In *Open Borders to a Revolution: Culture, Politics, and Migration*, edited by Jaime Marroquín, Adela Pineda Franco, and Magdalena Mieri, 67–90. Washington, DC: Smithsonian Institution Scholarly Press, 2013.

Vaughn, Bobby. "My Blackness and Theirs: Viewing Mexican Blackness Up Close." In *Black Mexico: Race and Society from Colonial to Modern Times*, edited by Ben Vinson III and Matthew Restall, 209–19. Albuquerque: University of New Mexico Press, 2009.

Velázquez, Marco, and Mary Kay Vaughan. "*Mestizaje* and Musical Nationalism in Mexico." In *The Eagle and the Virgin: Nation and Cultural Revolution in Mexico, 1920–1940*, edited by Mary Kay Vaughan and Stephen E. Lewis, 95–118. Durham, NC: Duke University Press, 2006.

Velázquez, María Elisa. "Afrodescendientes en museos de México: Silencio y olvido." *Gaceta de Museos*, no. 58 (2014): 27–31.

Velázquez, María Elisa, and Ethel Correa Duró, comp. *Poblaciones y culturas de origen africano en México*. Mexico City: INAH, 2005.

Velázquez, María Elisa, and Gabriela Iturralde Nieto. *Afrodescendientes en México: Una historia de silencio y discriminación*. 2nd ed. Mexico City: Consejo Nacional para Prevenir la Discriminación, 2016.
Vázquez, María Elisa. "Detrás de Memín Pinguín." *Diario de Campo*, no. 79 (2005): 65–68.
Villegas Torres, Fabiola Martha. *Alberto Beltrán y el libro ilustrado*. Mexico City: Consejo Nacional para la Cultura y las Artes, 2007.
Villela, Khristaan D. "Miguel Covarrubias and Twenty Centuries of Pre-Columbian Latin American Art, from the Olmec to the Inka." In *Miguel Covarrubias: Drawing a Cosmopolitan Line*, edited by Carolyn Kastner, 49–75. Austin: University of Texas Press, 2014.
Vincent, Ted. "The Blacks Who Freed Mexico." *Journal of Negro History* 79, no. 3 (1994): 257–76.
Vinson, Ben, III. *Bearing Arms for His Majesty: The Free-Colored Militia in Colonial Mexico*. Stanford, CA: Stanford University Press, 2001.
Before Mestizaje: The Frontiers of Race and Caste in Colonial Mexico. New York: Cambridge University Press, 2017.
"Fading from Memory: Historiographical Reflections on the Afro-Mexican Presence." *Review of Black Political Economy* 33, no. 1 (2005): 59–72.
Flight: The Story of Virgil Richardson, a Tuskegee Airman in Mexico. New York: Palgrave Macmillan, 2004.
"La historia del estudio de los negros en México." In *Afroméxico: El pulso de la población negra en México. Una historia recordada, olvidada y vuelta a recordar*, by Ben Vinson III and Bobby Vaughn, translated by Clara García Ayluardo, 19–73. Mexico City: Fondo de Cultura Económica, 2004.
"Introduction: African (Black) Diaspora History, Latin American History." *The Americas* 63, no. 1 (2006): 1–18.
"The Racial Profile of a Rural Mexican Province in the 'Costa Chica': Igualapa in 1791." *The Americas* 57, no. 2 (2000): 269–82.
Vinson, Ben, III, and Matthew Restall. Introduction to *Black Mexico: Race and Society from Colonial to Modern Times*. Edited by Ben Vinson III and Matthew Restall, 1–18. Albuquerque: University of New Mexico Press, 2009.
Virtue, John. *South of the Color Barrier: How Jorge Pasquel and the Mexican League Pushed Baseball toward Racial Integration*. Jefferson, NC: McFarland, 1996.
Vitalis, Robert. *White World Order, Black Power Politics: The Birth of American International Relations*. Ithaca, NY: Cornell University Press, 2015.
Wade, Peter. "Afterward: Race and Nation in Latin America: An Anthropological View." In *Race and Nation in Modern Latin America*, edited by Nancy P. Appelbaum, Anne S. Macpherson, and Karin Alejandra Rosemblatt, 263–81. Chapel Hill: University of North Carolina Press, 2003.
Blackness and Race Mixture: The Dynamics of Racial Identity in Colombia. Baltimore, MD: Johns Hopkins University Press, 1993.
"Conclusion: Race, Multiculturalism, and Genomics in Latin America." In *Mestizo Genomics: Race Mixture, Nation, and Science in Latin America*, edited by Peter Wade, Carlos López Beltrán, Eduardo Restrepo, and Ricardo Ventura Santos, 211–39. Durham, NC: Duke University Press, 2014.

Race and Ethnicity in Latin America. London: Pluto Press, 1997.
Wahlstrom, Todd W. *The Southern Exodus to Mexico: Migration across the Borderlands after the American Civil War*. Lincoln: University of Nebraska Press, 2015.
Wallace, Michele. "Modernism, Postmodernism, and the Problem of the Visual in Afro-American Culture." In *Dark Designs and Visual Culture*, 364–78. Durham, NC: Duke University Press, 2004.
Watts, Steven. "Walt Disney: Art and Politics in the American Century." *Journal of American History* 82, no. 1 (1995): 84–110.
Weinstein, Barbara. "Erecting and Erasing Boundaries: Can We Combine the 'Indo' and the 'Afro' in Latin American Studies?" *Estudios Interdisciplinarios de América Latina y el Caribe* 19, no. 1 (2008): 129–44.
White, Hayden. "The Historical Text as Literary Artifact." In *Tropics of Discourse: Essays in Cultural Criticism*, 81–100. Baltimore, MD: Johns Hopkins University Press, 1985.
Williams, Adriana. *Covarrubias*. Edited by Doris Ober. Austin: University of Texas Press, 1994.
Wood, Andrew Grant. *Agustín Lara: A Cultural Biography*. Oxford: Oxford University Press, 2014.
Revolution in the Street: Women, Workers, and Urban Protest in Veracruz, 1870–1927. Wilmington, DE: Scholarly Resources, 2001.
Wood, Marcus. *Blind Memory: Visual Representations of Slavery in England and America*. New York: Routledge, 2000.
Yankelevich, Pablo. "Explotadores, truhanes, agitadores y negros: Deportaciones y restricciones a estadounidenses en el México revolucionario." *Historia Mexicana* 57, no. 4 (2008): 1155–99.
Yelvington, Kevin A. "The Invention of Africa in Latin America and the Caribbean: Political Discourse and Anthropological Praxis, 1920–1940." In *Afro-Atlantic Dialogues: Anthropology in the Diaspora*, edited by Kevin A. Yelvington, 35–82. Santa Fe, NM: School of American Research Press, 2006.
Zelade, Richard. *Austin in the Jazz Age*. Charleston, SC: History Press, 2015.
Zeleza, Paul Tiyambe. "Rewriting the African Diaspora: Beyond the Black Atlantic." *African Affairs* 104, no. 414 (2005): 35–68.
Zolov, Eric. *Refried Elvis: The Rise of the Mexican Counterculture*. Berkeley: University of California Press, 1999.
"Showcasing the 'Land of Tomorrow': Mexico and the 1968 Olympics." *The Americas* 61, no. 2 (2004): 159–88.

Index

CPSIA information can be obtained
at www.ICGtesting.com
Printed in the USA
LVHW112022161122
733301LV00003B/142